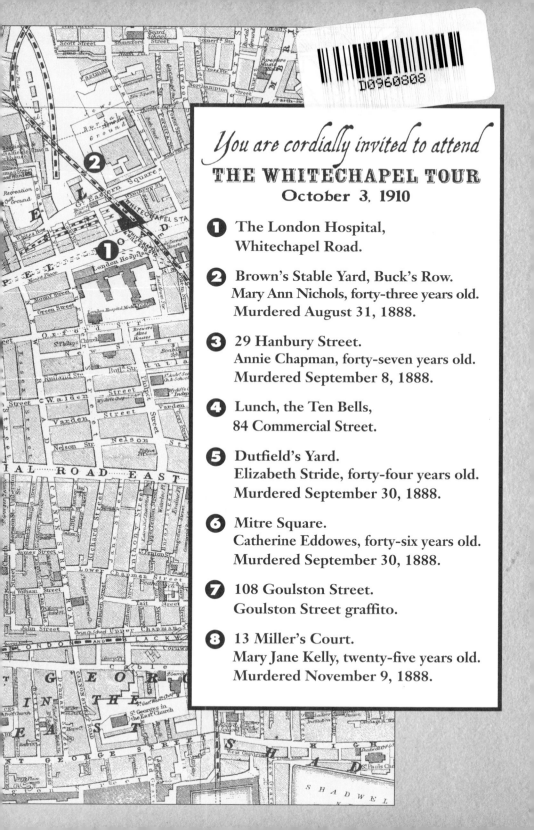

You are cordially invited to attend

THE WHITECHAPEL TOUR
October 3, 1910

1 The London Hospital,
Whitechapel Road.

2 Brown's Stable Yard, Buck's Row.
Mary Ann Nichols, forty-three years old.
Murdered August 31, 1888.

3 29 Hanbury Street.
Annie Chapman, forty-seven years old.
Murdered September 8, 1888.

4 Lunch, the Ten Bells,
84 Commercial Street.

5 Dutfield's Yard.
Elizabeth Stride, forty-four years old.
Murdered September 30, 1888.

6 Mitre Square.
Catherine Eddowes, forty-six years old.
Murdered September 30, 1888.

7 108 Goulston Street.
Goulston Street graffito.

8 13 Miller's Court.
Mary Jane Kelly, twenty-five years old.
Murdered November 9, 1888.

THE STRANGE CASE OF DR. DOYLE

A JOURNEY INTO MADNESS & MAYHEM

THE STRANGE CASE OF DR. DOYLE

A JOURNEY INTO MADNESS & MAYHEM

DANIEL FRIEDMAN, MD
EUGENE FRIEDMAN, MD

SQUAREONE
PUBLISHERS

COVER DESIGNER: Jeannie Tudor
EDITOR: Michael Weatherhead
TYPESETTER: Gary A. Rosenberg

Square One Publishers
115 Herricks Road
Garden City Park, NY 11040
(516) 535-2010 • (877) 900-BOOK
www.squareonepublishers.com

Library of Congress Cataloging-in-Publication Data
Friedman, Dan, 1970-
  The strange case of Dr. Doyle / Dan Friedman and Eugene Friedman.
    pages cm
  ISBN 978-0-7570-0348-6 (hardcover)
  1. Jack, the Ripper. 2. Serial murders—England—London—History. 3.
Doyle, Arthur Conan, 1859-1930. I. Friedman, Eugene. II. Title.
  HV6535.G6L65344 2015
  364.152'32092—dc23
                                        2014009012

Printed in the United States of America

10   9   8   7   6   5   4   3   2   1

Contents

We dedicate this book to our wives,
Elena Friedman and Sheryl Friedman,
who sacrificed their time and unconditionally
devoted themselves to ensuring that
this work of ours came to print.

Acknowledgments

We would like to begin by thanking Dominick Grillo, librarian extraordinaire, for helping us track down rare manuscripts and newspaper clippings, and for adding his own thoughts to the book. Without his help we could never have completed this Herculean task. A special thanks to Alan McCormick, curator of the Crime Museum of New Scotland Yard, and to Paul Dew of the historic collections of the Metropolitan Police Force, who corresponded with me during the early phases of this project and then serendipitously put me in contact with Keith Skinner, who, although he might not be aware of it, confirmed my hypothesis.

Many thanks to the gifted and talented *New York Times* best-selling author Ben Mezrich, who encouraged me to transfer my thoughts onto paper and guided me along the way. Thanks to Fiona Riddell of the Arbuthnot Museum located in Peterhead, Scotland. Your willingness to remain in touch during the entire project was an immense help, particularly in the section devoted to Doyle's Arctic adventure. Thank you, David Knight, archivist at Stonyhurst College, for sending me your personal notes on Doyle's years as a student there, and also for furnishing me with Doyle's academic records. Thanks to Sally Pagan and Claire Button of the University of Edinburgh for supplying me with medical school transcripts of Doyle and several of his contemporaries. I appreciate the difficulties you both faced in tracking down records that date back well over a century. Not only were they insightful, but they served to reinforce our suspicions.

Thanks also to Philip A. Magrath, curator of Artillery at Fort Nelson, Portsmouth, for supplying us with that wonderful map from 1884 of the "Review Grounds," as well as other invaluable information. Thank you,

Barbara Roden of the Arthur Conan Doyle Society for not only corresponding with me via email, but also enlightening me with your phone calls. Your help was greatly appreciated. We would also like to thank Jennifer Johnstone, assistant archivist at the University of Dundee, for providing us with Charles Doyle's admission and case notes at the time he was incarcerated at Morningside Lunatic Asylum. We would like to thank Evan Friedman for tracking down arcane genealogical information to fill in gaps in the chronological order of events.

Many thanks are due Cary Skalaren, Stan Newman, Doctors Stan and Leslie Friedman, and Dr. Martin Edelstein for reviewing and critiquing our manuscript. John Romita Jr., thank you for lending your artistic talent and creativity to the pages of our book. Although it is said that a picture is worth a thousand words, your pictures translate to much more than that.

In addition, we would like to express our gratitude to the staff of the Long Island Jewish Medical Center Library and the staff of the Hollis Library at Winthrop University Hospital, each of which allowed us a place to conduct our investigation within its treasure trove of books, for providing us with a stream of relevant information that helped put things into place. We must also take a moment to recognize the masterful detective work done by the Baker Street Irregulars and Ripperologists who have been so willing to share their discoveries in books and on websites, and who have given us a firm foundation for this book.

Of course, we would like to express our thanks to our wonderful editor, Michael Weatherhead, who kept us on the straight and narrow and tied this book's two alternating plots together, and to Rudy Shur, our publisher, who believed in and encouraged this project from its very inception. Special thanks to Sheryl Friedman for all the hours of researching, charting, note-taking, and writing she did right from the start of this project. Each and every page of this book has the mark of her excellence and brilliance.

I, Daniel, would like to thank my children—Amanda, David, and Andrew—who were the best helpers anyone could have asked for. These three "assistants" never complained or demanded anything from me, and were always there for me. I would also like to thank my wife, Elena, whose love, encouragement, and compassion allowed me to believe I could actually undertake this project. I knew I could do it only because she said so. She was my driving force and my inspiration.

My father, Eugene, would like to thank his wife, Sheryl, for her self-less commitment to this project, and for her efforts to bring this book to fruition. She has always been his inspiration, his biggest supporter, and the love of his life.

Introduction

In 1903, British stage actor Harry Brodribb Irving hosted a dinner party at his London home. The two prerequisites he had set for earning an invitation to this exclusive soirée were membership in London society's upper echelon and expertise in the art of conversation. He made sure the ambience of the evening would be conducive to relaxed discussions of the day's more controversial issues. Gradually, the group's focus shifted to a single topic—murder.

Irving himself had already achieved a degree of fame through several of the books he had penned on the subject, and his guests that night were a collection of Britain's best and brightest in the spheres of law enforcement, forensic medicine, journalism, and crime and mystery writing. Then and there, Irving decided that there was no way he would allow such lively exchanges on his favorite subject to end after just one night. By the evening's conclusion, he proposed that this small assemblage establish a dinner club dedicated to the formal study of murder and the criminal mind. Its mission would be "the propagation of truth and the communication of new ideas—rather from the necessities of things than upon any one man's suggestion."

This fraternity was not to be open to all who would want to join it, for, in the spirit of the day, it was designed to remain both exclusive and secretive. The roster was comprised of S. Ingleby Oddie, the City of London police surgeon; Norwich's Dr. Herbert Crosse, a medico-legal expert; James Beresford Atlay, a noted barrister and archivist of crime; Arthur Lambton, writer and journalist, and the club's first secretary; and, of course, Harry Irving himself. Almost immediately after its creation, the dinner club added to its members William Le Queux, the master of mystery writing; A.E.W. Mason, actor, author, and future spy; Max Pemberton, lawyer, mystery novelist, and journalist; John Churton Collins, Oxford professor and writer; George R. Sims, humorist, journalist, and poet; E.W. Hornung, creator of A.J. Raffles, the gentleman thief; and Sir Arthur Conan Doyle, the recently knighted author.

This diverse group of gentlemen brought to the table credentials that qualified each of them as an expert in the inner workings of the criminal mind. Soon, admission to the club became one of the most sought-after prizes in the realm. While these gifted individuals referred to their club rather snobbishly as "Our Society," the British press decided to tag the group with a somewhat more lurid label: the "Murder Club." Its dinner meetings were held four times a year at the Great Central Hotel on Marylebone Road, and in the early days, these gatherings were informal affairs, where celebrated cases were bandied about in a chatty yet sophisticated manner. Some of its members had unprecedented access to crime photographs, weapons, letters, and other authenticated evidence associated with sensational cases. Indeed, some of the clubmen had been able to obtain and amass the rarest of specimens from crimes that had occurred as much as a century earlier. Many of these items were assembled into special exhibits and transported to the club's dinner discussions, so these privileged associates could view and, in some instances, even hold them in their own hands.

Although Our Society was established as a sit-down dinner club, it refused to restrict itself to the confines of hotel dining rooms. Within a year of its formation, the Murder Club went on its first field trip. On Wednesday, April 19, 1905, the three members of Our Society who were alumni of the University of Edinburgh Medical School—Dr. Samuel Ingleby Oddie, Dr. Arthur Conan Doyle, and Dr. Herbert Crosse—along with H. B. Irving, John Churton Collins, and Collins's twenty-six-year-old son, Laurence—met up with Oddie's old friend Dr. Frederick Gordon Brown in front of the City of London Police Hospital in Bishopsgate. Brown, who was the current City of London chief police surgeon, owed his reputation to his knowledge of the burgeoning field of crime scene investigation, which had begun only three years before. He would take this select group on the excursion of a lifetime, a guided tour of one of London's roughest sections, Whitechapel.

Although criminal activity, debauchery, and murder had always been considered intrinsic components of the district, the name Whitechapel had not evoked universal fear and horror until seventeen years prior, when, in the late summer of 1888, the man who would become known as Jack the Ripper began his victimization of some of the area's female residents. Wanting to perform its own investigation of the still unsolved Ripper murders, Our Society had decided to enlist the assistance of Brown and two police detectives who "knew all the facts about the murders."

On this early spring day, the group of nine sallied forth to visit the sites at which it was said the Ripper had performed such terrible deeds. Moreover, Brown was not about to forfeit this rare opportunity to impress such an elite band of amateur crime solvers with his encyclopedic knowledge of non-Ripper related cases, sometimes taking the group to places that bore only peripheral relationships to the Ripper legend, hoping to create a better understanding of the neighborhood's social, economic, and emotional climate during Jack's reign of terror. This jaunt into unglamorous real life was exactly the type of thing in which all the members of Our Society reveled. In fact, according to the elder Collins, Doyle had been mesmerized by the hustle and bustle of the area.

As the group's first president, Arthur Lambton was the acknowledged leader of Our Society, but it was Doyle's association with the club that gave it its elevated status. Doyle, who had immersed himself in all of London's activities, always managed to become the center of attention wherever he went. Everyone wanted to share the limelight with him. Doyle was held in the highest esteem by the Crown, mostly for his work chronicling the Boer War. In 1902, King Edward VII awarded him a knighthood, which he would have turned down had his mother not insisted that he accept the designation of "Sir." As the most famous writer on the hottest topic of his day—crime—Doyle had the good fortune to find himself at a time when this subject was shedding its scruffy image and evolving into a refined science. He always seemed to be a half step ahead of the club's other members when it came to the details of so many noteworthy crimes.

While there have been many theories regarding Jack the Ripper's identity, over a hundred years later, his real name remains unknown. Perhaps a clearer understanding of the facts as they exist may shed light on this mystery. To this end, we have taken the liberty of bringing you, the reader, on a tour of Whitechapel similar to the one taken by Our Society in 1905. This book's rendition of the original expedition is set five years later, and is presented in such a way as to avoid any confusion regarding the order of Ripper events. And who is better qualified to conduct our tour than Sir Arthur Conan Doyle? Replacing the other original tour members are eight fictionalized surrogates who will serve to ask and answer the reader's questions along the way. Although this tour never happened, the facts of the murders as described are accurate, and the comments and opinions offered by Dr. Doyle and his guests are based on historical records. While the original tour visited nine documented murder sites on April 19, 1905, only the five Ripper sites recognized by Doyle are visited and discussed on this outing.

Along with our fictitious hunt for Jack the Ripper, we also offer a nonfictional look at the young Arthur Conan Doyle. To understand the man himself, and the ideas on which he expounds within our tour, we present a detailed biography covering the first thirty years of his life. We trace Doyle's roots back to his earliest days in Edinburgh and watch as his life unfolds. We witness his hardships, education, adventures, and entanglements, allowing us to perceive the renowned author as few have ever done before. Alternating between biography and tour, we hope to give you not only the chance to piece together the picture of a famous man, but also the opportunity to solve an infamous series of crimes. The game is afoot.

1

1839–1859

The Doyles

On May 22, 1859, in Edinburgh, Scotland, Charles and Mary Doyle witnessed the arrival of their first male offspring. But the birth of Arthur Ignatius Conan Doyle did little to ease the sadness and depression that had been afflicting his father over the past few years. At this time, twenty-six-year-old Charles Altamont Doyle was primarily focused on how to obtain money for his next bottle of Burgundy. The youthful optimism that had accompanied him just a decade before on his train ride from London to Edinburgh, the "Athens of the North," had given way to self-pity and hopelessness. The new father may have felt as though he were the unwitting victim of a conspiracy plotted against him by his own father to rid the family of its sole black sheep. The combination of Charles's introspective nature, religiosity, and candor had made it virtually impossible for him to conform to the complex family dynamics that had dominated his childhood, and the situation that faced him now was testing his resolve.

It seemed the Doyles were accustomed to confronting obstacles. Born in Ireland in 1797, Charles Doyle's father, John, was one of four children of a deeply religious family that had been dispossessed of its estate and impoverished by harsh laws against Roman Catholics. While his two sisters, Katherine and Anna Maria, became nuns, and his older brother, James, entered the priesthood, John Doyle's artistic nature precluded him from pursuing a life in the Church. He trained under Gaspare Gabrielli, the noted landscape painter. He then continued his education at the Dublin Society's Drawing Academy, where he gained local fame with his sketches of horses. At age twenty-three, he married Marianne Conan, the daughter of a Dublin tailor. To make ends meet, he used his innate talent for drawing, seeking commissions from wealthy Dubliners. Fortunately for him, he had good looks and a pleasant personality, which made it easy for him to attract patrons.

Brimming with confidence, and now with a baby daughter, he and his wife decided to move the family to London in 1822. Once there, the Doyles leased a home on Berners Street, but due to a lack of connections, John's career got off to a slow start. He was forced to house his growing family in some of the city's poorest sections during their first years there. Eventually, his keen intellect, quick wit, and skills as a draughtsman, illustrator, and lithographer led to his success as a political caricaturist who gently poked fun at members of Parliament. At the age of thirty-six, and with seven children, he was able to move his family into an elegant townhouse at fashionable 17 Cambridge Terrace, which was just north of Hyde Park.

Along with the acquisition of wealth came homeschooling, dance instruction, and fencing lessons for the children. All the Doyle offspring were talented, and some extraordinarily so. Annette, the oldest child, was an accomplished musician. James took to history and drawing. Like his father, Richard was attracted to politics and the art of caricature. While Henry possessed artistic talent, he was more interested in art history. Francis, Adelaide, and Charles looked up to their older siblings as role models. The Doyle clan soon found itself surrounded by a wide assortment of John's friends, many of whom enjoyed worldwide celebrity.

During the Christmas season of 1839, Marianne succumbed to complications of heart disease at the age of forty-four. Annette was able to cope with the loss of her mother by devoting herself to the Catholic Church, while Richard, James, and Henry were able to escape into drawing and writing. In fact, oldest brother Richard's journal from 1840, which would later be published, makes absolutely no mention of the passing of his mother. Fortunately, Marianne Doyle's brother, Michael Conan, who had moved in with the family just prior to his sister's death, brought a stabilizing presence to the younger children, Adelaide, Francis, and Charles.

Tragedy struck again with the premature deaths of Francis, who died at the age of fifteen, and Adelaide, who died a year later when she was only fourteen. Emptiness surrounded Charles and intensified after his father chose to continue homeschooling him. Left with no one his age to talk to, and with no one to provide him with any age-appropriate guidance, he risked developing into a self-absorbed young man. Although he exhibited precocious talent as an artist, his father constantly compared him to his remaining gifted, talented, and much older brothers, who were already making names for themselves in academic and literary circles. In fact, Richard, James, and Henry would socialize with some of the major intellectual stars of the time, often at their Cambridge Terrace home.

By the age of ten, young Charles had already become slightly cynical. In a letter to his father at the time, he officially declares no painting at the Royal Academy of particular interest to him. Later on, in another message to his father, he dryly describes himself as "Your diminutive son Charles, who watcheth"—an accurate interpretation of his place in the world. Whether John Doyle appreciated the sensitivity and seriousness of his son's statements remains unknown. Some inferences can be made, though; as the most famous political cartoonist of his era, John Doyle possessed the gift of being able to analyze personalities in the blink of the eye. Surely he would have noticed the delicate nature of his son, however hidden it might have been. After all, using the pen name H.B., John Doyle had managed to conceal his identity as a caricaturist from the public for twenty years, all the while flinging polite barbs at England's members of Parliament. Although the identity of the great H.B. should have easily been revealed, apparently no one was able to connect the dots that linked John Doyle to the artist. If it had not been for his seventeen-page signed confession to Prime Minister Robert Peel in 1843, the world might never have known the truth.

While John Doyle was forced into the limelight once he became known as the famous H.B., his young son Charles needed an outlet to "forget the cares of the world," finding solace in fishing. Charles's escapism and "distractible" nature might have played a part in his father's 1849 decision to use his status and influence to secure a job for the seventeen-year-old Charles in one of the four branches of Her Majesty's Office of Works. John Doyle felt it would be helpful for his son to be made "subject to the disciplines of formal office environment" in a place where "he could put his skills to productive use as a designer and draftsman." He concluded that Charles would be well suited to the vacancy that had opened in the Edinburgh office after the recent death of its chief draftsman, William Nixon.

The position was highly desirable, especially since it came with an excellent starting salary of £180 annually. For Charles, the timing could not have been better, as the Doyle townhouse had become even more of a beehive of activity—exactly what the introverted daydreamer Charles did not need. Even his adult siblings had chosen to continue residing there. Guests were continually going in and out of Cambridge Terrace. Socialites and intellectuals, who never tired of steeping themselves in controversy and heated discussions, buzzed around at all hours of the day and night. There was never a peaceful moment to be had. Although Charles appreciated the friendliness of his brothers, all of them were given to boasting, which conflicted with his personality.

Edinburgh had the potential to serve as a haven for Charles, an opportunity to secure some space of his own far from the madding Doyle compound. An added bonus was that his favorite pastime, fishing, would be readily available at the nearby lakes and streams. With his bags packed and his hopes high, Charles Doyle took a train to Edinburgh where, with the help of a local parish church, he found lodging at the home of Catherine Foley, the mother of two young daughters. Later on, in a letter written to a friend, he would describe the three as "very pleasant people and very Irish." Charles, a staunch Roman Catholic, was impressed by their piety. He hadn't realized that his new landlady was a convert who had abandoned her Protestant roots in order to be granted permission to marry her now late husband, who had passed away just six years into their marriage. With his untimely death, she had been forced to move back in with her rigidly Protestant family, who made it a point to remind Catherine of her unwise decision. But Catherine Foley had a will of steel, and instead of abandoning her new faith, she became more fervently pledged to it. Eventually the tension would reach the point at which, daughters in tow, she would decide to make the voyage across the Irish Sea and establish a governess training school on Edinburgh's James Street.

When Charles first laid eyes on Catherine's twelve-year-old daughter, Mary, he was struck by her beauty and charm, but before he was able to know her better, she was sent off to a strict convent school in France to augment her education and polish her social skills. Charles remained a lodger at the Foley house for a short time, but it is not known whether he corresponded with the young lady while she was away for five years. He spent most of his time by himself, getting to know every one of Edinburgh's landmarks and all of its many streets and wynds. At this stage of his life, he chose to view the city as a modern center of knowledge and culture. Later on, his perspective would change, and Edinburgh would become in his eyes a city of filth and illiterate curs.

Unlike his brother Richard, who tended to neglect his deadlines, Charles was compulsive about the punctual completion of his assignments. While he may have been slightly self-obsessed and often undisciplined in his social life, he was always highly conscientious in his creative life. Without any formal training in draftsmanship, he entered numerous competitions in order to show off his artistry and emerging technical skills. He took great pride in his work and was champing at the bit to demonstrate the progress he had been making under the tutelage of his boss, Robert Matheson. Nevertheless, there were two habits that he refused to abandon. The first was his father's Sunday custom of reviewing all of his offspring's work, from blueprints to illustrations and writings. Charles consistently sent samples of his current projects to London so that he could remain in the family circle. The second was his loyalty to the Catholic Church. Two years after he arrived in Edinburgh, he made sure to show up and become an active participant against the current government's anti-Catholic agenda. It mattered little to him that he was a government employee when he seconded the motion calling for Parliament to rescind the recently passed Ecclesiastical Titles Assumption Bill, which made it illegal for anyone outside of the United Church of England and Ireland to use an Episcopal title, such as bishop, in connection with any place within the United Kingdom.

Charles, having been impressed by Edinburgh's architecture, which so often made use of stone over common man-made brick, devoted himself to combining the robust with the delicate in his draftsmanship. Matheson, impressed by his assistant's progress, made it a point to place him on the project committee responsible for designing the fountain for Holyrood Palace, the official Scottish residence of Queen Victoria and her beloved consort, Prince Albert. When the Queen made an official visit there in 1850, it was the first time that a female ruler had set foot on Scottish soil since Mary, Queen of Scots, 300 years prior. And it had been none other than the eighteen-year-old Roman Catholic Charles Altamont Doyle who had been given the honor of being part of the team in charge of readying Her Royal Majesty's apartment. Moreover, Charles became a visible participant in the pomp and circumstance of that glorious day as he hoisted the Union Jack atop the magnificent fortress. Queen Victoria was so impressed by Holyrood's potential that she committed herself to renovating the castle, and to spending more time there and even further north, at Balmoral, near Aberdeen.

The Office of Works was given the responsibility of the massive project of Holyrood's renovation. It was Charles Doyle who was the designer of the figures that showcased Holyrood's spire, and Matheson was thrilled by his results, describing them as "more in the class of a work of Art than ordinary Building work." Although one trade magazine, the *Builder,* disagreed, calling them a "confused and miserable mixture, ugly in outline and puerile in detail," Matheson remained a firm advocate of their worth. He was well aware that dozens of architects were waiting in the wings in the hope of taking the lucrative and powerful job of clerk of works away from him. A few years later,

Matheson would ask Charles to come up with a proper design for the stained-glass windows that put the finishing touch on the restoration of the Glasgow Cathedral. Even though Matheson was able to gain the backing of James Ballantine, the nation's best and most ambitious maker of stained glass, the proposal was shelved, and Charles's designs never saw the light of day.

Charles's post as second assistant at the Office of Works was one he relished, so when his father informed him that he would try to secure a spot for him at the London office, Charles stated, "I have the greatest horror of being herded with a set of snobs in the London Office, who would certainly not understand and probably laugh at the whole theory of construction. . . ." Charles had established what would become a life-long friendship with his supervisor, Robert Matheson, and had also grown close to the man who ranked one slot above him in the office hierarchy, Andrew Kerr. In later years, Charles's relationship with Kerr would enable him, and eventually his wife and children, to mix and mingle with some of the country's most well-regarded people, including John Hill Burton and his family.

Charles's currently mixed feelings, however, about remaining separated from his London family may be inferred by his comment, "But if the present vacancy is anything in the way of composition, writing, or architectural work—where I would be left to myself, to do my best without any interference till I had done so—I would without hesitation accept the office." Charles's father, who had become unable to paint due to illness, had even tried to get himself a job in the Office of Works in London, but had been turned down. The attempt by John Doyle to find a place for Charles in the London office is notable, as it contradicts the idea that Charles Doyle's presence in Edinburgh was an attempt by his family to turn him into a social outcast.

In 1854, when Mary Foley returned from her five years in France, Charles decided to woo her. He was no longer a lodger at the Foley household, and Mary was seventeen years old. Within a year, he and Mary took their marriage vows at St. Mary's Church. After their honeymoon, the two tried their best to find a permanent home for themselves, but this dream was never to materialize. A year later, a daughter was born, Ann Mary Francis Conan, whom they called Annette. Less than two years later, another girl, Catherine Amelia Angela, arrived. Unfortunately, Catherine was born with a life-threatening condition known as "water on the brain," which, at the time, was untreatable. It is difficult to imagine the stress endured by the young Doyles as they heard her shrill cries, witnessed her convulsions, and observed her lack of development. After six months of suffering, and with Mary pregnant once again, Catherine died.

Mary was able to cope with her grief, but Charles proved less resilient. He slipped into a deep depression, finding solace in alcohol. This addiction would haunt him for the rest of his life. Seven months after Catherine's death, Arthur Ignatius Conan Doyle entered the world.

2

The Tour
The London Hospital, 8 AM

It was October 3, 1910, and the British Empire was at its pinnacle, so vast the sun never set on it. At the center of the Empire, its crown jewel, the city of London, was welcoming the new day. Just outside the ancient city walls, from the district known as the East End, which had become the unofficial repository of the less fragrant activities of the city—its tanneries, its breweries, its foundries, its slaughterhouses—malodorous, dirt-filled smoke was beginning to be coughed out. In Whitechapel, the East End's most poverty-stricken area, sweepers in their tattered hats and threadbare clothing had just completed their morning rounds, the dusty cyclones spawned by their brooms still swirling above the cobbles and sidewalks surrounding the London Hospital. Despite their efforts, the layers of filth and putrefaction that had been stomped into the stones and pavement over time seemed too thick ever to be scraped away completely.

At the hospital's northwest gate, a lone man stood blade straight, his powerful frame cutting a commanding figure. Indeed, the willingness of this model of British Imperialism, Sir Arthur Conan Doyle, to stand unaccompanied and wait for a group of strangers in a place such as Whitechapel might have seemed odd, but he had made a promise to the colleagues of a semi-secret organization called "Our Society," which he had joined in 1904, to guide a hand-selected group of their friends and relatives on a "certain tour" of this rugged neighborhood. Dubbed the "Murder Club" by the press, Our Society, which would later call itself the "Crimes Club," was essentially a supper club comprised of individuals of the highest intellect and influence, including authors, doctors, and lawyers, who met in private to debate popular criminal cases as well as the nature of the criminal mind.

Aside from the group's focus on criminology, the complete truth of what went on at its exclusive dinner parties was known to no one other than invited guests. The organization's objectives had once been ludicrously misrepresented in print, but the media's fabricated tale and its inaccurate account of the assembly's activities only served to compound the mystery surrounding the group. None of those who had been selected to rendezvous with Doyle this morning were remotely aware of anything that went on behind the club's closed doors.

Always the gentleman, Doyle had adorned himself in a camel-hair suit, complete with a fitted white shirt, fashionable gold cravat, plaid vest, and brown derby hat. Completing the portrait of Britannia's favorite son were ringlets of smoke that wafted from his calabash pipe, painting his handlebar mustache a distinctive whitish grey. Not even the raucous barks of the street vendors or the influx of beggars, street waifs, and other "miserables" who were beginning to crowd the area were able to detract from Doyle's majestic demeanor.

When a physician on his way to his morning rounds recognized Doyle and asked if he were there researching a new Sherlock Holmes book, Doyle answered that he was there only to meet up with a few of his friends. Doyle then looked up at the hospital building's face, which, except for a large round clock, was otherwise unadorned. He checked the hospital's time against his watch. When he saw that the two were in synchrony, he began tapping his foot on the ground and peering into the courtyard in the hope of spying someone who might be looking for him, but no one fitting such a description was apparent. Punctuality had always been of the essence to this Knight Bachelor. Just when he thought there might have been a failure in communication concerning the time of the meeting, two fashionably appareled men in their early thirties approached him on foot. One was dressed in a navy blue double-breasted suit, the other, in a grey pinstripe.

The gentleman in the grey suit recognized Doyle immediately. "Pardon our tardiness, Sir Arthur, but we were unaware of just how long it takes to walk here from our hotel," he said, extending his thin arm towards Doyle in greeting. "I am Matthew Stanton and this is my younger brother, Evander."

With that, the gentleman in blue offered his hand in salutation. "As is his usual fashion, my brother has taken the liberty of speaking for me," he said. "Allow me to introduce myself. I am Evander Stanton and it is my distinct pleasure to meet you."

Just then a carriage pulled up with its top down, allowing its passengers to enjoy the mild weather. Down from his perch stepped a liveried cabman, who offered his hand to the first of the two lovely ladies he had driven there. She gracefully accepted and was escorted from the treacherously uneven cobblestones to the smooth sidewalk, looking dainty in her yellow lace dress, her bonnet framing her well-coiffed blonde hair. Before the driver could turn around to make his way back, the second woman was one step to the side of him. The picture of refinement in her petticoated pink crêpe dress and large straw hat, she was not the type to accept assistance from any man. Once again, one member of the duo insisted on speaking for both. The lady in the straw hat confidently extended her hand to Doyle and firmly squeezed it. "Glad to meet you, Sir Arthur," she said. "I am Gertrude Pemberton, Max Pemberton's niece, and this is Adelaide Oddie." Adelaide curtsied demurely. Doyle was a bit taken aback by the forthright actions of Miss Pemberton, who by now was already in the process of introducing herself and Miss Oddie to the Stanton brothers.

Within a minute or two, a carriage carrying two finely dressed young men in their late twenties pulled up. They were just as eager to meet the legendary Doyle as were the first arrivals. They waited for the cabman to open their door and asked him to place a step down for them, so that they might avoid scuffing their expensive leather boots. The first one out was of average height, and his long sideburns, clean-shaven face, and morning coat with brass buttons gave him the appearance of a true dandy. Then the second gentleman dismounted from the cab. His manly face, with its finely groomed mustache and piercing blue eyes, made Adelaide's face flush. He seemed to make it a point to draw his gold-chained watch slowly from his inside pocket, allowing everyone to see his fine timepiece. After checking the hour, he slipped it leisurely back into his pocket. As he took his place next to the first man, his athletic physique and tall stature became even more apparent.

The dandy made it a point to introduce himself to Doyle with dispatch. "Sir Arthur, I'm Edgar Collins, nephew of your friend Professor John Churton Collins," he said. "I am quite honored by your invitation, and it is a privilege to be in the company of my literary idol, the man whose imagination gave birth to the world's greatest detective. Your stories provided me with a haven from my studies at Oxford and allowed me to reinvigorate myself after my examinations. Such fine studies of the human mind. My dreams were filled with visions of exploring Baker Street with the creator of Sherlock Holmes."

"I'm happy to know that my work has managed to enter that citadel of higher learning," Doyle said. "And who might be this handsome chap standing next to you, Mr. Collins?"

"Sir Arthur, I am Carrington Lambton, and I, too, am grateful for this extraordinary opportunity," the second gentleman said. "Like Mr. Collins here, I enjoy the good fortune of being related to one of your colleagues. My great-uncle Arthur Lambton has spoken glowingly of your myriad achievements on behalf of the Commonwealth. A Knight Bachelor! That speaks for itself."

"Quite kind of you, Mr. Lambton," Doyle said.

"But of all things, it is your status on the cricket field that impresses my uncle the most," Lambton said.

"Yes, among all things, my favorite pastime," Doyle said.

Soon another gentleman approached the designated meeting place. He wore a soft brown traveling suit, and his bearing suggested that he might once have been a military man. His gold-framed pince-nez was highlighted by its chain, which swooped down across his thick mustache, and his well-manicured beard extended a third of the way up his jaw, adding to his impressive figure. Brandishing a finely carved ebony cane adorned with a silver caduceus, the symbol of his medical trade, he walked with a swagger, heading straight towards Doyle and extending his right hand in greeting. But it was Doyle who spoke first.

"Dr. Hammond, I presume," Doyle said. "So nice to have you here on our side of the Atlantic. I hope you had a pleasant journey across the sea."

"In fact, I did," Dr. Hammond said. "There weren't too many rough spots, and the sea air was delightful. I arrived here fully refreshed and with a clear mind."

"I'm glad to hear that," Doyle said. "And with the advent of the transatlantic cable and the recent advances in shipbuilding, our two great nations will hopefully be able to forge the inextricable link that would rightfully permit us to dominate world affairs. Certainly such a strategic merger would create quite the combination of military and intellectual strength!"

"Dr. Doyle, I have not given much thought to that before, but now that you've suggested it, my interest has been piqued. You're right! Such a union would have its mutual benefits."

"Yes, despite arguments against relinquishing autonomy, which exist on both sides of the Pond. Nevertheless, nothing should be ruled out."

As Doyle was finishing his statement, an apparition dressed in a long trench coat sprung from out of nowhere. It turned and jumped in front of the group, startling the gathering with the greeting, "Cheerio, everyone. I hope you weren't waiting for me?" This strange salutation wasn't the only thing that shocked the guests. The giraffe-like figure appeared to be no more than eighteen years of age. Acne blanketed his cheeks and forehead, his Adam's apple bulged, and he had an apparent lack of shoulders. He was all legs. Doyle did not bat an eyelash, but in lieu of shaking the adolescent's hand, he placed his right arm around the boy's shoulder.

"Glad you could make it!" Doyle said. "Quite the deerstalker cap you have on."

"Thank you very much, Sir Arthur," the young man said. "My hope is to follow in your footsteps. I have read everything of yours that I've been able to get my hands on. And I hope I can measure up."

"Mr. Mitchell, I think you have a lot of potential. I have certainly enjoyed reading the treasure trove of letters you've sent me over the past few months. And some of your alternative endings for my stories have been rather entertaining. Let me hazard a guess: You're studying literature up at Cambridge?"

"Actually, Sir Arthur, my concentration is something more mundane: the history of Europe."

With his select group now complete, Doyle led the members into the hospital's courtyard, where it was quieter. "Ladies and gentlemen, a good morning to you all," he said. "Allow me to properly introduce myself. I am Sir Arthur Conan Doyle of Scotland and England. It is my pleasure to escort you on an excursion that I once took with some of your family members and friends. My perspective on certain events that occurred here a bit more than two decades ago in the neighborhood of Whitechapel and its surroundings gave them such pleasure that they asked me if I wouldn't mind taking a few of their loved ones on a similar tour. I was more than happy to oblige them, but I elected to restrict this little outing to eight people. You are all the beneficiaries of eight long straws drawn at a round dinner table. Those who sponsored you for this walk about town were granted permission to inform you of its purpose, but it is my suspicion that at least a few of you have no idea as to what is about to transpire. Before we embark on our journey, I would like you to introduce yourselves to each other. Let us begin with those who arrived first."

With this, the gentleman in the grey suit started things off. "I'm Matthew Stanton," he said, pointing his finger towards the man next to him, "and this is my brother Evander."

Evander's facial expression revealed his displeasure with his brother's action, but this didn't stop him from talking. "Once again, my older brother has insisted on speaking for me," he said. "Let me introduce myself to all of you. I'm Evander Stanton, and what Matthew neglected to tell you is that we are confectioners from York."

"Very good!" Doyle said. "And next we have our two fair ladies. Would you be kind enough to tell us your names and places of origin?"

"Sir Arthur, it is a pleasure to be here. I am Gertrude Pemberton from Kent, and my darling uncle Max, as I mentioned, is the one who provided me with this wonderful invitation. I must say that your historical works like *The White Company* enthrall me. Even more than Macaulay's."

"Thank you," Doyle said. "Quite a compliment, as he is my hero. It is unusual for people to remember me for anyone other than Holmes and Watson these days. By the way, your uncle Max possesses one of the brightest minds I have ever come across. And when you see him, please tell him he still owes me a visit. I want to show him my bicycles. He will understand."

Next, the other young lady introduced herself. "I'm Adelaide Oddie from nearby Wembley. My cousin Sam tells me that I'm in for a forensic treat and if anyone should know about that topic, it's Sam," she said.

"Oh, so you know the nature of my agenda! Capital! But please keep it to yourself for now. Suspense is good for some," Doyle said.

"Sir Arthur," Gertrude said, "as an aside, before you go on to the next person, I just want to personally thank you on behalf of all the women of Great Britain for championing our right to divorce."

With this laudatory statement, Doyle's chest puffed and his lips pursed. He sniffed in deeply through his nostrils. "My dear Miss Pemberton, it is only the misinterpretation of certain Biblical texts that has prevented members of the gentler sex to obtain what should be a natural right."

The disbelieving faces of all the male members, save Dr. Hammond, were a testament to the general attitude of the British male. But when

Gertrude demanded that Doyle take up the cause of women's suffrage as well, both he and Dr. Hammond recoiled in surprise. "Perhaps we shall discuss this over lunch some other day," Doyle said, closing the subject.

The next guest to introduce himself was Edgar. "Good morning, everyone," he said. "Edgar Collins is the name. After prepping at the King Edward's school in Birmingham, I went on to Oxford. I am now a solicitor back in my home city."

"Very good," Doyle said. "I know Birmingham very well as I spent several years in my early career in medicine up at Aston Villa. I have even met one of its former mayors!"

"You're a physician?" Edgar said.

"But of course," Doyle said, "although I am no longer engaged in clinical practice."

Next spoke the Don Juan of the group. "Carrington Lambton of London," he said, "although this is a section of the city I have never been to. Not only that, but Whitechapel was just a name to me till today. I didn't realize its proximity to my place of residence."

"And where might that be?" Doyle asked.

"Hampstead."

"Ah! Very good. One of the most beautiful spots in the entire city. I know every nook and cranny of that part of our 'village.' And what do you do there?"

"I'm a financier, but my great-uncle knows of my passion for Poe's Monsieur Dupin, and for your two sleuths. That's probably why I'm here today."

"Very well then."

Doyle then turned to his American visitor, Dr. Hammond. Dr. Hammond lifted his head high, adjusted his glasses, and took a deep breath, pulling his jacket slightly away from his body. "I'm Philip Hammond, and as all of you can easily tell, I am from the United States of America, specifically New York City, where, unlike Dr. Doyle, I continue to practice medicine. I regard it as both an honor and a privilege to be here with you today. When my friend and colleague Herbert Crosse offered me the opportunity to meet the acclaimed Dr. Doyle, there was no way I could turn it down. I want to tell our host that the chance to meet him was the sole reason I boarded an ocean liner and made this trip, and that once our adventure has been completed, I will be heading straight home. Apparently, I am the only one present here today who knows of Dr. Doyle's wizardry in the field of medical detective work, not to mention his sheer determination and dauntless nature. Are you aware that the man who stands before you had the grit to confront and expose the weaknesses of the tuberculin theory put forth by the acknowledged leader of western medicine, Dr. Robert Koch? Dr. Doyle is a clinical investigator and accomplished researcher of the first magnitude."

As Dr. Hammond lavished praise on Doyle, Sir Arthur placed one hand up in the air, signaling him to stop. "Although Dr. Hammond insists on elevating me to the status of a demigod, I have to interrupt him at this point," Doyle said. "Dr. Hammond is not just any old doctor, although I can see that he is a very modest one. During a medical career spanning more than thirty years, he has authored a substantial number of articles and books that address the subject of sociopathy, or what you might call the study of madmen—both those who act alone and those who act in groups. Dr. Hammond has served on innumerable select committees and has held very prestigious positions in both the private and the public sector. Dr. Hammond, it is a pleasure and a treasure to have you along with us today. But I must ask this question of you: What do you hope to gain from our stroll around Whitechapel?"

"My objectives for today's visit are twofold," Dr. Hammond said. "The first is my particular interest in Jack the Ripper, and the second, and more important one, has already been completed."

"What's that?" Doyle said.

"It is the opportunity to meet the only person in the world who has such hands-on experience with crime." Dr. Hammond now addressed the group. "My new friend, Dr. Doyle, is certainly not a mere armchair detective. Rather, he is the most respected and admired solver of crimes in all of the Americas, and, for that matter, the world."

Doyle, sensing the group's anticipation of what they were about to experience, felt compelled to add some comic relief to the moment. "Alas and alack! Now they know," he said. "I'm afraid, Dr. Hammond, my dear colleague, you have let the proverbial cat out of the bag. But of course, if you hadn't, I would have been forced to do it myself." The eyes of the group gleamed with enthusiasm. Doyle then spread both of his hands up and away from his body as if he were Moses parting the Red Sea. "We are in pursuit of Jack the Ripper."

Now they were all aware that they were to assist the creator of the world's greatest detective in an attempt to solve the most beguiling mystery of all time.

"I sense that you're excited about this journey into madness and mayhem," Doyle said.

"Oh. And one more thing, Dr. Doyle," Dr. Hammond said. "It is my hope that once this tour has ended, I will be able to put forth my own theory that will capture and encapsulate the warped personality of this murderer so that the authorities will finally be able to bring him to justice."

"Dr. Hammond, I wish you the best of luck, and it is my hope that this excursion will be of some service to you," Doyle said. "And last but not least, if I may employ a banal but useful phrase, our fellow in the interesting hat."

"I assume that would be me," the young man said. "I'm Stephen Mitchell, and I am quite pleased to meet you all. As you can see by my outfit, I have fallen under the spell of Sir Arthur's literary genius."

"Thank you! I am flattered," Doyle said.

"I regard this as the most important day of my life, never having dreamed that I would be invited to be in the presence of the greatest man of our age," the baby-faced lad said.

"Again, you flatter me, Mr. Mitchell," Doyle said. "Now, let us review today's particulars." As Stephen lifted his long cape, reached into his back pocket, and pulled out a notepad and pencil, Matthew softly chuckled. Doyle continued. "This tour, which will reach its conclusion at 6 PM, commences right here. But before we begin our journey into the sinister world of this real-life villain, I ask all of you to put aside, or at least to compartmentalize, anything and everything you think you know about this matter. I am going to furnish you with details heretofore unknown to you. I will also ask you to draw your own conclusions based upon the additional information with which you will be provided today. I will be taking you to the exact locations of the five killings that constitute the 'Ripper canon.' Some or all of you may be aware that the number of murders purported to have been committed by the notorious Jack range from as few as four to as many as two dozen, but I agree with the list of the 'official' five.

"If you should have any questions along the way, feel free to ask them. It is my hope that by the conclusion of this tour all of you will have a keen appreciation of just how fraught with difficulty this case was and remains. For the record, Scotland Yard, our nation's top police force, has diligently and fastidiously searched the world for any evidence that would lead to the arrest and hanging of Jack for the murders he committed almost twenty-three years ago. I certainly do not expect us to crack the case in a period of a few hours. At this juncture, it is my duty to inform you that this tour is not for the faint of heart. If you are not prepared to steel yourself against the more grisly and macabre aspects of this butchery, feel free to leave now."

Doyle paused for a moment. As there were no takers of his offer, he made ready to start. "Now, my dauntless ones, if there are no questions, let us begin!"

"Hold, sir. One moment," Stephen said. "Are we going to be proceeding chronologically or in some other order?"

"This tour will be conducted sequentially so that it may end at the appointed hour of 6 PM," Doyle said. "It appears to me that this is the proper way to attempt to unravel the terrible events that took place during the infamous autumn of 1888."

"Don't you mean summer and autumn of 1888, Sir Arthur?" Stephen said.

"I stand corrected. Summer and fall, it was indeed. And so we begin."

"Before we start, Sir Arthur, may I ask you a question?" Edgar said.

"Certainly, Mr. Collins."

"Were either you or Dr. John H. Watson trained here?"

"Although I met the criteria for admission here, it was my home city of Edinburgh's medical college that I chose for my education. At the time, it was a better fit for me. And as for Dr. Watson, he is purely fictional. Good question, though. Now we have to get back to the nightmarish reality of Jack the Ripper. In order for us to proceed down these streets without interfering with other pedestrians, I am going to divide us into groups of two."

With that, Doyle paired Stephen with Dr. Hammond, Edgar with Adelaide, Carrington with Gertrude, and Matthew with his brother, Evander. The duos then fell in line behind Doyle. Whitechapel's reputation had filled most of them with at least some trepidation, but the confident look on Sir Arthur's face helped to relieve almost all of their apprehensions. As Doyle led them towards Turner Street, he sped up his pace.

"This area's reputation for violence and poverty may have prevented you all from appreciating its many historic sites, churches, and pioneering factories, which have been here for centuries," Doyle said. "Whitechapel is also a contemporary hotbed of activity, and more than several societal changes have had their origins right here inside its buildings and outside on its streets and lanes. Some local color before we reach the scene of the first crime! Diagonally across the street on Baker's Row is the Pavilion Theatre, which was built almost 100 years ago in 1828, and which has the capacity to hold almost 3,000 patrons. It was rebuilt once and today . . ."

Edgar's voice interrupted Doyle's monologue. "If that's Baker's Row, is Baker Street nearby?" he said.

Doyle quickly replied that he had never been down Baker Street in his entire life and had no intention of ever setting foot on it, and that it was not nearby. He politely but firmly made it clear that any further mention of either Baker Street or Dr. Watson was strictly forbidden. Only the factual elements of the Ripper murders were open for discussion at the moment. He mentioned that there were many tours devoted to the characters Holmes and Watson, but also issued the disclaimer that he had not the slightest affiliation with any of them. Doyle then pointed out that they had already passed the shop in which, only twenty-five years before, that beleaguered soul, Joseph Carey Merrick, the "Elephant Man," had been placed on exhibition.

A few seconds later, a massive crowd of the most poverty-stricken members of Whitechapel society came into view. It was so tightly packed that its constituents seemed to be glued together. When Doyle's entourage stopped in their tracks to gawk at them, Doyle said that what they were witnessing was the daily quest of the unwashed poor to get some breakfast for themselves.

"The so-called Salvation Army that Dr. William Booth founded will give these unfortunates a bit of sustenance," Doyle said, "provided they agree to attend this new religion's services. These downtrodden start gathering at night, so that they may be the first in line for food. There are no seats here, and so they are forced to stand erect, hour upon hour, for two pieces of bread, a wafer of cheese, and a mug of 'water bewitched,' or weak tea, which they are not permitted to consume until almost noon, when the attempt to convert them has ended. I do hope that Mr. Booth might one day devise a kinder method of feeding the hungry.

"Thankfully, Dr. Thomas Barnardo has already tried to get around this vicious circle of misery, removing as many of the children of Whitechapel from the depths of poverty as he is able and sending them to Canada. There they are the recipients of something to which they have no access here: an education. When they return to London as adults, they are properly equipped to escape from the stagnant depth of poverty in which they were previously mired. I concur with the good doctor that this approach may provide them with the only way they can return to London to function as productive members of society."

The tour began to move, and Doyle continued his narration. "Although we won't be passing it, the Whitechapel Bell Foundry is nearby. Its workers produced the bell that informed Dr. Hammond's brothers across the sea that the Declaration of Independence had been signed. And a hundred or so years later, this same foundry cast Big Ben, which is now one of the salient landmarks of this great city. As we will soon be reaching our first stopping place, I'm going to provide all of you with a bit more background information. In the late summer of 1888, a murderer was stalking the women of Whitechapel. Somehow, this dastardly coward was able to kill at least four prostitutes out in the open, eviscerating three of them. An even more grisly element of these assaults was that on four occasions he left them on the sidewalks right where he had committed his foul deeds. Only one of the victims was found indoors. Perhaps unsatisfied by his ghoulish actions, he may have had the audacity to leave clues in the form of letters, body parts, and even a wall graffito at the various crime scenes. He issued a challenge to both our Scotland Yard and the Metropolitan Police Force to 'catch me when you can.' But there was to be no conviction in the wake of these horrible and terrifying events, even though many men were questioned by the police."

"Sir Arthur, you made it a point to tell us that only men were interrogated," Gertrude said. "How is it that no women were questioned? All the victims were prostitutes, a fact that suggests they were business rivals. As it is said, all is fair in love and war."

"I simply cannot believe that," Adelaide said.

"Ladies," Doyle said, "this is not the proper time for bringing up a 'Jill the Ripper.' As a matter of fact, one of my biggest contributions to the Yard is my theory that a 'Jill' of sorts may have had something to do with this hideous series of crimes. When the time is right, my hypothetical 'Jill' will make an appearance. For now, let us limit ourselves to the Yard's assumption that a minimum of five women were randomly selected for death, and that no ulterior motives like robbery or sexual assault were involved."

Dr. Hammond asked Doyle's permission to speak, and Doyle granted it. "Dr. Doyle, the Yard's assumption is most probably wrong. My many years of clinical and investigative work have made me a firm believer that there is no such thing as a random or motiveless murder. Otherwise there would have been no rationale for these murders to have taken place at all. Perhaps the evildoer who slew these women possessed an intrinsic propensity to kill his fellow human beings, while also having the where-withal to conceal it. Sometimes the underlying forces that impel a killer to commit his heinous acts cannot be altogether understood by normal members of humankind. Maybe Jack's motives were invisible to those whose minds are set to the rational interpretation of things."

"My friends," Doyle said, "Dr. Hammond has just brilliantly suggested that murders without apparent motives tend to be understood by the police and the public as being the products of the perpetrator's insanity. In reality, however, there is always an underlying basis for such killings. In the cases involving the Ripper, the immediate reason simply couldn't be discerned by those who looked at things from what we consider to be a normal perspective. Perhaps some insight into the workings of the Ripper's twisted mind is still to be found, and maybe the murderer will be brought to justice! Thank you, Dr. Hammond, for sharing that with us. But now we are at the exact site where the Ripper made his premiere performance, where poor Mary Ann Nichols, Jack's first victim, met her end. Right here.

"Prior to Mrs. Nichols's unfortunate demise, two other murders had been committed within 300 yards of this particular location. They, too, remained unsolved, and as they were performed in a Ripper-like manner, they also became attached, for a time, to Jack. My work with Scotland Yard has borne out my theory that the murders of Emma Smith and Martha Tabram could not have been his work. Therefore, for all intents and purposes, the murder of Mrs. Nichols must be considered the first of the five East End killings. On the last day of August, at 3:30 AM, as Mary Ann Nichols was making her way back to her place of lodging, or perhaps to some other location, she wound up here on Buck's Row."

When Adelaide asked what Mary Ann Nichols was doing out in the streets at that time of night and why she had been unaccompanied, Doyle let out a halting laugh. "My dear Miss Oddie," he said, "this woman was conducting business in her usual manner. Hers was the traditional way of plying her trade, the world's oldest profession."

"I guess I've never given any thought to it until this very moment," Adelaide said. "I understand."

"A cabman named Charles Cross was on his way to work when he spotted something right here at the entrance to Brown's Stable Yard," Doyle said. "Can any of you tell me what might have passed through his mind when he saw a large object stretched out in the street in the middle of the night?"

"Perhaps Mr. Cross thought the object was an inebriated man," Adelaide said.

"Very good guess," Doyle said.

"Maybe a lame or dead animal," Matthew said.

"Another good guess," Doyle said, "but Mr. Cross actually thought that he had noticed a tarpaulin lying in the gateway to the stable yard. When he walked over to check on it, however, he saw that it was no tarpaulin, but rather a woman lying supine on the muddy cobblestones. Another cabman named Robert Paul was also on his way to work at the time and was hailed by Mr. Cross for assistance. The two of them thought that this was just one more of the many intoxicated homeless women who line Whitechapel's streets after visiting the local pubs during the warm nights of summer. Upon more careful inspection, they noticed that her skirt had been lifted and that her legs were slightly apart. They concluded that she had been attacked and may have also been the victim of a sexual assault.

"When Mr. Cross summoned the courage to touch the victim's hands, he told his fellow carriage driver he thought her extremities were too cold for her to still be alive. Paul refused to accept the finality of all this, and he placed his own hand on her face and hands. Next he crouched down and listened to her chest to see if she had any breath left in her body. As he brushed her chest with his ear he convinced himself that he heard shallow breathing sounds. Fearing for his reputation and livelihood, he lowered her raised skirt in a gentlemanly gesture to preserve her modesty. This having been done, the two men began walking towards their stables, but made sure to inform the first constable that they came upon of what they had seen, and of what they had done on her behalf."

Edgar was amazed at what he had just heard. "Are you implying, Sir Arthur, that they really believed this woman was still alive?" he said. "That's unfathomable to me, and also, I am sure, to others here."

"In the recent past, such an inference was fathomable my dear Mr. Collins," Doyle said. "Unlike the constabularies, cabmen did not carry lanterns with them, and so they could not have properly inspected the wounds sustained by this woman. On the contrary, they would have been forced to rely on the dim lighting thrown off by the alley's homes and factories, which amounted to almost no light at all. Thomas Edison had yet to become a household word, and it was the old lamplighter who illuminated the streets of Whitechapel. But let us continue where our story left off. When the two cabmen came upon Constable Jonas Mizen, they told him of what they had seen. He immediately raced towards the crime scene. But when he arrived, another constable, John Neil, was already in the midst of his own investigation. Constable Neil had just signaled with his lantern for the assistance of another officer who was in the vicinity, Constable John Thain. Thain and Mizen arrived nearly simultaneously, and when all three of them directed their lanterns on the victim, they discovered that her throat had been brutally slashed from ear to ear. Word went out to fetch a local physician, Dr. Rees Ralph Llewellyn."

Doyle paused. "Let us stop here for just a minute and assess the situation with which the constables were confronted. Had you been in their shoes, which clues would you have addressed first? Keep in mind, blood was still oozing from her throat and, although her upper extremities were reportedly cold, her lower extremities were, to their collective surprise, still rather warm."

Carrington was the first to volunteer. "I would want to know if anyone in the neighborhood had heard or seen anything that would have drawn their attention," he said.

"Capital!" replied Doyle. "And that is precisely what these constables did. They immediately set about the area and questioned as many people as they could, even if it meant waking them up. As you can see, only one side of this street is inhabited, and the constables made sure to ring the doorbells of each and every apartment so that they could interrogate the residents, in an attempt to discover whether anyone had heard the cry of murder or had seen anything even the least bit suspicious. There was a universal consensus that there had been no disturbances whatsoever. Constable Thain went over to a nearby abattoir and questioned the slaughterhouse workers. His queries were met with similar responses. Once Mrs. Nichols's body had been carted away to the mortuary, Inspector Spratling came to examine it. When he lifted up her clothing, he observed that she had sustained deep abdominal wounds and that her entrails had been ripped out."

"So that's how Jack got his surname," Edgar said.

"Maybe, maybe not," Doyle said. "Now, as I was saying, to Spratling's surprise, her stays and her buttons were still fastened."

Stephen slowly took out his notebook, made some sort of entry in it, and without bothering to lift his head, nonchalantly stated that it must have been terribly dark outside if three constables were unable to observe the butchery that had been performed upon Mrs. Nichols. Doyle agreed. "I have a question," Stephen said. "If Jack had to work with the same paucity of light, how would he have been able to commit such a violent and specific attack so successfully? He certainly could not have been carrying a lantern. And what adds more weirdness to this particular case is the fact that the killer was able to carry out this attack so quickly."

"Mr. Mitchell, a small point," Doyle said. "According to the information gathered by the Yard, Jack would have had up to twelve minutes to complete his attack upon the dear woman."

"But, Sir Arthur, you yourself have told us that Mr. Cross listened to the lady's chest with his ear, which would have put him at a distance of less than a few inches from the body at most, yet he did not notice the victim's neck wounds or abdominal wounds. This seems almost impossible, even in dim lighting, unless the cabmen did not do what they said they did, or perhaps they did something they shouldn't have."

"Ah! I see. Are you implying that they didn't even attempt to assist Mrs. Nichols, and that they left her there without ever coming to her aid?"

"More than that! The possibility remains that they worked in tandem to put an end to her."

"You are correct, Mr. Mitchell. It is possible." Doyle addressed his next comments to the group as a whole. "The lighting throughout Whitechapel tends to be uniformly quite poor, and yet it must be assumed that Jack carried no lantern. With the moon serving as his sole light source, he must have had the eyes of a cat."

"His excellent vision suggests he was a young man," Dr. Hammond said, "or that his retinas contained extra rods and cones!"

"Just extra rods, Dr. Hammond," Doyle said. "Rods give us our night vision. Cones are for color only."

"Very good, Dr. Doyle."

"So you agree that Jack did not carry a lantern?" Stephen said.

"He would never have been so careless as to draw attention to himself in such a way. Jack relied on his own two eyes," Doyle said. Stephen quickly jotted something down in his notebook. Doyle, ever the perfect host, waited for him to finish writing and place his notebook back into his pocket. He then continued. "In regard to any possible involvement of Mr. Paul and Mr. Cross, I am hard-pressed to imagine that they had anything at all to do with this crime, as they were the very ones who informed a constable that a crime might have taken place. That there was no blood on their persons is sure, for the constable would have observed it. So, these two are not our Jack, just unfortunate pedestrians who were at the wrong place at the wrong time. It's odd, but your question served to bring another portion of this case to mind, something I must have suppressed for years. At the time this crime took place, it was the press that printed a bold-typed theory that a gang of blackmailers might have been involved in these murders. I say 'these' because, as I have already told you, Mrs. Nichols was believed to have been Jack's third victim. As an expert on pathological behavior, Dr. Hammond, what opinions can you offer in regard to such a theory?"

"Such a theory doesn't make much sense at all," Dr. Hammond said, "because gangs desire to do their bad work, if you will, without inspiring the wrath of the community that surrounds them. While a confederacy of criminals may wish to plunder or to terrorize, it also knows that it can be easily broken by scientifically conducted cross examination and the promise of reward."

"I couldn't have said it better myself," Doyle said. "Although it remains questionable as to how scientifically the police conducted their cross examinations of potential wrongdoers, and as for the issuance of rewards, we shall get back to that a little later. But it is plain and true that this killer worked alone. Now, going back to my original question, what are other clues for which one might look?"

"I would look for carriage tracks," Gertrude said confidently and assertively.

Doyle, slowly bobbing his head up and down, prodded her for further explanation. "And why is that?" he said.

"If nothing so much as a whimper was heard, then maybe she wasn't killed at this spot. Maybe she was transported here by carriage already dead."

"Wonderful thought process, Miss Pemberton," Doyle said. "And you'll be happy to know that Constable Neil did just that. He searched the ground for scents and for fresh carriage tracks, but he came up with nothing of significance. But I must confer a collective bravo on all of you. Yours is certainly a virtuosic performance that rivals the Yard's."

"Are you sure that is a favorable comment?" Carrington mumbled.

"In fact, it is, Mr. Lambton," Doyle said. "While at first many held to the theory that Mrs. Nichols was transported here from somewhere else, it was proven to be without any foundation. She was killed on this very spot. On their first view of the scene, the apparent absence of blood on the ground led the police astray. But when the victim's body was lifted onto the simple handcart that served as a makeshift ambulance, the body-bearers watched their hands become saturated with blood as the liquid leached out from her clothing."

Dr. Hammond spoke. "Dr. Doyle, when a throat is slit, are not massive amounts of blood typically ejected? I am asking you to opine as to whether the spurting, not the oozing, of blood would have been observed by the constables. And further, would it be your opinion that blood would have dripped down Mrs. Nichols's bodice and skirt if she had been attacked and killed in the erect position? It was only after the unfortunate woman was moved that any blood was discovered, which implies that it had been trapped and pooled underneath her body, correct?"

"Yes, my American friend," Doyle said, "a valid point. And I am in total agreement with your hypothesis. Several explanations of how the attack may have been carried out were soon forthcoming. One scenario suggested that the killer had attacked Mary Ann Nichols from the front while a second scenario had her being killed only after she had been forced to the ground." Doyle now addressed the group. "The eminent Dr. Hammond's assertion that Mrs. Nichols's neck was ripped open while she lay in the supine position seems to be most logical, as there was absolutely not even a spot of blood visible on the ventral, or anterior, surface of her body. In fact, after his review of the scene, Dr. Llewellyn arrived at this same conclusion."

"Not exactly," Dr. Hammond said. "There were two discrete parts to her murder, and what I am suggesting is that Mary Ann Nichols was murdered while standing in the upright position."

"Dr. Hammond, I'm a bit confused," Doyle said.

"Please grant me a moment to clarify my thoughts. What I am saying is that the victim was slain while in the orthostatic, or upright, position, but her killer, for some reason, was driven to slash her throat after she had been placed on her back upon these filthy cobblestones."

"But there would be no need to do something so anticlimactic."

"The word here is not 'need.' Mrs. Nichols was placed on the ground after death, when her heart would have been asystolic, which is to say, not pumping. With the cessation of a beating heart, her blood would not have left her body in throbs. Rather, it would have trickled out. This would have left Jack a clean surgical field, if you will, somewhat akin to a surgeon performing an elective procedure. Would you not agree?"

Doyle congratulated Dr. Hammond on his ability to merge his medical knowledge with great detective work. He clapped his hands and yelled out, "Bully for you! Keen reasoning! My conclusion exactly!" The electricity in the air was charged even further when Doyle revealed that, in all likelihood, Mrs. Nichols had been the victim of a technique known as "throttling," basing his argument on the bruises that covered her face and her slashed tongue, which suggested she had attempted to ward off her killer as he was smothering her face to asphyxiate her.

"Thank you, Dr. Doyle," Dr. Hammond said. "Perhaps, the 'throttling' concept lends even more credence to my clean surgical field theory. After all, the full extent of the savagery wasn't appreciated until her autopsy. Only then was it discovered that her upper body had remained fully clothed with her bodice stays in place and her buttons buttoned. Yet, while her insides had been brutally mutilated, there was a certain neatness to the killer's approach that might make one think that he came to the site with a well-rehearsed scheme."

The other seven members looked on in bewilderment as the two physicians continued their great debate. Dr. Hammond did not stop his barrage of questions and opinions. "I'm on Mr. Mitchell's side when it comes to the actions of Mr. Paul and Mr. Cross," he said. "Those two blatant liars never intended to help that wretched woman."

"Just how have you arrived at that conclusion, Dr. Hammond?" Doyle said.

"Mr. Mitchell told us that Mr. Cross listened to the victim's chest in the hope of hearing the sound of breathing. In other words, he would have knelt down beside her in the street. Wouldn't his clothing have been soaked by the pool of blood that surrounded her? And if Mr. Paul had really touched her hands, wouldn't he, too, have crouched down next to her?"

"Not necessarily, Dr. Hammond. They likely bent their knees to gain access to her, but probably didn't make contact with the blood in the street. After all, Mr. Paul's statement that her hands were cold to the touch was borne out later. As for Mr. Cross's statement, the man was probably so laden with guilt that he felt duty bound to tell the police that he had tried to see if the poor lady was alive. We must forgive him if he failed to listen to her chest."

Dr. Hammond's only response to Doyle's theory was to cross his arms and tap his right foot rhythmically. After a ten-second interval, Doyle informed everyone that Mary Ann Nichols's clothing had absorbed a great majority of her blood, preventing the two cabmen from noticing it. He implied that this validated the story told by the three constables, which stated that there was a paucity of visible blood in the crime area until the body was moved. Doyle then asked the tour group to look around the area for anything that might be relevant to the case. While the eight amateur sleuths began to comb and scrutinize the area, Doyle stood apart and watched. A few moments later, Stephen separated himself from the group and came over to Doyle. Something was bothering him, and he was hopeful that Doyle could solve the problem.

"It appears to me that this side of the street would have been darker than the other because everybody lives over there," Stephen said, pointing at the rows of tenement buildings directly across from where they were standing. "There is always some random light emitted by lanterns or candles in apartments. Do you think the murderer might have known this, or do you think it was sheer luck that took him to the darkest spot in the alley? I get the feeling that Jack may have known that this was the side of the street with the least light, and that it would have been less traveled than the other side."

Doyle's eyes lit up and he smiled. "You may be on to something," he said, "but unless we come back here one night, I really cannot draw any conclusions. You do know that in a span of less than ten minutes, a minimum of three people managed to walk past her body, even though the area was regularly policed at all hours of the night."

"I know that Cross and Paul came upon her. But what do you mean by at least three?" Stephen said.

"There is a third person who saw Mary Ann Nichols after she was murdered and before the police arrived at the scene. The only thing we know about him comes from the statement of Mr. Mulshaw, a night watchman who had been on guard on a neighboring street that night. Although he had fallen asleep during his fourteen-hour shift, he swore that he had been awake at the time when the murder had purportedly taken place. Evidently, a gentleman passing his guard post had told him that he believed someone had been murdered down the street, only to vanish immediately upon offering the information."

"What would rule out the possibility of that person being the Ripper?"

"Nothing at all would negate it. I am quite upset at myself for having buried this incident so deeply in my mind."

By this time, the group had reassembled around Doyle, who informed them of Stephen's question regarding the illumination of the street.

"Sir Arthur, you've mentioned more than once that it was quite dark that night. I am assuming that the moon was new that night, and I have heard theories that lunatics are strongly influenced by this particular phase of the lunar cycle," Carrington said.

Doyle responded that while the moon does exert substantial effects on tides and weather patterns, the phase of the moon associated with lunacy is that of the full moon. No one questioned this statement.

Now Sir Arthur questioned everyone on how they would have gone about trying to determine the identity of the Baker's Row victim. Carrington suggested that placing the victim's picture in the newspapers might have yielded results; Adelaide was more inclined to canvas the immediate area by going door to door; and Evander proposed that the local churches might have been repositories of information. Doyle was of the opinion that, although all of these approaches had their merits, in this case, it was the victim's clothing that had been the key to determining who she was. Apparently, two of her flannel petticoats had borne the mark of the Lambeth workhouse, a place of refuge for London's poorest souls. As soon as these stenciled stamps were discovered, the police went over to interrogate the matron of the shelter and brought her down to the morgue in an attempt to jog her memory. Nothing new was derived from her visit. Once word had spread that another woman had been killed in Whitechapel, two Lambeth women came forward and tagged the victim with the nickname "Polly," revealing her to be a forty-three-year-old prostitute who had been recently staying at a common lodging house over in Spitalfields. When the police questioned the deputy keeper of the place, he told them that on the night of her death she had been evicted by him personally for lack of rent money.

The man identified "Polly" as Mary Ann Nichols, a middle-aged woman who had not long ago become a member of the "unfortunates." Although she had been lucky enough to leave Lambeth to work as a domestic servant, she had made a poor decision in stealing £3 and some clothing from her employer. She had been left with no choice other than to run away and become a street wanderer. Indeed, the deputy recalled that her addiction to clothes superseded anything else, including finding shelter. In fact, when the police questioned him, he thoroughly enjoyed reenacting her parting words to him, which were something to the effect of, "I'll soon get my doss money; see what a jolly bonnet I've got now."

"Now, can anyone interpret that phrase?" Doyle said. His question was rhetorical, as he immediately went on to explain that the typical East End woman would part with all her worldly possessions—would sell herself, body and soul—to become the proud possessor of a velveteen hat or bonnet. It was obvious that Mrs. Nichols's statement alluded to the sad fact that, as someone who possessed a new bonnet, she had already plied her trade with some success earlier that night.

"There but for fortune and a few pence go I," Adelaide whispered. A few members of the group nodded their heads in agreement, although Doyle did not.

"This is not the time to sink into the quicksand of ancient history," Doyle said. "Let us move on, my new friends."

3

1863-1875

Young Arthur

June 1863

Things continued to deteriorate for Mary Doyle. Charles remained mired in alcoholism, and in June of 1863, just one year after the passing of her mother, Mary's two-year-old daughter and namesake succumbed to complications of diphtheria. Instead of submitting to these depressing events, Mary managed to pull herself together and eventually found solace at the Philosophical Institution, Edinburgh's most prestigious intellectual haven. Headquartered at 4 Queen Street, this building, with its well-stocked library and newsroom, was a place where Mary could spend her time reading and debating contemporary issues with some of the most brilliant minds of "New Athens." It was a place in which the strict constraints of Victorian society were conspicuously absent, a place where women were able to remove their aprons and step up to the podium. There were even moments when Mary Doyle's spouse was sober enough to participate in the proceedings and interact with her new friends without embarrassing himself or his wife.

Among the learned individuals of the Philosophical Institution, there was one with whom Mary Doyle formed a close bond. John Brown was a noted physician and writer who, along with Joseph Lister, had been chosen as co-assistant to Dr. James Syme, the leading consulting surgeon of the era. Dr. Brown was in the midst of coping with domestic problems of his own. His wife was in the throes of depression and mental illness. He found in Mary Doyle a kindred spirit. He became her confidant and she became his. Their mutual admiration was apparent.

Although Charles had periods of remission from alcoholism, they were always short-lived, and soon Mary was forced into making a major decision— one that ran counter to the social etiquette of the time. She decided to pack her bags and relocate to the home of her friend Mary Burton, who was more than willing to throw a lifeline to Mary Doyle and her two children and tow them to the safety of Liberton Bank House. That same summer saw the birth of Mary Burton's nephew Cosmo Innes Burton. On many occasions, Mary Doyle and the children accompanied Mary Burton over to Old Craig House, the home of Cosmo's father, John Hill Burton, Mary Burton's very famous brother. The house itself was a mansion majestically situated atop a hill "embosomed among venerable trees," lofty and massive, and replete with stately rooms. Four-year-old Arthur, who had already been steeped in genealogy and heraldry by his mother, must have felt as if he were a great lord as he walked through the estate. It was here at Old Craig House that his intellect would be further stimulated.

John Hill Burton enjoyed a fine reputation as an eminent biographer, legal expert, historian, and secretary of the Scottish Prison Board, but to Arthur his stature came strictly from being the keeper of a grand old house that dated back to the sixteenth century. The impressive home had become a gathering place for intellectuals and Spiritualists. With its countless nooks and crannies, Old Craig House offered Arthur unending opportunities for exploration. It also contained a wonderful library, with books arranged in such a fashion that Mr. Burton "knew where to find any one, even in the dark." The library was open to all visitors with only one exception: the "Green Lady," who, it was claimed, had haunted the place for centuries. For some unknown reason, this female specter was forbidden entry to the library's interior, a regulation that must have come from the "other side." This was the first time that Arthur had heard an adult other than his father and relatives warning him about the existence of another world. As it was John Hill Burton who had uttered these words, young Doyle must surely have taken them seriously. An impressionable Arthur found himself inhabiting a world in which even esteemed members of society believed in the continuing existence of the soul after death.

Arthur soon met John Hill Burton's two daughters, thirteen-year-old Eliza and three-year-old Mary, and his son, seven-year-old William, who immediately took Arthur under his wing. Willie, as he was called, provided young Doyle with a guided tour of the house, including a visit to the chemical and photographic laboratory this child prodigy had set up all by himself. He quickly deputized Arthur to help him track down and forever banish the elusive ghost from the premises of Old Craig House. This youthful partnership was destined to evolve into a lifelong friendship.

Meanwhile, under Mary Doyle's tutelage, Arthur absorbed tremendous amounts of information. He became enamored of the printed word, and even wrote his first tale of adventure, that of a hunter who was unwise enough to follow a Bengal tiger into its cave. Mary, bedazzled by this literary achievement, sent her son's story to his godfather and great-uncle, Michael Conan, a respected art critic who had made a permanent move to Paris after having divided his time between England and the Continent for many years. He was as impressed as Mary had been by his "Dearest Laddie"'s vivid imagination, comical illustrations, and grasp of mature concepts. Struck by Arthur's ability to weave a complex tale with a minimum of words—the gift of a natural-born storyteller—Michael Conan would be prompted to write to Mary, "With regard to that philosopher, Master Arthur, whose sympathy with the carnivorous tiger is so ultra comical. I shall look to his development with great interest." In this same letter, Michael responds to Mary's request that he offer his opinion on where a boy of such promise should be educated, saying:

The question you ask about his schooling can have scarcely yet arisen. Keep him at your apron strings for two or three years more, at least. You can teach him much of the initiating and more necessary matters. Win him into multiplication, division, and the rule of three and make him practically familiar with geography. I would soon familiarize him with maps. His more serious schooling gives to a nice question. I perfectly accord with you, in all your expansive geniality of opinion—in all your unexclusive humanity—remembering your friend Burns' prophetic record—"It's coming yet for a' that, that man to man, the world over, shall brothers be, for a' that." And I do encourage my old acquaintances, the Jesuits, for their devotion to the per-centa creed—but in matters of education—I mean mere secular education, they are, from experience and their employment therein, of the highest order of mind, unmatched. Therefore the question will assume this form—viz, have you any school at Edinburgh where a boy of gentle birth can be thoroughly well instructed on terms as reasonable as those which you would have to disburse in consigning Master Arthur to the Jesuits—and that gives rise to the further query—have you in Edinburgh, as they have in Dublin, a good Jesuit day school? But this question, as I have said, cannot be ripe for decision for two or three years more. In the meantime, keep your attention awake on the subject and be ready for the final move, when made it must perforce be. As to Arthur's future development, that, apart from Nature's endowments, will much depend upon the mother who cherishes him and at once secures his love and respect.

Over the course of the next two years, Mary dedicated herself to carrying out Michael Conan's implicit mandate. She immersed her son in a home curriculum of geography, history, French, pageantry, and genealogy—subjects that ran parallel to her own interests. Arthur absorbed the material like a sponge and became even more creative.

On February 22, 1866, Mary Doyle gave birth to Caroline Mary Burton, also known as Lottie. Four months later, Mary, unaccompanied by Charles, took her three children across the Irish Sea to visit the wealthy Foley branch of her family near Waterford. While this visit had ostensibly been designed to reconcile some longstanding differences, its true objective was to extract some much-needed tuition money from her relatives to benefit Mary's sole male heir. Despite her best efforts, however, by the trip's end her pocketbook remained unfilled, leaving her with no option other than to downsize to less expensive and less spacious living quarters so that Arthur might be able to attend a fee-based private school, known in the United Kingdom as a "public school."

The family took up residence in Sciennes Hill, a working-class suburb of Edinburgh, with Charles showing up every so often. This once proud neighborhood had fallen on hard times. Less than a century before, it had hosted the initial meeting between Scotland's two most famous literary sons, Sir Walter Scott and Robert Burns. Now, its stately homes were being partitioned into inexpensive multiple-dwelling units. The location's one saving grace was its proximity to the Meadows, the park-like expanse that separated the old part of town from the new and served to make Sciennes Hill a bit more sanitary than the rest of the city. It was only by her willingness to live in such a place that Mary would be able to save enough money to secure an education for her son.

Once settled in Sciennes, Arthur joined up with a neighborhood group of kids known as the Sciennes Hill Place Boys. Doyle was a tough boy, always on the lookout for a skirmish, and frequently called upon to be the gang's knight in armor, its champion. He often found himself enjoying one-on-one combat with different members of the Sciennes Garden Boys, a rival group. After one particularly unsuccessful bout, he returned to his cramped apartment battered and bruised. His mother, however, held fast to her belief that her son was an innocent who had been unfairly bullied and assaulted by one of the local ruffians, crying, "Oh, Arthur, what a dreadful eye you have got!" He responded triumphantly, "You just go across and look at Eddie Tulloch's eye!" No one was ever prouder than Arthur to be an official member of the gang. Doyle would write of his experiences in Sciennes Hill, "My comrades were rough boys and I became a rough boy, too. If there is any truth in the idea of reincarnation—a point on which my mind is still open—I think some earlier experience of mine must have been as a stark fighter, for it came out strongly in my youth, when I rejoiced in battle."

The move to Sciennes Hill led to a temporary reconciliation between Charles and Mary, although Charles resented the loss of proximity to the beach, the sea air, and his art studio. Charles also felt that his wife was giving too little thought to his needs, caring only about the agenda that Michael Conan had laid out for Arthur, and so his bitterness became directed at his only son. In order to shield Arthur from his father's unpredictable behavior, Mary thought it best to send her son over to Liberton Bank House. Mary Burton was the perfect choice to act as a surrogate mother. After all, Mary Doyle could easily convince others that her son was moving in with Burton, an early suffragette and educational reformer, to benefit from a relationship with the renowned educator. It would be easy for her to deceive any questioning individuals by telling them how close Liberton Bank House was to Arthur's school, Newington Academy, where he had recently been enrolled—leaving out the fact that her house was equally close to the establishment. But the separation from his mother, father, and siblings would come with an emotional cost, as Arthur would see them with much less frequency. Thankfully, Arthur's life at Liberton Bank House included visits from Willie Burton, who did his best to spend time with his young friend as often as he could. The two of them loved fishing in the Braid Brae and climbing up to the top of the majestic sycamore that greeted all who visited the house. Bright and resourceful, Willie proved an excellent instructor, displaying his great comprehension of photography as Arthur gloried in the role of Willie's apprentice.

At Newington Academy, pupils were expected to be seen but not heard unless called upon. Arthur's first lesson in the importance of keeping silent came at the hands of the schoolmaster, Patrick Wilson, a "pock-marked, one-eyed rascal" who gleefully subjected Arthur's hands to the vicious lashes of the leather strap known as a tawse. This was not to be Arthur's final experience with teacher-induced pain. Arthur's second year at Newington, however, would be his last at the school. His mother, acceding to Michael Conan's plan for Arthur, had filled out applications to the only two public schools in all of England that were under the auspices of Catholic orders. Downside was run by the Benedictines, while Hodder Place, the lower school of Stonyhurst College, was run by the Society of Jesus. In her attempt to secure her son's future, Mary sent off letters to the Doyle clan, asking them to support their gifted nephew's education. They were all willing to partially subsidize what they regarded as a sage decision on her part, and when Hodder Place awarded Arthur a fifty-pound annual scholarship, Mary's trepidation in regard to finding tuition money subsided. The increasingly influential Michael Conan decreed that Hodder—and later Stonyhurst College—would be the best place for Arthur, not so much due to its emphasis on theology, but because of the time-tested ability of the Jesuit Order to prepare their students for both the secular and ecclesiastical worlds. It was Michael Conan's expectation that one day in the not too distant future Arthur would join the ranks of the other Doyles as an accomplished artist and gentleman. With his tuition now paid, a teary-eyed Arthur set off by train to Lancashire's Preston Station, where a horse and wagon would drive him to his new school.

Beginning at eight years of age, Arthur would spend two years at Hodder Place preparing himself for the main school, Stonyhurst College. The campus of Hodder Place was only a mile from Stonyhurst, but the two divisions were thousands of miles apart in the way they treated their students. Unlike the dirty streets of Edinburgh, the setting in which he found himself was a veritable paradise. Hodder Place overlooked the picturesque stream from which the school borrowed its name. Contrary to the policies of most other public schools, here the practice of fagging, a form of hazing in which the younger students are made the servants of the senior pupils, had been banned. This rule kept bullying to a minimum and prevented many injustices from being perpetrated on the new boys. Arthur eased into the routine with no difficulty, and was able to boast in a letter to his mother that he had won "a nice little Bible picture for winning" a debate. The rough boy from the mean streets of Edinburgh was a natural when it came to intellectual pursuits.

At Hodder Place, Doyle "could hold his own both in brain and strength" with his fellow students. He played many sports, with cricket and football becoming his favorites. He was fortunate enough to "get under the care" of Father Cassidy, the greatest left-legged kicker of the school. Arthur performed even better in his second year than he had in his first. He was granted the label "distinguished" and found himself in the running for a multitude of prizes, which was appropriate, as he seemed innately competitive in all aspects of life.

September 1869

At ten years of age, Arthur was ready to enter Stonyhurst College, Great Britain's premier Jesuit school. As he boarded the train for the familiar four-hour ride to the premises, his thoughts turned to his mother and ever-increasing number of sisters, which now included fourteen-year-old Annette, four-year-old Lottie, and the newest member of the clan, two-year-old Connie. With an adventure novel to occupy his time, Arthur found that the two-hundred-mile journey passed quickly. Although he had visited the upper school at Stonyhurst on two occasions while at Hodder, he hadn't realized how different things were to be at his new school. Stonyhurst was an age-old bastion of Jesuit conservatism, anti-Darwinism, anti-materialism, and most of all, total adherence to the concept of papal authority in all matters secular and ecclesiastical.

Unlike his previous train rides up to Lancashire, when he had been met personally by the priest of the local parish of St. Wilfred's Church upon arrival, there was no one to meet him when he stepped off the train. In fact, not a single member of his grade, or form, could be found. The only person Arthur saw as he exited the locomotive was a cabman sitting upon his carriage seat. As the cabman's only passenger, Arthur found he would have plenty of time for sight-seeing on the thirteen-mile trip to his new school. His journey came to an end as the carriage pulled onto a wide path flanked by enormous rectangular ponds. As soon as his vehicle passed between two huge gateposts, Arthur spied the intimidating grey towers of Stonyhurst. Next to Stonyhurst was a regal cloister, which stood between a Gothic church and a huge Elizabethan building. But it was the Shireburn Shield draped over the school's entry arch that made the biggest impression on Arthur. This old shield had been the emblem of the staunchly Roman Catholic clan, whose county seat, Shireburn Castle, had once been proudly located on Stonyhurst's present site. As he continued along, his mother's wistful stories of the chivalry and bravery that had been displayed by certain Catholic families of the not-so-distant past came to mind. He thought of the noble deeds and great accomplishments of the Doyles, of the Conans, and of his mother's family, the Foleys. The magnificence of this ancient place held Arthur in thrall.

The carriage came to a halt and Arthur found himself in front of a massive courtyard with an expansive stairway that led to the school's main entrance. While scores of both new and returning students surrounded him, his eyes focused only on the impressive mullioned windows that dominated the institution. The rector, Reverend Edward I. Purbrick—a tall, handsome, bespectacled gentleman with a prominent nose—stood in front of the boys. He had a smooth style and an easygoing manner. Purbrick looked at Doyle and instructed him to join his companions. When Arthur hesitated, the rector gave him a guiding push. Arthur was younger than the vast majority of the boys in his class, having been admitted one year early. Many of the other boys had enjoyed recent growth spurts, but as of yet, Arthur had not. Even more significant to Arthur was the disparity between most of the boys and himself in terms of social class and financial resources. He did not have access to extra pocket money, as his father had drunk it all away. In fact, his father's condition was so bad that Arthur had seen Charles crawling around the house like a dog and smashing open his piggy bank, as well as those of his sisters, for the few coins his children had placed inside them. Arthur had also seen his father carrying off his own artwork to be bartered away at local pubs as payment for his bar tabs. But nothing was sadder than watching his own father imbibing furniture polish for its alcohol content. Although Arthur was aware and proud of his family's rich heritage, the poverty his immediate family was enduring in Edinburgh put him ill at ease. After all, his inability to access funds when needed could be a stumbling block to full acceptance by his peers.

Soon, one of the boys he knew from Hodder approached him and asked him to join a game of football that was being played on the nearby great lawn. Arthur agreed to play. As he headed towards the playing field, he saw three black-robed priests pacing up and down what was known as the Prefect's Walk. They were keeping a strict and cautious eye on the students during this, the first day of school. Arthur sensed that they would be monitoring the movements of the students from this moment on.

The next morning a terrible racket of stomping feet and a sudden lighting of gas lamps shocked him from his sleep. Within a few minutes, hundreds of boys milled about him as he scurried down to the washing place along with the other students. He had no truly close friends, no confidants, and no family here—no one to whom he could turn. He knew he could depend only on himself, and that self-reliance would be his passport to survival at Stonyhurst. The spectacle of the school's elite undergraduate students, known as the "Gentlemen Philosophers," who paraded about in a special uniform consisting of a blue tail-coat with gold buttons and fine leather shoes, filled Arthur with awe. It was not just a matter of academic performance that ensured admittance to this special program of Catholic university education; social standing and wealth played their parts. Arthur regarded the Gentlemen Philosophers as the ultimate representation of success for a Roman Catholic boy in the British

Empire. These older boys were worshipped and envied. Buoyed by his wish to become one of the Gentlemen Philosophers, Arthur accommodated himself to the routines of the school.

October 1869

By the end of his first month at Stonyhurst, Arthur had successfully made the adjustment to the daily rituals of this celebrated institution and was enjoying Stonyhurst's massive library. In a letter written to his mother just a few weeks after his arrival, he states, "I have bad news to tell you two poor boys have died at Stonyhurst within the last 3 weeks from getting croup. To my great delight 50 new books have been bought for the library." Helping him to combat any homesickness was the short period of time known as "the walking days," when each entering student was assigned to two of the older boys. These boys, in turn, introduced the newcomer to the customs and nuances of the college.

At the close of each class, the boys would enter a corridor known as the "long room," where their playful banter broke the silence maintained by the prefects positioned there to monitor their activities. Although impressive display cases filled with precious stones and rare minerals lined the hallway, most of the boys were interested only in the collection of taxidermied animals and exotic birds that had been donated by the school's most noted alumnus, Charles Waterton. Dubbed "the dauntless one" by his classmates during his time there, Waterton had already attained legendary status even before his graduation. After all, this was the young man who had risked life and limb to climb to the summit of the Old Tower just to satisfy his urge to reach out and grasp the sculpted eagles perched at its top. Doyle wanted to follow in Waterton's footsteps, but his first attempt to emulate his predecessor by climbing to the top of the gymnasium did not go as planned. He plummeted to the floor below, injuring his ankle as well as his pride. Nevertheless, it would not be the last time he would attempt to reach such great heights.

Waterton's daredevil exploits continued long after his Stonyhurst days had ended. He achieved well-deserved celebrity and acclaim as a naturalist-explorer of the first magnitude when he voyaged to South America in search of the lost city of El Dorado. Although he was unable to locate the city, Waterton's reputation would influence young naturalists such as Charles Darwin and Alfred Russell Wallace. Waterton also achieved more than a bit of notoriety with his "discovery" of human evolution's "missing link." His "nondescript," as he called it, was in actuality nothing more than a red howler monkey, which he had reconfigured to resemble a customs inspector who had overcharged him for his collection of artifacts and animals upon his return to England. Despite the uncovering of this falsification, his reputation soared. Arthur was attracted to a richly colored feather and porcupine quill cap seen in the Waterton display case. It bore a caption written by the great man himself: "Made by me in Rome, for a fancy ball, 1818. Charles Waterton." How uneasy those elegantly dressed attendees must have been when the debonair Waterton strutted into the room wearing that ridiculous hat!

Once the students passed the exhibits, they entered the "do-room," where they ate their meals, which included "dry bread and hot well-watered milk." The school's well-equipped gymnasium featured a vast array of exercise equipment, including Indian clubs, dumbbells, sword-sticks, and an assortment of the newly introduced boxing gloves. The school's mission was to produce men of sound mind and body, so professional instructors were hired to teach the proper techniques of fencing, gymnastics, and pugilism. Young Doyle, who was already an expert in street fighting, was attracted to the boxing ring. In addition to learning the physical components of the "sweet science," he also immersed himself in the study of the recently introduced Queensberry rules. In the process, he became acquainted with the new employee who served in the dual capacity of boxing instructor and superintendent of "penance-walks." As Arthur ranked amongst the most frequently disciplined students, he soon grew accustomed to these isolated disciplinary walks, which took place along a designated path in the playground under the watchful eye of the instructor. One time, when Doyle told a particular teacher that he wished to pursue a career as a civil engineer, the teacher replied, "You may be an engineer, Doyle, but from what I have seen of you, I should think it very unlikely you will be a civil one." Apparently, his activities on campus had endeared him to very few. An unexpected benefit of his many atonements, however, was the improvement of his physical conditioning.

When their instructor led the boys on grueling "long walks," which were often marches of twenty-five miles through the rivers, hedges, and ditches of Pendle Mountain, Arthur was not bothered by these treks in the least. Such was not the case with the other members of his form. Almost all of them were exhausted by the difficulties of these journeys. An incident in his second year at Stonyhurst involved one of the Guibara boys, who, as Arthur explains in a letter home, had to be placed on a hastily made litter of tree branches after succumbing to the rigors of one of the hikes. The boys lugged him for more than two miles until they came upon a man with a dog cart who was willing to transport the young Guibara back to school. The boys were then allowed to wade in the river Ribble to cool off after their heroic effort. Arthur was one of the few boys capable of keeping pace with the instructor, who would spin strange tales about the area's history as he sped through the countryside. It was through these stories that Doyle learned about the witches of Pendle Mountain and their trials, which had taken place more than two centuries before.

Arthur's Stonyhurst years coincided with the college's golden era in the field of astronomy. The observatory, which was in the center of the formal gardens, had earned a worldwide reputation as a respected place of learning and scientific research in the fields of solar and stellar physics. Indeed, two of its priest-scientists were considered leaders in those spheres of study. Father Stephen Perry headed the observatory for many years, with the exception of a three-year religious hiatus known as a tertianship, during which Father Walter Sidgreaves served as the observatory's interim head. Father Sidgreaves hailed from nearby Preston, and, to his credit, had been handpicked by the British Government to repeat Captain James Cook's 1769 mission to observe the transit of Venus in the South Pacific. Perry and Sidgreaves epitomized the Society of Jesus's ability to work in conjunction with the secular world in its efforts to promote scientific advances. These two faculty luminaries had studied at Stonyhurst as young students under another priest-scientist, Father Angelo Secchi, who would later become the Vatican's official astronomer. Secchi was the first person to confer the label of "star" upon the sun, and the first to photograph a solar eclipse. He invented the multipurpose meteorograph, with its uncanny ability to simultaneously measure barometric pressure, temperature, wind velocity, and rainfall. He also developed a spectroscope to determine the composition of distant stars.

Perry, a member of the elite British Royal Society, was known throughout the world for his invention of the self-recording photographic magnetograph. His accomplishment in the new discipline of weather forecasting had led his peers to dub him "the prophet." As a teacher, Father Perry was aware that if a subject was made interesting and kept simple, there was a greater likelihood that his students would learn it sufficiently. One of his favorite teaching devices was a photographic slide projector, which he used to cast giant images onto the wall, a technique that always enhanced the learning experience of his audience.

There is no doubt that the students of Stonyhurst received a first-rate education in all the sciences, especially astronomy. With a huge telescope right on campus, students were afforded the opportunity to see firsthand the rings of Saturn, the moons of Jupiter, and other objects of the solar system. Thanks to Sidgreaves and Perry, Arthur and the other boys would be taught the three basic premises of Copernican theory as well as Newton's gravitational laws.

Arthur's next few years at Stonyhurst were much the same as his first. The ledgers of his professors were continually filled with unflattering and derogatory comments, with words such as "quarrels," "buffoon," "dirty habits," "greedy," "stubborn," "scatterbrain," and "slovenly" appearing multiple times. At the end of his second year, the administration commanded Arthur to write a letter home regarding his appearance. He would write, "I have been requested to ask you, Ma, if I may get another suit of clothes. I can get them very cheap & good here as the Rector has a private tailor. . . ." After completing his second year, Arthur returned home, though his presence was not much acknowledged and he was often forced to fend for himself.

On their first day of their third Stonyhurst year, Doyle and James Ryan worked in cahoots to set off a salvo of firecrackers on the Lancashire train. Doyle would later describe the incident, writing, "Ryan and I let off crackers and romped till we came to Carstairs." A year later, Ryan would again play with firecrackers aboard the train, this time without his confederate. The results of his prank would be nearly disastrous, however, and Ryan would have to seek medical attention at school, becoming forever known as "Gunpowder" by the masters.

Arthur's teachers' descriptions of him and of his pleasure in behaving badly may indicate that something was bothering him. In fact, a letter written by Arthur to his mother in October of 1871 suggests he may have believed that he was being left in the dark about matters back in Edinburgh, as he writes, "You have not written to me for a very long time. I am awfully uneasy. Tell me if anything is wrong and don't conceal it." Thankfully, the unfavorable comments written by the faculty about Arthur proved inversely proportional to his academic performance, and in this same letter he would admit, "I am getting on famously, am in the extraordinary," which was the expression used to describe boys who did very well in their lessons.

September 1873

Arthur arrived back at school in the late summer of 1873 and soon banded together with a group of boys who didn't mind poking fun at their teachers and fellow classmates in a handwritten magazine called the *Wasp*. As its name suggests, the magazine offered stinging attacks on anything the boys perceived as oppression and tyranny at the school, though it also made fun of certain boys who were disliked by its contributors. The fact that the magazine lasted five issues can probably be attributed to the prefects being able to use it to their own benefit. The *Wasp* was unknowingly furnishing those in charge with information they could never have obtained any other way, permitting them to use student dissension and rivalries to the administration's advantage. Eventually, however, the prefects put an end to it, but no punishment was exacted against its writers.

Apparently, Arthur felt there was no lesson to be learned from the fact that the magazine had been shut down, and after the demise of the *Wasp,* he and a fellow student named Roskell launched a new publication called the *Stonyhurst Figaro*. The two boys refused to be restrained by the prefects. The publication's name was probably selected as a tribute to *Le Figaro,* the satirical French daily whose motto was, "Without the freedom to criticize, there is no true praise." According to a letter written to his mother in October of 1873, the new magazine was "how [he] signalized [his] entrance into the higher line." Arthur, who was trying his best to impress the older boys, thought this was the most effective way to curry favor with those he admired. As the publication's "correspondents," Doyle and Roskell wrote enough poems, essays, and what he described as "wicked jokes" to fill a "large 2penny themebook," boasting that "nearly all the higher line have seen it." In a message to his mother, Arthur would confess that he "produced verses that were poor enough in themselves but seem miracles to those who had no urge in that direction." This same letter also implies Arthur's loneliness and longing for home, as he writes, "I was a little frightened in not receiving any letter from you for so long, but your note today calmed my fears." In a later letter, Doyle may have been trying to reveal these sentiments again, as it states:

> We have had a great commotion here lately, from the fact that our third prefect has gone stark staring mad. I expected it all along, he always seemed to have the most singular antipathy to me, and I am called among the boys "Mr. Chrea's friend." Ironically, of course. The first signs of madness were at Vespers the other day. I was near him & I saw him, just as the Laudate Dominum began, pull out his handkerchief and begin waving it over his head. Two of the community took him and at once led him out. They say that in his delirium he mentioned my name several times. A story is going about that before entering the society he fell in love with a maiden, but the maiden absconded with an individual named Doyle, and Mr. Chrea in his despair entered the society, and the

name of Doyle has ever since had an irritating effect on him. I can't
however answer for the truth of this. We are having the most
detestable weather possible over here. Rain, rain, rain, and nothing but
rain. I shall soon at this rate die of ennui, my great comfort however is
the thought of seeing you all again at Xmas.

Stonyhurst has always insisted that no one by the name of Chrea ever
functioned there as a prefect, and so it may be that the events described by
Arthur in the letter had an ulterior motive. Perhaps Arthur conjured up this
tale to gain the attention of either Mary or Charles Doyle, neither of whom
ever managed to visit him at school. His apparent lack of concern with the use
of the Doyle name as the cause of the mysterious Mr. Chrea's wrath, and the
manner in which he writes about the prefect's madness, is bizarre. He glosses
over so much of the sordid event and the rumors that accompanied it that
there is difficulty in believing any of it, especially when a trite account of the
local weather conditions, a statement that a death induced by boredom may
be imminent, and the notion that his "great comfort however is the thought
of seeing [them] all again at Xmas" are all squeezed together in the letter's
final sentence. The concluding words of the missive leave any potential problems that might be related to the incident in Mary Doyle's lap. Surely any
mother would have been dismayed by her son's predicament and possible lack
of safety. As a member of a family who loved word games, Arthur may have
gained an extra bit of satisfaction in coming up with the name "Chrea," an
anagram of the German word for revenge, "rache," which he had heard from
his teacher Father Cyprian Splaine in "a jolly story translated from the
German . . . called 'The Avenger' about a lot of horrible murders." This word
would even appear as a clue in Doyle's first Sherlock Holmes novel, *A Study
in Scarlet.*

What this letter represents is a gifted narrator and writer's initial effort to
show at least one of his parents the life of solitude he perceived himself as
enduring as a student far from home. In 1872, Stonyhurst had issued a new
policy, permitting families to decide whether their children would leave or
remain on campus during the Christmas season. Arthur was one of the very
few non-foreign students who had not gone home for Christmas that year.
Instead, he had remained inside the walls of Stonyhurst during the "long vacation." By 1873, it had been a half-dozen years since he had observed
Christmas in Edinburgh. Perhaps the Chrea letter was meant to plant a seed of
guilt in his mother for having left him stranded at Stonyhurst. Perhaps Stony-

hurst's denial of any instructor named Chrea was merely an attempt to cover up an actual event that could have had potentially embarrassing repercussions to the school's reputation. This scenario seems rather unlikely, though, as there are no other reports known to confirm it.

According to Doyle's personal recollections, he was singled out for corporal punishment by his teachers more than any other boy. At Stonyhurst, the most feared instrument was the birch rod, which had been used when the school was located at St. Omer in the former Spanish Netherlands at the end of the sixteenth century. Luckily, it rarely found the buttocks of any of the students in Arthur's day. Instead, the ferula, or tolley, as it was known to the boys, was the device of choice to "correct" the students when they strayed from the path of righteous behavior. This eight-inch long India-rubber slab was in the possession of First Prefect Thomas Kay, whose role was to maintain discipline. If Arthur was caught "dodging the rules" or his misbehavior was "found out," he would accept the penalty of corporal punishment without protest and report to the "lictor's" room promptly after dinner or, at times, after evening classes. He soon got used to hearing the phrase, "Doyle, get twice nine ferulas!"—the maximum number of smacks permitted—and walking to the prefect's office, where he would wait outside with any other perpetrators until it was convenient for the prefect to start calling each one inside, one at a time, to receive punishment.

There was a certain sound that emanated from the prefect's room each time rubber met flesh. When it ended, the door would open and the repentant one would exit the torture chamber, allowing the next penitent to enter and ask for his ferulas. Doyle would ask, "Please, sir, would you give me twice nine?" and Father Kay would oblige him by removing the ferula from the cupboard next to his desk, and smashing the tolley nine times on each of his hands. Arthur bore his punishments with willful stubbornness and never shed any tears in front of his schoolmates or his teachers.

During one period of several weeks, Arthur's mother received no letters from her son, after which Arthur would write, "Got injured playing again. Excuse my writing. I hurt my thumb at hockey and cannot bend it properly." Another letter written around this time states:

You would have heard from me some time ago, only I lately got my finger hurt so much that it rendered it very painful for me to write. It was the last football match this year, and everyone was playing very hard. I was rushing after the ball, when suddenly I tripped up, and fell with outstretched hands. Before I could get up someone, not being able to stop himself, stood on my hand, with such violence that for every nail in his shoe, there was left a little hole in my hand. My forefinger also was hurt and the nail came off. I have however had a lot of remedies applied to my hand and it is much better now.

These injuries to his hand may well have been due to the tolley and not to any on-field activities.

As he got a little older, Arthur began smoking a pipe—a privilege officially reserved for the Gentlemen Philosophers—and joining the more daring students to venture to the area on the east side of the gardens known as the "dark walk." This pathway was one of the most beautiful places in all of England, a "grand and magnificent avenue of trees, full of shadowy beauty and overhung by the richest foliage." Arthur began spending a good deal of time beneath the silent arch of yew trees, despite having been told the story of the Shireburn Ghost, who was said to haunt this remote section of the school. Local legend states that nine-year-old Francis, heir apparent to Nicholas Shireburn's family estate, lost his way one evening in the bushes and trees that lined the "dark walk." In order to sustain himself, he picked up a berry from one of the yews. Unaware of its poisonous effect, he ate it, fell to ground, and convulsed until all the life was out of him. Even those boys who displayed the most bravado lived in fear of this ghost, but if Arthur was the least bit concerned that anything might happen to him, his feelings were not revealed to anyone. When the boys wanted to smoke, they veered off the dirt avenue and headed down a narrow path, which also led to the kennel where the dogs belonging to the Gentlemen Philosophers were boarded. These dogs were not raised to be pets; they were hunting dogs—"well-fashioned, well-bred, hound like creatures . . . which can make ever so much noise."

The four years Doyle spent under Father Cyprian Splaine were not necessarily conducive to later success. Although the two never engaged in any verbal altercations, they had very different academic and theological points of view. Doyle approached all subjects in general terms, particularly Latin and Greek, which occupied a substantial portion of the curriculum. Father Splaine was preoccupied with minutiae. In regard to religious topics, the same clash in personalities existed, with Doyle favoring a broad, flexible approach, and Splaine once again focusing on the intricate theological details that may have caused Doyle to reject his faith in later years.

While Doyle was younger than any other member of his class, he was nevertheless strong and energetic. Father Splaine, on the other hand, was his polar opposite. He certainly would not have been amused by the rough-and-tumble games in which Doyle liked to participate. These differences usually led to the involvement of Father Kay, whose job was to dole out Father Splaine's requested ferulas. Unfortunately, Arthur's youth failed to protect him from Father Kay's wrath. Doyle's frequent class disruptions were in direct proportion to the number of tolley lashings he received.

December 1874

The students sat in the solitude and silence of their unheated dormitory while Lancashire was being battered and brutalized by a long week of snow and ice. Cold, cruel winds blew in from the northwest, penetrating the branches of the trees outside with force enough to crack the dormitory windows and allow the gusts to assault the chamber walls. Most of the boys endured the wintry blasts in the knowledge that they would soon be going home to their families for the three-week Christmas recess. Once again, Arthur would be amongst the few students who would not be going home for the holiday. While he knew that the school had recently decreed that it was best for the boys to go home if possible, somehow plans were never formulated for him to visit Edinburgh. His mother's letters were becoming more and more distant, terse, and uninviting, and indicated her preoccupation with things other than Arthur. Moreover, her correspondence did not intimate that Arthur should come home for the break, even though there was now a little baby brother named Innes at home.

Arthur's only hope of rescue from this deserted citadel came from his mother's suggestion that the London-based Doyle clan might invite him there for the holidays. His uncles Richard and James and his aunt Annette had written a note to Mary informing her that their brother Henry Doyle would be arriving from Dublin at the same time. The four of them thought it would be a good idea to have Arthur in London, as they had not seen him in several years. Arthur seized the opportunity to write to his aunt and uncles, stating that there was nothing he would appreciate more than seeing them and the great city of London.

The will of John Doyle, Arthur's grandfather, had designated the soon-to-be-married oldest male sibling, James, as the official owner of the old Doyle place at 7 Finborough Road in London. But all the Doyles had access to the home that had been the meeting place of so many prominent artists and

writers of the period. When the greatly anticipated response arrived for
Arthur, his despair lifted. He immediately wrote back, saying that he could not
wait to join his favorite relatives in the world's "premier city."

Even the harsh winter weather was beginning to cooperate with Arthur's
travel plans. The temperature was rising and the snow and ice that had covered Stonyhurst in angelic white was beginning to thaw. Train travel, which
had come to a grinding halt during the snow storm, was gradually being
restored in the region. Nevertheless, there was still one obstacle remaining in
Arthur's path: the requisite money for his fare and expenses. Arthur was
keenly aware that his future might be dramatically affected by the impression
he made on his father's siblings. This branch of the Doyles had always been
one of the most respected names in the city. The Doyles managed to be one
of the first families of London, despite their staunch Roman Catholicism. Most
urgently, Arthur needed to learn the source of the money that would carry
him from Preston Station to London. He immediately sent the following letter
to his mother:

> I am sorry not to be able to see you all, but I have no doubt I will enjoy
> myself very much in London; I told Uncle Richard that I expected him to
> take me to see the sights. I have to get my traveling expenses for Xmas;
> am I to get them from home or London?

Mary Doyle did not send Arthur the train fare. Instead, she wrote to the
Doyles in London, hinting that if they showed no willingness to cover the trip,
Arthur would not be able to join them. Arthur's Christmas box, which would
have contained food enough to sustain him over the holidays at Stonyhurst,
and with which Mary would have been required to provide him, would have
been similar in cost to the train fare in question, but still Mary claimed she
could not manage the ticket. Thankfully, Arthur soon received a letter from his
Aunt Annette, a secular nun, who tendered the news that she and her brothers
would be happy to furnish him with the fare. Arthur's anxiety about the
holiday season was thus eased. He thought about his upcoming trip every
moment of every day, and eventually it dawned on him that his relatives might
not be able to recognize him, as he had not seen them in years. He dashed off
a letter to them, making sure to furnish an exact description of himself and the
clothes he would be wearing as he stepped off the train, writing that he would
be "five feet nine inches high, pretty stout, clad in dark garments, and, above
all, with a flaring red muffler round my neck."

When his train arrived on schedule at central London's Euston Station, Aunt Annette was waiting there for him. From there, the young gentleman from Stonyhurst and his adoring aunt boarded the underground train to Earl's Court, and then climbed into a carriage, which took them to the Doyle home. The second he crossed the threshold, he was instructed by Aunt Annette to inform his mother of his safe arrival. He dutifully complied with her order, but oddly enough, he made sure that his missive included a vivid, detailed description of three accidents that had supposedly marred his rail trip on the very efficient Lancashire railway. It is highly unlikely, however, that Arthur would have arrived on time had there been so many accidents along the way. Perhaps Arthur's creative writing skills had become developed enough for him to use them to inflict some degree of guilt upon his mother for her failure to invite him home.

Life for the Doyles of London was quite the opposite of life for the Edinburgh Doyles. Although Uncle Richard had resigned from *Punch* magazine a quarter-century before, his financial situation had hardly suffered. A successful freelancing cartoonist, he was a man about town who hardly ever spent an evening alone. As Uncle James, a formerly dedicated bachelor who had finally tied the knot, had recently moved out, Arthur had plenty of room in this large yet cozy residence. He looked around the comfortable stability of the Doyle compound and compared it to his family's unstable situation back in Scotland. Why his father's family would have sent Charles to a place that must have felt so foreign to him, Arthur could not guess. And now, in what would be his last year at Stonyhurst, Arthur was being evaluated by his family members in much the same way his father had been a generation before, and in the same exact location.

Nevertheless, Arthur had to admit that his relatives were treating him well, and the next several days were busy ones. He saw two theatrical productions, accompanied on both occasions by Uncle James. The young man from Stonyhurst sat in a private box—a present from Uncle Richard's friend Tom Taylor, who was the newly appointed editor of *Punch.* While Arthur was quite impressed by Henry Irving's portrayal of the Dane in *Hamlet,* he would describe the rest of the Lyceum production as "very poor." As for the Haymarket Theatre production of *Our American Cousin,* Arthur had already seen this show in Edinburgh.

During his trip, Arthur visited a "Stonyhurst boy and great friend of mine" on three separate occasions. Curiously, the name of this great friend is never mentioned. On one of these occasions they went to the London Zoo to see the "seals kissing their keeper." Another day they went to a "Luncheon at

Clifton Gardens." On the third occasion they went to the theater. Arthur was learning his way around town rather rapidly. Uncle Henry took him to the renowned Crystal Palace, and Uncle Richard took him to Hengler's Circus, and also down Baker Street to the internationally acclaimed Madame Tussaud and Sons' waxworks. There, lifelike wax statues of the most celebrated people of the past and present filled what had become an extraordinary museum. Richard had been among the satirists and cartoonists of *Punch* who had helped Madame Tussaud gain publicity for a certain apartment inside the place, that they called the "Chamber of Horrors." This section of the exhibition hall had gained such notoriety that a separate admission fee was required to view its "residents." What Richard would not have willingly revealed was that eight years prior to the use of the term by *Punch,* the phrase had been coined by the *New Monthly Magazine.* The room had become a magnet to the public, drawing in thousands of people a day. After all, Madame Tussaud's "palace" was the closest most people would ever come to viewing royalty, celebrities, or criminals of any kind "in person."

Arthur may have been puzzled by the fact that, despite his uncle's status, the two of them had to stand in a very long cordoned queue to enter the museum. His uncle may have even anticipated this question and volunteered that Madame Tussaud never gave anyone, no matter what his rank or lineage, permission to go in front of anyone else. The Doyles were no exception. Once Arthur and Richard had gained entrance to the elegantly appointed space, they opened their catalogues so that they could pick out which figures to see. Huge gas chandeliers cast a delicate light on the objects in the room, which, combined with the heavily pleated plush crimson drapes and ornate mirrors that concealed this former factory's plain brick walls, mesmerized the crowd.

There was no avoiding the stunningly realistic young woman whose gown was daintily appliquéd with fine jewelry. An exquisite pendant adorned her neck and multiple bejeweled bracelets were wrapped around her slender wrists. Her elegant countenance made it clear to Arthur that he was gazing at either a queen or a princess. By matching the number on the statue to the number in his catalogue, he would have known he was looking at the ill-fated Princess Charlotte of Wales, who had died at the age of twenty-one during childbirth, along with her male heir. Next they may have cast their eyes on the magnificent re-creation of her Majesty, Queen Victoria. Richard may have told Arthur that he had met the Queen on several occasions, and that when she had married her beloved Albert in 1840, he had been the illustrator chosen to draw the cake for posterity.

Arthur would have seen lifelike renditions of King Leopold of Belgium, who was currently brutalizing the people of the Congo in his attempt to build an empire that would rival that of Britain. He also would have seen the unimpeachable Arthur Wellesley, Duke of Wellington, whose military prowess had brought down the great Napoleon at Waterloo. And surely he would have noticed England's George III, who had enjoyed a lengthy but nonetheless erratic reign. In fact, Doyle's future writings would touch upon some of these figures.

As they moved through the gallery, a head inhaling snuff suddenly stared Arthur in the face. Arthur's catalogue informed him that he was looking at William Cobbett, the man responsible for the abolishment of the "rotten boroughs," those corrupt parliamentary townships that once plagued England. What Arthur did not know, and what the catalogue did not tell him, was that Madame Tussaud had not cast Cobbett from a live model, but rather from an illustration drawn by Arthur's grandfather, John Doyle.

Uncle Richard paid one shilling so that Arthur could gain admission to the Chamber of Horrors. Ushers were strategically placed there to make sure that no one with a faint heart could pass through the huge curtain that hid the room from view. Seven severed heads were mounted on a wall to greet the ticket holders, and visitors seemed caught in a current that propelled them deeper and deeper into the chamber's heart. Arthur looked upon some of the great villains of the French Revolution, including Robespierre, Carrier, and Tinville. He also saw Louis XVI and Marie Antoinette, who had been dragged up to the guillotine in Paris. Arthur associated this tableau with his college, which had been driven out of France across the channel into England during the "Reign of Terror."

Arthur's next stop was in front of the Austrian soldier and father of martial music, Baron Franz von der Trenck. As he scrutinized the rear wall of the chamber, his eyes must have been attracted to a group of men of noble appearance but not of noble garb, whose statues had been placed on an elevated platform. The inscriptions engraved on their plaques revealed their names: Edward Oxford, James Greenacre, James Goodfield Rush, John Nichols Thom, and Daniel Good. Arthur found it hard to believe that such distinguished-looking gentlemen could have had any association with murder or villainy of any kind, but nevertheless, there they stood. As Arthur turned, he would have crossed paths with the statues of the notorious William Burke and William Hare, surely recalling how the mere mention of their names back in Edinburgh had made even the most hardened residents of the city tremble in fear. He opened his catalogue to the brief biographies of figures 289 and 290. First he would read about figure 289:

BURKE (the model of Burke, taken within three hours after his execution). Burke, a murderer, with his associate Hare, became notorious for a series of murders, perpetrated for the purpose of gain. There was a demand in the schools of anatomy for bodies as subjects to be used for the demonstrations and at lectures, and for the practice of the students. Burke and Hare were in the habit of waylaying strangers, suffocating them by a pitch plaster fastened tightly over the nose and mouth, and selling the corpses to the professors of anatomy. This practice was carried on for upwards of ten months, during which numbers of persons disappeared in a manner that could not be accounted for. A discovery was at length made; Burke was convicted on the evidence of Hare, and executed at Edinburgh, January 27, 1829. Hare, in consideration of his having turned King's evidence, was again let loose upon the world.

Arthur would then read about figure 290:

HARE, the accomplice of Burke. Though he escaped the just penalty of his crimes, this miscreant did not go unpunished. He quitted Scotland with all secrecy, and made his way to the neighbourhood of London, where, under a feigned name, he obtained employment at some lime works. But his identity was discovered, and the indignant workmen flung him into a lime pit, whence, he escaped with the loss of his sight. For many years a blind beggar with peculiarly long hair and beard generally accompanied by an elderly woman, was a familiar figure in London Streets; but few who encountered him, suspected that the harmless looking mendicant was the miscreant Hare who had escaped the gallows by betraying his companion in guilt.

When Richard Doyle saw the excitement on his nephew's face as the two of them exited the room, it may have been hard for him to resist quoting from his own book of 1850, *Manners and Customs of Ye English,* saying, "Methinks it is of ill consequence that there should be a Murderers' Corner, wherein a Villain may look to have his Figure put more certainly than a Poet can to a Statue in the Abbey." These words were a response to the streams of love letters that *Punch* had been in the habit of receiving from admirers of these perpetrators of evil "currently residing" in Madame Tussaud's. Interestingly, they would also predict the treatment of his famous father, John Doyle, in death. Once a famous cartoonist, John Doyle was met with less respect than any infamous villain of the day when, in 1868, it took an unbelievably long three months before the *Art Journal* deemed it appropriate to post Doyle's obituary. Years later, in 1882, due to a dearth of potential buyers, Christie's would cancel an auction that had been arranged to sell John Doyle's original caricatures. The great John Doyle, who had popularized and refined the political cartoon, was consigned to the scrap heap of history all too quickly, proving the fleeting nature of fame, and perhaps the indelible nature of infamy.

The next day, Arthur's first priority was to visit the pride of Britain, Westminster Abbey, with a specific agenda. He headed straight to the tomb of Thomas Babington Macaulay, the historian and poet, which lay in Poets' Corner at the foot of the statue of essayist and poet Joseph Addison. After paying homage to his idol, Arthur also paid his respects to Addison, another of his literary heroes. He noticed that there were far fewer people gazing at the monuments of the great poets and writers than there had been staring reverently at the scoundrels of the Chamber of Horrors the day before.

Upon leaving Westminster, Arthur raced over Tower Bridge to pay his first visit to the Tower of London. Once there, he studied each section of its battlements and scrutinized every peripheral building before he entered its epicenter, the White Tower. Once inside the keep, he was overwhelmed by the richly ornamented passages, walls, ceilings, and beams. He was fascinated by the finely crafted swords, bayonets, lances, and pistols, most of them featuring priceless jewels and ivory. But the greatest imprints on Arthur were made by the Council Chamber and Banqueting Hall. He marveled at the thousands upon thousands of Martini-Henry rifles, which were mounted on racks at the ready, and the thumbscrews, bilboes, and iron shackles that had been used as instruments of torture during medieval times. He had seen these objects before in pictures on the walls at Stonyhurst, but to view them up close was a very different experience.

By the end of his visit to his London relatives, Arthur could navigate much of the world's largest city with relative ease, and was actually looking forward to returning there in a few months to take his matriculation examination.

January 1875

As his winter break came to an end, Arthur had a different outlook on life. His grades reflected his new optimistic attitude towards academics, despite that semester's challenging syllabus, which included "English Language, English History, French Latin and Greek grammar, a book of Homer, Sallust's *Cataline,* Natural Philosophy, Chemistry, any French author, Algebra, arithmetic and Euclid." Father Cyprian Splaine, who had been a thorn in his side for four years, had finally been replaced by Father Reginald Colley, a respected descendant of the Duke of Wellington. Colley was to become and remain Doyle's lifelong confidant, and Doyle would correspond with him for the rest of Colley's life. When the new master suggested that Arthur obtain a book called *The Civil Service Examination History of England,* young Doyle immediately wrote to his mother and declared it a matter of paramount importance for her to find it. Colley instilled confidence in Arthur, telling him, "You have talents enough and we have every reason to hope that you mean to make the most of them." Arthur realized he was under the wing of someone who actually cared for him, a figure who would guide and support him.

Unfortunately, March brought with it some troubling news. His financially burdened mother had a new mouth to feed, Jane Adelaide Rose, known as Ida, and his oldest sister, Annette, the one person he truly adored, was about to be shipped off to Portugal to work as a governess. Mary Doyle told her that any salary she earned must be sent home in its entirety. This demand served only to magnify Arthur's trepidation over his family's dire financial straits and, most importantly, the distinct possibility that he might never see his sister again, although he claimed to be "very pleased to hear of her success."

There were just four or five weeks to go before he was to take the London University Matriculation Examination. A passing grade on this test would guarantee him admission to many universities within Great Britain. Despite Colley's enthusiasm, there were those who voiced their skepticism about Arthur's prospects. His progress reports were littered with unfavorable comments, and his rhetoric teacher went as far as to inscribe "matriculation doubtful" on his transcript. Arthur started experiencing debilitating headaches and stabbing jaw pain, which would come out of nowhere and reach the point at which he was unable to concentrate on anything. He called it "neuralgia," and claimed that he had "got it from sitting near an open window in the schoolroom, the draught acting upon the nerves of the face." He was deathly afraid of failing his preliminary tests, for that would preclude his taking the actual examination in June. Thankfully, he passed his trial exams with ease. Leading up to the London Examination, Arthur conveniently reverted back to Catholicism, if asking God for a favor is true religiosity. In a letter written just days before the test, Arthur would ask his mother, "[O]ffer up a communion for me on Sunday, I will go myself on that day and so get a blessing on my examens." It is amazing to think this was the same person who claimed in later years to have "privately renounced Catholicism before leaving school." Perhaps he was ready to reach out to anything that might help him attain his goal.

After taking the exam, Arthur predicted that his highest score would come in the mathematics portion, but he was less confident about his performance in natural philosophy. In the end, he need not have been concerned. When the post from London arrived in late July, he discovered that he had passed, along with twelve of the remaining thirteen boys in his class. The news was officially announced by the old and grey prefect of studies, who climbed onto a chair and proudly proclaimed that this was the all-time moment of triumph for the school. Never had such a high percentage of the boys done so well. Arthur, who had surprised many of his fellow students and faculty, was glad-handed by almost everyone. A few days later the "classified list was read out," and Arthur learned that he was among the top 10 percent of takers of the exam who had been declared as completing the test with "honours." This was his greatest moment at Stonyhurst. With exhilaration, he proudly informed his mother of his accomplishment, writing, "I nearly got a hole worn in the back of my coat by being clapped on it, and some enthusiasts carried me round the playground."

In early August, Arthur entered one of the college's few highly decorated rooms known as the Great Academies. The "Programme of Entertainments," as the graduation ceremony was called, was soon to begin there. Arthur's parents, however, would not be in attendance on this important occasion. He had already posted a letter to them anticipating his temporary return to Edinburgh, stating:

> I fear that we will come in so late that you will not be able to meet me conveniently. The train starts at four and comes in at ten I think. I am sorry to leave the old place after such a long residence, but I will be glad to get home again and see you all and Ida. Seven years continued routine becomes monotonous eventually.

Why he would have missed the "old place" is difficult to comprehend, considering the lack of respect he had engendered in most of his teachers and the absence of any close friends there, and especially after he had been turned down by the Gentlemen Philosophers program. But he had grown accustomed to the "routine" and "monotony" of the place and now had to leave the only sure path to success available to Roman Catholic students. Father Purbrick had made arrangements for Arthur to travel to Feldkirch, Austria, and spend his university-prepatory year at Stella Matutina. This institution, although run by Jesuits, did not enjoy the academic reputation that Stonyhurst had earned.

On graduation day, with the strains of Schubert's "Ave Maria" reverberating in his ears, Arthur must surely have found it difficult to cope with his disappointment at not being admitted to the Gentlemen Philosophers program. While his classmates were enjoying the commencement day festivities, which featured dramatic dialogues and political speeches in Greek and English, as well as readings of scenes from Shakespeare, Arthur would have been forced to maintain his composure. He would have remembered Purbrick's simple "fact" that he was a bit too young and immature to be granted admission to such a "serious" program as the Gentlemen Philosophers. The curriculum was too grueling for someone who lacked the requisite skills. His excellent score on the London Examination, however, makes this latter reason questionable. Nevertheless, Purbrick "convinced him" that a few months abroad on the Continent would do him a world of good. This may have been the moment that Arthur finally rejected, once and for all, Roman Catholicism. With the exception of one or two members of the Stonyhurst faculty, he viewed the rest as socially inept.

Once intermission had come to an end, Arthur braced himself for the second portion of the commencement ceremonies, which included the recitation of a scene from Moliere's *Le Misanthrope,* some tedious English poems, and a monotonous reading of Cicero. Finally came the reading and awarding of the Stonyhurst prize ode. Arthur certainly should have been a candidate for the award, but to his chagrin, he had to accept that he had been strategically overlooked because of his prior involvement with the *Stonyhurst Figaro* and the *Wasp.*

The presentation of a book to those few boys who had made "honours" on the London University Matriculation Examination brought the ceremony to a close. The thirteen boys who had brought distinction to Stonyhurst were granted the privilege of hearing their names called aloud, and each of them mounted an elevated platform where they were greeted by the highest-ranking faculty members—Fathers Purbrick, Colley, Kingdon, Splaine, Payne, Lander, and Kay. Each of these key individuals shook hands with the honorees as they passed on their way to receiving the gift. When Arthur walked across the stage, he made sure his vise-like grip would be remembered by all of them.

Once the presentation had ended, the entire student body and their families gathered in the gardens outside to pay tribute to their dear old Stonyhurst, though Arthur would later state that he would never "send a son of [his] there." Arthur quickly gathered his belongings and readied himself to leave Stonyhurst forever. The next morning, he climbed aboard a horse-drawn carriage and made the thirteen-mile journey back to Preston Station, where he boarded the train for home. He opened up a book on supernatural phenomena and immersed himself in its pages. He had come to terms with the fact that he could temporarily escape the biting gales of reality by becoming lost in literature. Unfortunately, when he arrived back home at 10 PM with no one there to meet him at the station, he immediately understood what the next few weeks in Edinburgh had in store for him: screaming babies, a drunken father, the departure of his older sister, and financial unrest. He would also learn that his mother had taken in a lodger.

4

The Tour
Hanbury Street, 9 AM

Sir Arthur proceeded to lead his coterie into the dismal area of
Whitechapel, where the cobblestone streets around the London
Hospital subtly transformed into muddy unpaved paths that somehow managed to insert themselves between the dirty and dilapidated
houses nearby. An unfamiliar sight to the tour members, windblown
laundry waved overhead in a valiant but vain attempt to fend off the soot
that puffed and billowed out from the pipes of the surrounding factories.
Brazen street peddlers overwhelmed the eyes and noses of passersby with
unappealing and smelly merchandise, and then assaulted their ears with
a cacophony of obscenities when their wares went unsold. Several of
Doyle's crew placed their fine silk handkerchiefs over their nostrils and
lips in a failed attempt to keep themselves from being affected by the rancid odor of both human and animal excrement. Adelaide was wearing a
fragrance-laced ring, which she had brought with her for just such an
eventuality. She pressed it against her nostrils and proceeded to take a
deep breath, but found no relief. Doyle seemed impervious to all the
unpleasantness that surrounded him. Women with dirt-smeared faces,
looking older than their years, scrounged through the garbage in search
of any bit of discarded food, and when they found some, they devoured
their edible treasures on the spot.

Sir Arthur kept his group moving through the East End, and within
minutes they came upon a group of half-starved boys engaged in a game
of urban cricket. A broken broomstick served as the bat, while balled up
stockings tied round with sundry pieces of string and rope stood in for

the ball. Doyle stood motionless, studying their every move. It was a full minute before his face lit up and he broke his silence.

"Great game, cricket. Great game!" Doyle said, turning to face the onlookers. "These lads are doing their collective best to cope with the dismal environment they have been forced to endure every moment of their lives. This modified version of the world's greatest pastime affords them a brief respite from outrageous fortune's slings and arrows. And yet, here before you in this wretched alley may be a future professional cricketer. Who knows? And maybe, by dint of his ability, fate will smile on him, and he may gain admission to 'respectable society.' Down here, in this hell, it is survival of the fittest. Each of these children is forced to rely on his instincts and, most importantly, his acquired skills, to ward off the pickpockets, the lowly thieves, and worse yet, the Rippers who inhabit the area. But I am intruding on our precious time. Let us forge ahead."

Doyle began walking the tour towards its next destination. A few minutes later, he did an about-face and stood like a sergeant addressing his troops. "We are about to enter the 'Sweating District,'" he said, "an area that twenty-five years ago teemed with thousands of miserable and oppressed workers who labored from dawn till dusk, cutting and sewing piecemeal garments at subsistence wages. These items were then sold to distributors at high prices, resulting in huge profits for employers and virtually nothing for workers. After 9 PM, this area would be nearly deserted, with only those who resided within its confines remaining. These were dangerous and mean streets, and even the local trollops looked for the shelter offered by the local pubs. We are just several yards away from the exact spot where Annie Chapman's body was discovered on September 8, 1888. This building was one of many that were originally built for the Spitalfields weavers back when many laborers were needed to operate the hand-looms that produced the goods. Once steam and electricity became the dominant sources of power, these factories and their workers became obsolete, innocent victims of modern technology. The empty buildings were soon converted into dwellings for the poor.

"Getting back to Annie Chapman, one of the tenants of such a residence was Mr. John Davis who, on September 8, after having his morning tea with his wife, made ready to set out to his place of employment. As the clock struck 6 AM, he exited his apartment at 29 Hanbury Street, only to find a body lying supine a few feet behind this very door in front of us. After his initial shock had passed, he craned his neck and saw that the victim was a woman whose throat had been deeply cut. Mr. Davis enlisted the help of Mr. James Green and Mr. James Kent, who were the first two people to pass him. He left them in charge and raced off to a nearby police station to report what he'd found. An investigation was immediately begun, and within a few hours, an arrest warrant was issued for one John Pizer, known to many of the locals as 'Leather Apron.' By the way, is there anyone here who can tell me the source of this nickname?"

Edgar blurted out, "Yes, I can. The killer removed a fragment of cloth that he had excised from the poor woman's apron and then placed it right outside a tenement door so as to . . ."

"Curb your enthusiasm, my dear Mr. Collins," Doyle said. "You're getting ahead of yourself. The details to which you are alluding are not of the murder in question. A jolly good try at linking things, though." Within seconds, Doyle, with a magician's sleight of hand, thrust an old newspaper clipping in front of the faces of his entourage. He read, "Ghastly murder in the East End. Dreadful mutilation of a woman. Capture of Leather Apron." He proceeded to pass around the clipping for all to see. "In those days of fear," he said, "highly colored pictorial advertisements such as these would be plastered all over London. But now let me tell you all of the aftermath of the second Whitechapel murder.

"Initially, the aforementioned John Pizer, a Jewish bootmaker, was the prime suspect. He had attained local notoriety in the district because of his history of abusive behavior towards the women of the night. A small delegation of the local prostitutes had gone to several of the district's police stations and told them that a man fitting Leather Apron's description had been seen at 29 Hanbury Street that night. None of them knew his given name, but a police sergeant named William Thicke insisted that Leather Apron was indeed John Pizer, and that the two had known each other for almost twenty years. Mr. Pizer's friends and acquaintances refuted Thicke's claims and denied that Pizer was known by that moniker. When Pizer was interrogated, he furnished an alibi that was confirmed by other members of the police force, stating that he had made his way down to the London docks that night to witness a spectacular fire, which had threatened to envelop a large portion of the city's wharves. He claimed to have gone over to the residence of one of his relatives shortly after that, where he spent the remainder of the early morning hours. His story satisfied the Metropolitan Police and he was released from custody. I ask you, my dear friends, what could possibly have motivated Sergeant Thicke to point his accusatory finger at Mr. Pizer?"

Carrington suggested antisemitism as having been at the root of Thicke's actions, but Evander disagreed. He was convinced that Thicke regarded the matter as an opportunity to attain instant fame—payment for his many years of unappreciated and uncelebrated service.

"A second person of interest was William Henry Pigott," Doyle said, "a fifty-two-year-old wanderer, although he was the son of a well-known Gravesend insurance agent. A group of young men told the police that the man later identified as Pigott had asked them where he could get a beer, as his long walk home from Whitechapel had exhausted him. They added that he was pained by a bad hand, and that they thought it odd that he was carrying a black bag in his good hand. Pigott was spotted all over town that night. According to reports, he had jumped into a tramcar going towards Northfleet, ending up at a Mrs. Beitcheller's fish shop. When the police questioned her, she recalled that Pigott had told her he was going across the Thames to Tilbury, adding that a paper parcel had been left by him at her store. Whether this package had been left there accidentally or by design is a question that remains unanswered. What we do know is that Mr. Pigott did not cross the Thames to Tilbury, but instead walked into the Pope's Head pub, where he unleashed a vitriolic tirade against all women, a verbal barrage so intense that the pub's patrons thought it proper to call the authorities.

"In the meantime, Superintendent Berry traced Pigott's path to his previous stop at the fish store and, once inside the shop, opened the package Pigott had left behind. In it were two blood-stained shirts, one of which had been torn about the breast. It also contained a pair of stockings. When the police entered the pub in response to the call for help, they found Pigott in a dazed state and brought him down to the precinct for interrogation. He asserted that he had been merely walking down Brick Lane when he spied a woman in the throes of a fit. When she fell to the pavement, his attempt to come to her aid had been misinterpreted as a physical attack. Before he knew it, he was in agonizing pain, blood was spurting from his hand, and he reflexively struck her."

"There must have been a full moon that night," Evander said. "It seems that all the vampires and werewolves of London were out and about."

"While we do not have time to discuss everything that went on that night," Doyle said, "Dr. Whitcombe, the police surgeon, did a meticulous examination. His report states that blood was also present on Pigott's boots, and that an attempt had been made by Pigott to remove this blood. When three so-called witnesses failed to pick Pigott out as 'Leather Apron,' the authorities concluded that Pigott was not the man for whom they were looking, but nevertheless deemed it in the best interest of society, and of Mr. Pigott, to detain him further and observe his mental state. He was later declared insane by a Dr. Phillips, but the police still would not consider him a Ripper suspect."

"Why not?" Dr. Hammond said.

"They did not feel he had the wherewithal to commit such acts," Doyle said. "His physical and emotional state seemed to make it impossible for him to have done so." Doyle immediately moved on to the grim details of Annie Chapman's murder. "At approximately 1:45 AM on Saturday, September 8, 1888, Mrs. Chapman, who had been in the kitchen of the Crossingham Doss House since 7 PM, decided to leave the premises," he said. "Before she departed, the deputy of the house, Timothy Donovan, was told by Mrs. Chapman, and I quote, 'I haven't any money now, but don't let the bed; I will be back soon.' On that evening, the bed that Annie Chapman usually occupied became the sole potentially vacant one. The night watchman, John Evans, witnessed Annie walking down Little Paternoster Row in the hope of obtaining enough money to retain it."

Matthew confessed his ignorance in regard to what a doss house was. Doyle explained that doss houses were places that offered cheap daily lodging to male and female transients, describing how, at certain times of the year, people would be crammed into these dwellings from cellar to roof. When Matthew asked if the doss house might have been used as a secret hiding place, Doyle responded, "That is an absolute possibility, Mr. Stanton, for it is a matter of common knowledge that the night watchmen take little notice of those who enter or exit from this type of place, especially in the wee hours of the morning. All that is registered is whether these 'miserables' can pay for their shared rooms."

"Apparently, Annie Chapman went to Ringer's pub," Doyle said. "Three hours later she lay dead on these very steps. Alas, Mrs. Chapman had the misfortune of plying her trade to the wrong person. Now, I must tell you, the Ripper was either very daring, very stupid, or both to have killed her here, for he would have been forced to lead her through the passageway of a house filled with tenants. He would then have had to kill her within a few feet of occupants who were sleeping next to the windows, which were typically kept open to allow air to circulate. We must assume that the victim did not utter even the tiniest whimper, for it would have woken the occupants. To add to the difficulty of what he did, Jack was somehow able to return through the same passageway and vanish into a street that was now filled with early morning market goers. I am almost certain that Jack had blood on his hands and clothing. Although there are those who contend that Chapman's death was due to strangulation, it is my belief that it was suffocation by facial compression that killed her. The autopsy report revealed that she had a swollen tongue and that two of her teeth had been knocked out of her mouth, findings which tend to dispute the strangulation hypothesis. It is more than likely that sufficient pressure was exerted on her face to assure that she would lose consciousness, and that once she became hypoxic, or completely deprived of oxygen, she was placed down on the ground. Her neck was then severed and almost decapitated by a powerful sweep of the knife.

"The killer's blade splayed the victim's abdomen and exposed her intestines. Next, her innards were dissected, moved away from their mesenteric attachments, lifted from her body, and carefully placed adjacent to her right shoulder, while her stomach was placed above her left shoulder. More gruesome discoveries were made when her body was moved to the morgue. The coroner discovered that the Ripper had removed Annie Chapman's uterus and its appendages, along with the posterior two-thirds of her bladder. And by removed, I mean just that. These organs were taken from her poor, mutilated body, and not a trace of them was to be found at the scene. For those of you who do not know the proportions of the organs taken, they weren't very much. They would have fit nicely into a teacup. To this day, the Yard is convinced that Jack took them home with him as trophies, while others believe that Jack intended to sell them to a pathology museum.

"That time was not of the essence to this heartless and methodical killer is evident by the care he took to go through Annie's personal belongings. With the precision of a Swiss watchmaker, he neatly arranged the following items by her feet: a fine-toothed comb, a paper-wrapped pocket comb, and a small swatch of coarse muslin. A portion of an envelope with the words 'Sussex Regiment' embossed in blue was placed under the occipital area of her cranium. In the envelope were two pills. This dedication to order and arrangement adds another macabre element to the case."

Carrington wondered if Mrs. Chapman might have been a victim of poisoning, and if the killer might have left the pills there to tantalize the police. Doyle answered unequivocally and curtly in the negative. Evander, who had been made queasy by the description of poor Mrs. Chapman's body, managed to ask if the military seal might perhaps have led the police to the killer, and if anything else had been written or stamped on the envelope.

"Good questions," Doyle said, "but the Sussex Regiment had nothing to do with this, and neither did the letter 'M' on the front of the envelope, nor the letters 'Sp,' which were found on the back. The police investigation concluded that the pills had come from the London Hospital pharmacy, and that the envelope had been found by Mrs. Chapman on the street and was being used as a replacement for her medicine box, which had fallen and shattered earlier."

"How do we know that?" Stephen said.

"I neglected to tell you that an acquaintance of Annie Chapman named William Stevens vividly recalled Annie picking up the torn envelope at random from the cobblestones to use as a container for her medication," Doyle said.

"The performance of the police far surpassed what I would expect of them," Carrington said. "I look upon their work with a sense of incredulity. They were able to garner great amounts of information from that which I would have interpreted as nothing at all. And I am doing this with twenty-five years of hindsight."

Doyle seemed to agree with Carrington's comments. "As a rule, the perpetrator of a crime will leave something behind, which serves as the starting point of pursuit," he said. "The police and detectives have no method of approach other than what is there at that moment in time. It could be something as small as a bit of gravel in a horse's hoof, or as thin as a piece of thread on a lady's dress, or a pinch of tobacco ash."

"I have seen a few Jack-like homicidal maniacs back in the States," Dr. Hammond said, "but none are his match. This breed of criminal enjoys watching the failure of those who endeavor to discover the evildoer, and thoroughly relishes seeing the sense of irritation that so often overcomes those who are intent on bringing the criminal to justice. It loves tarnishing the reputation of these pursuers."

Doyle nodded his head in approval, but uttered not a word.

"Speaking of fabric, that swatch of coarse muslin, did it belong to Annie Chapman or to Mary Ann Nichols?" Stephen said.

"I am not sure if anyone has ever thought of the possibility that a piece of muslin might represent a clue to the prior murder," Doyle said. "I must say that if the police had successfully traced that piece of gauze, they may have made a connection. But they did not, and so it goes."

Matthew asked if the police were able to ascertain if any valuables had been removed from the victim's person.

"Yes, if you call some paltry brass rings valuable," Doyle said. "The police had been informed by some of the area's residents that Annie always wore several brass rings. If the authorities had failed to find them on her fingers, then surely someone had removed them, they thought."

"But sir," Stephen said, "earlier on you specifically told us that robbery is never a motive when it comes to the members of the unfortunate class."

"And my opinion has not changed an iota," Doyle said. "The taking of the rings was a ruse employed to throw the 'bloodhounds,' which is to say, the criminal investigation detectives and Metropolitans, off the trail. The organs are the story here, and how fortunate we are to have had such a diligent coroner assigned to this postmortem."

Dr. Hammond, who always seemed to offer a dissenting viewpoint, inquired as to what might have been the cause of the bruises that Annie had on her face and chest. His facial expression was one of puzzlement as Doyle began to explain that of the many possible explanations for the marks on Annie's body, the one he felt was correct suggested a lodging house brawl. Evidently, several days before her death, Annie and a young man named Ted Stanley had gone to the Britannia pub, where they had met a pensioner known as "Harry the Hawk" and a woman named Eliza, both of whom Annie knew. The Hawk was drunk, and when he put down a florin, a coin worth two shillings, to pay for some drinks, Eliza palmed it and replaced it with a penny. Supposedly, Annie then told Harry what Eliza had done, and later that evening, after Harry had accused Eliza of theft, the lodging house kitchen became a virtual boxing ring. Eliza got the best of Annie, blackening her eye and bashing her chest.

"Therefore, the bruising is irrelevant to the case," Dr. Hammond said.

Doyle agreed. "Several days after the murder of Annie Chapman, a certain 'special detective,' a little girl of the neighborhood, noticed some strange marks on the wall and ground where the murder had taken place. She was confident these marks had not been there prior to the incident. She ran over to Detective-Inspector Chandler, who was there investigating the crime scene for the coroner's office. The little girl excitedly informed him that she had found something scary. He followed her back to the site and realized that there was a six-foot-long trail of blood that led from the back door of the house to the fence. The detective was sure that these were the killer's tracks, and that he had passed through or over the fence that divided numbers 29 and 27, and then had entered the garden of number 25. He was certain that the 'splotch' of blood found, which he described as being more than a sprinkle but less than a smear, was the product of a bloodied coat that the killer had taken off and whipped against the wall in an effort to rid it of any telltale evidence. Shortly after this discovery, the police found a crumpled piece of paper in a remote corner of a neighboring yard."

"Pardon the intrusion, Sir," Matthew said, "but what could explain this near smear?"

"As Dr. Doyle said, Jack had to out the damn spot, if you'll pardon my witticism," Dr. Hammond said.

"Wouldn't beating the coat in the middle of the night tend to rouse people from sleep?" Stephen said.

"That's right," Doyle said. "He would not have done such a thing."

"Dr. Doyle, Jack could have obliterated the blood from his jacket by employing friction as his agent of removal. Any residue would easily have blended into his coat and been made indistinct, if not invisible," Dr. Hammond said.

"That depends on the coat's fabric," Doyle said. "If it were a traditional overcoat, especially of light color, such an act of abrasion would make it more blatantly obvious that something was amiss. On the other hand, if the coat were dark and made of densely woven wool, I would imagine that simply rubbing it against the wall would have removed any superficial blood."

"I thought you suspected that the perpetrator of these crimes wore a midwife's uniform." Stephen said.

"I haven't changed my mind, Mr. Mitchell," Doyle said, "but could not a midwife wear a coat over her uniform?"

"Touché, Sir. I failed to think of that."

"Not a problem. Now, where was I? Oh yes, the crumpled paper. According to a credible report in the September 12, 1888 edition of the *Saint James Gazette*, the police linked the killer to a bit of discarded paper they had found in a remote corner of 25 Hanbury Street's yard. It had been saturated with blood. Evidently the Ripper had used this paper to wipe his hands. The purported 'blood stain' found on the wall, however, turned out to be nothing more than dried-out urine according to laboratory testing."

Having finished with the details of the Chapman murder, Doyle then concluded the visit to Hanbury Street and moved the group on to its next stop.

5

1875–1876

To Feldkirch and Back Again

August 1875

His time at Stonyhurst behind him, Arthur finally returned to Edinburgh. There his family was living in a cramped apartment at 2 Argyle Park Terrace. The dingy quarters were a reflection of Charles Doyle's continuing downward spiral. Arthur did not bother to unpack very many items from his box, as he knew that within a month he would be off to Stella Matutina, a Jesuit college in western Austria, where he would be completing a preparatory year before his entry into a royally chartered university.

During his few weeks at home, there was no discussion of his father, who had vanished into alcoholism. Sixteen-year-old Arthur did his best to fill the role of surrogate father to his younger siblings—nine-year-old Lottie, to whom he had written letters while at school; seven-year-old Connie; two-year-old Innes, his only brother; and six-month-old Jane Adelaide Rose, or Ida. Unfortunately, his older sister Annette's departure for Portugal had left him with no one close in age with whom to speak and share his feelings. Before she had left for Portugal, however, Annette had made an impression on a young man who was boarding with her family.

Bryan Charles Waller was the twenty-two-year-old scion of one of Britain's most distinguished families. Hailing from Yorkshire, he was an Oxford graduate who, having recently completed his medical school education at the University of Edinburgh, had been granted a junior position there as a lecturer in pathology. He was also in the process of preparing his thesis for his MD, for which he would be eligible in three years. Mary Doyle had taken him in as a lodger in much the same way that Catherine Foley had taken in Charles Doyle twenty-five years before. Both Mary and her oldest daughter must have been quite impressed by the dashing and sophisticated Waller's "eager, cultured face, his fine old world courtesy, and his eighteenth century manner." But why Waller, a man of considerable means, would have chosen a lodger's life, particularly one at the Doyle residence, is hard to understand, especially in light of his profound aversion to young children.

"Annette's Music," a poem Waller had dedicated to the oldest of the Doyle children, suggests that he had been in the Doyle household prior to 1875. As the school calendars of Stonyhurst and of the University of Edinburgh ran parallel to each other, it is easy to visualize Arthur and Bryan during their respective summer breaks as ships passing in the night. The often absent Charles Doyle had a degree of involvement with the young doctor. Waller even contracted Charles to prepare two wood engravings for his medical school thesis, "The Microscopic Anatomy of Interstitial Nephritis." Six years later, Waller's intensive labor and research would prove their worth, with the University of Edinburgh Medical School naming his work the "Gold Medal Thesis" of 1881 and conferring the degree of MD on him. Upon receiving his doctorate, Waller would depart Edinburgh for good, and Mary Doyle would follow him, taking up residence at Masongill, Waller's Yorkshire estate, for virtually the remainder of her life. Despite Arthur's future wealth and celebrity, she would choose to stay with the man who had once been her lodger. Mary Doyle would remain there as Bryan's confidante even after his marriage to Ada Roberts in 1896.

Initially, Bryan and Arthur got along well, discussing literature and their future careers. A dreary collection of poems by Waller called *The Twilight Land* had been released by George Bell and Sons, and Waller had been savvy enough to dedicate it to his well-known uncle, Bryan Waller Procter, which would automatically generate some sales. Waller may have inspired Doyle to submit some of his own work for publication. After all, Arthur had seen Bryan opening envelopes containing payment for his published work. Arthur, who relished the thought of having some extra money in his pockets, may have begun to consider more seriously becoming a writer as a result. When Waller suggested that medicine would be the perfect profession to combine with a writing career, Arthur discarded any ideas he had entertained about becoming a civil engineer. He now wanted the title of medical doctor.

Arthur was convinced he possessed the innate intelligence, the penchant for reading, and the perseverance necessary for a career as a physician. The self-sufficiency and financial security that were part and parcel of a well-run medical practice intrigued him. He was hopeful that his superb performance on the London University Matriculation Examination would gain him admission to the University of Edinburgh or the University of London, provided he did well enough at Stella Matutina. Although London's medical school was more prestigious than Edinburgh's, both were excellent options, and in either case he would not have to pay for room and board. If he went to London, he would be able to stay at his aunt and uncle's, and if he remained in Edinburgh, he could live at home. Waller told him that he would personally investigate all the available scholarships and grants offered by the community and the medical schools.

Before he was to leave for Austria, Arthur wanted to reestablish his relationship with his closest friend, William Burton. Burton, who had chosen not to leave his home city, was now in the second year of a five-year apprenticeship at Brown Brothers and Company at the Rose Bank Ironworks. His winning personality, fierce independence, multiple talents, and profound intelligence had gained him a reputation all over England and Scotland as someone with whom to be reckoned in the fields of hydraulics and mechanical engineering. Soon, nations all over the world would recognize his achievements in architecture, water sanitation, and photography. As Arthur and William walked down Drummond Street, they would have been jostled by the crowds of people who swarmed the libraries and stalls that lined this book-lover's paradise. Turning onto Hanover Street, they passed the famed Tait book auction rooms, "the great haunt of bookhunters of all degrees, from the peer to humblest bookseller's apprentice." Nearby, at the shop of Mr. Le Sage, printseller, a famous H.B. caricature would have been stuck up on the railings in front of the store, guaranteeing a crowd of onlookers. As H.B.'s grandson, Arthur must have felt a sense of pride, though his joy may have been tempered by the thought that his father might have sold the print to Mr. Le Sage to buy alcohol. As long as Charles was able to get his hands on one of his father's works, he could always raise some much needed capital.

The weeks passed quickly, and by late August, Arthur was packing for his year-long stay at Stella Matutina. He made certain to place two pairs of boxing gloves inside his trunk. Like many young British lads of the time, he had become a proficient practitioner of the sport, and regarded his gloves as his prize possessions. His intention was to begin training as soon as he arrived at his new school.

September 1875

The Jesuits at Stella Matutina had made Arthur's travel arrangements, which included providing him with a companion, Charles Rockliff, on the 1,200-mile journey to Feldkirch. This time, when his train stopped at Preston Station, Arthur remained in his seat and looked out on the stunning mountain range known as the Pennines. For the first time in seven years, he would not be getting off here. The huge doors of Stonyhurst were now closed to him forever. He finally made it to Birkdale Station and stepped onto the platform, where he "saw a hoary headed old chap," Mr. Francis Rockliff, his traveling companion's father. The two of them headed off by carriage to Mr. Rockliff's home on Oxford Road in Birkdale, about eighteen miles north of Liverpool. There Arthur was introduced to Mr. Rockliff's sons Henry, Francis, and Charles, as well as his daughters, Ellen and Alice. The cheery reception Arthur received at the Rockliffs was in stark contrast to the air of depression and melancholy that had greeted Arthur on his last visit home.

The next morning, Arthur attended Sunday Mass with the Rockliffs, and likely made an attempt to circumvent any discussions related to religious matters. There was no need to make the Rockliffs aware of his skepticism towards Catholicism in general or the Jesuit order in particular. He prepared himself for a long day of "observance," but as soon as the Rockliffs and he returned to the family hearth, the mild-mannered Mr. Rockliff lit up a cigarette and offered one to Arthur, who was thrilled to partake in this adult activity. A long walk soon followed and was topped off with an invitation to play a "friendly game" of billiards. Arthur must have thought it quite a novel way to observe the Sabbath.

In the middle of the night, the biggest hurricane in almost forty years stormed in. "Nearly the whole top of the house was carried off like a feather, tiles and chimney pots were flying about and in the midst of the turmoil a messenger arrived from Mr. Rockliffe's [sic] brother, who was to take [Arthur and Charles] to London, saying that he would not risk [their] lives by going in such weather." It would be two days before Charles's Uncle Robert arrived. He was accompanied by his sons William and Robert, who were already students at Stella Matutina and would be heading back to the school along with Arthur and Charles. On Wednesday morning, the boys were off "to London, then to Newhaven, Dieppe and Paris." Charles's uncle left their company on the English side of the channel and the quartet continued their journey by themselves. A surprise visit to Arthur's great-uncle Michael Conan was rendered impossible by their nighttime arrival in Paris and the early departure of their train to Feldkirch. Arthur voiced his profound disappointment at this state of affairs.

Many hours later, when the conductor announced that Feldkirch would be the next stop, Arthur looked out his window and gazed at the imposing castle of Schattenburg looming in the near distance. A few miles later, the train crossed the high bridge that spanned the river Ill and entered Feldkirch Station. As soon as he and Charles stepped onto the platform, they noticed that the churches and homes of the village were placed so closely together that it was difficult to imagine any street fitting between them. The towers of the city gates dwarfed the medieval town's old walls, while picturesque rooftops and gabled windows recalled a bygone age. The river Ill, which had appeared to be flowing so gently when Arthur had viewed it from the train, now rushed torrentially through the center of town, powering the many cotton mills that dotted the city and neighboring villages. The boys soon noticed that their new school was standing directly ahead of them. It was one of the few structures in the village that was devoid of all beauty and charm—a large white building whose one adornment was a statue of Our Lady Stella Matutina, which appeared to have been unceremoniously plunked down on a turret. Arthur, having tacitly renounced Roman Catholicism, must have found himself in a quandary. There was no way for him to know how strictly the tenets of the Church would be enforced here. His common sense led him to adopt the role of "the observant student" and suppress his rebellious streak, which he had been unable to do at Stonyhurst.

Arthur and Charles mounted the school-owned carriage that was waiting for them and took the short ride to Stella Matutina. Arthur's first impression of the Feldkirch institution was a favorable one. Here the students were catered to by the administration, and unlike the Stonyhurst student body, there were a substantial number of local boys who actually went home to their families each evening. These "day scholars" were assigned to the second pensionnat, or division, and were kept physically segregated from the 150 students who boarded there and made up the first pensionnat. Almost every boy was from the European continent, except for a dozen or so students who were English or American. A beautifully manicured playground surrounded by light railings stood in front of the school. The field was open to public view, so the townspeople were able to observe the students at play. Cricket, a game of British origin, was unexpectedly popular, but Arthur felt even more fortunate that rugby, his second favorite sport, was also a well-regarded pastime. While there were several games that the students were forced to play, by far the most popular was stilt football, in which the boys would run on foot-long heavy stilts and try to "kick" the ball into the net. Leg trauma and other injuries were a natural part of the game, and spectators could not wait to see a player hopping about on one foot, holding one stilt in the air until he had an opportunity to withdraw from the field to readjust it.

Charles and Arthur were assigned to different dormitories and went their separate ways after orientation. Arthur was taken to his sleeping chamber by a German boy wearing a large, ornate cross. When Arthur entered his new quarters, he was overwhelmed by the dank smell of mold. Although the building's walls were in better condition than those of Stonyhurst, they were completely devoid of any decorative features. Once he had been shown his small cot, he considered the feelings a prisoner must experience when first incarcerated. Arthur opened his valise and proceeded to unload his clothes and books, depositing them into his minuscule cubicle. Despite the accommodations, he quickly fell asleep. Before long, he was awoken by a loud rumbling, which was coming from the cot directly across from him. Being sleep deprived, Arthur had no tolerance for this assault on his senses. He grabbed one of the wooden bed shears used to keep the bed sheets from bunching, walked over to his snoring roommate, and jabbed the boy directly in his belly.

It had taken just one night at his new school for Arthur to be summoned to appear before the Feldkirch disciplinary committee. He was castigated for his violation of the school's code of behavior. He was advised in no uncertain terms that any further violation would lead to his immediate expulsion and the forfeiture of all tuition paid. Despite the administration's strict interpretation of the rules and regulations, there would be no corporal punishment. The Jesuits now regarded his transgression as resolved, and Arthur would later write that his misdeed had been "met with far more human kindness than at Stonyhurst." From this moment on, as Arthur would recollect, he "ceased to be a resentful young rebel and became a pillar of law and order." Despite this belief, however, Arthur remained unable to resist the irrepressible urge to lampoon others in his writings. This time, his magazine's name was the *Feldkirchian Gazette,* which bore the potentially inflammatory motto: "Fear not, and put it in print." While his poetry and short stories were showcased in his new publication, once again, Arthur could not miss the opportunity to be controversial. He used the magazine to disclose the fact that all incoming mail was reviewed by the faculty prior to its distribution to the boys. Just how he obtained this vital information is unknown. His "printing press" was immediately shut down by the school's administration, and the publication disappeared. Thankfully, Arthur endured no further repercussions from the event.

Despite the language barrier he faced, Arthur managed to do an admirable job in most of his official studies, which included history from the German perspective, French, and Latin. Most of all, he excelled in chemistry. Outside the confines of the classroom, he remained almost completely aloof from those students for whom English was not their primary language—a group that included virtually his entire class. Hikes were the norm at Stella Matutina, and foreign students were mandated to walk side by side with their German-speaking classmates at least twice a week, so that they would become more proficient in their conversational skills. Arthur showed a willingness to conform to this regulation, and eventually was able to "keep up an unbroken conversation [in German] for three hours."

October 1875

The annual Fall Vine Harvest, one of Stella Matutina's time-honored rituals, took place approximately one month into Arthur's stay at the school. The entire student body and most of the faculty made the three-mile pilgrimage to the quaint village of Rankweil in the nearby Rhine Valley to mark this perennial highlight of the school year. While it was not particularly long in distance, the trek was not without its hazards. It was a challenging journey through a thick pine forest, where dangerous ice and snowy slopes had to be carefully navigated. Attention to detail was a must, and the ability to reach and maintain a grasp on tree limbs, roots, and rocks was necessary to avoid a potentially deadly fall off the mountain. Although the hike was often marred by minor to moderate injuries, thankfully there were never any tragic endings. Once the combined faculty and student body had successfully completed their mission of standing atop the isolated rock formation on which St Mary's Church was situated, Arthur was able to look down upon the village of Rankweil. There he saw hundreds of others attempting to do that which he had just done. A short series of prayers and a fun-filled grape festival followed. Afterwards, everyone was taken to the Carina, a large country house owned and operated by the college.

Later that month, Arthur was drafted by the music director to play the bombardon, the heaviest and largest of all brass instruments, in the marching band. Doyle attributed his selection for the task to his powerful and muscular build, and not because of any particular musical talent. At first, he respectfully declined the "offer," but when he learned that the band stayed at the country house every two weeks, he had a sudden change of heart. Even though the bombardon was a forty-pound mass of solid brass, Doyle took to it like a duck to water. Within three months, his stamina had increased to the point where he could hike the forty-two miles from his school to the band camp with ease. Fearless, he would exact a cruel punishment upon any of the gigantic oxen that dared interrupt his path. He would march right up to it, point the aperture of his massive horn directly into one of the poor beast's ears, and blow into the bombardon's mouthpiece with all the force he could muster. His already powerful body completed its metamorphosis into a self-confident, chiseled physical specimen. When he ventured into the gym in his spare time, his improved agility, flexibility, footwork, quickness, and strength were noticed by all.

By November there had already been some significant snowfall, which had transformed the campus into a winter wonderland. Arthur joined in the construction of a twenty-foot-high wooden stage with a planked slide. The students dubbed this man-made slope the Russian Mountain. Once it had been completed, the crew of the school's fire engine took out its hoses and sprayed water on it until the Russian Mountain became a virtual ice sculpture. The students then extended the track from the base of the slide to the full length of the playground. Heedless of any potential danger to life or limb, Arthur went headlong down the treacherous slope on a single-bladed sled. He brimmed with excitement after surviving his downhill ride and refused to get off his sled until his schoolmates acknowledged his achievement with bravos and cheers. By day's end, he was competing in a game in which rings were hung from a bar placed just above the bottom of the slope, where they were picked off with a large stick that resembled a medieval lance.

Arthur honed his skills in skating, sledding, and ring sticking, and in the process, enhanced his coordination, strength, and dexterity. Later he extended his repertoire to include downhill skiing, and became the first Briton to popularize the pastime, about which he would write, "You let yourself go, gliding delightfully over the gentle slopes, flying down the steeper ones, taking an occasional cropper, but getting as near to flying as any earthbound man can. In that glorious air it is a delightful experience." What these words fail to mention was that in order to ski down the mountains of Switzerland, he had to carry his skis up to the top of a mile-and-a-half-high mountain pass without the benefit of a ski lift.

Although these activities tended to brighten up Arthur's early months at Feldkirch, by the time Christmas approached, the same sadness and despair he had known in the past returned. It was his destiny to spend the holiday season by himself, practically forgotten. What added to his dismay was the grim realization that there would be nothing for outcasts like him while the other students were home for the holidays.

At the same time, Arthur was quickly realizing that the Feldkirch syllabus was inadequate. It lacked Euclidean geometry, and what geometry it did contain was literally foreign to him. In a note home, he would write to his mother, "I think Dr. Waller will agree with me that it will be hard work getting up the subjects, when he hears that I have never learned any trigonometry or conic sections, nor read the books V and VI of Euclid." He would then ask his mother to try as best she could to get her hands on some of the previous bursary exams, so that he might figure out how much remediation was needed for him to perform well on future bursary exams. Interestingly, it was the lodger, Dr. Bryan Waller, who would answer on Arthur's mother's behalf. Bryan Waller, having researched the possible upcoming scholarships and bursary prizes, guided Arthur along the proper path, helping him prepare for the examinations for which he was eligible. Unlike the situation in London, grant money at Edinburgh was scarce, which made competition for any of the awards extremely fierce. Arthur found himself backed into a corner with no realistic option other than to remain at home and enroll in courses at his city's major university. But without any bursary prize or scholarship money, even this choice would be fraught with financial difficulty.

April 1876

As the semester at Stella Matutina was nearing its close, so, too, was the twenty-five-year career of Arthur's father. Unfortunately, the relatively young forty-four-year-old Charles Doyle had never been promoted beyond second assistant, and his drinking and failure to capitalize on his natural talent had caught up to him. There is a certain sense of denial in Arthur's April letter to his mother, in which he ingenuously writes, "I was indeed surprised and sorry to hear that papa is leaving the office; has he been unwell? Or is there any other particular reason for it?" And it is hard to conceive of his next sentence, "He ought now to be able to finish the skating picture soon at any rate," as being anything but the blocking out of a sad truth. The remainder of this same letter suggests an attempt to put off the inevitability of facing up to his family's dire straits, as Arthur considers traveling "sumptuously alone" throughout Europe. His words also hint at a desire to go to Paris to share in his godfather's largesse.

It was thanks only to the generous nature of Robert Matheson that the Doyles avoided winding up in the poor house. The termination letter he had written included the inaccurate statements that Charles Doyle had completed his projects with "diligence and fidelity" and had never missed a day of work. The new regime at the Office of Public Works gave Charles the choice of "resigning," which would ensure a lifelong annual pension of £150, or of remaining and facing the indignity of getting fired and losing everything. For once, the debilitated Charles Doyle made a judicious decision. He accepted the first proposal.

Faced with the scary thought of not being able to pay the tuition fees for his future studies at the University of Edinburgh Medical School—or at any school, for that matter— and concerned about the fate of his brother and sisters, Arthur found himself backed into a corner, a victim of extreme stress and mental anguish. He was able, however, to set his problems aside, and followed every single instruction he had received from Bryan Waller to a tee. Waller even shouldered the expense of sending Arthur his old chemistry textbook, an act about which Doyle would write, "It was very kind of Dr. Waller to send me his own chemistry book, with such splendid notes too in his hand writing on the margin. Of course I wrote to thank him." Arthur, who had won first honors in the London University Matriculation Examination, claimed that he was working harder than ever to receive a bursary for medical school, and that "the twelve labors of Hercules were child's play" when compared to the amount of work he was doing.

He adopted a strict study schedule, often reading by the faintest of light into the wee hours of the morning. He found he was able to see well enough by moonlight, but he still had to make sure never to oversleep by mistake, and begged his mother to send him an alarm clock. Soon enough, he applied for and obtained the enviable position of study room doorkeeper, which had the added perk of a private office with a lamp. No longer would he have to be concerned about incurring the wrath of his dormitory roommates by telling them they were snoring too loudly, nor would he have to worry about having enough light by which to study.

Towards the end of his year abroad, Arthur received a brief but strange letter telling him that neither his mother nor Bryan Charles Waller would be present when he returned to Edinburgh in August. Rather, the two of them would be summering at the Waller family estate at Masongill, while his siblings and father would be remaining in Edinburgh with the housekeeper. Mary Doyle had decided to travel with her young lodger down to Yorkshire for the purpose of meeting Waller's mother, Julia. Coincidentally, Arthur's two previous schools, Hodder and Stonyhurst, were a stone's throw away from the Waller country estate, and yet Mary had never visited Arthur at either place during his years away. Mary's current decision to journey away from Edinburgh could not have come at a more inopportune moment, with Charles losing his job and her oldest son returning home.

When the school year finally ended, Arthur, under the guise of seeking the most "economical arrangement" in terms of traveling home, set out for Paris by train. After seventeen years, he would at long last meet the man for whom he had been named, his godfather and great-uncle, Michael Conan. Surrounded by a group of classmates, Arthur boarded the train that would take him to Paris on his roundabout journey home. When the train stopped at the small Austrian town of Strasbourg, Arthur and the boys made sure to visit many of the local taverns, where they drank away the night and their money. When he staggered back onto the train, Arthur was alone, destitute, and stripped of his companions, all of whom had boarded different trains to travel to different destinations.

When his train arrived at the Paris train station, Arthur found himself an impoverished stranger in a strange land, his lack of restraint in Strasbourg having reduced him to a state of vagrancy. He had no choice but to walk to his great-uncle's apartment at 65 Avenue de Wagram, even if it meant dragging his massive trunk across half the city. With each step he took in the heat of the summer sun, his trunk got progressively heavier and he got progressively weaker. Thirsty, he purchased a glass of "coco" with his last pennies. Although this cheap beverage looked like some sort of dark ale, it was, in essence, a derivative of licorice, and as such, a natural laxative. Within minutes, he was to learn of its adverse effects. First came a mild cramping sensation, and then a distended belly, and finally, excruciating abdominal pain. Knowing he was in trouble, he walked as quickly as he could between agonizing spasms. Young Arthur was about to suffer the ultimate humiliation: an ungodly gastric accident in front of crowds of people on the streets of Paris. Just as he was about to drop his suitcase and run, he realized he was standing right in front of the Conan house. What appeared to be a house servant in shredded shirt sleeves and worn trousers was sitting on the porch. When the ragamuffin stood up and extended his hand in greeting, there was no time to reciprocate. Arthur asked where the water closet was and sped to it. Once he had finished ridding himself of the effects of the dark drink, he returned to the porch where the ragamuffin introduced himself. He was none other than Arthur's great-uncle, the famed Michael Conan.

Arthur tried the best he could to atone for his rude entrance, but he must have been quite surprised and somewhat disappointed when he looked upon his renowned family member. Could it have slipped his great-uncle's mind that he would be visiting him that day, or did he simply not care about a distant relative of no particular importance? What soon became clear to Arthur was that France, his great-uncle's adopted land, was the thing that Michael Conan cared for most, not the formalities of greeting family members. After a proper introduction to Susan Conan, Arthur's great-aunt, Arthur was shown to his "bedroom," which was essentially a stuffy library of old worn books and a long couch. The chamber's only redeeming quality was the scads of old editions of works by Scott, Poe, and Macaulay, among others, which had been stacked and stashed all over the place, likely reminding Arthur of John Hill Burton's Craig House.

Although Michael Conan was now a full-time resident of France, in the past he had been based in London, where he had worked for a newspaper, the *Morning Chronicle*. It was actually he, not John Doyle, who had introduced Richard Doyle to Mark Lemon, the editor of *Punch*. During this glorious three-week period in Arthur's life, Arthur and Michael engaged in long talks about genealogy and heraldry. Michael would both amaze and amuse Arthur as he traced the Conan clan's lineage back to the Dukes of Brittany. Arthur learned about the original Arthur Conan, the young Duke who, according to Shakespeare's *King John*, died while trying to escape imprisonment and death at the command of his ruthless uncle.

During his sojourn with the Conans, young Doyle devoured the astonishing collection of literary masterpieces his great-uncle had acquired. Indeed, despite having the City of Light at his doorstep, Arthur rarely left the house. His great-uncle, who had a reputation of being "a mild-mannered and unobtrusive man who was more disposed to listen than to talk" and "rather averse to thrust his opinions upon others," surprised Arthur with his loquacious nature. Arthur's perception of him was as "a dear old volcanic Irishman" who made it an absolute point to take his great-nephew away from the more popular works to which he was attracted. Instead, he introduced him to a treasure trove of rare manuscripts and magical works that had been produced by the most respected scholars and religious authorities of the past millennium. During this same visit, Michael Conan also expressed his misgivings about the direction in which the Society of Jesus and the Roman Catholic Church itself were headed. Arthur's great-uncle's skepticism about the validity of Christian doctrine magnified his own doubts, moving him more and more towards Spiritualism.

In Michael Conan, Arthur saw a kindred spirit, and ingested, absorbed, and accepted his godfather's rather odd ideas, ideals, and beliefs without question. Judging by Arthur's description of their time together, Michael Conan viewed his seventeen-year-old great-nephew as a young man with considerable promise. Three weeks after his arrival, Arthur found it difficult to leave the man who had revived his mind by providing it with so much intellectual stimulation. Arthur felt a strange connection to Michael Conan, as if he himself were in some way "built on the lines of body and mind of the Conans rather than the Doyles."

Arthur left Paris for London, where he could not wait to tell the Doyles of Finborough Road about his Parisian experience. But his aunt and uncle voiced their displeasure with what their eccentric and heretical cousin had imparted to their innocent nephew. When his London relatives told him they feared he was on the road to eternal damnation, Arthur remained steadfast in his recently solidified unorthodox views. He let them know that he would not be a practicing Catholic any longer. Uncle Richard and Aunt Annette were aghast at this rejection of their faith. And even though he had been counting on them to help pay a portion of his medical school tuition, Arthur maintained his position, despite their threats to withhold financial aid. Had he been able to hold his tongue, the money would most certainly have been his, but he just could not suppress the urge to tell his uncle, a man who had given up his career at *Punch* for his faith, and his aunt, a woman who had devoted her life to the concept of poverty, chastity, and obedience, that he had turned his back on the religion to which they had committed themselves. Somehow Arthur had convinced himself that honesty, integrity, and independent thought would make a favorable impression on them. He was incorrect, and found himself departing London a bit earlier than planned.

Upon his return to Edinburgh, the first thing he encountered was a flute that Bryan Waller had left for him—perhaps the lodger's humorous attempt to contrast Arthur's former marching band instrument with a lighter option. Arthur must have found the scene in front of him surprising when he saw that the current members of the household were his four siblings and a housekeeper. His mother and Bryan Waller were out in the country, and his wandering father was nowhere to be found. Although he did the best he could to reacquaint himself with his brother Innes and the three sisters who still lived there, most of the time he holed himself up in his room and studied for the upcoming bursary exam. He would send a letter to Bryan Waller at Masongill, informing him that his daily readings included "a Greek and Latin exercise," "a chapter of Livy and Simpson's *Cyropaedia*," and a "certain quantity of Euclid and Algebra." According to Doyle, he left his room only to eat or to scare his "small family circle by reading Poe's tales."

One of the first things Arthur did when he got back to Argyle Park Terrace was to hire someone at two guineas per month to tutor him for the upcoming scholarship examination. Just how Arthur managed to pay his tutor, Mr. Walker, for his services is difficult to figure out, for according to Arthur, he had squandered his money on his return trip home. In addition, his father had imbibed his pension fund money, and had also disposed of the money he had received as payment for some illustrations he had done for an up-and-coming art weekly, the *Graphic.* Most likely, Mr. Walker received his fee from Bryan Waller. The young tutor almost broke Doyle's spirit when he cautioned him that Arthur had little chance of winning any prize, as the test he was about to take was geared towards the curriculum of Edinburgh's school system. Doyle immediately dispatched a desperate letter to Waller at Masongill. Waller's response was rapid and reassuring. He restored Arthur's "equanimity" by gently explaining to him that the university had "so many competitions," and that the majority of his fellow competitors would be going in "without a vestige of a chance."

With Waller absent from the premises, Arthur trespassed into Bryan's room and took "the liberty" of snooping around, searching for anything that might help him in his studies. Although he was probably looking for books, he came across Walker's copy of Edinburgh's "university calendars." He thumbed through the papers until he found something interesting: a listing of all the bursaries offered by the school. After carefully analyzing the available prizes, he decided that the one he would seek would be the lucrative Grierson, and not the one that Waller had handpicked for him. If Arthur had read the prerequisites of this test, he would have known that there were, in fact, two Grierson bursaries—one for medical students who had already successfully completed the winter semester, which Arthur had not done, and another for fine arts students who had completed a year of college. There were other medical bursaries available, such as the Sibbald medical scholarship, which was only awarded to "sons of duly registered medical men," and the Abercrombie bursary, which was set aside only for those students who had "been brought up in Heriot's Hospital." Doyle must have read the entry requirements of each exam, as he did not consider these other prizes. Nevertheless, in late October, Arthur sat for the Grierson Fine Arts examination.

Walker's methods proved effective. Doyle purportedly received word that he had won the much-coveted seventy-five-pound bursary prize, which would be paid over two years. He strode down to the University of Edinburgh's Office of the Bursar to claim his reward, but quickly received the unwelcome news that only students of fine arts, not medical students, were eligible for the prize. Perhaps he had not read the exam requirements closely enough; perhaps he had hoped the university would see his actions as an honest mistake and award him the money regardless. Whatever the truth, the best the school could do was to give him a one-time consolation prize of £7. This paltry sum was little consolation to him. He became bitterly irate at what he perceived as a mammoth slight, and told Waller and his mother that he planned to sue the school's administration. Calmer heads prevailed, however, and he backed off. Mary knew that this would be an exercise in futility, and would surely bear no fruit.

Although Arthur told Waller and his mother that he had won the bursary, and that the university had refused to grant him his just reward, a look at the list of students who took the Grierson Fine Arts examination actually places Doyle a distant twelfth out of twenty-six contenders in the order of merit. This fact suggests that Arthur would not have been offered any prize, whether in the fine arts or medical division of the university. Perhaps his complaints were merely a way of trying to guilt his mother or Bryan Waller into giving him money to make up for this supposedly egregious wrong that had been inflicted upon him.

6

The Tour

The Ten Bells, 11 AM

Doyle led his group a short distance to the Ten Bells pub, where he had made arrangements for lunch. Before they walked in, he had the group look at the church across the street and said, "Across the street is Christ Church. It has four illuminated clock faces on it. No one has to own a pocket watch to know the time around here. The reason why we have such an accurate chronology of the Ripper crimes is that many of the witnesses simply and instinctively looked up at one of these clock faces. By using this clock, the police were able to avoid being confused by conflicting accounts of when events occurred."

"On Saturday night you can pay and play, and then the following morning you can come right back and pray," Edgar said. "Very convenient!"

"May I have your permission to borrow your poetic wit for my next book?" Doyle said, chuckling along with the group.

The tour members walked through the pub's oak double door and waited for Doyle to give them permission to sit down. Dr. Hammond decided to look at the beautiful tile mosaic of a couple visiting a weaver's shop. Doyle walked over to him. "So, what do you think of it?" he said.

"A sad remembrance of things past," Hammond said.

"Where are the snows of yesteryear?" Doyle said, inspecting the mosaic. "It's all too easy to forget how quickly glory can fade away. This wonderful work of art serves as a poignant reminder of the prosperity and prominence this part of town once enjoyed. In fact, we are no longer in Whitechapel, but now in the Spitalfields part of the East End. Its name is actually a combination of the words 'hospital' and 'fields,' with the omission of the first two letters of the word 'hospital.' More than a half a millennium ago, the Priory of St. Mary Spital, a medieval hospital, stood nearby."

"Hospital fields," Evander said, nodding.

A hostess brought the group to a large table. Doyle motioned to the barmaid to bring drinks for everyone. He took his seat last, sitting next to Gertrude on one side and Stephen on the other. Carrington had pulled a seat out for Adelaide and made sure to sit next to her. Once everyone had been given their drinks, Doyle said, "Why do you think I've brought you here?"

"For the food, of course," Stephen said.

"Actually, the food is quite good," Doyle said with a laugh, "but I've brought you here for a completely different reason. The Ripper's victims used places like this as their offices, and some of them used this place in particular. They stationed themselves outside pubs, and if anyone dared move in on their territories, the result would be pulled-out hair, blackened eyes, or lost teeth. Patrons didn't have to go too far to witness great boxing matches. All they had to do was find a seat near a window. Ten Bells is a symbolic starting point for the Ripper murders."

"Oh, I understand," Adelaide said. "To be serviced by a woman of the night, a man would have to come down here to a tavern."

"More or less," Doyle said, "but business was usually conducted on the streets and sidewalks outside."

"Didn't these women have any friends who might have kept an eye on them?" Gertrude said.

"The victims were street women, my dear. A breed apart from the suffragettes of Manchester, although members of each group managed to land in jail cells from time to time, didn't they?"

"Pardon me, Mr. Doyle, but we militants, as we like to call ourselves, are not at all like those women. We are engaged in a campaign for justice and equality. And we are fighting for a worthy cause."

"You've taken my words out of context, Miss Pemberton. What I am saying is that these women were fighting to survive. To come up with doss money. All I meant by my statement was that these women acted alone, not in bands, to defend their territory. Out here, you were on your own. What happened to others quickly became irrelevant, no matter how idealistic you may have been when you started. If my comments offended you, I do apologize. Now, where was I? As I implied earlier, on the night of each murder, Jack would have made his way to a tavern such as this one, found a suitable companion, and then, sometime later, taken her life."

As Doyle spoke, sandwiches were served to each of them and their empty glasses were refilled.

"Sir Arthur, you mentioned that all of Jack's victims were from this area, but where do you believe the Ripper was from?" Stephen said.

"There is a distinct possibility that he may have been both born and raised right here in the East End," Doyle said.

"I am a bit perplexed by your response," Stephen said, "for if Jack had lived in this area, would not he have been worried that someone might recognize him? After all, the potential for an eyewitness to his misdeeds was enormous, especially as he committed these atrocities out in the streets."

"There are more than half a million people who live in this poverty-stricken morass, and as I have told you previously, at least one-fifth of them subsist solely by participating in criminal activities. Those who do not are compelled to work long and hard just to provide a small parcel of food for their tables. So, there is no true socialization here, nor is there any compassion for those who get attacked or even killed in the streets. It's a dog-eat-dog world, in a way."

"But Sir Arthur, I have seen many of the people of Whitechapel during my current sojourn here in London, and most of them appear to be decent, though impoverished, human beings."

"Of whom do you speak? The prostitutes and beggars of this rancid slum? There is only one thing in this entire world that holds their interests, and that is money. The entire basis of their society revolves about its acquisition, and whether it is legally or illegally obtained is irrelevant to them. If one prostitute dies, the remaining ones pounce on her clients and augment their earnings."

Stephen pressed Doyle once again. "While Jack may have been somewhat familiar with this area, my initial impression is that he more likely would have been an outsider. It is quite difficult to keep a low profile in these crowded neighborhoods, and as there are no regular working hours, there are always people up and about. I have been told that Whitechapel never sleeps. If Jack had lived here, his comings and goings would have been noticed by his neighbors or passersby. Certainly, when he returned to his flat after committing these murders, he would have had to accomplish the difficult task of entering his building through its front door without leaving any trace of blood evidence behind. His neat and tidy slashings would still have shown up in some way on his clothing, or on a door handle, at the very least. Something in his demeanor would have aroused suspicion. His posture, his footfalls, his vocal cadence, or perhaps the lingering odor of the victim's blood—something would have screamed out 'murderer.' No, if he were a familiar figure, someone would have taken notice of these clues. Sir Arthur, he may have worked here, but I do not believe that Whitechapel was his home."

"You put forth quite an interesting argument, Mr. Mitchell," Doyle said.

"Another possible scenario comes to mind," Stephen continued. "The London Hospital is close by. Perhaps we should look into the possibility of a house physician or surgeon being our Jack, or consider the remote possibility that the Ripper was someone who worked at the hospital in another capacity. This would have enabled him to walk through this district openly, yet, by not residing here, he had the anonymity he required."

"Let's investigate this while employing your logic," Doyle said. "Imagine this scenario: Jack kills his victim, proceeds to run down the street with blood dripping from his hands, and then nonchalantly walks through the front entrance of the London Hospital. No one notices anything amiss. In fact, an orderly hands him a towel so he can wipe the blood from his hands. Now, having just committed a brutal crime, the humanitarian side takes over and compels him to hurry back to his hospital duties to render care to his needy patients! Ha! Ha! What a brilliant piece of detective work and a marvelous study in deductive reasoning."

"That is not at all what I meant."

"Then what did you mean?"

"What I am saying is that it is more than possible for a physician to have some blood on his hands without it being perceived as something unusual."

Dr. Hammond joined in the conversation. "After all, it's only been about twenty years since organized medicine brought itself to accept Dr. Semmelweiss's controversial view that the spread of infection can be curtailed by hand washing," he said. "All too many of my older colleagues have resisted this notion, and regard mandatory hand washing as an egregious infringement on the limited time they have to spend with their patients."

Doyle shook his head in disbelief and voiced his opinion. "I was a young physician when the Ripper went on his rampage, and I can tell you with utter certainty that I and my colleagues would have been keenly aware of any physician whose hands were steeped in blood outside the confines of the operating room. Once the morning papers had reported that a murder had been committed right here in this area, I certainly would have informed the authorities that I had seen a physician bathed in blood walking into this hospital. Is what I am saying correct in your opinion, Dr. Hammond?"

Dr. Hammond nodded in agreement. Doyle looked Stephen's way and said, "And Mr. Mitchell, I know I've been more than a bit exacting, but after all, I have been caught up in the Ripper case for more than two decades, and up until this moment, I have never allowed myself to give even the remotest consideration to the theoreticians who suggest Jack could have been a physician. What cannot be ruled out is the possibility that an orderly, or even a man disguised in a midwife's uniform, could have been the perpetrator. But a physician? Totally and absolutely out of the question. Nevertheless, your sharp mind and sheer determination have earned you my sincere applause. In fact, you remind me of my esteemed surgical professor and mentor, Dr. Joseph Bell, back in Edinburgh. He, too, had an obsession for analyzing and sifting through that which seemed of no particular consequence to others in his search for a correct diagnosis. There was very little that escaped his watchful eye, and apparently very little escapes yours. You may take these words as an earnest and supreme compliment. I wonder, Stephen, are you familiar with any of the great American writers of detective stories, such as Mr. Poe or Mrs. Green?"

"Actually," Stephen said, "I have read their works, and I like the Dick Stanhope dime novels as well, but I am most impressed by Gaboriau's Monsieur Lecoq, with his ability to blend into the crowd and solve the most complex cases."

"Yes, Gryce, Stanhope, and Lecoq are certainly worthy of being included in the pantheon of great detectives of modern fiction," Doyle said. "But let's get back to Poe, the father of the modern detective story. Even he made occasional errors in reasoning, "The Murders in the Rue Morgue" being a prime example. After all, how could any rational person accept the concept of an orangutan being a murderer! Now, let us return to the matters at hand."

Carrington then joined in. "Sir, I believe that I've come up with a unifying theory, one that would be acceptable to you, me, and our fellow members."

"And what's that?" Doyle said.

"Perhaps Jack did not reside in Whitechapel," Carrington said. "Maybe he was a salesman or a merchant seaman who had easy access to the district's places of lodging. If he had been at all familiar with the East End's streets and back alleys, but had chosen to stay in Whitechapel for only a short period of time, wouldn't he have been able to carry out these crimes without arousing any suspicion, whether physician or not? After all, when the killings were taking place, the constabulary was calling on doctors to report to the various crime scenes all the time. Apparently, there were a lot of professional people who lived in Whitechapel."

"An interesting thought, and yes, the police surgeons were often able to get to the crime scene in a trice," Doyle said.

Doyle made his way over to the Stantons. Hovering over their shoulders, he asked for their opinions. "We're just amazed at how little we knew about these matters," Matthew said, "whereas we thought ourselves so knowledgeable on the subject prior. Everything is crystallizing now."

Taking a break from the matters at hand, Doyle took the opportunity to tell the brothers that he had spent a significant portion of his life in the Pennines region, regaling them with a few quick but humorous anecdotes regarding his time there as a student before transitioning back to the subject of the tour. "Any questions at all about what has transpired thus far?" he said, his gaze singling out Evander.

"Well, my first question is the elementary one, of the exact number of Jack's victims," Evander said. "I have heard estimates ranging from as few as five to as many as eight."

"What my brother is trying to say is that we have heard there were as many as a dozen prostitutes who became Jack's prey," Matthew said.

"There are actually those who attribute two dozen gravestones to his terrible spree," Doyle said, "but the correct answer is five."

"With such a large discrepancy, how can you be so sure of your number?" Matthew said.

"I appreciate your diligence, but five is the number that I and the Yard's most respected men have come up with," Doyle said. "You see, gentlemen, when the Ripper scare was at its height, Jack was tagged with every Whitechapel murder. With the proper technique and analytical skills, it is easy to eliminate the ones that do not bear his trademarks. So, I am reiterating that which I told you at the outset: Please disregard all that you thought you knew."

"We most certainly will, won't we, Evander?" Matthew said.

Evander nodded his head in agreement. Before Doyle moved on from the Stantons, he added, "And by the way, when I did this tour a few years ago, even my club was under the impression that Jack had done away with seven women." He then sat himself between Gertrude and Adelaide. "You know, my fair ladies, the summer of 1888 was a red-letter year for criminologists and for women, too," he said.

"And how is that, Dr. Doyle?" Gertrude said.

"Does the term 'matchgirls' strike' ring a bell?" Doyle said.

"No, it doesn't," Gertrude said.

"I haven't heard the phrase either," Adelaide said.

"Of course it doesn't. I realize that you two ladies are too young to remember, or possibly were not even born yet. But just prior to the onset of Jack's activities here in the East End, a well-known feminist named Annie Besant, the owner of her own periodical, the *Link*, published an inflammatory article, "White Slavery in London," which elicited a swift reaction from the public. Its contents were a bitter indictment of the management practices of Bryant and May, a match factory located only a stone's throw from here. Mrs. Besant accused this firm of forcing their laborers to work excessive hours at low pay in premises that were unsafe. The 1,400 female workers were continuously exposed to the known toxin white phosphorus while making matches, resulting in severe health problems. They were also faced with exorbitant and unreasonable fines on a regular basis. In their attempts to whitewash what was going on, Bryant and May demanded all its employees sign a document denying that working conditions were anything but acceptable. When one brave 'matchgirl' stood up and refused to sign, she was fired on the spot. Her dismissal ignited a strike that shut down the factory. The strikers, lacking a leader, sought out Mrs. Besant's guidance, and soon her support of the struggle helped the workers find the courage to remain steadfast. Within three weeks, Bryant and May were brought to their knees."

"My group is quite similar to those girls, in that all we are asking for is fairness in our ongoing battle for women's suffrage and divorce reform," Gertrude said.

"My dear Miss Pemberton, these two topics are not necessarily tied to each other. Let us discuss them," Doyle said. "I am in total agreement with you that our divorce laws are unjust and unfair in their current forms. They are so arranged at present that many people are tied to lunatics, drunkards, and criminals without hope of release. Certainly when a husband has been convicted of a crime and condemned to a long period of imprisonment, a woman should be granted a speedy divorce if she so desires it. And certainly when a husband has been confined in an asylum for many years because it has been determined that he suffers from incurable insanity, likewise, his spouse should be granted a quick divorce. When it comes to divorce proceedings, men and women should be treated equally. But when militants demand suffrage, they take things too far. If women were granted the vote, a powder keg within marriage would be created. Political arguments would be an inevitable consequence of such an experiment, and would surely lead to unkind words, to the disruption of the conjugal bed, and potentially to violence. The foundation of the Empire would be shaken to the core if this frivolity was put into law, and divorce would become an even greater problem than it is currently. Such legislation you propose poses an imminent threat to the future of Britain."

Gertrude had held herself back long enough. She glared into Doyle's eyes like a matador staring down a bull, flared her nostrils, and pursed her lips. "Statements like yours are the reason why women must fend for themselves in order to ensure their rightful place in society," she said. "We are willing to sacrifice our lives for the freedom to take part in the crafting of society. Your fears will be proven incorrect in a very short time."

"When foolish hooligans feel it is their obligation to commit violent acts in the name of progress and women's rights," Doyle said, "their civil disobedience only serves to diminish what they deem to be a just cause. What do you think this is, America's Wild West? Your next step will probably be to blow up a blind man and his dog to get your point across?"

Gertrude sprang from her chair as if she had been stung by a bee. She whirled around, pointed a finger at Doyle, and began to berate him. "We militants have had no choice but to engage men of your ilk in battle," she said. "Now the lines have been permanently drawn. No longer will we remain in a subservient position. We refuse to tolerate unfair treatment anywhere, whether in the workplace or in the home, and there is only one way for us to realize our full potential, and that is by capturing the ballot box. Those 'matchgirls' of whom you speak were ahead of their time. In fact, they were not girls; they were women of the first order. You, Dr. Doyle, are a wolf in sheep's clothing, but I am no lamb. And I have had enough of your demeaning statements."

"I'll have a cab pick you up," Doyle said.

"No need for that. I'm quite capable of making my own arrangements," Gertrude said.

Adelaide was now forced to make a quick decision in regard to leaving with her traveling companion or remaining with the tour group. The balance tilted quickly as she saw Carrington Lambton staring in her direction, seemingly oblivious to the altercation that had just taken place. While Adelaide's heart agreed with Gertrude's goals, her mind could not condone the abrupt insults heaped on Sir Arthur. After taking a second look at Carrington, Adelaide made the difficult decision to carry on with the group. Gertrude waited for Adelaide to rise from her chair and join her, but Adelaide remained in her place. Not a word was said when Gertrude exited through the tavern's door and vanished.

Doyle, who had already resumed his meal, remained pensive for a few moments. The others continued on with their lunch and engaged each other in light conversation. Once the group had finished eating, Doyle rose calmly from his seat, proceeded to thank the pub-keeper for her hospitality, settled the tab, and then, as if nothing of import had just occurred, simply said, "From this time forth, Miss Pemberton will no longer be a member of this tour. Apparently, she has had more than her share of walking and talking for the day. But we have not. As my fellow Boer War correspondent Richard Harding Davis would say, everybody up and at 'em."

With that, the tour marched into the slums of Spitalfields.

7

1876-1878

The University of Edinburgh

September 1876

In the fall of 1876, Arthur Doyle began his five years of study at the highly regarded University of Edinburgh Medical School. The vast majority of the school's accomplished faculty had also trained there. These professors maintained a fierce loyalty to their fellow alumni, to their alma mater, and to the city itself. These tight bonds worked together to earn the college a respectable reputation in Great Britain and internationally. Students from all over the world coveted acceptance to this school. In Edinburgh, there were two medical schools, one called Edinburgh Medical School and the other being the University of Edinburgh Medical School. Although their names were similar, they had separate charters and campuses. While the University of Edinburgh had the better reputation, students were free to take classes at both schools, which led to a healthy dynamism between the interacting student bodies and professors. While most of the London schools had outstanding faculties, not a single one of them could match the University of Edinburgh's clinical and academic strengths in each and every department.

For Arthur, there were apparent and hidden advantages to living at home. He would have no roommates, and his expenses would be reduced dramatically. Textbooks, which were hard to come by, would be readily available to him through Waller and Waller's friends. Unfortunately, by remaining in Edinburgh, Arthur would also be taking on at least some of the responsibility of preventing the Doyle household from disintegrating due to the unpredictable behavior of his father and the family's ever-present financial problems. Moreover, when Arthur's mother returned to Edinburgh from Mason-gill at the beginning of the school semester, it was obvious that she was preg-nant and would soon be adding another mouth to feed to the Doyle family.

The Doyles were living a short distance from the medical school, just a brief walk through the large expanse of greenery known as the Meadows. The orderliness and structure of Stonyhurst and Feldkirch differed greatly from the inherent disorder and chaos of this urban medical school, where a student had to be self-reliant in order to ensure his success. Students were left to their own devices to make arrangements for their classes and to pay their teachers for the lectures they chose to attend. Unlike the medical system of England, which provided living quarters for its students, Edinburgh provided none, and had no structured lectures or after-school activities. The university was indif-ferent to its student body, and no "official" help was available along the difficult path that led to a well-respected bachelor of medicine degree, and later on to a very prestigious MD degree.

The medical school was faithful to the ideals of the nation of Scotland. Its environment was unembellished and austere. Lectures tended to be lengthy and detailed, and there were many overworked professors who found them-selves compelled to call upon teaching assistants to fill in for them. For the most part, only students disciplined enough to place their social lives on hold could hope to make it through the rigorous and challenging five-year course of study. The first year's curriculum required students to pass "an examination in Natural Philosophy, Chemistry, Physiology, Botany, and Zoology." All but the strongest were weeded out. Those who remained were required to attend lec-tures in "Anatomy, Chemistry, *Materia Medica,* Institutes of Medicine or Phys-iology, Practice of Medicine, Surgery, Midwifery and the Diseases peculiar to Women and Children."

Doyle was one of the few who dared test the necessity for self-discipline. From day one, he demonstrated his unwillingness to make classwork his only priority. Instead, he became a man about town, regularly attending the theatri-cal performances and dances so readily available to people his age. He tried out for and was accepted by the university's rugby team, played in several cricket and football leagues, and continued to work on his boxing skills. According to Doyle himself, he "missed nothing in the way of fun," yet he still managed to get by academically.

On March 2, 1877, Mary Doyle gave birth to her last child, a daughter. With her husband nowhere to be found, it was left to her to register the child's birth, a role that Charles had always performed. Mary chose the name Bryan Mary Julia Josephine for her baby girl. Arthur referred to her only as Dodo. It may have been disquieting for Arthur to gaze upon an infant named after Bryan Waller and Bryan's mother, Julia, but who lacked any reference to Charles Doyle aside from his surname.

Arthur was most critical of two of his teachers: Dr. John Balfour, who taught botany, and Professor Charles Thomson, who taught natural history. He described their courses as being a "long weary grind," even though both professors had superb reputations. Thomson had returned only months before from exploring the Atlantic onboard the H.M.S. *Challenger.* Interestingly, the man who was to become Doyle's surgery professor a year later, Dr. Joseph Bell, had used similar terms to describe those two particular subjects five years prior, in his introductory remarks to the student body of the university:

> I am unable, however, to see that botany and natural history are necessary parts of a medical curriculum. Every well-educated gentleman ought to have his mind expanded and his taste improved by an acquaintance with the flowers and fauna of his native land, if not of the world, and is none the worse—indeed, may sometimes be much the better—of a knowledge of geology and mineralogy.

Dr. Bell had also added:

> Botany and natural history should, I believe, be included in the preliminary examination, and put on a level with mathematics or physical science, so that the student may have the privilege of choosing which subject he likes to be examined on, the board being satisfied if he proves himself a well-educated gentleman, with a fondness for some branch of scientific study, and not a schoolboy who has been compelled against his will to grind up a smattering of many subjects.

Bell's comments of 1871 are mirrored in Doyle's autobiography, *Memories and Adventures,* which was written many years later, and which might induce the reader to wonder about the extent to which Bell's personality, opinions, and prejudices influenced the ideas and ideals of his disciple and admirer, Arthur Conan Doyle.

Doyle, who had always loved working with chemicals, especially enjoyed the lectures and demonstrations given by Dr. Alexander Crum Brown. Despite being the developer of the first system to represent molecules and their iso-mers graphically, Dr. Brown was regarded by the students of the school as a safety hazard. On many occasions, his demonstration would go awry, and more than a few of his students would be forced to hold their ears and duck for cover. Sometimes there were explosions, and other times, when nothing hap-pened, the students would yell, "Boom!"

There was an especially high dropout rate during the first year, but Arthur managed to remain. He always looked forward to attending clinical lectures given by Dr. Joseph Bell. Bell was a paradigm of the "compleat physician," who, in that era, conducted his own experiments, mixed his own pharmaceuti-cals, and performed his own blood work and urinalyses. Held at the Royal Infirmary off campus, Bell's class was by far the most popular among the stu-dents. A select few who met Bell's high standards of academic and clinical achievement would be chosen to act as his dressers or assistants. These posi-tions automatically conferred elite status on the lucky recipients. Doyle desper-ately wanted one of these positions for himself, but, thus far, passing Dr. Bell in the chemistry lab had been his only contact with him.

Arthur began to voice his desire to travel to the island of Arran, a sports-man's and bird-watcher's paradise located just off the southern tip of Scotland. It could not have been a coincidence that Bell, a serious dabbler in poetry, lit-erature, ornithology, and hunting, had already made plans to make the short ferry ride to Arran, which had come to be known as "Scotland in miniature." Somehow, the poverty-stricken first-year student managed to obtain permis-sion and funding from his mother by convincing her of the absolute necessity of his going on holiday. Mary Doyle was willing to pay for the trip, but Arthur would have to take his eleven-year-old sister, Lottie. Having no other option, he acquiesced to this demand.

Now that his mother had burdened him with a little extra baggage, Arthur wisely invited his old schoolmate James Ryan along. Ryan had been a year behind Arthur at Stonyhurst but had caught up to him during Arthur's preparatory year at Stella Matutina. James was happy to accept the invitation. Doyle's offer to James must have included the added bonus that he had made arrangements to stay in Brodick, the island's main village and its most fre-quented ferry stop. Strangely, Doyle had chosen a holiday location that boasted many activities, yet he did not possess fishing tackle, hunting gear, bird-watching equipment, or sufficient money to purchase or rent any of these items, which suggests that running into Dr. Bell may have been his only motive for the trip.

August 1877

On a warm afternoon in late August, the trio of Arthur, Lottie, and James went down to the Kilwinning docks, where the *Elysian II* ferried them across the Firth of Clyde. During their trip, Arthur resolved that the three of them would make it to the top of the highest peak of the beautiful Goatfell Mountain, which took their collective breath away as they sailed towards it. As evening approached, the boat pulled into Arran's small island harbor at Brodick, and its two dozen or so passengers disembarked. Arthur marched Lottie and James to an inn at which he claimed to have made a firm reservation. But when he got to the desk, he was told that the entire place was already "engaged," and that he would have to look elsewhere for lodging.

Hours later, and after multiple failed attempts to secure a place to stay, they arrived at a "darling little cottage up on a hill." When they entered, they were accorded the same welcome they had received from the other establishments. Fortunately, a rather buxom, but bearded, motherly creature named Mrs. Fullerton came out from behind the desk after seeing the forlorn expression on Lottie's face. She told them they could stay so long as they could pay her fourteen shillings a week for room and board, plus a gift of their choosing as payment for Lottie. James and Arthur agreed to her terms, and then Mrs. Fullerton offered them tea and biscuits, which they gulped down in a matter of seconds. She took them to a small but pretty room that would be theirs for the next few weeks. When Lottie called herself a princess and claimed the big bed, the boys politely carried her to the room's small sofa, on which she immediately fell asleep. Arthur would write to his mother, recommending that she send a shawl for the landlady, which he felt would be a most appropriate payment for Lottie's stay.

The following day, Arthur was eager to lead the way up Goatfell, and asked Mrs. Fullerton for the easiest route up the mountain. She warned him how risky and "feckless" such "an undertaking" would be with a small child in tow. Although Mrs. Fullerton was doing her best to protect them, Arthur was unwilling to be denied the thrill of climbing the island's highest point. He borrowed three stout walking sticks that were in the lobby in a basket, handing one to Lottie and one to James, and keeping one for himself. The three young wanderers began to make their way to the "Hill of Wind," and had the serendipity to come across someone who could furnish them with accurate directions to the open space at Goatfell's foot, where they began their ascent. The three mountaineers kept coming upon potentially deadly deep morasses and rugged crags, and also encountered a labyrinth of rocks that led nowhere and left them totally disoriented for a time. Nevertheless, they regained their bearings, and with each passing hour their confidence grew and they were better able to navigate the terrain.

Their battle with gravity and fear lasted almost six hours, but once they reached the top and gazed down upon the island itself—a great part of the Scottish mainland, and the wide expanse of blue sea that stretched to the horizon—they were immensely proud of their achievement. After resting for an hour, Arthur led them down the mountain, attributing the success of this expedition to his training in alpine activities back at Feldkirch, Stonyhurst, and Hodder.

In the first days of September, Arthur, Lottie, and James took a boat out and somehow "managed to lose the hooks and weights from each of the lines." Amazingly, the owner would not hear of taking any compensation, and only laughed at their disaster. Just a few days later, on September 8, "guests on board Lord Glasgow's steam yacht *Valetta* observed a strange sea monster about half a mile distant. The *Valetta* was steered for the monster, and ran close along side of it where upon it dived, but about 16 or 18 feet of the tail end was afterwards distinctly seen, being only two or three feet below the surface. The body was of a greenish colour. The fish was again seen about an hour and-a half afterwards, near the same spot, just off the Sannox Rock, on the north-east side of Arran." While the two incidents may have been completely unrelated, it is somewhat uncanny that just four years after stumbling upon the exploits of Stonyhurst's noted alumnus, scientist and master of hoaxes Charles Waterton, Arthur would have lost his fishing gear inexplicably in the same spot where a mysterious sea creature would be spotted. Ten days later, after having gone fishing again, this time with "very original & primitive apparatus," he would ask his mother if she had seen any article in the *Scotsman* that described the sighting.

Not long after this incident, James returned to Edinburgh to prepare for the new school year. Arthur had given no prior thought to the reality that there would be no one around to help him with Lottie once James left. He came up with a potential solution to the problem, writing a letter home to invite his father and his sister Connie to join him on the island. He enticed his father with a free opportunity to go fishing, explaining that James had already paid his part of the rent for the vacation lodging. Charles Doyle answered in the affirmative, and he and the nine-year-old Connie arrived at Arran a few days later. At the same time, Mary Doyle was moving the two smallest children from Argyle Terrace to a new residence at 23 George Square, a house that had been rented by Bryan Waller for the hefty sum of £85 per year. In addition to taking care of little Innes and baby Bryan, Mary also had to pack up and move all of the family's possessions to this new dwelling.

Unfortunately for Arthur, there was some sort of unexplained problem with his father's return ferry ticket, which apparently would be expiring within a few days. This situation made it impossible for Charles to remain on the island without having to pay another fare. Arthur delayed informing his mother that his father was on his way back after having been banished from the island by "some stupid official," who had said his return ticket "would not do for the return unless he left soon." What is difficult to explain is why Connie, whose ticket was presumably set to expire shortly as well, would have been allowed to stay, unless children her age were granted free passage. Nevertheless, according to Arthur's frequent correspondence during his sojourn at Arran, Connie remained with him and Lottie for the remainder of the trip.

Arthur's actions during the last few days of his trip further suggest an ulterior motive for the vacation. Putting his sisters at profound risk, he made Connie and Lottie accompany him through fifteen miles of steep hills and glens to Lochranza, the island's prime area for grouse and deer hunters. Arthur knew full well that Joseph Bell was a sportsman who hunted these two animals at Arran. Doyle had already scouted Brodick's nearby hunting areas, finding "real red deer in a state of freedom," but no Joseph Bell. Several hours into this trying journey, Connie, according to Arthur, "became slightly tired." The always resourceful Arthur spotted an old but functional wheelbarrow in a peat cutting. Seeing no one around to stop him, he "did not scruple to clap the young woman in." Taking hold of its wooden handles, he rolled it over to his nine-year-old sister, picked her up, and plunked her down in it. But the road was rough, and after wheeling her for as long as he could, he removed her from the barrow, making her walk the rest of the five-hour trek. Doyle then "left the vehicle on a conspicuous place near the road." Once the exhausted trio had made it to Lochranza, they spent only one hour walking through the seaside village before beginning the long journey back.

At roughly the halfway mark along the way home, they came upon a farmer who engaged them in conversation. Spying the wheelbarrow he'd used, Arthur merrily told the farmer that the vehicle in the hands of "that old ugly woman over there" had earlier served to transport his baby sister for a distance of a half a mile over the rocky soil. To Arthur's "horror [the farmer] answered with a broad grin 'Oh aye, th' auld wuman is just my wife, and the barry's my barry.'" In an almost unbelievable account of the matter, Doyle states, "[H]e was very good natured and laughed at the way I had insulted his wife & his 'barry.'" Had Arthur not been escorting two children, it is possible that the farmer might have reacted differently.

On September 17, with his trip nearing its end, Arthur Conan Doyle somehow "recognized" and "met up with Joseph Bell in Brodick." Arthur would grossly underplay the significance of this meeting in a letter to his mother, asking, "I wonder what he is doing here?" The conclusion of his trip also signaled the end of his shoes, which were now so ragged that they appeared a sight for "men to wonder at, not to see."

September 1877

When Arthur returned home, it took him a few days to adjust to the stench that surrounded his new living space at 23 George Square, and even more time to accept the fact that his family had been relegated essentially to "lodger status" by their former lodger, who was now their landlord. He soon left to attend a lecture given by Dr. Bell. Joseph Bell was a celebrity in many worlds— literature, golf, hunting, academia, and surgery. He had gained a reputation for his ability to utilize his keen powers of observation to make extraordinary diagnoses. Doyle often heard the upperclassmen waxing poetic about the charismatic legend that was Bell, and was almost certainly relying on his recent encounter with Bell at Brodick to help him become the doctor's assistant.

Bell was riding a wave of favorable publicity as the school year began. Less than a year before, in his role as consultant to the Edinburgh police, he had quickly discovered that foul play had been involved in the death of Marie Chantrelle, a young woman who had been found dead in her home. Bell and his colleague Dr. Henry Littlejohn had worked together to determine that it had been Marie's husband, Eugene, a former medical student, who had employed opium to bring about her demise. Although Bell's involvement in the case had been kept under wraps, when Eugene Chantrelle was executed, his last words were, "Bye-bye Littlejohn. Don't forget to give my compliments to Joe Bell. You both did a good job of bringing me to the scaffold." With this statement, Joseph Bell's legend was born.

Doyle walked quickly towards the Royal Infirmary, where a growing throng of students had queued up, anxious to pay for the opportunity of watching the great Dr. Bell in action inside the old gaslit surgical amphitheater. He found a space for himself on a horseshoe shaped bench. At precisely 1 PM, Bell, a thin gentleman of about forty years of age, wild-haired and red-faced, made his way down the aisle, waving his white towel, and proudly took center stage. His audience peered at his piercing grey eyes, beak-like nose, and determined chin. Only the truly observant would have seen that his hands bore stains of myriad colors from the chemicals with which he had been working in his lab immediately before the lecture. Even more difficult to detect would have been the limp he always tried so hard to conceal. He rolled up his sleeves and placed his hands in a basin of water for a full minute, revealing his eerily slender fingers.

Bell called for the first patient to be brought in to the amphitheater. The doctor's voice was raspy and airy, and its pitch and volume fluctuated. Doyle, who had noticed Bell's strange manner of walking, suspected his abnormal vocalization and strange gait to be the results of diphtheria, which was prevalent in Edinburgh at the time. Only a few years before, Dr. Bell had saved a boy from the consequences of this dreaded illness by removing the infectious membranes from the back of the young victim's throat through suction. Bell had considered his actions an integral part of his sworn adherence to the Hippocratic Oath. Arthur was reminded of one of his classmates at Hodder, "little Guibara," who had almost succumbed to the ravages of the same beastly affliction.

Whenever Bell was presented with a new patient, he would press his fingertips together and then make extraordinary use of his five senses to determine the patient's prior whereabouts, occupation or trade, and family history. Dr. Bell could decipher the meaning of any tattoo he came across, and could determine the origin of any dirt or soil sample. He was an expert in body language. Not only could he come up with complicated clinical impressions in the blink of an eye, on occasion he was able to impart his gift to some of his brighter students. What he failed to tell his rapt audiences, however, was the fact that he often gathered substantial information about his patients beforehand.

Henry Jones, one of Doyle's contemporaries at Edinburgh, wrote that Bell gave their class a "long talk on the necessity for the members of the medical profession" to develop their five senses. He recalled how Professor Bell had placed a "large tumbler filled with a dark amber-colored liquid" on the oak surgical table, announcing to the class that the glass contained a "very potent drug," which "to the taste it is intensely bitter . . . is most offensive to the sense of smell. Yet as far as the sense of sight is concerned—that is, in color—it is no different from dozens of other liquids." With this warning, he tested the students' "powers of perception" by asking them to "smell and taste" the liquid. Of course, he added that he wouldn't "ask anything of [his] students which [he] wouldn't be willing to do [himself]." After having "dipped his finger in the liquid and placed it in his mouth," he passed the tumbler around the room. "One after another tasted the vile decoction; varied and amusing were the grimaces made." Once each and every student had been made to taste the unknown sample, Bell laughed at them, saying, "I am deeply grieved to find that not one of you has developed this power of perception, which I so often speak about; for if you had watched me closely, you would have found that, while I placed my forefinger in the medicine, it was my middle finger which found its way into my mouth." Jones said that Bell's methods "impressed Doyle greatly at the time." Among other things, Doyle learned from Bell the power of sleight of hand. Bell knew that the hand is always quicker than the eye.

Dr. Bell feared nothing, and an incident that Bell once described illustrates this fact. A short, muscular male patient "walked into the room where [Dr. Bell] was instructing students." By studying him carefully, paying close attention to the man's fingers and lips, and smelling his breath, it was only a matter of seconds until Dr. Bell haughtily put forth his conclusion, stating, "Of course, gentlemen, this man has been a soldier in a Highland regiment, and was probably a bandsman." Bell then pointed out that "the swagger in his walk" was "suggestive of a piper; while his shortness told [Dr. Bell] that if he had been a soldier, it was probably as a bandsman. In fact, he had the whole appearance of a man in one of the Highland regiments."

When the patient protested that he had been "nothing but a shoemaker, and said that he had never been in the army in his life," Bell regarded his words as "rather a floorer." Dr. Bell went on to state:

> But being absolutely certain I was right, and seeing that something was up, I did a pretty cool thing. I told two of the strongest clerks, or dressers, to remove the man to a side room, and to detain him till I came. I went and had him stripped. Under the left breast I instantly detected a little blue "D" branded on his skin. He was a deserter. That was how they used to mark them in the Crimean days and later, although it is not permitted now. Of course, the reason for his evasion was at once clear.

Bell let his class know that his method of operation relied on common sense. According to him, when reason and logic could not be denied, one had to dig deeper to learn where the error lies. If no error appears, then the subject must be engaged in deception.

Having become focused on obtaining the coveted position of assistant to Dr. Bell, Arthur committed himself to studying more diligently than any of his fellow students so that he could capture Bell's attention. He felt that the only way to ensure the professor's notice would be to compile a list of Bell's interests and accomplishments, and then to attain enough proficiency in all of them to impress the doctor. He practiced and perfected the surgical techniques described so elegantly in the textbook Bell had written, *Textbook of Surgical Practise,* and even adopted some of Dr. Bell's mannerisms, speech patterns, and style of dress.

On Fridays, Arthur skipped lunch in order to take the time to visit the local bookshops. His favorite haunt was James Thin's Bookseller, which was located just a short distance from the university. It was one of only two places in all of Old Town that had retained its original medieval windows. Whenever Arthur entered Mr. Thin's magical world, he never failed to be mesmerized by the sheer magnitude of its twenty-six book-filled rooms. People came from far and wide to browse its shelves and to experience the sense of intellectual power conferred on them by being within its friendly confines. Doyle was always hoping to find a well-conditioned secondhand copy of a work by one of his favorites—Scott, Macaulay, or Thackeray—at a good price. This shop was where the intellectual elite were most likely to cross paths, and that group included Dr. Joseph Bell. While Doyle had "run into Bell" while traipsing through Arran with his siblings, he later recollected that he had first met Bell on his way to chemistry class, though it is quite possible that it was here, at James Thin's Bookseller, that the two had had their first encounter, browsing the bookstalls in search of some stimulating reading.

Another of Doyle's favorite lecturers was Dr. Henry Duncan Littlejohn, a pioneer in the emerging science of forensic medicine, which uses scientific and medical knowledge to answer questions in legal cases. A homegrown talent who had come to prominence as the city's first Medical Officer of Health, Littlejohn, now in his early fifties, was known throughout Britain. Not only was he a masterful actor who was fully capable of portraying all sorts of characters, he was also a highly trained physician and researcher whose reputation exceeded that of the younger and less experienced Joseph Bell.

Dr. Littlejohn had a habit of arriving late for his lectures, but "his boys," as he called them, would never consider leaving their seats. They eagerly awaited the opportunity to be the audience for one of the great Littlejohn's one-man plays. On one occasion, Littlejohn uttered not a single word during the course of a lecture, nor did he write on the blackboard. Instead, he pantomimed an entire murder case that had been tried against Madeleine Smith, a beautiful Glaswegian socialite. The students looked on in disbelief as Littlejohn became the accused, "denying indignantly the accusation" that she had tried to poison her lover with arsenic. Moments later, he became her ill-fated "lover creeping through the window." And then, his "ever-changing" face transformed itself into the face of Scotland's leading defense attorney, Lord Inglis, the person Littlejohn had respectfully dubbed, "that great man." Despite having restricted himself to body language, expressions, and gestures, Littlejohn was still able to win over the imaginary jurors, just as Lord Inglis had done in Glasgow when he had "got her off in a trial which ended in a 'Not Proven' verdict."

Dr. Littlejohn was unlike any other University of Edinburgh professor, according to Doyle, for "no teacher ever took a greater interest" in his students, both within the walls of the school and most especially outside of them. His specialty was guiding his students on field trips to places apart from the "routine museums." He exposed them to the realities of the city and gave them a firsthand look at the grime and filth of its slaughterhouses, as well as its unhygienic reservoirs and sewage systems. As Doyle and his fellow students trailed behind Dr. Littlejohn, the professor discussed the need for better rules, regulations, and enforcement of urban mandates, which, in the role of Police Surgeon, he had often seen the authorities overlook.

Littlejohn would take his students to the scenes of recent crimes. There he would discuss the salient features of each case. Whenever Henry Littlejohn was called to testify regarding his findings on behalf of the Crown, the courthouse would be besieged by his students and admirers. The best anyone could hope to gain was standing room, but most people ended up being left out in the halls or even out in the streets. Littlejohn "never got the worst of the argument. He was never entrapped by the smartest of lawyers, and never disconcerted by the severest of cross-examinations." The school's reputation thrived on the greatness of the man, growing with every case in which Littlejohn was involved.

Doyle happened to be present at one of Littlejohn's most exciting lectures, in which the professor put on a performance for the ages. Dr. Littlejohn transformed himself into Dr. William Palmer, a London-trained physician and compulsive gambler, who was later to become known as the Prince of Poisoners. Littlejohn raced to his desk, picked up a glass of water, and feigned slipping something into it. He then became Palmer's friend and associate John Parson Cook, who was handed the same glass by his chum, and who drank down its entire contents. Within seconds, "Cook" screamed, "Good God! There's something in it; it burns my throat!" Dr. Littlejohn "returned," explaining that

Palmer had poured strychnine into Cook's brandy. Littlejohn then recreated Cook's grisly death. As his knees bent and his hands trembled, he frantically patted his neck and chest. "Cook" painfully gasped, "I can't lie down; I shall be suffocated if I lie down. Oh, fetch Mr. Palmer!" With that bitterly ironic phrase, Littlejohn's creation fell to the floor and lay motionless on the planks for a full minute. When Littlejohn finally stood up, he addressed his audience regarding the details of Palmer's trial and how the Crown had managed to gain a conviction of the unrepentant perpetrator of the crime. He closed with a reenactment of Palmer's death on the gallows. Placing an imaginary noose around his neck, he looked down at the "trapdoor beneath him."

Many of the students rolled on the floor with delight. After things had quieted down, Dr. Littlejohn's authoritative countenance and demeanor were restored. He addressed his class, revealing that this was not the only time a physician had been a doer of unspeakable acts. The case of Dr. Edward William Pritchard of Glasgow, in which Dr. Littlejohn had played a part in securing a conviction, had disgraced the medical profession. Pritchard had murdered his wife and his mother-in-law, and may have been involved in the premature departures of several others. Dr. Littlejohn, who had already seen just about everything under the sun, had been a bit surprised by Dr. Pritchard's ability to appear so calm in the face of such serious charges. Littlejohn was forced to admit that Pritchard's stately appearance had made him wonder at the time if perhaps he was wrong to presume Pritchard's guilt. Neither Dr. Pritchard nor Dr. Palmer ever admitted any culpability in the incidents, which meant that either they had been falsely accused or they were the most original liars who had ever lived. Dr. Littlejohn told the students that which he had already determined, that both men were indeed liars, stating that the training and privileged status of physicians afforded them the ability to undertake criminal acts without detection, and had almost allowed these two men to avoid justice.

January 1878

One of the controversial issues of the 1870s was the practice of vivisection, which involves surgically opening a living organism in order to view its functioning internal structure. In fact, at the outset of Doyle's medical studies, Parliament had recently passed a new Cruelty to Animals Act, which sought to limit experimentation upon animals by physicians and veterinarians. The champion of this piece of legislation was Dr. Lyon Playfair, a former chemistry professor at the University of Edinburgh, and an influential member of Parliament

Dr. William Rutherford

The model for Arthur Conan Doyle's fictional character Professor Challenger, noted professor of physiology Dr. William Rutherford was a vocal proponent of vivisection and a critic of the Cruelty of Animals Act 1876, which had placed strict regulations on the practice. Although Doyle seemed to admire Dr. Rutherford while under his tutelage, he would later describe his former professor as a "rather ruthless vivisector" and express his appreciation for the aforementioned law, which had been designed "so as to restrain such men as he."

at the time. One of the items of the law was a ban on the use of curare, a South American poison that inhibits certain receptors found at the junctions of nerves and muscles. Antivivisectionists argued that this substance, commonly used on the tips of arrows, was not truly an anesthetic, stating that it failed to take away the sensation of pain. They insisted that curare was merely a paralytic agent, and as such, it allowed the animal to feel the cut of the knife upon its skin and the handling of its internal organs. Playfair regarded all vivisectionists as inhumane torturers. Interestingly, it had been none other than Stonyhurst's favorite son, Charles Waterton, who had introduced this exotic substance to Europe, and it had been Charles Waterton who had been the first to keep a curarized animal alive through artificial respiration by using a bellows inserted into a tracheostomy, or hole in the trachea.

The most vocal opponent of Playfair's initial proposal to abolish vivisection and the use of curare, which eventually led to the Cruelty to Animals Act 1876, was a distinguished member of the University of Edinburgh's physiology department, Dr. William Rutherford, who would later be acknowledged by Doyle as the model for his "fictitious character of Professor Challenger," with his "Assyrian beard, his prodigious voice, his enormous chest and his singular manner." Rutherford retaliated against Playfair's original bill in words that were plain and clear, declaring, "It is wonderful what you may do to a sheep-dog without the animal making any commotion." He would also state, "[A]bout half the experiments I have done are on animals not under anesthetics." Rutherford denounced the legislation as being "extremely objectionable," and said that it had been "drawn up by the Anti-vivisectionist party." He defended the practice of vivisection as being noble in purpose, and suggested that the incredible advances in the prevention of human suffering could never have been made without it. Rutherford's defense of vivisection was countered by Scotland's Lord Advocate, William Watson, who remained steadfast in his refusal to acknowledge that vivisection had any justifiable scientific purpose. He painted a scathing portrait of vivisectionists as zealots who did not "have a due regard for the suffering of dumb creatures," and launched a rancorous attack on them in the *Medical Gazette*, stating, "[E]xperiments on animals have no direct value for medical science, that it is an aimless torture, brutalizing the mind, and that distinguished scholars have denounced it." Rutherford lashed back, writing, "We are conscious of having faithfully done our utmost to advance the scientific treatment of disease, and while steadily pursuing this object we have been most careful to avoid the infliction of all pain that was not absolutely necessary."

Even after the Cruelty to Animals Act had passed, Rutherford and his cohorts refused to be shut down by a ruling they regarded as a hindrance to progress. They soon created an underground operation to advance medical physiology, recruiting others who were willing to work in secret. Doyle was one of these new recruits, as was another student, George Turnavine Budd. Rutherford, displeased with the barriers Parliament had put in the way of men of science, issued a decree to his followers that it was incumbent upon each of them to apply for a vivisectionist permit after being granted their medical degrees. Before long, Dr. Rutherford gave Doyle the opportunity to learn a very particular surgical skill, allowing him to assist in the dissection of a canine's portal triad, a structure in the liver containing veins, arteries, and bile ducts.

Adopting a method pioneered by George Budd's uncle, also named George Budd, Dr. Rutherford set out to determine whether the bile stored in the gallbladder could be forced out by using mercury as a cholagogue, or stimulant for gallbladder contraction. Rutherford made certain that the procedure was followed to a tee from start to finish. Dogs were not given food for "eighteen hours. The animal was first paralyzed by injecting a solution of curare into the jugular vein; the windpipe was then opened, a tube fixed within it to connect it with a machine for maintaining artificial respiration; then the abdomen was opened, the stomach and duodenum were moved aside," the liver raised, and the common bile duct dissected out. Of course, each student knew not to touch the small nerves that allow the gallbladder to release its contents of bile. Although the dogs felt the sharpness of the scalpel's blade, they were unable to respond to the pain, their muscles having been paralyzed by curare. After a preparatory period of thirty minutes, each student sewed the common duct to his animal's skin and sutured up its abdomen. Each dog was given a different dosage of mercury, and the students were told to record any volume of bile produced.

Doyle's experience in Rutherford's lab inspired him to compose this little ditty, which parodied the man who would become "Professor Challenger" a generation later:

> Said Rutherford with a smile,
> "It's a mass of solid bile,
> And I myself obtained it, what is more,
> By a stringent cholagogue
> From a vivisected dog,
> And I lost it on the Portobello shore."

Inside Rutherford's classroom, things weren't quite so jaunty. Adherence to strict orthodoxy was obligatory, as was his textbook, *Outlines in Practical Histology.* Dr. Rutherford stressed the importance of documenting observations and offered students suggestions that were not to be disregarded. His textbook states that "making drawings of microscopical objects necessitates a thorough inspection of an object, and it impresses its features deeply upon the memory." A nitpicker with regard to the importance of having the right tools for the job, Rutherford not so subtly informed his students that "[e]xcellent paper for drawing is the smooth but not too highly glazed 'antique note paper' made by Pirie and Sons, in Aberdeen," and even suggested which two types of pencils he expected them to use in his laboratory, namely "H.B. and H.H.H.H." Although as a student he seemed to worship Rutherford, in his autobiography, Doyle recalls Dr. Rutherford as a "rather ruthless vivisector," and downplays his own participation in the practice of vivisection, saying, "Though I have always recognized that a minimum of painless vivisection is necessary, and far more justifiable than eating meat as a food, I am glad that the law was made more stringent so as to restrain such men as he."

8

The Tour
Dutfield's Yard, 1:30 PM

With lunch completed, it was time for the group to begin negotiating its way through the East End's winding streets. They soon walked past a narrow, garbage-filled alleyway, where they saw a collection of ragged homeless men and women sleeping side by side. When Adelaide asked why these "miserables" were asleep in the middle of the day, Doyle said, "The survival ethos of the downtrodden poor decrees that they be nocturnal, that they be people of the night. In actuality, the criminal statutes of this city explicitly read that anyone found sleeping outdoors past curfew is classified as a 'vagrant' who can expect to find himself or herself at the fat end of a billy club. The implicit risk that attends dozing off after dusk serves as a constant reminder that discretion is surely the better part of valor."

"Sir Arthur, were any of these 'vampires' questioned by the constabulary about Jack's crimes back then? It seems logical that at least one of them may have borne witness to his evil deeds," Stephen said.

"My dear Mr. Mitchell," Doyle said, "even if any of these street people had been tortured, none of them would have offered any valuable information to the authorities. They, too, are members of an exclusive 'club.' They adhere to a strict code of silence, which prohibits them from assisting in any way those who are responsible for carrying out the city's mandates against them. While I do not rule out that, for a shilling or two, one or two of them might have acted as secret informers to the police, such information would have been of limited value. But even under the best of circumstances, there is an inherent problem when one obtains information from multiple sources, which is that one receives conflicting versions of events. In the case of the street people, you would be unable to tell whether you were being led off the track out of spite or revenge."

Suddenly the group's attention was drawn to Dr. Hammond's index finger, which was pointed straight up like Lady Liberty's torch. Doyle gave him the floor. "Surely, if you are aware of this creed, then it can reasonably be assumed that Jack knew it, too," Dr. Hammond said.

"Most probably," Doyle said. "What makes this an item of importance, Dr. Hammond?"

"He must have been certain that he had nothing to worry about, even if he were to be spotted by one of them," Dr. Hammond said, pointing to the huddled mass.

"I happen to agree with you."

It was a fifteen-minute walk to the next stop, and Doyle had prepared a little educational seminar on his favorite topic to hold the group's interest along the way. With the zeal of an evangelist, he gave a sermon on the benefits and logic of Spiritualism. Ten minutes into it, Dr. Hammond became agitated. He just could not tolerate any more of the bizarre phraseology, which to him represented an overt attempt at converting the group to this weird science. Staring directly into Doyle's dilated blue eyes, as if he were gazing at a loon, he interrupted him.

"So, Dr. Doyle, do you believe in fairies, too?" Dr. Hammond said. "You are aware, of course, that to this day, no medium has ever been lifted into the air by spirits. And no one has ever lifted tables or chairs except by trickery. No one has ever read unknown writing through a closed envelope, and no one has ever been tied or untied by spirits of any kind. No one has ever heard the knocks of a spirit, and no one has ever spoken through the power of a spirit other than his own."

Doyle, fearing that his entire effort at educating his entourage might be washed down the drain, tried to cut Dr. Hammond off at the proverbial pass. As soon as this man from New York paused to take a breath, Doyle began to speak.

"Dr. Hammond, am I to accept that you are not at all interested in your own nature or in your own fate?" Doyle said. "I have always held that people like you insist too much upon the palpable. What direct proof do we have of most of the great facts of science? We simply take the word of those who have examined these facts. Dr. Hammond, have you ever seen the rings of Saturn?"

"No, I haven't."

"But you do believe they exist?"

"Why of course, I do. And they do exist."

"And how do you know this with certainty? Who or what has assured you that they are indeed there? And why have you accepted these assurances?"

"Please, Dr. Doyle, each and every one of us knows that our astronomers have telescopes that are quite capable of seeing Saturn's planetary rings."

"But you haven't seen them, and yet you are not at all skeptical about their reports. As strong telescopes are rare, we cannot expect to see the rings with our own eyes. In the same way strong mediums are rare, and we cannot expect to experience the higher psychic results."

"Such logic does not do the trick, Dr. Doyle. Mediums suffer from mental illness or diseased nerves. They cannot talk to the dead, and neither can you or I. We must summarily reject such balderdash."

The tour members did their best to feign that they weren't seeing or hearing the debate raging right in front of them. While they made their best efforts not to antagonize their host, they were thankful that Dr. Hammond had thrown himself onto the sacrificial altar. Yet it was clear to them that Doyle had the utmost confidence in the validity of his wild theory, and that he remained absolutely convinced that if his words were properly interpreted the intelligentsia who stood with him that day would embrace these ideas and reject the American's ill-considered barbs.

"As I come from a long line of distinguished neurologists," Dr. Hammond said, "I can state with absolute certainty that it is possible for the most careful and experienced judgment to be deceived by false sensorial impressions of real objects, and even by illusions created by the mind. A gleam of moonlight passes for a ghost, the stump of a tree becomes a robber, and the rustling of leaves blown by the wind is imagined to be the whispering of voices. As no one possesses an absolute perfection of sensation, nothing is ever seen, or heard, or smelt, or tasted, or felt exactly as it exists. In the dark, or in the uncertain light of the moon, the liability to self-deception is very much increased. I now have to wonder if in fact Jack the Ripper had been a convert to Spiritualism, and having been converted was a zealot malevolently influenced by its tenets."

"And how, pray tell, have you arrived at this conclusion?" Doyle said, rubbing his jaw.

"When the Ripper planned his crimes he had already armed himself with the ability to maneuver others into compromised positions," Dr. Hammond said. "Just as illusionists and magicians are able to exploit the senses of their victims, perhaps Jack did the same when he managed to make himself disappear from the scene of the crime without being detected by the authorities."

With the tension between the two heading towards a crescendo, Edgar thought it wise to insert himself into the conversation, hoping that a third party might calm down the proceedings. Without really caring about the answer to his question, he said, "Sir Arthur, maybe I missed this somewhere along the line, but do you consider Spiritualism to be a religion, a creed, or perhaps both?"

"It is none of the above, Mr. Collins," Doyle said. "Rather, it is a revelation that confirms and makes absolutely certain the fact of life after death. And after all, this fact is the basis of all religions. Spiritualism alone removes many of the crude conceptions that are held by a poorly informed religious public. But I have a question for you: Have you ever lost a loved one? An uncle, perhaps?"

"Yes, I have. My favorite uncle died just two years ago."

"And shortly after he left you, did you not try to communicate with him?"

"Yes, I did."

"But if you are certain that we cannot communicate with the inhabitants of the spiritual world, why then did you bother?"

"I must confess, I thought I could reach him."

"And did you reach him?"

"I did."

"Splendid! And did he not appear exactly as he had been before he departed?"

"Yes, he did."

"My dear boy, you have just confirmed Spiritualism's fundamental premise. And yet you still consider yourself to be an Anglican, do you not?"

"I do, Sir Arthur."

Doyle raised his hands in triumph, lifted his chin, and looked to the sky. "All of you can see that Spiritualism and your religious beliefs are not incompatible and are not mutually exclusive," he said. "Instead, you can see that the two can peacefully coexist in our universe. Indeed, it is only through Spiritualism that the basic principles of all of the world's major religions can be shown to be true. We must recognize that in recent years there has come to us from divine sources a new revelation, which constitutes by far the greatest religious event since the death of Christ—a revelation that alters the notion of death in the fate of man. Failure to accept this revelation as the absolute truth would compel us to believe that there has been an outbreak of lunacy—a lunacy that assails men and women who are otherwise eminently sane."

Shaking his head in apparent disbelief, Dr. Hammond stood there, and then uttered a statement that reflected his disappointment in what he had just heard. "My new friends, it is my unpleasant duty to inform you that there has, in fact, been an outbreak of lunacy," he said. "Soon, psychiatric asylums will be forced to make room for those who adhere to the questionable philosophy of Spiritualism, which is fraught with danger."

"Hopefully everyone here understands that the absence of proof is not necessarily proof of absence," Doyle said, doing his best to remain composed. "Just because neither you nor I have seen a white bull does not mean there isn't one. Nevertheless, let us lighten things up a bit and not force anyone to take sides. Off we go now, as we have lots to see and so little time."

Doyle's entourage arrived at the third crime scene and he began a well-rehearsed speech. "Although there were no murders attributable to the Ripper during the three weeks that transpired between the death of Mrs. Chapman and the ones about which I am ready to tell you," he said, "Jack was anything but inactive at the time. In fact, during this interval, he peppered the police with taunting letters and proudly assigned 'the Ripper' epithet to himself. His employment of the definite article suggests how the killer perceived himself, and how he wished to announce his importance to the public. He was not simply a murderer, he was the murderer."

"For all of you who are not students of psychiatry, what Dr. Doyle has so brilliantly alluded to is the concept of the megalomaniac," Dr. Hammond said.

"Good use of a not-so-appreciated word, Dr. Hammond," Doyle said. "You have certainly not missed the mark here! Let us continue. Today's subject insisted on affixing upon himself the name Jack the Ripper."

"I was told that it was not the killer who coined this phrase, but rather the London press," Adelaide said.

"That some journalist came up with this phrase is a misconception, and a serious one at that," Doyle said. "On September 17, 1888, Jack sent off the following letter, which I am about to read to you verbatim. It is imperative that you listen most carefully to its words and sentence structure. After you have done so, I will pass it around, so that you may see its spelling and punctuation errors."

Doyle then read:

17th Sept. 1888

Dear Boss

So now thay say I <u>am a Yid</u> when will thay lern Dear old Boss? You an me know the truth dont we. Lusk can look forever hell never find me but I am rite under his nose all the time. I watch them looking for me and it gives me fits <u>ha ha</u>. I love my work an I shant stop untill I get buckled <u>and even then</u> watch out for your old pal Jacky. Catch me if you can

<u>Jack the Ripper</u>

Sorry about the blood still messy from the last one. What a pretty necklace I gave her.

Having mesmerized the group with the theatricality of his delivery, Doyle proceeded to pass around the facsimile of the letter and asked everyone to refrain from making any comments for the moment. After everyone had read the letter and it had been handed back to him, he placed it into Carrington Lambton's hands and asked him to offer his interpretation of the missive.

"To paraphrase Sherlock Holmes, it's quite elementary," Carrington said. "Apparently Jack was no stranger to the art of letter writing. He begins with 'Dear Boss,' and employs the uppercase 'D' and 'B.' He also dates the letter properly, which demonstrates that he had been at least partially educated. What capture my attention, though, are the apparent discrepancies between the first part of the letter and the second."

"And what are these discrepancies?" Doyle said.

"The amount of syntactical errors diminishes dramatically by the letter's end. In the first sentence there are three overt spelling errors, almost as though the writer is trying to convince us that he lacks proper schooling. But in the last few lines, with the exception of the word 'rite,' there are only minor errors."

Dr. Hammond tapped Carrington on the shoulder, an indication that he wanted to take another look at the letter. While Carrington complied with his request, Doyle said, "And to what do you attribute this evolution in writing?"

Dr. Hammond chimed in. "Obviously, by the time he neared the end of his writing, his focus had changed," he said. "Perhaps he wanted to toy with the police and simply forgot to maintain the ruse. Such behavior is what we neuropsychiatrists refer to as an act of the subconscious."

"Ah!" Doyle said. "But if we were to follow your logic, my good doctor, we would easily see that Jack soon realized it would be wise to spell at least some of the final words incorrectly. This is what your colleagues refer to as an act on the conscious level. We can safely make the assumption that the words 'rite' and 'untill' were purposely misspelled."

"Unless he meant the word 'rite' as a double entendre," Stephen said.

"And you passed over the word 'an,'" Doyle said, "which lacks the letter 'd.' I believe there is a consistency to the letter that rules out the theory of the subconscious."

Dr. Hammond looked down at the letter one more time and conceded victory to Doyle on this particular point. Stephen then took out his notebook and pencil and asked Doyle if he thought the phrase "pretty necklace" had any significance, especially in light of Mrs. Chapman's cruel fate.

"I can think of at least two ways to interpret this phrase," Doyle said. "It may have been a reference to the necklace of skin that Jack's blade created when he severed the poor woman's neck. The more probable explanation of these words, however, may have something to do with Mrs. Chapman's intestines having been removed and placed in close proximity to her neck. This graphic reference may be the writer's attempt to prove himself the real killer and not some cruel hoaxster."

Evander was uneasy with both hypotheses and added a third one to the pot. "Maybe the scarf that she was wearing that night represented the 'pretty necklace,'" he said.

"What my brother is doing his best to say is that Jack may have been the one to furnish Mrs. Chapman with the scarf," Matthew said.

Both Stephen and Dr. Hammond issued a gentle but firm rejection of the idea put forth by the brothers Stanton, but Matthew wasn't done yet. He extracted the letter from Hammond's hand and viewed it again, and in a whispering voice read each and every word aloud. He then lifted his gleaming eyes up from the letter and said, "I am especially drawn to the phrase 'catch me if you can,' which I interpret as being the work of a cunning adult afflicted with nostalgia. It is almost as if he was looking back wistfully to times past, remembering the power, the beauty, and the horror evoked in him by those five words, which he had first heard in a nursery rhyme recited to him by his mother. You will note that the letter excludes most punctuation marks but somehow manages to capitalize properly those words that require capitalization."

When Carrington facetiously asked Matthew if he thought the letter might have been written by a child's hand, Dr. Hammond rose to Matthew's defense. The doctor had no use for banter. "No, Mr. Lambton, let's not get diverted from Mr. Stanton's fascination with this taunt," he said. "This is an adult who may be reverting back to his childhood scrawl, an adult who is regressing, either consciously or subconsciously, to plant the seeds of terror into his correspondence with the police. This Jack is someone whose psyche was indelibly stamped with the words of those scary nursery rhymes when he first heard them. We may be dealing with someone who is more than able to recall his early literary memories, a man who is able to accomplish the difficult task of applying these memories effectively to an adult theme."

"You mean Jack was able to frighten the police using children's terms as a vehicle?" Adelaide said.

"Exactly!" Dr. Hammond said.

Stephen quickly reached for his notebook and made another entry. Evander, puzzled by his brother's theory, asked him which nursery rhyme he was referencing. He had no recollection of their mother having read such a tale to them.

"Evander, you do realize that I am two years older than you," Matthew said. "I vividly remember sitting on Mother's lap without you in the room when she read it to me. While I do not recall its title, I do remember it being about a 'Jacky' who ran away. Perhaps she never read it to you once you came along because she liked me best!"

"That was cruel!" Evander said.

Doyle ended the sibling rivalry by telling Matthew that his recollection was cute but likely off track, as the phrase "catch me if you can" was not derived from any story involving "Jacky," but rather from the well-known "Little Robin Redbreast." The rest of the group concurred with Doyle, with the exception of Matthew, who remained insistent that "catch me if you can" and "Jacky" also had some other source, which eluded him at the moment.

"Jack displayed such bravado in his ability to evade the police and had such obvious disdain for them; why take a three-week break between murders?" Carrington said. "Don't you think he would have continued his butchery and perhaps even increased his activity?"

"Mr. Lambton, there is something about this season that I neglected to tell you," Doyle said. "Things in the East End undergo a dramatic change in September, and I am not merely referring to the year 1888. Each and every year sees a rapid population decline here in Whitechapel during this particular month. Can any of you offer a reason for this?"

Doyle waited, and when no one responded he answered for them. "Not unexpected. Of course you wouldn't know it," he said. "You see, each September, a staggering percentage of the people of this district, especially those who live in the workhouses, invade the county of Kent to enjoy the sweet fragrance of the countryside, and to engage in an activity with which most of you are unfamiliar. I'll get to that in a minute. In all probability, the Ripper was one of the tens of thousands of strangers who decamped to Kent's rural paradise at the time, where they would have enjoyed what has been described as the lightest and most pleasant variation of the toils of tramping. All these paupers get paid a handsome reward for their hopping . . ." Dr. Hammond immediately stopped Doyle and asked him to explain what hopping was.

"Ah! Yes, my American colleague," Doyle said, "our killer may have traveled in a jam-packed train or by some other mysterious mode of transportation to arrive at those perfumed gardens where hops, the main component of beer, are gathered. Hence the terms hopping and hop picking. During early autumn, everyone, except for the very youngest or the most aged and infirm, works on these farms, where even twenty-five years ago they received a full shilling for every five bushels they were able to pick. While it is impossible to determine whether Jack ventured alone to these plantations or if a wife and family accompanied him, his lack of activity for more than a fortnight suggests that he was a member of this band of temporary migrants."

"Sir Arthur, do you mean to tell me that Jack could have had a wife and maybe even children? You can't be serious!" Adelaide said.

"Miss Oddie," Doyle said, "I am quite serious. As I have said before, any one of us might know a murderer, and sometimes that person might be your very own spouse. And yes, it is possible that Jack had a family. I am not implying that his family would have had any inkling of his nefarious deeds, for surely he would not have disclosed such an awful secret to them. But yes, Jack being a family man is completely within the realm of possibility."

Stephen opened his notebook again and scribbled down a few things. "Yes, Sir Arthur, *My Friend the Murderer*," he said.

"Capital reference!" Doyle said.

Dr. Hammond jumped back into the conversation. "Getting back to your previous statement, the one about Jack being out hopping," he said. "You mentioned that Jack had sent off letters from London proper during this time. How could he have been out in Kent? It doesn't make any sense at all."

"True, Dr. Hammond, but it is not difficult to visualize Jack asking some unsuspecting soul to post the letters on his behalf. And Dr. Hammond, the county of Kent is but a short distance from the city. Does this explanation satisfy you?"

"Indeed!"

"Let us discuss what Jack did after he ended his three week 'holiday,' shall we?"

Whispering to Dr. Hammond, Stephen said, "If Jack had gone off to Kent to make money for himself, he would have never have returned to London to post letters. That would have been counterproductive. And to give the letters to a friend seems a bit ludicrous."

"And if the letters had been given to someone else to post for him, what would have been the outcome if the police had released a copy of these letters to the press and his friend had happened to see them?" Dr. Hammond said.

"Had it been me," Stephen said, "I would have quickly been on the receiving end of a handsome reward."

"Me, too!" Dr. Hammond said. "So, it is quite improbable that Jack was a hopper."

"I'm with you," Stephen said, placing another entry into his book.

After the two of them had stopped talking, Doyle, who had been waiting patiently, recommenced his talk. "Jack resumed his activities on September 30, when he did away with Elizabeth Stride at this very location," he said. "Once he had finished here, he immediately went to a different location, where he committed another murder. But any discussion of that case will have to wait for now. I'm going to recapitulate the events that occurred here in Dutfield's Yard during those early hours.

"A few minutes before 1 AM, a peddler named Louis Diemschutz was seated in his carriage on his way back home from the market at Westow Hill. Usually he stopped here, where he stored his unsold wares. When his carriage entered the yard, Diemschutz's pony veered left and refused to continue on any further. This was out of character for his little steed, and the puzzled peddler soon realized that the cause of his pony's stubborn refusal was the motionless figure that lay on the side of the road. In an attempt to rouse what he believed to be an inebriated man or woman, Diemschutz flicked the straps of his whip and created a loud cracking lash. When this maneuver failed to do the job, the merchant employed the handle of his whip to jostle the person out of harm's way. When this too failed, the peddler alighted from his carriage and struck a match to see if he could identify the obstacle. Although the wind quickly extinguished the flame, what Diemschutz had managed to see in that split second frightened him to the core. To his consternation, he observed that the person lying in the dirt was a woman. As the body was located close to the building where he and his spouse resided, he feared that his wife might have been the victim.

"Diemschutz hurried past a nearby social club, where thirty or so men and women remained after having attended a lecture on why Jews should be socialists. He headed towards his apartment to check on his wife, but stopped short when he spotted her among the crowd of people who had stayed in the meeting hall after the talk. Now that he had been relieved of his darkest fear, he was able to attend to the task at hand, which was to acquire some assistance from the club members. Initially, only his best friend, Isaac Kozebrodsky, accompanied him outside the club, while Diemschutz's wife stationed herself next to the door. With the aid of the light shed by her husband's candle, she was able to conclude that the dark heap she saw before her was the body of a woman who had been murdered. Mrs. Diemschutz let out a bloodcurdling scream that reverberated through the yard and into the club itself, rousing many of the other members to action. A man named Gilleman informed those members who had remained to sing and talk upstairs of the unpleasant discovery, while Mr. Louis Stansley and Mr. Morris Eagle raced off in different directions, each in a frantic search to find a constable. It wasn't long before the victim had been identified by several of the club members. She was a Swedish-born local prostitute known to them only by her nickname, 'Long Liz.' No one knew her real name."

Entrance to Dutfield's Yard

An 1888 newspaper drawing of the entrance to Dutfield's Yard, in which Elizabeth Stride's body was found, and a nearby social club on Berner Street.

Adelaide interrupted Doyle's lecture by asking him whether this "Long Liz" had been a member or a guest in the club that night.

"No, this woman was exactly what I told you she was," Doyle said, "a registered local tart. But let us proceed. Soon, Morris Eagle came upon two constables, one named Lamb and another bearing your surname, Mr. Collins. Mr. Eagle blurted out that a woman had been found lying dead on the pavement outside his club. Constable Lamb delegated assignments to the other constable and to Mr. Eagle. Constable Collins was instructed to fetch Dr. Frederick Blackwell, who resided nearby at 100 Commercial Road, while Mr. Eagle was told to run to the Leman Street Police Station for help. But Dr. Blackwell did not leave his home right away. Instead he sent his medical assistant, Edward Johnston, while he got himself dressed and gathered up his medical material. When Dr. Johnston arrived on the scene, he was able to observe only one identifiable injury, a slit throat. His notes indicate there were no other areas of active bleeding visible. Placing his hands on the corpse's extremities, he noticed that the hands and feet were cold to the touch. Next, he unfastened the victim's blouse, which his notes describe as being intact and unruffled. His entries also mention that the victim's chest was still warm. Making sure not to move her extremities from the positions in which he had found them, Dr. Johnston made an announcement to those who had gathered around the crime scene. He warned them that the killing had taken place quite recently, and that the murderer might still be in the vicinity. He then matter-of-factly informed the constable that the victim's bonnet lay precisely three inches away from her head, and that her knees were close to the wall of the club next to a ventilation grate."

Doyle pointed out the ventilation grate in question to his followers. "Less than three minutes later," he said, "Dr. Johnston's employer, Dr. Blackwell, arrived. Unfazed by the chaos about him, he calmly took out his pocket watch and documented his time of arrival: 1:16 AM. His records state that the woman lay on her left side, facing the right side of the club wall, and that her feet were three yards away from the club's open gates. His statements seem to corroborate Dr. Johnston's findings. The victim's blood-smeared right hand was in the open position atop her chest, with her left hand partially clenched and resting on the ground. His curiosity having been aroused, Blackwell gently opened her palm, only to find her grasping a packet of cachous wrapped in tissue paper. More of these cachous were scattered about on the cobblestones."

"Pardon my ignorance," Matthew asked, "but what is a cachou?"

"A cachou is a South American tree nut that was introduced to Europe by Portuguese sailors," Dr. Hammond said.

"What you are describing is a c-a-s-h-e-w," Doyle said, "but not exactly the cachou we are talking about here. We are talking about a cutch."

"A cutch?" Matthew said.

"A cutch is merely a Malayan term for a pastille," Doyle said.

"And what is a pastille, Sir Arthur?" Matthew said.

"You must forgive me," Doyle said. "I am just making words dance a little jig. Pastille, cutch, and cachou are all synonyms for a breath-sweetening lozenge."

"Aren't you and your brother in the candy business, Mr. Stanton?" Carrington said.

"We have our little niche," Matthew said. "But we are chocolatiers, not confectioners. These specialities are not the same."

Stephen thought this might be the right time to challenge a theory Doyle had put before the group earlier. "Do you still believe that Jack might have been a Jill?" he said.

Doyle responded that he was ready to clarify his previous comment, so that it would not be misinterpreted. "What I meant by Jack being a Jill," he said, "is that a man could have easily disguised himself as a midwife had he wanted to divert attention from his blood-stained clothes and blood-soaked hands. But no woman could have mustered up the sheer power required to accomplish this series of crimes with such swiftness. Remember one of the official definitions of the word power: the accomplishment of work during a prescribed period of time."

"You don't think there are any women at all who are strong enough to have done something like this?" Adelaide said, adopting a bit of Gertrude's personality.

"I'm not saying that females are incapable of murder, but I am stating that the methods used by Jack preclude anyone but a most physically fit male from doing this dirty work," Doyle said.

"Sir Arthur, I do not believe nor do I accept any theory that has Jack donning a disguise," Stephen said, unable to contain himself.

"I respectfully disagree with you, Mr. Mitchell," Doyle said.

"Mrs. Stride would never have taken out a breath-sweetening mint if she had thought she was being approached by a midwife and not by a potential client," Stephen said. "The cachous were a fortuitous clue provided to us by Dr. Blackwell's innate curiosity. Mrs. Stride's tenacious grip on them may have been a last ditch effort on her part to furnish the police with a clue regarding how Jack approached his victim."

"Excuse my ignorance, but I don't follow you," Edgar said.

"Their presence in her palm implies that Mrs. Stride was a priestess of the night who was desirous of ridding herself of the fetid breath of her class," Stephen said. "A more pleasant aroma might have persuaded her client to purchase her services for a longer period of time. It follows that Jack was in full view when he approached her. She was not a victim of a sneak attack. She must have been under the impression that she had ample of time to ready herself for her client."

Doyle, finding it difficult to follow Stephen's line of reasoning, asked him whether a solicitor of prostitutes would really care if she had sweet breath.

"It certainly wouldn't have harmed her potential earning power," Edgar said.

"Really?" Doyle said. "I have never considered that. Perhaps I shall go out and buy some cachous for Mrs. Doyle. Her breath is a bit stale. Ha! Ha!"

"Returning to the more salient matter at hand," Dr. Hammond said, "I must tell you that I am in total agreement with Mr. Mitchell's assessment of things. These cachous tend to rule out the involvement of a pretend midwife."

"Au contraire, monsieur," Doyle said. "Nothing is disproved here. We have to consider the before and after of the scenario, in which the killer would have committed the crimes as a 'male' but exited the scene as a 'female.' It would have been no problem at all to conceal the attire of a midwife within the confines of a coat or an umbrella, especially on a night with rain in the forecast."

"I understand it now!" Edgar said. "As Jack approached Long Liz, she took out a breath mint. Then, before she could even put her cachous back into her pocket, Jack cut her throat, placed her on the ground, put on a midwife's outfit, and left the scene dressed as a woman."

Dr. Hammond remained steadfastly opposed to such a hypothesis. "Let us recapitulate a bit," he said. "From what I have gathered thus far, it would have been necessary for the killer to be young, strong, agile, and in possession of the skills needed to decapitate someone and remove their viscera with lightning speed. There are two segments of society that fit this bill—those whose members are adept with knives and those who possess the detailed anatomical knowledge needed to carry out such crimes—namely surgeons and butchers. I ask you, Dr. Doyle, would not someone trained in one of these professions become your most likely suspect?"

"Dr. Hammond, weren't we just discussing Jill the Ripper?" Doyle said. "But since you've veered off that subject, I ask you, what great anatomical knowledge was needed to murder Mrs. Stride? What great knowledge or training or schooling is required to simply slash a throat?"

"None at all," Dr. Hammond said.

"Need I remind you, Dr. Hammond, that we physicians are gentlemen? Doyle said. "I know of no member of our noble profession who might be capable of committing the acts ascribed to Jack the Ripper. Years ago, I learned firsthand that even the most skilled surgeon requires an adequate and orderly period of preparation before an operation, and a team of assistants to achieve the best possible outcome in each case. Gaining membership to the fraternity of physicians must always be regarded as a calling from the divine, while butchery, a far from noble trade, is its very antithesis."

"Dr. Doyle, it seems as though the first three victims we have discussed were positioned in a manner commonly seen in an operating room or a mortuary," Dr. Hammond said. "This method would have been learned and practiced in medical school during the course of surgical training."

"Dr. Hammond, if you recall, Mrs. Stride was not found on her back," Doyle said. "Her killer rolled her towards the wall and placed her on her left side, or on what we call the left lateral decubitus position. So, what would have been the purpose of this?"

"You may have me there," Dr. Hammond said. "But we do know that all three victims were killed in the same manner, a method that may not be deviated from in the surgical theater. Specifically, by cutting their necks from left to right, the killer circumvented the inconvenience of staining his clothes, as his victims' blood flowed away from him. That all of them were dead and gone prior to having their necks cut is a given."

"I thought we agreed that Long Liz was killed the moment Jack approached her. There was no delay," Edgar said.

"Actually, Mr. Collins," Dr. Hammond said, "if any of the ladies had been alive when their throats were cut, the force exerted by their beating hearts would have sprayed blood all over the walls, onto the sidewalks, and onto the killer himself. Scotland Yard's keen observation that the blood oozed but did not spurt from each of the bodies indicates that the killer knew that by suffocating the victims first he could avoid this complication. It follows that Long Liz's neck was severed only after she had been asphyxiated."

"What could have motivated Jack to employ two such drastic measures to bring about death when one would have sufficed?" Edgar said.

"Precisely," Doyle said. "This superfluous repetition lends even more credence to my argument that Jack was not a physician. Any medical man would have known that by severing the internal carotid artery, jugular vein, and windpipe, the victim would have been rendered aphonic, that is to say, she would have been unable to let out a scream. Once the blood vessels had been severed, the victim would have held onto her throat reflexively in a vain attempt at salvation. This is one particular aspect of the case that has held my interest for almost a quarter century. While there certainly may have been a specific reason why the killer chose to use two completely different methods of murder, it will have to wait until later to be discovered."

"Maybe Jack's priority was neatness, and the attainment of silence was a distant second," Edgar said.

"That the Ripper was a man of genius and talent goes without saying. But let us reconsider Dr. Blackwell's report for a minute." Doyle pulled a piece of paper out of his jacket pocket and started to read from it. "The woman's face was placid," he said, "with the mouth slightly open, and she wore a checked silk scarf around her neck with its bow pulled tightly around to the left. There was a huge incision in her neck that began on the left side and actually cut through the lower edge of the scarf as it continued through the trachea, or windpipe, and then stopped." Doyle put the paper back into his pocket and continued. "My friends, no other part of Mrs. Stride's body was touched. No viscera were removed. No organs were taken. There was only one incision. Does anything strike you here?"

"The killer might have been spotted by someone or, at the very least, thought he was going to be," Carrington said. "Fearing that someone might be able to describe him, he might have thought it in his best interest to complete that night's work at another site."

"Why do you feel his work was incomplete? Wasn't that enough for one day?" Evander said.

"Obviously not enough for him," Carrington said. "Surely his agenda was not limited to a mere throat slashing. Liz Stride's murder does not conform to the fate of the other victims and may offer a bit of an explanation as to why Jack committed another murder directly afterwards."

"Hold on," Doyle said. "Rein yourselves in. This was not a simple slashing. Jack stopped just a centimeter or two before decapitating her. Such vicious work takes time and effort. The Ripper must have stationed himself on the ground to gain the proper leverage and mechanical advantage. But let us go on to what transpired next.

"Within a half hour, the official police surgeon, George B. Phillips, arrived at the scene and stated that, based on the depth and extent of Mrs. Stride's wound, her measured body temperature, and the current time, he was in agreement with Dr. Blackwell's assessment that she must have been attacked between 12:44 AM and 12:54 AM. Fortunately for us, an influential member of the Whitechapel community came forward to confirm the victim's identity. It was Dr. Thomas Barnardo, the Dublin-born director of an organization that bore his name, who identified 'Long Liz' as being Elizabeth Stride, and only then were the police willing to attach a name to the victim. Dr. Barnardo told them that he had seen Mrs. Stride at a temperance meeting he had recently held in the Flower and Dean lodging houses, and that he recalled having spoken to her in the shelter's kitchen a few days prior to that."

"If Dr. Barnardo knew this area so well and also knew Elizabeth Stride, why wasn't he considered a suspect?" Carrington said.

"Do you know the kind of man on which you are casting the shadow of suspicion?" Doyle said. "Dr. Barnardo was a man of unimpeachable character, a physician trained right here in London, a man who devoted himself to the Church, a savior to thousands of children, women, and men. His was the voice of the poor. He was their political advocate, the acknowledged leader of the temperance movement that tried so desperately to remove the scourge of alcohol from the East End. In this part of town he would have been recognized more quickly than Queen Victoria herself. If he had been seen here by even one person, any potential veil of secrecy would have been lifted. That the great Dr. Barnardo happened to have spoken to Elizabeth Stride that week was merely a coincidence. And besides, Dr. Barnardo would never have killed someone without giving her one of his little Bibles. But I must apologize for my facetious quip and lapse of judgment. Sometimes I can't help myself."

Edgar asked Doyle in private if he had heard the rumor about a certain knife having been left at this spot.

"I hope Mr. Collins won't mind if I repeat the question he just asked me," Doyle said. "Have I heard the story about a knife having been left here the night of Elizabeth Stride's death? Of course I have, and I must confess that this rumor was one of the few whose foundation rested on a sound base. And because it was more than just common talk, clarification is needed.

"It was 12:30 AM when Mr. Thomas Coram left the house of a friend and headed home on Whitechapel Road. As he was walking towards Aldgate on the odd-numbered side of the street, he decided to cross over and saw something white on the first step leading up to house number 252, just a few yards from where we are right now. Constable Joseph Drage, who was on fixed-point duty, noticed Mr. Coram in a stooped position looking down at something and, of course, walked over to him. In an instant, Mr. Coram sprang up and made a summoning gesture with his finger to the approaching officer. Mr. Coram greeted the officer by saying, 'Policeman, there is a knife down here.' Constable Drage then turned on his light and the two of them looked upon a long-bladed knife smothered in blood. Curiously, a bloodstained white handkerchief was bound around the handle and tied with string."

"Then it is clear who owned it," Carrington said.

"Mr. Lambton, please tell us," Adelaide said.

"Miss Oddie, I would be happy to comply with your request," Carrington said. "It is quite simple, indeed. If Constable Drage had been standing at the spot where he claimed to have been, then Mr. Coram must have planted the knife himself. The constable recognized that something was amiss when he saw Mr. Coram apparently looking at some sort of object, which turned out to be a knife. It can be assumed that if the knife had been placed there earlier, Drage would have caught a glimpse of the person who had placed it there, and of the weapon itself, especially since it had been wrapped in an attention-calling white handkerchief, as Sir Arthur just told us."

"Excellent, Mr. Lambton," Doyle said. "My congratulations on your brilliant detective work. But there is something I neglected to mention. Just minutes before the knife was found by Mr. Coram, Constable Drage was forced to leave his fixed position when a most funny thing happened. A horse had reared up and fallen on the odd-numbered side of the street.

As was his duty, the good constable lent his assistance to restoring the horse to the upright position."

"Ah, I see," Evander said. "I guess that is when the Ripper got rid of his knife."

"The point Evander is trying his best to get across," Matthew said, "is that in the ensuing commotion, Jack would have had the perfect opportunity and amount of time to blend into the crowd and deposit his handkerchief-wrapped knife on the stoop."

"What makes you able to conclude that the knife could not have been there before?" Edgar said. "You may be jumping to conclusions. It was after midnight, you know, in an area that is always dark. Most probably the incident involving the horse had nothing at all to do with it."

"Mr. Collins, while I happen to agree with you that all this was a mere coincidence, Constable Drage had witnessed the landlady, who possessed the key to number 252, let out some of her tenants," Doyle said. "At least one of them would have seen the knife while walking down the steps, had it already been there. This was one of those rare exceptions when Whitechapel's lighting was adequate enough, as described in Mr. Coram's testimony."

"Dr. Doyle, how long was this knife?" Dr. Hammond said. "One inch? Five inches? Ten inches? Do we know?"

"In fact, we do," Doyle said. "Although Constable Drage judged it to be nine inches in length, I have been told by reliable sources that it was twice as long as this measurement."

"Then we have a problem here, in the fact that a knife of this type would not have been used as a murder weapon."

"And why is that, Dr. Hammond?"

"The length of its blade would have been too long to employ as a surgical instrument, and it would most likely have precluded its use as a concealed weapon."

"There is no reason to assume that Jack could not have placed such a knife inside his coat. However, I am in accord with your impression that the knife was too long to be used as a weapon."

"Sir Arthur, if you wouldn't mind, I would like to go over a few things," Stephen said, taking out his notebook.

"No problem at all," Doyle said. "As a matter of fact, it might serve us well if you would give us a brief synopsis of what has happened up to this point."

Stephen extended his right hand as if it were a pointer and spoke to the group. "Let's make sure I get things straight. A group of women are let out of an apartment by their landlady. They see nothing unusual as they descend the steps. Then, minutes later, a horse falls down in the middle of a street where an officer is stationed on fixed-point duty. The officer participates in righting the horse, which has fallen for no apparent reason. He then returns to his assigned post, where he sees Mr. Coram looking down at an object. He begins to cross the street and is summoned by Mr. Coram, who has just sprung to his feet, and the two of them gaze down upon what reveals itself to be a knife once Constable Drage turns on his light. You don't find this to be a little strange and disconcerting?"

"In what way, Mr. Mitchell?" Doyle said.

"Isn't it rather odd that a horse falls down on one side of the street and then, minutes later, a knife gets discovered directly across from where the poor beast had jumped and landed on its back?"

"You can't just make a horse fall down in the middle of the street, Mr. Mitchell," Edgar said.

"Maybe not, but the Ripper would not have forgone such a perfect opportunity to put down his knife."

"Are you saying that he waited for a horse to fall down?"

"No. Just anything that might have served as a distraction. It just so happened that the Ripper had such good fortune that night."

"Why, pray tell, would he have left his knife there?" Doyle said.

"As a decoy, Dr. Doyle," Hammond said, chiming in.

"Explain," Doyle said.

"If Mrs. Stride's murder occurred close to 1 AM, and the knife was discovered a half hour before, it would have clustered the police around Whitechapel Road, drawing them away from the murder scene in the process."

"So, Dr. Hammond, you are suggesting that this knife was just a clever ruse used by the Ripper?"

"Exactly, Dr. Doyle."

Doyle then addressed the group. "Yes, Mr. Collins was correct when he mentioned that a knife had been left on Whitechapel Road, but what he failed to realize was that it was found on the morning of Monday, October 1—a full twenty-four hours after the Ripper had been here. But I must congratulate you all on your well-considered analyses of the event. Now let us move on to the next of Jack's murders."

Stephen's notebook was still open, as he had one more question he wanted answered. "That white handkerchief that was so carefully wrapped around the knife bothers me," he said.

"And why is that?" Doyle said.

"It just might be the handkerchief that was of primary importance to the killer, and not the knife itself. The handkerchief might have been a calling-card of sorts."

"I've never thought of the handkerchief as a clue, but now that you mention it, I do recall reading that two handkerchiefs were found on Mrs. Stride, and at least two people who knew her told the police that they had never seen her with these handkerchiefs before."

"If that's the case, Sir Arthur, I wonder if the Yard has ever tried to match the three to determine if they were of the same manufacturer."

"An interesting question, but I do not know its answer. For now, it is time to pay a visit to Mitre Square."

9

1878-1880

Apprentice and Arctic Adventurer

May 1878

One of the university's requirements for earning a diploma was the successful completion of a clerkship in the office of a licensed practitioner at any time during the five-year course of study. Although these clerkships did not pay well, or at all, they were considered an integral part of a doctor's education. Getting the right job with the right physician could lead to future opportunities and success. Doyle certainly could have found a local position, but instead sent his applications out only to physicians in England. Ironically, during the entire period that he was away from home in Hodder, Stonyhurst, and Stella Matutina, Doyle had longed for the family hearth, but now that he had returned, he could barely tolerate the surroundings in which he found himself. He had become a subordinate to his landlord, Waller; a babysitter to siblings he barely knew; and a nursemaid to his drunken father, Charles. It must have been with great relief that he received a clerkship offer from Dr. Charles Sidney Richardson, a Scotsman who had trained at the University of St. Andrews, and who ran a general practice in inner-city Sheffield.

Arthur was woefully unprepared for the responsibilities that went with his position. When he was given the simple assignment of placing pills inside pill-boxes and sending them out to patients, he somehow managed to forget to place the pills inside the boxes. How mortified Dr. Richardson must have been when his patients remarked upon the incompetence of his office. After just three weeks, Doyle was unceremoniously dismissed and told to go home. This was to be the first of several apprenticeships for him. Arthur employs his best defense mechanisms to explain his expulsion in a letter to his mother, saying that the people of this Yorkshire city had mistakenly judged him to be "too young." He continues, "Those Sheffielders would rather be poisoned by a man with a beard, than saved by a man without one." Arthur goes on to paint an unkind picture of his first employer, whom he describes as being ungenerous and overly frugal. "He made me pay my washing bill, and never allowed me a farthing for cab fare in my journey," Doyle states.

After his dismissal, instead of heading north to Edinburgh, Doyle headed south to London, where once again he stayed with Aunt Annette and Uncle Richard. Not only would he have ample time to roam about London, he would also be there to celebrate his nineteenth birthday, although his mother would forget to send him any birthday wishes. Arthur would soon write to her, stating, "I was surprised at not getting a letter on my birthday, however that is all right now. I have seen a good deal of London. On my birthday I went to see [Henry] Irving in his latest success 'Louis XI.' A most ghastly sight it was and has made quite an impression on me. The death scene is an awful bit of dramatic art, no vulgar horror about it, but the general effect nonetheless thrilling for that."

What had impressed Arthur most during his birthday rounds in London was a toy he had seen children playing with in the streets. It was a water launcher that could drench anyone who came within twenty feet of its path. On May 23, 1878, the day after his birthday, he walked to Piccadilly Circus and purchased one of these "Lady Teazer Torpedoes." Filling the toy's leaden bottle to the brim with water, he lay in wait for his first victim. It happened to be a beautiful young lady exiting her carriage. Arthur struck with deadly accuracy and roared at the unpleasantness he had created for the now-waterlogged damsel. He then took off down the street with lightning speed, listening gleefully to the expletives being hurled at him by the lady's escort.

Arthur spent the next few weeks down at the East End docks, where he was fascinated by the anatomy of the ships, especially the architecture of the new steamers, and the harp-like sails and masts of the older vessels. He was intrigued by the patterns created by the waves as they undulated. But what made the biggest impression on him were the passengers, both boarding and disembarking—he could not get over the fact that so many men and women had so much to do in such faraway places. He made it a point to seek out and speak to the sailors and merchants, who were going out on or making their way back from their distant journeys. Her Majesty's Navy seemed to be beckoning to him and he was succumbing to the lure of the sea.

As his only prospect at the time was a low-paying job as a hospital dresser back in Edinburgh, Doyle even gave consideration to heading off to fight in the second Afghan War. But when he received three letters, each offering him a chance at redemption from his ineffectual stint in Sheffield, he reconsidered, writing to his mother, "I went today and found that our bait had caught 3 fish, Dr. Bryan of Leicester, Dr. Brady of Derby, and Dr. White of Snodland, Kent. The last one I have chosen, as looking most promising." For some unknown reason, however, he did not show up at Dr. White's clinic. Instead, Doyle secured himself a position in the fledgling practice of a young Edinburgh alumnus named Dr. Henry F. Elliot, to whom he had also applied.

It seems as though Mary Doyle had helped in the writing of the curriculum vitae that had been sent out to those doctors with whom Arthur had sought employment, as is evident from the following communication between Doyle and his mother:

> By the way I had a small triumph over you the other day. Elliot told me that the reason he preferred me to the other candidates, was not in account of my testimonials, they all had those, but on account of my clean legible fist. (Not this one, you know, but your version, the characterless one.)

These words, along with the idea of Arthur calling his letters "our bait," imply that mother and son had worked together in the writing of these applications.

Doyle was hired to serve as an assistant to Dr. Elliot for four months. The office was located in a remote English village near Wales called Ruyton-XI-Towns, and Doyle seemed to regard the people of the area with mild disdain, often going so far as to call them "hulking ruffians" right to their faces. On one of the rare occasions when Dr. Elliot left Arthur to manage the office by himself, an unexpected caller rang the bell and then pounded on the door. When Arthur pulled it open, he saw before him a frightened woman who was babbling that her husband had been involved in some sort of terrible accident. She grabbed Doyle by the coat sleeve, giving him just enough time to pick up his trusty black medical bag. She then raced him off to her spouse, who was lying in the middle of a muddy field, screaming in agony. A large piece of metal was sticking out of his head, and Doyle quickly knelt down next to the man and assessed his wounds. Doyle determined that somehow a cannonball fragment had pierced the poor fellow's skull, winding up in his brain. With absolutely no idea of what he was doing, he took the largest forceps he could find and clamped them onto the shrapnel, extracting the chunk of metal from the man's head. Doyle breathed a sigh of relief when he saw that the injury would not be that much of a problem, despite the bloody mess that was now the poor man's head. Somehow, the unguided projectile had lacked the power to penetrate the victim's skullcap. He calmly closed the wound, telling no one of its triviality. With the assuredness of a veteran, he informed the large audience of bystanders who had now assembled there that, although the gentleman had suffered a severe injury, that he would be back to his plow in a short while. Yes, it seemed that Arthur Doyle had learned the art of showmanship very well from Professor Littlejohn.

After this miraculous performance, Arthur decided that Dr. Elliot would have to treat him as a peer, not as a subordinate. When his employer returned home from his outing, he had already been informed of his assistant's exploits and called Arthur in to congratulate him, adding that his great work would be quite beneficial to the development of his new practice. Arthur wanted more than mere kudos. He sat himself down in Dr. Elliot's prize armchair and proceeded to engage Elliot's family in an opinion-laden conversation, violating the unwritten rule that medical assistants were not to interact with a doctor's family members, except at mealtime. But Arthur had no qualms about entering into heated discussions about Spiritualism and politics, and did not hesitate to voice his opposition to capital punishment. This faux pas was more than Dr. Elliot could bear, and he berated Doyle for such an obvious lack of tact. Once again, Arthur refused to yield, stating that he had every right to express his thoughts. Elliot warned Doyle that discussions with either his pregnant wife or him were strictly forbidden. One month after this incident, Dr. Elliot decided to make arrangements for another young medical student to take the place of Doyle. He gave Arthur two weeks to leave.

With his tail between his legs, Arthur returned to Edinburgh, where he was forced to wait for the next school session to begin. His arrival coincided with one of his father's infrequent stays with the family. Waller was alternating between the estate he had just inherited and Edinburgh, where his professional career was now skyrocketing. Arthur had barely reconnected with his sisters and his only brother, Innes, when he learned that he had been accepted for another apprenticeship, this time in the large industrial city of Birmingham. This time Arthur made sure that the position would be a paying one, and found some relief in moving on, as he did not want to be part of the circus that was sure to ensue as the result of Waller's return.

September 1878

During the summer session of 1878, Bryan Waller taught pathology at the Medical College of Edinburgh, where Dr. Bell had been teaching anatomy. The two of them certainly would have known each other, and perhaps Waller may have suggested that Doyle was smart enough to serve as Bell's surgical assistant, although Arthur had not yet proven himself one of the best and brightest at the university. Alternatively, it might have been Doyle's physique that helped secure him the position. Bell was careful to choose assistants who were strongly built, so that any uncooperative patients could be adequately restrained, and Doyle certainly was powerful. Most likely, however, it was simply a fortunate alignment of the stars that led to Arthur being chosen as Dr. Bell's assistant. Once picked, Arthur was not about to let his talents remain dormant. He devoted himself to proper preparation and meticulous observation—two qualities he knew were essential for him to remain in Professor Bell's good graces.

His first assignment was to prepare a patient schedule that included every minute detail of their case summaries. He was further instructed to make every effort to learn the vernacular of all districts from which Bell's clinic drew its patient population. Joseph Bell's mentor had been Dr. Syme, and Bell enjoyed reciting the former chairman's three maxims to his new assistants:

> First, never look surprised at anything. Second, before stating your opinion of a case on your second visit, ascertain whether your previous directions have been complied with and do not compliment your patient on the excellent effect of your sleeping potion till you find he has taken it. And third, never ask the same question twice, for if you do, your patient will either be hurt at your inattention, or impressed by your stupidity.

Doyle put these rules to memory on day one, and he and Dr. Bell got along famously from the start. Indeed, thirty years later, Dr. Bell would be one of Doyle's supporters during his unsuccessful run for Parliament.

Doyle joined Dr. Bell in caring for Edinburgh's poor in the dreary, cavernous room of the Royal Edinburgh Infirmary. Although doctor visits, care, and medications were not entirely free, by and large they were provided at considerably reduced rates. The city's tradesmen were the prime recipients of care there, and they were able to maintain a sense of dignity by being allowed to pay for their care.

A short time after being named an assistant to Joseph Bell, Arthur got the chance to play a key role in the very class in which he had first seen Dr. Bell. The routine was for Arthur to set up the charts and equipment that Dr. Bell would be using that day, thirty minutes before class was to begin. Once Professor Bell arrived in the amphitheater, Arthur would usher patients in and out, and deliver equipment and chemicals to the good doctor's desk. Bell was well aware that the application of his methods to the affairs of everyday life produced a deep and everlasting impression upon the imaginations of his pupils. But it was Doyle who "was one of the aptest" at picking up the art of careful observation. Years later, Bell would recollect with a grin an incident that he had shared with him:

> He was amused once when a patient walked in and sat down. "Good-morning, Pat," I said, for it was impossible not to see that he was an Irishman. "Good-morning, Your Honor," replied the patient. "Did you like your walk over the links to-day, as you came in from the south side of the town?" I asked. "Yes," said Pat, "did Your Honor see me?" Well, Conan Doyle could not see how I knew that, absurdly simple as it was. On a showery day, such as that had been, the reddish clay at bare parts of the links adheres to the boot, and a tiny part is bound to remain. There is no such clay anywhere else round the town for miles.

Dr. Bell's young assistant tried to learn about every sort of rock, clay, flower, and animal, making it a point to study the most minute and arcane subjects. Doyle's commitment to his profession must have reminded Joseph Bell of his own days as a student in Edinburgh.

May 1879

After completing his second year of clinicals, Doyle, who was under severe pressure to provide for his younger siblings, moved to Birmingham, the home of Dr. and Mrs. Reginald Ratcliffe Hoare. Hoare guaranteed him a salary of £2 per month. This time Arthur thought it wise to hold his ego in check and got used to calling his "fine little fellow" of an employer "boss." Dr. Hoare ran two practices, which took in £3,000 a year and, according to Doyle, provided him with "plenty of spondulick," an Americanism for money. Dr. Hoare was no ordinary physician, for he had successfully completed the tedious examination that granted him the diploma from the Royal College of Surgeons of Edinburgh. This degree was unlike all other medical degrees, for the recipient of it was "enabled to register three Diplomas . . . Licentiate of the Royal College of Physicians of Edinburgh, Licentiate of the Royal College of Surgeons of Edinburgh, and Licentiate of the Faculty of Physicians and Surgeons of Glasgow." Dr. Hoare was qualified to instruct medical students in three fields, namely "Medicine, Surgery, and Midwifery," and those fortunate enough to work for him at his Midland facility were the beneficiaries of credit towards their degrees. Very few students in all of Scotland were as lucky as Doyle.

Just as he was settling in to his new quarters, however, Doyle received a letter from his mother indicating that the situation at home had taken an unexpected turn. Shortly after having reestablished a cordial relationship with his father during his brief visit, Arthur was now informed that Charles had managed to destroy any chance of regaining his "rightful" place in the Doyle household. Mary wrote that their new lodgings at 23 George Square had somehow caught fire, and that Charles Doyle had been forcibly removed from Edinburgh and escorted north to Blairerno House, a "Home for Gentlemen in the North of Scotland of very old standing" whose primary mission was to cure those afflicted with dipsomania, also known as alcoholism. Interestingly, Arthur would choose not to comment on the plight of his father or family in his reply, focusing instead on his own perceived misfortunes by writing, "Nothing but rain, splashing in the streets, and gurgling in the gutters, everything sloppy and muddy, that's my experience of Birmingham." Perhaps his world was colored by the events his mother had described, and perhaps his refusal to acknowledge these events in his writing was a simple case of denial. Additionally, Doyle's facial neuralgia symptoms, which seemed to appear at times of stress, were now back in full force, threatening his physical and mental health.

As part of Dr. Hoare's agreement with the University of Edinburgh, each of his assistants was granted access to the impressive library he had in his house. It was there that Arthur must have seen the issue of the *American Journal of Pharmacy* that contained an article by Dr. Theodore G. Wormley describing a detailed recipe for easing the symptoms of certain types of neuralgia. After he had read the mini-treatise, Doyle headed for Dr. Hoare's small but well-supplied laboratory to make sure that all the apparatuses, reagents, and other materials he would need for the concoction were in stock. Emulating the methods that his unorthodox professor of physiology, Robert Christison, had unabashedly practiced on Arthur's fellow students, Doyle began to use himself as a guinea pig to rid himself of his facial neuralgia. Using gelsemium, an extract of the root of yellow jasmine, he recorded every last detail of his work in a notebook for possible publication in prestigious medical journals. With each passing day and each failure, Doyle increased the dose of gelsemium, confident he would soon be able to determine its therapeutic concentration, not its lethal one. One can only imagine just how terrible his pain must have been to cause him to take such a chance with his life.

Whether it was one of Dr. Hoare's other two assistants, Smith and Hues, or Dr. Hoare himself who discovered Doyle's madcap venture into unsubstantiated medical practices is not known, but we do know that Dr. Hoare's wife, Amy, threatened to inform Doyle's mother about his activities if he failed to stop immediately. Surely, Dr. Hoare had to have been anxious about getting into trouble himself, as one of his previous assistants had already brought about the death of a patient by using one of his concoctions incorrectly. This assistant had made the sad mistake of neglecting to tell a patient afflicted with a painful joint disorder that the linimentum aconiti he had dispensed to ease his rheumatism was only a salve and not meant for oral use. Unfortunately, the patient ingested the preparation instead of applying it to the affected areas and quickly experienced a precipitous drop in his heart rate, succumbing within minutes to its toxic effects. But Arthur beat Mrs. Hoare to the punch by writing a letter to his mother confessing, "I have been experimenting upon myself with Gelsemium. Mrs. H said she would write to you unless I stopped it." He even becomes boastful about his devil-may-care attitude, stating, "I increased my dose until I reached 200 minims, and had some curious physiological results." He goes on to rant:

> There is a pestilent little quack here, or rather a firm, Smith and Hues. The latter is a qualified man but a sleeping partner. Smith is the perfect type of quack. I have written out a most preposterous case and sent it to the Lancet in Hues' name. It is told most gravely and scientifically. If the Doctor sees anything about an eel in the *Lancet* that is the letter.

Miraculously, Arthur was not asked to pack his bags by the even-tempered Dr. Hoare. Even more incredibly, Doyle continued to occupy his usual seat at the family dinner table, where he had become a favorite of the two Hoare children, Cecil, a boy of six; and Josephine, a girl of ten. They loved his scary ghost stories, much as the boys at Stonyhurst had. It was from this house in

Aston Villa that he submitted his first non-medical tale for publication, "The Haunted Grange of Goresthrope." Although *Blackwood's Edinburgh Magazine* rejected this story, along with its "bloody" title, for being too juvenile, some of its characters would serve as templates a few years later. Doyle was all too aware that his job would not be in jeopardy so long as these two "spoiled" off-spring of Amy and Reginald Hoare remained spellbound by his stories.

Around this time, Arthur was introduced to Herr Gleiwitz, Amy Hoare's German teacher. Doyle would describe him as "a doctor and professor, and one of the very first Arabian and Sanskrit scholars in Europe. . . ." Despite Professor Gleiwitz's credentials, however, the poor man had only one client and no other prospects on the horizon. He and his family were trapped in financial quicksand. Doyle would relate this to his mother, telling her, "I did a rather foolish thing the other day . . . I gave him my watch and chain and told him to go and pop them, which I am bound to say he was very unwilling to do. However he sailed away with them at last, and I hope got something decent for them. . . ." When Doyle gave his watch to Gleiwitz, he knew that the only way he would ever see it again would be to "get the ticket from him . . . and rescue the watch" from the pawnbroker, in the hope that Gleiwitz would later pay him the money back. Doyle's mother must have wondered why her son, who was always pleading for money, would have been so reckless to give his watch to a person who obviously had no way of reimbursing him the funds to retrieve it.

November 1879

Despite his participation in cricket, rugby, and football while in medical school, Doyle established very few friendships during his time at the University of Edinburgh. One of his only friends there was the aforementioned George T. Budd. According to Doyle's semi-autobiographical work, *The Stark Munro Letters*, one day, the newly married Budd invited Doyle over to his apartment, which was located directly above a grocery. Upon his entrance into the building, Doyle noticed that the staircase reeked of an unidentifiable rotting cheese, which he assumed was inappropriately housed inside the store. When he knocked at the apartment door, Doyle was greeted by a cacophony of clicks, springs, and snaps, which represented the unlatching and unbolting of an array of locks. This was to be Doyle's introduction to Budd's paranoia. Once Arthur had been granted admittance to the dwelling, Budd began the process of ritualistically refastening the locks. He asked Doyle if he was sure he had not been followed. Arthur answered that, as far as he knew, he had not been.

Recently married, Budd and his seventeen-year-old wife, Kate, who until their union had been a ward of the state, were leasing a four-room suite, although only three of the rooms were being used. The fourth one had been completely closed off by Budd, who felt that some sort of virulent agent of death lay inside. Not only had he secured it with every type of imaginable lock, he had also placed "gummed varnished paper over all the cracks of the door, to prevent the imaginary contagion from spreading." Disregarding these eccentricities, Doyle became a frequent visitor to Budd's apartment. His seat was often a giant pile of old issues of the *British Medical Journal*, and his meal was usually a single apple dumpling. One day, Doyle noticed that the smell of cheese had been replaced by the odor of canine liver. Budd apprised Doyle of just how he had managed to smuggle this organ from Dr. Rutherford's ice chest. He had casually draped his overcoat "round the dreadful glistening mass" and simply strolled off with it. At no time did Doyle give any thought to turning in the perpetrator of the theft to the chairman of the Department of Pathology. Instead, he was all too pleased to join the culprit in conducting experiments on the nature of glycogen. Budd had set up a makeshift laboratory in the apartment, which included a microscope and a vast and colorful supply of all the apparatuses and materials needed to carry out chemical reactions and make slides. Arthur used his drawing ability and his observational skills to document a three-week period of investigations into the pathology of the liver and its ducts. Budd, however, sent out their documented findings to the most prestigious medical journals in the land with only his name attached.

If Arthur was angry or disappointed by Budd's attempt at achieving celebrity status for himself alone, he said so to no one. Despite Budd's irrational and unethical actions, this was not to be the last Doyle-Budd partnership.

January 1880

In a letter addressed to his mother and posted on January 30th, 1880, Arthur chides his mother for not responding to "[t]wo letters and an Xmas card all unanswered and unnoticed," adding, "It's enough to make a fellow cynical." He also lays blame at his own feet, however, for appearing ungrateful for the "pretty necktie" his sister Connie had given him. He then writes of a fellow student named Currie and the upcoming Arctic whaling expedition in which Currie would be taking part as ship's surgeon, stating, "So Currie goes in the

Hope. I shouldn't think Currie will care much about sleeping with the mates—I should strongly object. I must write to him before he goes." Coincidentally, Doyle would later describe being approached by Currie at school a few weeks before the trip and offered the opportunity to replace him as surgeon of the *Hope.* The first oddity regarding this recollection is that Doyle seems to have been in Birmingham at the time, not at school. After having learned of the imminent departure of one of his fellow assistants at Dr. Hoare's practice, Doyle had agreed to stay on until mid-March to "put the newcomer through his facings," which would rule out the possibility that he was at the university when his fellow student and friend supposedly walked in and implored him to take his place on the whaler. Additionally, there would have been no reason for Doyle to send his concerns in a letter had he known he would soon see Currie. If the letter had been sent, it would also seem to fly in the face of reason to think that Currie, knowing of Arthur's bias against the mates, would have bothered to ask him to take his place.

Ultimately, any account of how Doyle replaced Currie must be viewed as poorly remembered at the very least, or as a tale designed to justify his early departure from Dr. Hoare's practice. Interestingly, research of the roster of the *Hope's* previous voyages yields no record of anyone named Currie having ever sailed on that ship in any capacity at any time, so Doyle's statement that the trip would have represented a "second tour" for Currie is curious indeed.

No matter how he ended up with the position, it came with the handsome sum of "two pound ten" shillings a month and "three shillings a ton oil money," as well as Currie's expensive Arctic kit. Although Doyle's surgical skills could be described as being rudimentary at best, the chance to get out of dreary Birmingham combined with the prospect of earning a decent sum of money led him to take the job. While the position of ship's surgeon was not regarded as anything special, it paid well enough and gave Arthur an opportunity to indulge his love of the sea. He was in a mad rush to make it to Scotland's most northeastern point, but made sure not to leave behind his most prized possessions: his collection of Macaulay's essays and other "books, a journal, and two pairs of boxing gloves."

Just a few miles from Peterhead, the home port of the *Hope,* stood Blairerno House, the place where Charles Altamont Doyle had been sent after allegedly trying to burn down the apartment the Doyle clan had been renting from Bryan Waller. Blairerno was run by the Forbes family, which was headed by David Forbes, and a small staff, which cared for the eighteen male residents. Those interned at Blairerno ran the gamut of professions, from tobacconists and accountants to medical students and artists. Not even the wonderful care afforded those who dwelled there, however, proved sufficient to stop Charles from climbing down "water spouts" to make his escape to a nearby town in search of wine. Although most of the time he was well-behaved and sober, there were other moments when he became violent and even "dangerous." To combat his anxiety, he would take "refuge in his prayer book" and meet with the Blairerno priest. At other times, he would "lie down & die" in front of Mr. Forbes, Mrs. Forbes, or their children, but somehow, he always managed to "come to life again."

February 1880

At about 11 AM on February 28, 1880, Doyle arrived in Peterhead, which until a decade prior had been the northern hub of the whaling and sealing industries. Now, the overexploitation of the Arctic Ocean's whales and seals had driven these animals to near extinction and was threatening to turn this once-thriving village into a ghost town. Only the continued presence of the legendary Grays, the first family of Peterhead, had kept the place alive. Even the citizenry's willingness to invest in the complete modernization of the wharves and the increasingly lucrative herring trade would have been insufficient to stave off the town's demise. At present, a mere six whaling ships were nestled in port when, just ten years before, there had been scores of vessels clogging the harbor. Hunting grounds for whales had shifted to the Antarctic, taking all but the Gray family's ships to different ports of call.

Two of the half-dozen vessels in the harbor, the *Alert* and the *Perseverance*, were of an earlier vintage and had no engines at all. The next two, the *Jan Mayen* and the *Windward*, had been modified with steam engines to make them more seaworthy in the treacherous waters of the North Sea and Arctic Ocean. The remaining two, the *Eclipse* and the *Hope*, were modern steamers equipped with sails to be used only as backup. It was on the *Hope* that the fledgling and woefully "unqualified physician" would make his first voyage. Never on any of his frequent visits to the wharves of the Thames had Arthur Conan Doyle seen anything that even remotely rivaled "his ship" in appearance or power. The person in command of the ship was none other than fifty-year-old John Gray himself, the most distinguished member of the Gray family. Doyle was immediately impressed by his grizzled white beard, ruddy face, and erect muscular figure, but he was made uneasy by the light blue eyes that appeared to fix themselves on the horizon instead of on the person standing right in front of him.

That afternoon, at precisely 2 PM, the *Windward* and the *Hope* weighed anchor for the Shetland Islands. The captain of the *Windward*, Alexander Murray, went out on deck and treated a large cheering crowd to a minor spectacle. Bellowing out the words "starboard" and "port," he played to the appreciative throng that had queued up on the pier. The crowd acknowledged his showmanship, the gentlemen raising and tossing their hats in the air, the women waving their handkerchiefs, all bidding their fond adieus to the friends, relatives, and spouses who would be away for the next six months. Doyle was caught up in the event, and when he spied a young lady looking at him flirtatiously, he could not resist tipping his hat to her, even though he was quite aware that Captain Gray did not approve of such behavior from the ship's "gentlemen." Captain John Gray was not one to accept the least amount of tomfoolery on board his vessel when it was on public display. In contrast to the pomp and circumstance of Captain Murray, Doyle would describe the launch of Captain Gray's *Hope* as being "set about in a quieter and more business-like way."

Once the phrase "anchors aweigh" had been uttered and the ship had sailed out of the harbor, Doyle went back to his cabin to unpack, escorted by Jack Lamb, the ship's steward. A short and burly golden-bearded man of about thirty, Lamb was surprised to see two pairs of boxing gloves occupying a prime position in the young physician's suitcase. According to Doyle, it was then that Lamb challenged him to a fight, though it would be more in keeping with Doyle's personality to assume that it was he who challenged Lamb. Although there are conflicting accounts as to where the bout took place, we do know that the two warriors fought it out in front of a group of cheering spectators, and that Doyle overwhelmed the tough but unschooled steward. As he was being attended to by his second, Lamb issued the following assessment of Doyle's medical abilities to the first mate, Colin McLean: "So help me, Colin, he's the best surrr-geon we've had! He's blackened my e'e!"

Doyle's successful ring debut gained him a prize much bigger than he had ever imagined: the respect and admiration of the men of the *Hope*. From this time on, he had unprecedented access to their inner circle and was invited to join them at their midnight meetings, where they discussed any and all topics of interest. Doyle had the best of both worlds, as he also enjoyed the hospitality of Captains Murray and Gray. Captain Gray even granted him permission to join his mates in exploring the rough Shetland village of Lerwick, where they made their first stop on the way up north. There was more than just a bit of danger that went with being a *Hope* or a *Windward* man, as the members of the other thirty boats in Lerwick that week regarded Gray and Murray as snobbish aristocrats whose crews were a bunch of arrogant windbags in need of some deflating.

Doyle would write to his mother about an incident that occurred in the Queens tavern, involving the first mate, Colin McLean. Apparently, while he and his fellow whalers were drinking there, six officers of the rival whaler, the *Dundee*, were engaged in spewing derogatory comments about the men of the *Hope* to anyone willing to listen. McLean, who was usually a man of few words, put down his drink, rose from his seat, and announced, "I'm a *Hope* man myself," and then "floored a doctor & maimed a captain & got away in triumph." The next morning, McLean, who was still in an agitated state, ranted to Doyle, "It's lucky I was sober, Doctor, or there might have been a row." Doyle was so peeved that he had missed the brawl that he made sure to ask Captain Gray for "leave to go with a few of the biggest of the petty officers to the Queen's today to see if we can't have a row."

The position of ship's surgeon was, on most voyages, easy to handle, but things were about to change. In the early morning hours of March 8, Doyle was woken by Captain Gray himself and ordered to get over to the *Windward* to assist in a surgical emergency. Grabbing his lantern and black medical bag, Doyle made his way over the pitch-dark wharf towards the *Windward*. Although his oil-fueled lamp gave off some light, the black Arctic night made it virtually impossible to see where the planks of the Lerwick dock met the water of the harbor. Doyle adapted quickly to this lack of luminosity, and as soon as he spotted the gangplank of the *Windward*, he quickened his pace and dashed to the infirmary. Its surgeon, Dr. Brown, informed Doyle that two of the chief engineer's fingers had been crushed by machinery. The two doctors worked together and managed to save both digits, ensuring that the voyage would not reach a premature end. When they parted, Dr. Brown congratulated Doyle on his excellent performance and apologized to him for having previously rejected his application to work with him in his London office.

It was during this period that Doyle began experiencing the same throbbing pain in his lower left jaw, strange sensation in his lower lip, and brutal headaches he had experienced in the past. Once again, Arthur was caught in the constrictive web of neuralgia. Instead of remaining in his bed, however, he forced himself out onto the deck. McLean soon surprised him by saying, "I am going to have every man working hard when we start sealing. I've no fears of you, Surgeon. I'll back you to do a day's work with any man aboard. You suit me, and I liked the style of you the first time I saw ye. I hate your clean-handed gentlemen." Arthur regarded this testimonial from the usually taciturn Scotsman as the highest compliment anyone could receive, and was happy to join the sealing party. While McLean and the crew regarded Arthur as one of them, Doyle was still told he had to go to the captain to obtain official consent.

Initially, Captain Gray kept him off the ice, but he eventually granted him the minor task of pulling the sealskins up the side of the boat. Doyle performed more than competently in this task, causing Gray to have a change of heart. He told the crew to hand Doyle a club and then ordered Arthur to go to the locker where sea gear was kept. Doyle was officially one of the crew now. Gray surely must have warned Doyle that the bladdernose seal is capable of fighting like a bulldog and can rip off the legs and arms of its hunter in seconds. He also would have told Doyle that the seal protects and fights for its young with astonishing courage, and that if Arthur failed to pay careful attention to it each and every movement, or if he failed to move quickly enough, he would, in all probability, meet his end. Yet Doyle must have so impressed Captain Gray with his athleticism and strength that he was permitted to perform one of the most dangerous jobs in the world without any apprenticeship.

The young physician-turned-seal-hunter was led to a raft of ice. When he spotted a baby seal stranded on an ice floe, he used his club as a balance pole, cautiously making his way toward the pup. He struggled to maintain his position on the floating ice, but when a mother seal swam under it and lifted it out of the ocean, Arthur was sent hurtling into the freezing waters of the Arctic. The icy water did not scare Arthur as much as the jagged pieces of ice, which he knew could cut him to ribbons. After what seemed to be an eternity, a frightened Arthur was pulled to safety by two of the crew members. His mittens frozen solid, he thought he would have some fun by cutting off two hind flippers of the seals he had skinned, putting them on his hands as replacements. He must have looked like a walking seal as he made his way back to the boat.

Before long, Arthur was once again with his comrades out on the ice. Brandishing his club, he cautiously made his way to a floe where a ferocious bladdernose seal had stationed herself to bathe in the Arctic sun. Doyle looked her straight in the eye and swung his mace directly at her head with cricket-bat speed. Arthur clubbed her numerous times, oblivious of the fact that his initial blow had instantly put an end to the mother seal's life. According to Doyle's own account, no one was there to bear witness to his onslaught against the seal, and no one was there to help him when, once again, he lost his footing and plunged into the blood-red sea he had created. He tried to grab hold of a large piece of ice, and although he kept clawing at it, it was too slippery for him to get a firm grip. He managed to grasp the seal's hind flipper, but as he pulled on it, the seal slid towards him. He realized that the only way to escape death was to somehow scale the seal's slick back quickly enough to grab the ice floe before the seal fell backwards into the sea. Amazingly, he was able to summon the strength needed to escape Davy Jones's locker. When Captain Gray beheld the frozen "savage" covered in dirt, sweat, and blood, he proclaimed Doyle the "Great Northern Diver," after the bird of the same name, which swims slowly along the water and then, in a flash, plunges into the water after its prey.

Arthur quickly returned to the ice, but this time Captain Gray ordered the first mate to stick to Doyle like glue. After all, intelligent conversationalists and adequate physicians were hard to find. Arthur had swapped his mace for a rifle loaded with bullets and stood there with McLean, observing the off-target shots the harpooners were firing at a pair of bladdernose seals. Arthur silently steadied his weapon and from a distance in excess of 200 feet hit both seals with deadly accuracy. That night, an eleven-foot-long seal bone was brought to Doyle's cabin, where it served as a souvenir of the day's glory.

By April 7, Doyle apparently thought himself more of a seaman than a physician, for his journal entry reads, "[P]oor work today, seals are scarce and we only took 133." Upon his return to the ship, however, he found Andrew "Haggie" Milne in bad shape, which should have excused him from any other duties. Just a few days before seal season had begun, Doyle had been asked to evaluate the ship's oldest member for recurrent bouts of excruciating abdominal pain. Although he was seventy years old, the man more than earned his keep aboard the whaler. But now he was suffering in silence. Doyle had already performed an initial examination, ruling out surgery at the time. Although the possibility of an incarcerated hernia, or perhaps even the more serious strangulated hernia, had crossed Doyle's mind, he had convinced himself that Milne's condition could be effectively managed by "medicine," utilizing his magical analgesic chlorodyne—a mixture of Indian hemp, prussic acid, chloroform, and morphine. Why Doyle did not elect to tackle the surgical procedure is difficult to understand, as he had assisted with this type of operation numerous times back in Edinburgh, and since Milne's condition was disintegrating with each passing day. It may have been that the ship was too poorly equipped to accommodate such surgery.

Doyle must have been able to convince Captain Gray that Milne's condition was not critical, for otherwise a man of Gray's nature would never have allowed a ship's doctor to leave such an ill member of his crew. Doyle reexamined the mariner and concluded that his "foecal vomiting & constant pain" was the consequence of intussusception, which is characterized by one portion of the intestine collapsing into another part of the intestine, much like the sections of a hand-held telescope. Despite the enemas, castor oil, and chlorodyne he administered to Milne, he somehow gave the patient permission to eat and walk around the ship. The next four days found Doyle out with the sealing party or in his cabin logging his experiences.

On April 11, having enjoyed a grand old time picking "up seals all day," Doyle returned to the *Hope*. He was immediately told to report to mess hall and attend to Milne, who had taken a turn for the worse. Haggie, who earlier that day had been "very cheery and very much better," had devoured a thick concoction of molasses, flour, and raisins known as plum duff. Now he was in utter agony and appeared to be slipping away.

Doyle held Milne in his arms and the bewildered crew encircled them with their lanterns. Within minutes, Milne was dead. No one dared move until Captain Gray made his entrance, looked down silently at the corpse, and dismissed everyone save for Doyle, who was told to remain behind. Later that evening, a telegraph was dashed off to Peterhead, informing the local press that the oldest member of the S.S. *Hope* had died of congestive heart failure. Whether it was Captain John Gray or Arthur Conan Doyle who had assigned this incorrect cause of death to Andrew Milne remains unknown, along with the reason for this decision. Doyle was instructed to prepare Milne's body for burial at sea, which was to take place the very next day. He was also given the assignment of compiling a complete list of Haggie's personal effects.

Early the next morning, the entire crew assembled on deck. The Union Jack was hoisted to half-mast. A bag of old iron parts was tied around Andrew Milne's ankles. The canvas-wrapped corpse was then lowered onto one of the rowboats. Captain Gray read the Church of England burial service and, as he completed it, the body of the old sailor was slid gently into its watery grave with "hardly a splash." The service ended, the crew dispersed to their assigned posts, and the daily routine began anew. Arthur walked over to Captain Gray and suggested that it would have been a good idea to give Milne a "hearty fare-thee-well" with a three-cheer ovation. Despite the events of the morning, Doyle was back on the ice that very day.

The next few days proved relatively uneventful. Except for one man with heart palpitations and one with a lacerated eyelid, Doyle had few patients. With so little to do medically or surgically, Doyle was able to join the crew at breakfast mess each morning. There, the day's agenda was discussed before the crew went out to station themselves on the floating ice. Doyle became as fast and proficient as any of the men aboard at performing the daily ritual of sharpening his knife, and so never missed a minute of the kill. He was able to pounce upon his prey with lightning speed, and his mace always struck home. He had a significant advantage over his crewmates in readying the seal for skinning, as he incorporated techniques he had learned from Dr. Bell and Dr. Rutherford into the time-honored art of stripping a seal of its blubber, also known as flinching. While most of the sealers struggled to properly position their "meal ticket," Doyle's strength and skill enabled him to "roll" a large seal onto its back with minimal effort. He also modified the straddling position used by the others to gain a maximal mechanical advantage in each aspect of the task before him. Once he had drained the seal of its blood, Doyle, in one elegant motion, would thrust his razor-sharp knife blade through the seal's neck, chest, abdomen, and tail. The skinning was accomplished in less than five minutes.

Even though his back and thighs ached at the end of each day, the Great Northern Diver had neither the time nor the inclination to complain. He was too busy loving it all—boxing, running hundred-yard dashes across the ship, and trying his hand at taxidermy. Evenings saw him engaged in conversations "on zoology, murders, executions, and ironclads" with Colin McLean, Jack Lamb, and the Mob, his mates from his assigned rowboat. Doyle always managed to be the center of attention in the seven-by-four-foot cubicle in which they sat. His ability to scare the wits out of the superstitious mariners with tales of apparitions and murders was without equal. The men shivered when Doyle provided them with the graphic details of the high treason plot against their beloved Queen Victoria, or when he gave them the gory details of the manner in which a man had decapitated his wife, dismembered her body, and then scattered her parts about town. He enchanted them with tales of a self-proclaimed messiah who had successfully led his little army against oppressive tax collectors.

But every time the men gathered in this way, there was almost always an altercation between McLean and the hard-drinking Mr. Lamb, an altercation that threatened to break the spell Doyle had been weaving. Lamb's inhibitions were lowered by rum, and as a result, the phrase "No offense, Colin" was heard practically every night. Once said, it was as though a bomb was about to go off, and the berth would empty out accordingly. Doyle, who was always positioned farthest from the door, was consistently trapped. If Lamb continued with, "But all I says is that if you had been a bit quicker on the fush," Doyle would be forced into action because McLean would grab Lamb's throat. Doyle would then be required to grab Colin's waist to bring about an end to the mayhem, and the three of them would wrestle until they were on the brink of exhaustion. When things settled down a bit, the men would come back in, and Doyle would begin where he had left off. Apparently, the physical activity could not diminish Doyle's desire to be in the thick of it.

Every so often, when there was nothing much happening, Doyle would enter ink drawings into his journal. His illustrations depicted daily life at sea aboard a whaling vessel. Doyle restricted his colors to just four: black, yellow, blue, and an occasional red. Two weeks after Andrew Milne's death, Milne's brother boarded the ship, and Doyle proudly showed him the drawing he had made of Milne's memorial service. His brother was so taken by it that he asked if Doyle would do him the favor of making a similar drawing for him. Arthur was more than happy to oblige.

It was not until the middle of May that things began to be stirred up again. This time it was an invasion of privacy at the source of the commotion. One evening, one of the stokers brought up the subject of Doyle's seemingly inconsequential opinion that he did not like "Boiled Beef day," or as Doyle called each of these Tuesdays, "Tough-day." It is not hard to imagine the surprise Doyle must have felt as he heard these words uttered aloud, words that he had written in his journal but not shared with anyone else. Doyle soon discovered the source of the leak, and the culpable party was none other than the chief engineer, John McLeod.

Doyle knew that the ship could not afford to lose its chief engineer, but he also was not going to tolerate any violation into his personal life. He constructed a plan to put the fear of God into McLeod. Knowing that McLeod would read his next entry, Doyle decided to write:

> I hear from the engine room that Mr. McLeod, our chief engineer, has done me the honour to read my private log every morning, and make satirical comments upon it at table, and among his own firemen. Now I would as soon that he read my private letters as my journal, in fact a good deal sooner, and it is just one of those things which I won't stand from any man. If any man meddles with my private business I know how to deal with him . . . If he does it after this warning he shall answer for it to me . . . I hope this may meet his eye in the morning.

Never again was there any commentary by Mr. McLeod to the crew about Doyle's journal.

Over a week later, on May 22, Arthur Conan Doyle spent his twenty-first birthday on board the *Hope* as it crossed 79 degrees north latitude and officially entered whale country. Doyle celebrated his coming of age by getting dead drunk. Captain Gray was forced to fill in as the ship's surgeon and prescribe two mustard emetics to rid Doyle of the curse of alcohol. Multiple episodes of vomiting followed shortly thereafter.

The weather remained brutally cold, despite it nearly being summer. The crew's collective heart, however, was warmed by the Greeenland whales that had been spotted by Captain Gray. The whalers, Doyle among them, swung into action and lowered four of their eight rowboats into the water in what was to be Doyle's last great adventure at sea. Jack Coull, one of the members of the crew, encouraged Doyle to take the oars, while the others kept a close watch on a mysterious man known as the "Outlaw." The man's hand gestures had to be followed to a tee if the whale hunt was to be successful. His origins were unknown, and no one dared ask him where he was from. He was extraordinarily handsome, and extremely tall and swarthy, with dark eyes and a blue-black beard. Although Doyle had suggested that the Outlaw was a North England Highlander and was probably on the run for a murder he had committed in the past, this only increased the amount of respect the man received from everybody.

The Outlaw raised his hand and everyone knew to cease stroking immediately, as even the slightest movement might allow the pursued whale to spot them. Then the Outlaw lowered his hand and uttered the command, "Give way, boys! Give way, all! Hard!" A bevy of oars hit the water. When the whale was "end on" and unable to detect the presence of the boats, the click of harpoon gun triggers resounded off the water. Although the harpooners managed to inflict a mortal wound, the whale was still a threat to the lancers. When they went to work on the leviathan, they were suddenly seized by terror. A huge fin of immeasurable heft and size went above their boat and appeared to be on the verge of crushing both it and its crew. Each of the seamen reflexively held a hand up to ward it off, knowing full well that if that fin crashed down upon them, or if the whale went down below them, their boat would capsize. It was blind luck alone that allowed Doyle to survive this assault.

On the last day of May, with little to do, Arthur decided to perform an experiment upon the "maulies," a group of birds for which he did not particularly care. He took out four pieces of bread, which he had stored in his room for a week. He soaked one in strychnine, one in carbolic acid, one in zinc sulfate, and one in turpentine. He made his way on deck and hurled the bread over the railing to see which of the birds would die the quickest. He hadn't counted on the leader of the flock beating all of his brethren to the feast and leaving nothing for them to enjoy. To Doyle's amazement, after consuming all four pieces of bread, the bird flew faster and higher than he had ever done before. What Doyle neglects to mention in his journal is that the maulie was looked upon by sealers as a sacred bird, believed to carry the souls of dead sailors, and no sailor-sealer would ever think of killing one, for to do so would shower misfortune upon a ship. The fact that Doyle performed this experiment alone suggests that he may have known about the legend and did not want any eyes upon him. If any member of the *Hope* had seen Doyle's activities, or had gained access to his diary again, there would have been a panic, as the ship would have been regarded as cursed.

By July 11, Arthur, who prior to this trip had never spent a night aboard a ship, had been away from land for almost a half a year. That evening, the expedition yacht *Eira*, which had been built purposely to travel up to the North Pole, anchored on an ice floe next to the *Eclipse* and the *Hope*. The discovery vessel had departed Peterhead on Doyle's birthday with a well-dressed crew of twenty-four Scots and Shetlanders. The owner of the *Eira* was Leigh Smith, a wealthy bachelor. Doyle was included in the elite group that received an invitation to eat dinner with Smith; Johnny Grant, the world-famous polar photographer, and William Neale, the ship's surgeon, were also present. Smith thanked both Grays for their indispensable work in drawing up the specifications for the construction of his yacht. John Grant took a photograph that commemorated the occasion of the meeting of the three ships in the far north, and Doyle was one of just seven people to appear in it. Doyle, at his tender age, and with no official credentials of any type, was smoking cigars, dining on mock turtle soup and fresh roast beef with potatoes, and sipping champagne with a group of some of the most talented and respected men in the world.

One month later, on a hot mid-August day, a pilot boat greeted the *Hope* and escorted it back to Peterhead, with the *Windward* following close behind. Arthur gathered his belongings and said his goodbyes to the men of ship. Captain John Gray, in his serious manner, asked Arthur to reconsider the offer he had made, which was for Doyle to return to the *Hope* on its next voyage. To quote words Doyle would write of himself at a later date, "I went on board a big, straggling youth, but I came off it a powerful, well-grown man."

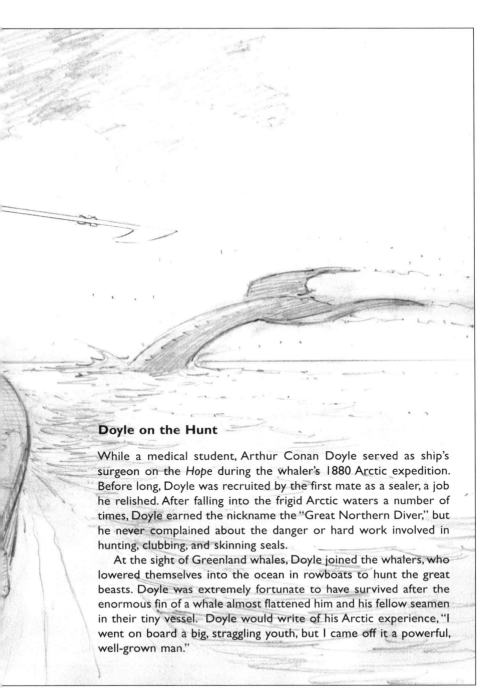

Doyle on the Hunt

While a medical student, Arthur Conan Doyle served as ship's surgeon on the *Hope* during the whaler's 1880 Arctic expedition. Before long, Doyle was recruited by the first mate as a sealer, a job he relished. After falling into the frigid Arctic waters a number of times, Doyle earned the nickname the "Great Northern Diver," but he never complained about the danger or hard work involved in hunting, clubbing, and skinning seals.

At the sight of Greenland whales, Doyle joined the whalers, who lowered themselves into the ocean in rowboats to hunt the great beasts. Doyle was extremely fortunate to have survived after the enormous fin of a whale almost flattened him and his fellow seamen in their tiny vessel. Doyle would write of his Arctic experience, "I went on board a big, straggling youth, but I came off it a powerful, well-grown man."

August 1880

Upon returning from his adventures at sea, Doyle decided to go back to Birmingham rather than return immediately to the University of Edinburgh. The six months of dangerous work had broadened his shoulders, enhanced his now powerful forearms, trimmed his waist, and made his thin legs more muscular. Since Doyle's departure, Mrs. Hoare's beloved brother, the renowned tenor Cecil Handel Tovey, who had been an integral part of their domestic life, had died. Cecil's death had removed the music from their residence. Thankfully, Arthur's return to Birmingham was regarded by Amy Hoare and the children as a harbinger of better things. He easily re-established himself back within the family hearth, and soon was concocting potions, writing stories and medical articles, beguiling the Hoare offspring with his tall tales, and smoking cigars with Amy Hoare. In a letter to his mother, Doyle would write of Dr. Hoare, "Hoare is the only man I ever met who has no fault in his character— a plain straightforward jolly fellow without pride, affectation or anything else. A difficult man to abuse as Johnson said of Reynolds."

Around this time, Doyle would also accuse his mother of abandoning him, writing, "Why don't you write? You have no excuse." Not knowing whether he would get any response from Mary Doyle, he would inform her that it was his intention to "run down to Budd's somewhere about March" so he could do some reading, adding that Budd had "a lot of notes and things which I can get nowhere else." Arthur would soon receive a response from his mother, along with a ten-pound note, enough to cover his expenses for the next three months.

Arthur was a master of entertaining himself at the expense of others and had no compunction about making people uneasy, disappointed, or inconvenienced, especially if they were rich. On one occasion, he pulled off a major hoax. As it was his duty to "send out ointment and pill boxes with elaborate directions on the lids" to Dr. Hoare's clientele, he had access to every name and address in the practice. One day, when he had a little free time available to him, he had invitations printed for an "upcoming mayor's ball." It must have been quite a scene when a parade of carriages arrived at their destination for the gala event. Men dressed in formal attire and women wearing their most elegant gowns made their way down to the pavement without any footmen to assist them. Imagine their shock and humiliation when they realized they had been the unsuspecting victims of a cruel practical joke. There was no ball. Doyle was likely somewhere in the shadows, watching the proceedings with delight.

When Birmingham police arrived at the Hoare residence, Dr. Hoare probably thought something horrible had happened to one of his patients. But the police were not there to speak to Dr. Hoare; they were there for Doyle. After they told Reginald Hoare about the scandalous hoax that had been carried out against Lord Mayor Chamberlain and Birmingham's high society, and that it had been traced back specifically to his medical assistant from Edinburgh, the police must have brought Doyle down to the station for further questioning. It is reasonable to assume that this unwelcome and potentially practice-destroying prank precipitated Doyle's return to Edinburgh, and that Reginald Hoare must have been infuriated by this turn of events.

10

The Tour
Mitre Square, 3 PM

It was becoming more and more obvious that the pace of the tour was a bit too much for at least some of the group. The portly and poorly conditioned Dr. Hammond was constantly stopping to catch his breath, while Adelaide, who was a sight for sore eyes in her fashionable attire, had made a bad choice of footwear. Her high-heeled shoes were not suited for a lengthy trek over uneven pavement and cobblestones, so her feet were killing her. Carrington Lambton offered her physical support by holding her under the arm, and gave her vocal encouragement by telling her she could do it. Doyle was forced to slow down and even stop on a few occasions so that everyone could catch up. Stephen Mitchell, unfazed by it all, now stood at Doyle's right shoulder. Doyle thought it only right to engage him in conversation, having already been impressed by his intellect.

"You play cricket on a high level, don't you?" Doyle said.

"I do, but who told you?" Stephen said.

"Told me? No! It is quite plain to see you are a bowler."

"Odds bodkins! You've hit the nail on the head. How in the world did you figure that out?"

"Well, it is certainly not your physique that reveals your favorite pastime. Rather, it is a constellation of signs associated with those who engage in this noble sport. When we began this little outing, almost everyone was able to keep up with me. As the hours have passed, you have been the only one to maintain the pace—an indicator of top-notch conditioning. But you have begun to rub your left side a bit, and I have spotted you massaging your right shoulder, which made you wince. These are signs that are pathognomonic, in physician's jargon, of what has been labeled 'young bowler's syndrome.' Are you aware of the source of your pain and discomfort?"

"No, I am not."

"Well, somewhere along the line, you sustained a subtle tear of the external oblique muscles of your four left lower ribs, which has forced you to compensate by overusing the muscles responsible for the rotation of your dominant shoulder."

"Jolly impressive, Sir Arthur. Quite a tour de force! And how many pounds do I owe you for your superb diagnosis?"

Doyle chuckled. "The first consultation is free," he said, "but if you want me to supply you with the medication that will help you, it will cost you dearly. Ha! Ha! I, too, enjoy the sport, and it is easy for me to recognize a cricketer. Not too long ago, I played on a team supported by the largesse of my fellow Scot Jim Barrie. Our team enjoyed a successful run, unlike the opera I collaborated on with J.B., which audiences met with frozen hands. But what has impressed me most is your scholarly approach to these tragic events of 1888. Tell me, is it just this case in particular, or do you have a general interest in unsolved crimes?"

"No, I have a general interest in you, Sir Arthur. Due diligence is an innate component of my personality, just as it is of yours. I'm compulsive, and everything I do must be done in an orderly and arranged fashion. So, Sir Arthur, there is no room or time for dabblers in a case like this."

"And why is that?"

"Because it was not only foul play that was involved in this case. These crimes were well rehearsed, ordered, and arranged by a deft hand. The police and the public at large were left with subtle clues and multiple challenges, which tantalized them. Almost everything remained beyond their intellectual reach and grasp."

"Don't most murders involve such things?"

"To some extent, most of them do, but this string of murders had patterns that were complex—almost like the plots of your stories! If I could just interpret the murders properly, the two of us might be able to bring some vindication to those lost souls."

"You have a strong sense of self, Mr. Mitchell. I like that. So let us start from the beginning. Is there anything that suggests that the patterns you were talking about truly exist?"

"Of course there is. There is more than one thing, actually. For one, the Ripper was nocturnal. But the question remains as to why specific nights or dates were chosen."

"Mr. Mitchell, most of us would assume that murders are easier to carry out in the dark of night rather than in the revealing light of day."

"Sir Arthur, while that goes without saying, burning questions still remain. Why did the murders occur in sporadic bursts and not on consecutive days or weekends? Was there a method to this madness?"

"Perhaps there were other failed attempts in which Jack's frightened victims were able to escape but thought it best to say nothing. Or perhaps Jack was only able to operate when conditions were optimal. As for specific dates, they have little or nothing to do with anything that occurred."

"Sir Arthur, if we opt to follow things chronologically, next you'll be taking us to the site of the second of the two murders that night. It puzzles me as to why there were two in a single night, unless both ladies met some sort of eligibility criterion. Maybe the Ripper couldn't bring himself to pass up such a serendipitous opportunity. This might be part of a pattern that has eluded both the London Police and the Yard all these years."

Doyle looked at his pocket watch. "You may or may not be right," he said, "but we'll have to get back to your 'pattern theory' at a later time. I had never thought of eligibility as being a criterion of admission into such an unlucky club. We'll get back to it, if time permits. Otherwise we can correspond by letter."

A few seconds later, Doyle halted and waited for everyone to assemble around him. "Gentlemen and lady," he said, "we are now at Mitre Square, the site of the fourth murder. This plaza you see before you was once the site of the Holy Trinity Priory cloister, until old Henry VIII, in a moment of Anglican fervor, insisted that it be razed to the ground. And it was here that the dynamitards of the Fenian Brotherhood incubated and hatched their plot to destroy the Tower of London. This was a mere three years before Jack's venture into the Square Mile. Let me explain what I just said with a point of information. This crime was the only one that did not take place in Yard territory, for you see, the City of London has its own designated police force."

"It has been my impression, up until this very moment, of course, that the Yard had been involved in each and every one of the Ripper murders," Evander said.

Doyle asked for Evander's patient indulgence, reassuring him that his question would be answered. But Matthew could not hold himself back. "What my brother really meant to say is perhaps Jack added an extra victim to his roster strictly to inject chaos into the situation by adding a second police force into the case," he said. Dr. Hammond suggested that Jack's would have thrived on creating disorder between two rival forces.

Doyle then encouraged the group to take a walk around the Square. "If you were the Ripper, where would you have conducted your dirty business?" he asked, reminding them that Jack had made it to Mitre Square from Dutfield's Yard and murdered his next victim within a forty-five-minute window of time.

"The Ripper must have been very athletic to cover such a distance and perform his evil deed without being terribly winded," Adelaide said. "Perhaps he took a cab here rather than running, for at least part of the way. It certainly would have been difficult to travel by foot to Mitre Square, find a victim, and then lead her to her demise in less than an hour."

"I doubt that anyone with blood-covered garments would have risked being identified by a carriage driver," Doyle said.

"I seem to have forgotten; how much time did you say elapsed between the two murders, Dr. Doyle?" Dr. Hammond said.

"Approximately three-quarters of an hour."

"Then, Dr. Doyle, Miss Oddie's theory is on a firm ground. Jack must have taken a cab from there to here. After all, it took us about twenty minutes of walking simply to arrive here, and we have not taken any time to hunt down and murder anyone."

"All right, Dr. Hammond. Let us temporarily accept the proposition that Jack took a cab from Dutfield's Yard to Mitre Square. By the next day, would not the driver of that cab come to the harsh realization that he had picked up a passenger who had traveled from one murder site to the other during the hour corresponding to the murders? Don't you believe he would have been morally obligated to make a statement to the police regarding such a passenger?"

Doyle took out his pipe and lit it, allowing himself the luxury of a few short puffs. "However," he continued, "it is possible that the driver might not have remembered such a passenger. Or he may have been illiterate, without the ability to read about the crime in a newspaper. Either way, I find it difficult to believe that Jack would have risked being identified by a cabman. He walked these streets just as we have, and when he reached this spot, he committed his next murder."

"But if the Ripper had taken a cab, he could have been picked up somewhere else along the route, not necessarily at Dutfield's Yard," Dr. Hammond said. "And he could have been dropped off in the vicinity of Mitre Square, but not directly at this location."

"So you are firmly attached to your version of events, Dr. Hammond?" Doyle said.

"I am convinced that directly after the evening's first murder, the killer made his way to his permanent residence, or to the place where he was sojourning, probably in the vicinity of Berner Street. Once inside, he cleaned himself up, returned to the street, and hailed a cab."

"An interesting theory. As a matter of fact, very interesting. So, from what I gather, Jack hailed a cab, climbed into it, and sat down next to the night cabman, where the two of them talked politics and perhaps even picked up a fare along the way, and then, after discharging the patron, Jack asked the driver, whom he knew by name, to take him to Dutfield's Yard so that he could commit his first mutilation. Having completed the initial phase of his agenda, Jack jumped back into his cab seat, where he sat in a bloodied coat and resumed his conversation with the driver while making his way to Mitre Square, where, once again, he got out of his seat, took out his knife, committed a murder, reentered the cab, and had his driver return him to his lodgings. For the cost of a few extra shillings, he also bought the driver's assurance of silence regarding the night's events. By Jove, Dr. Hammond, I think you have solved the mystery in one fell swoop. Congratulations!"

As the group laughed with delight, Doyle went on. "Enough of this disparaging whimsy," he said. "Look around this area and see if you can find the location that would have fit Jack's plan."

Everyone in the group raced off, with the exception of Dr. Hammond, who was trying his best to calm down, having been offended by Doyle's speech. Doyle realized that Hammond hadn't gone into the alley, so he walked up to him, put his hand on his shoulder, and apologized for his faux pas. He ended the short conversation by saying, "You are the most impressive person here, Dr. Hammond. I could see that the group was starting to become a bit intimidated by your fascinating analyses and theories, so I purposely turned things around on them. If I hadn't stripped you of some of your infallibility, you would have lost your ability to walk unencumbered around the square. Everyone would have been clinging to your every move. Now I have given you back your autonomy, so that you will be able to complete an independent investigation of the square. I hope you understand. It would astonish me not at all if you made some brilliant discovery."

Dr. Hammond proudly made his way to the courtyard. After the allotted time had passed, the group reconvened in the middle of the empty square. Doyle asked if any of them could suggest the area that would have been most conducive to Jack's style of attack.

"Over there!" Carrington said, pointing to the church passageway.

"Why there in particular?" Doyle said.

"While I was out reconnoitering, I noticed that the street lamp over there would have provided Jack with sufficient illumination to carve somebody up. It also would have provided a well-lit escape route had someone come upon him."

"Good thought, Mr. Lambton. Anyone else?"

Edgar chose the other passageway. It too had a lamp, as well as easy access to an even larger courtyard at its terminus.

"Also a good choice, and yes, this passageway leads to St. James's Place, where Jack would have had no problem vanishing into the shadows of the night," Doyle said. "Yes, a better-than-good choice, but Jack didn't think so. Dr. Hammond, I always look forward to your analyses. Where would someone with Jack's psychological makeup have chosen to commit the crime?"

"Let me state from the start that neither lighting nor escape routes had any bearing on what he did," Dr. Hammond said. "As a matter of fact, either of these passageways would have worked against the proper execution of his plan. Whether you're a New Yorker or a Londoner, the residents of a neighborhood habitually walk in those areas that are best lit and most accessible. If Jack had chosen either of these two passageways, chances are someone would have stumbled upon a murder in progress. Furthermore, any constable making his rounds would have been able to apprehend a man who had placed himself in the light. So the two choices put forth by Mr. Collins and Mr. Lambton would not have been chosen by Jack. He would have avoided them like the plague. The way I see it, Jack would have operated in an area that was not illuminated, and one that was not in close proximity to any point of egress. Like this area directly to the right of us."

"A capital observation, Dr. Hammond," Doyle said. "Brilliantly calculated. Of all things, the darkest corner in the entire courtyard. No street lamps. No way out. That would be Jack's choice. Let us go there."

As they walked over to this spot, Stephen jotted something down in his notebook. Jack's apparent willingness to run the risk of cornering himself bothered Stephen, and he felt compelled to ask a question. "What would he have done had he been seen by someone?"

All eyes were upon Doyle, but it was Dr. Hammond who fielded the query. "He would have killed him," Dr. Hammond said, "whether the observer was an innocent civilian or a police officer. No qualms about it!"

"Dr. Hammond, you're right," Stephen said, only now understanding the nature of the beast. "You're right. He certainly would have. Not only that, but Jack was akin to a lion on the African savannah: strong enough, bold enough, hungry enough, and wholly devoted to his mission. He was more than willing to fight someone to the death. And when you're willing to fight to the death, you must be prepared for any eventuality."

"Mr. Mitchell," Dr. Hammond said, "while I do agree with your thought process, it doesn't necessarily follow that the Ripper had trained himself for a situation like this one. My years of clinical practice and psychoanalysis have taught me that the propensity to kill exists to a greater or lesser extent in the mind of every human being, without exception. This irrepressible urge is hedonistic, something actuated by the love of pleasure. While most men succeed in keeping this instinct buried, there are those who yield to it—men like the Ripper."

"Good work, both of you," Doyle said, regaining control of his group. "You are really getting to his essence. And I concur with your assessment of the situation. No one was getting in his way. So that we can understand more about him, let us keep things moving. This is where poor Catherine Eddowes met her end. Nothing has changed very much about this part of town in these last twenty years. It is bustling during the day and virtually abandoned by night.

"At 1:30 AM on September 30, 1888, Constable Edward Watkins walked through an empty square, or so he said when questioned. Yet fifteen minutes later, as he was making his second circuit, his lantern happened to cast its light on the body of a mutilated woman sprawled out in this very corner. Watkins ran across to Kearley and Tonge's tea warehouse over there, and finding its door open, immediately notified George Morris, the night watchman, of his discovery. Morris, who happened to be a retired police officer, grabbed his own lantern and accompanied Watkins over to the body. Morris darted out of the square and blew his whistle in the hope that other police officers would come to his aid. In the meantime, Constable Watkins stood guard over the corpse. Within ten minutes, two police constables, James Harvey and James Holland, responded to Morris's call. Harvey went over to the crime scene while Holland knocked on the door of Dr. George Sequeira and summoned him to the scene. When Sequeira looked upon the dead woman, he decided it would be prudent to wait for the police surgeon to show up, rather than perform a less-than-adequate examination—a judicious move for a dermatologist."

Doyle reached into his pocket and carefully unfolded a piece of paper for effect. "I believe that this is the appropriate time to provide you with some of the information contained in the autopsy report that was generated when Dr. Frederick Brown arrived on the scene," he said. "Some of it is quite graphic, but I am sure you will all be able to handle it."

Doyle paused and then began to read descriptions from the report. "The throat was cut across to the extent of about six or seven inches. A superficial cut commenced about an inch and a half below the lobe below, and about two and a half inches below and behind the left ear, and extended across the throat to about three inches below the lobe of the right ear. All the deep structures were severed to the bone, the knife marking intervertebral cartilages. The liver was stabbed as if by the point of a sharp instrument. Below this was another incision into the liver of about two and a half inches, and below this the left lobe of the liver was slit through by a vertical cut. The abdominal walls were divided in the middle line to within a quarter of an inch of the navel. The cut then took a horizontal course for two and a half inches towards the right side. It then divided round the navel on the left side and made a parallel incision to the former horizontal incision, leaving the navel on a tongue of skin."

Adelaide, frightened by what she was hearing, grabbed hold of Carrington, who responded by pulling her in close to his body. Oblivious, Doyle continued reading. "The cut was made by someone on the right side of the body, kneeling below the middle of the body."

There was an eerie silence as Doyle folded up the paper and returned it to his pocket. Carrington released his grip upon Adelaide, allowing her to stand up straight. Now that the formal portion of his presentation was over, Doyle went on with its informal component.

"Both her arms lay at her sides, her palms facing upwards," Doyle said. "There was a thimble next to her right hand. Her bonnet lay at the back of her head, and her intestines were just above her right shoulder. Let me rephrase that a bit. Almost all her intestines were there, except for a two-foot-long segment, which had been excised and placed between her body and her left arm. Not a drop of blood was seen on the anterior, that is, the frontal aspect of her clothing. The killer had cut the victim's eyelids with incredible precision, but for reasons known only to him, her nose, cheeks, and face had been destroyed by the ferocity of his blade. Her right ear was cut so deeply it is possible that Jack had intended to take it home with him. Her left kidney, it seems, was taken home by Jack to serve as his dinner."

"Sir Arthur, what are you implying here? That he ate it like a cannibal?" Edgar said.

"In a few minutes, Mr. Collins, you'll have the opportunity to make your own judgment," Doyle said.

While all of this was going on, Dr. Hammond was busy creating a mental image according to Dr. Brown's post-mortem report. With the end of his cane, he drew some sort of design in the dust and dirt of Mitre Square. All eyes turned to the two cartoonish shapes he had carved into the ground: one a large oval, the other a small circle.

"Everyone, observe—and observe carefully," Dr. Hammond said. "Dr. Doyle, you have certainly presented us with the vivid and gory details of Catherine Eddowes's autopsy. Now let's try to put everything together. This small circle over here represents the victim's head, while the larger one is a simple representation of her body. Correct me if I'm wrong, but the Ripper's incision commenced at xiphoid process, the lowest portion of the breastbone, and continued directly towards her navel."

Dr. Hammond used his cane to illustrate what the Ripper had done with his weapon and then went on with his point. "Jack's blade then made a detour," he said, "a semicircular hook around her navel, and once it had returned to the mid-line, its perpendicular path recommenced, terminating at the pubic bone. The Ripper then lifted his knife and moved it back towards the navel, where he completed the circle around it. His blade continued to cut in a downward and lateral direction towards the poor woman's right hip." He paused for more than ten seconds, giving his audience a chance to digest what he had just described, and then continued by asking, "Are we to believe that in the blackness of this recessed corner the killer was able to leave Mrs. Eddowes's navel suspended on a flap of skin? I ask you, why would someone who sought to maim his victim have slowed himself down by making a circumferential cut around the umbilicus?"

"You're losing me, Dr. Hammond. Why is this of any significance?" Doyle said.

"Because it flies in the face of logic and reason to consider that anyone other than a trained surgeon could possibly have been the perpetrator," Dr. Hammond said. "Such a cut is taught only at medical schools at the cusp of clinical advances. And Brown's report proves it. More than that, what I am suggesting is that this physician had an agenda, an agenda consisting of only two objectives. The first was to open her abdomen, and the second was to remove her organs. This could not have been the Ripper's first venture into abdominal surgery."

"While it is possible that Jack might have had some surgical training, I am hard pressed to grant him a medical degree," Doyle said. "However, I will tell you that the Yard investigated the possibility of a murderous physician right from the start. I recall a story that ran in one of our local newspapers in which a physician-turned-amateur-detective decided to comb the streets of Whitechapel in a one-man search for the Ripper. On a fog-shrouded night, just several days after one of the Ripper killings, he bumped into a woman who was out walking in George's Yard—a location that had been associated with some recent murders, a few of which were being attributed to Jack. The frightened woman screamed murder, and her cry reverberated into all the alleys and streets of the area, generating a large crowd, which soon attacked the doctor. Fortunately for him, the police arrived at the scene quickly enough to rescue him from certain death at the hands of the frenzied mob. He was very happy to be arrested, and a few hours later, he was set free, of course. This is not the only such story of a suspected doctor, in fact.

"Moreover, I can offer a likely explanation for the so-called 'surgical cuts.' Most probably, Mrs. Eddowes had scarring, or abdominal adhesions, covering her bowels. Many of this class of women have histories of multiple miscarriages, multiple pregnancies, and diseases that lead to inflammatory changes in the pelvic area. This was one of those instances. The killer was forced to redirect his dissection. But I do agree with Dr. Hammond's assessment of him as a person absolutely hell-bent on removing her intestines and one of her kidneys. While Dr. Hammond has put forth a plausible argument for a 'Dr. Ripper,' his theory cannot be validated. We must remember that we are in the slaughterhouse district here, and there were many people who were capable of making these incisions. I assure you the Ripper had no intention of surgically closing Mrs. Eddowes's abdomen, so no cuts would have been made for cosmetic purposes."

"Please, Dr. Doyle," Dr. Hammond said. "My argument is more than plausible—it is quite provable. Not only did the Ripper possess surgical expertise, he was also as quick as a flash. The fact that he knew how to perform a ventral nephrectomy, or kidney removal—one of the most difficult operations, particularly at the time—would seem to be strong evidence that he was a trained physician."

"My dear American colleague," Doyle said, "the Ripper may have been many things, but he was not a man of medicine. All we know, and all we need to know, is that he committed unspeakable crimes against humanity. You'll soon see that the Ripper didn't have an iota of surgical skill."

"I don't think so, Dr. Doyle. Cutting off an ear or a nose is one thing. It happens all the time in the taverns of my city. But the removal of intestines and kidneys far exceeds the limits of a simple barroom brawler."

"Dr. Hammond, Jack just ripped and tore at her without any regard for technique."

"What makes you so sure? Maybe taking out someone's intestines doesn't require much training, but locating a kidney, a retroperitoneal organ that is obscured from ready view even when the abdomen is cut open, absolutely requires a good amount of anatomical knowledge, especially if you remove it in the dead of night."

"Dr. Hammond, while I agree with the notion that when one is operating one must be extremely cautious so as not to dissect the wrong artery or the wrong organ, the same rules of engagement do not hold when one is killing somebody. He just dug around until he completed his quest for her kidney."

At this point, Stephen got into the middle of things. "Dr. Doyle, we are allowing ourselves to be diverted from the central question here: Why was this woman's kidney targeted by Jack?"

"I must admit I can offer you no explanation, which only adds another layer of mystery to it all," Doyle said.

"Never mind her kidney," Dr. Hammond said. "What was he doing poking holes in her liver? It's almost as if he wanted to take liver samples home with him. That's quite a bit unusual, even for a mutilator. Now what profession takes hepatic samples on a daily basis?"

Before Dr. Hammond could answer his own question, Doyle put up one finger and said, "I might be able to offer an explanation for that one. Dr. Hammond, would you be kind enough to afford me a moment to take a letter from my pocket?"

Dr. Hammond nodded his head. Doyle reached into his coat pocket, and opened and closed a few letters until he came to the right one. "What I am about to read to you is from a copy of a missive sent to the London Police immediately after the death of Annie Chapman," he said. "Listen to its contents without concentrating on its grammatical errors. See if you detect any reference to why it was the liver that Jack selected to sample."

Doyle read:

Dear Boss,

I keep on hearing the police have caught me but they wont fix me just yet. I have laughed when they look so clever and talk about being on the <u>right</u> track. That joke about Leather Apron gave me real fits. I am down on whores and I shant quit ripping them till I do get buckled. Grand work the last job was. I gave the lady no time to squeal. How can they catch me now. I love my work and want to start again. You will soon hear of me with my funny little games. I saved some of the proper <u>red</u> stuff in a ginger beer bottle over the last job to write with but it went thick like glue and I cant use it. Red ink is fit enough I hope <u>ha. ha</u>. The next job I do I shall clip the ladys ears off and send to the police officers just for jolly wouldn't you. Keep this letter back till I do a bit more work, then give it out straight. My knife's so nice and sharp I want to get to work right away if I get a chance.
        Good Luck.

        Yours truly
        Jack the Ripper

        Dont mind me giving the trade name

        PS Wasnt good enough to post this before I got all the red ink off my hands curse it No luck yet. They say I'm a doctor now. <u>ha ha</u>

Doyle paused and then spoke. "Friends, let us return to my previous question. Is there a relationship between the contents of this letter and the liver samples? Perhaps, Dr. Hammond, you have some thoughts you'd like to share with us?"

Dr. Hammond shook his head, indicating that he was stumped by the question posed by Doyle.

"Nothing for now, Dr. Hammond?" Doyle said. "Then I'll continue. In the letter, Jack writes of his desire to employ Annie Chapman's blood as ink, but says that it had coagulated in a ginger beer bottle before he could make use of it. Perhaps the killer knew that uncooked liver contains lots of fresh blood that takes a long time before it coagulates, making it a suitable substitute for ink."

"Ah! Just like in the case of Burke," Stephen said.

Doyle quickly turned his gaze to Stephen. "Capital!" he said. "For those who do not know the person of whom Mr. Mitchell speaks, back in the 1820s, two men, William Burke and William Hare, were arrested for killing women and selling their bodies to the local medical school for money. They were eventually caught and brought to justice. Although Hare escaped with his life, Burke was publicly executed. After his hanging, his body was brought over to the medical school to be dissected in front of the students. It was there that Professor Alexander Munro dipped his quill into blood that he had drained out of Burke's head and wrote his message."

Doyle chose to remain silent for a second or two, which prompted Adelaide to raise the question on everyone's minds. "What did he write?" she said.

"If I remember correctly," Doyle said, "he wrote, 'This is written with the blood of William Burke, who was hanged at Edinburgh. This blood was taken from his head.' An excellent reference, Mr. Mitchell. But now to change subjects, have any of you noticed potential clues regarding Jack's upbringing in this letter? Are there any unusual phrases that might be found in certain geographic locations? Actually, Dr. Hammond, I am specifically directing this question to you. Are the phrases 'fix me just yet' and 'the right track' familiar terms to you?"

"They don't seem out of the ordinary, Dr. Doyle," Dr. Hammond said.

"Dr. Hammond, in 1888, these phrases were not used by residents of the United Kingdom. I have concluded that Jack was teasing his readers with these Americanisms, and that he had likely spent some time across the pond."

Although Edgar and Matthew were impressed by Doyle's statement, Stephen was not. "Sir Arthur," he said, "I don't share the same impression, I must say. All I heard was a rather disjointed writing style that is so . . . English."

"I beg your pardon?" Doyle said.

"First of all, the great Robert Browning used the expression 'fixed me just yet' in his poetry, and I'm quite certain that he was not an American. And the phrase 'the right track' is certainly of British origin, as we were the ones who introduced the railway. I remember my father using the term 'get buckled' all the time when I was a child, and he had absolutely no American roots of which to speak. As for ginger beer, I believe it is a chiefly British drink." Stephen turned to Dr. Hammond. "Is this correct, Dr. Hammond?"

"I would have to disagree with you. We also drink ginger beer in America," Dr. Hammond said.

"Yes, but was it popular twenty-five years ago?"

"No, it is a new beverage to us Yankees."

"We have had ginger beer here for years, Dr. Hammond. Jack even had a can of it lying around his house in which to store things."

"All I am saying is that Jack is either an American or, at the very least, a man who had spent some time in the States," Doyle said. "Just look at the valediction, 'Yours truly,' at the end of his letter. Americans finalize their letters with those words as an indication to the recipient that they are of the same social status of the writer. This implies that the Ripper regarded himself as the equal of any and all members of the Yard."

"I have to differ with you there, Sir Arthur," Stephen said. "The Ripper had a much higher opinion of himself than that. He used this phrase to indicate that he, the signatory, was higher in social position than they were. Clearly the intention of this letter was to denigrate the efforts of Scotland Yard."

"Let me attempt to put an end to this debate," Doyle said. "All things must be interpreted in their proper contexts. The use of the salutation 'Dear Boss' would tend to negate the second theory and confirm the first because 'boss' is strictly an American term. Do you not agree, Mr. Mitchell?"

"I offer no objections to that."

"The fact that 'Yours truly' and 'Dear Boss' appear in the same letter implies that its author was an American. But let us move on, shall we? The people of Scotland Yard were kind enough to grant me the opportunity to study the original letter in their Black Museum. Upon my analysis of Jack's handwriting, I observed that the missive had been written with a round, easy hand, not unlike that of a clerk, and on very good paper. So we may assume that Jack was accustomed to using a pen and could afford fine stationery. Sadly, after I scrutinized the letter for the Yard, it vanished without a trace and has not been seen since."

Stephen made another entry in his notebook.

"Well, if he was someone who worked with a pen, his marks in syntax must have been quite poor," Adelaide said.

After a few seconds of quiet laughter, Doyle unfolded another letter—one that had been addressed to Mr. Lusk, the chairman of the Mile End Vigilance Committee, also known as the Whitechapel Vigilance Committee, a local neighborhood watch established at the time of the Ripper murders. Before he could begin reading its contents, Stephen had some words of his own.

"I cannot suppress my impulse to discuss what Jack wrote in the last part of this 'Dear Boss' letter, only because it lines up so closely with something you wrote about in one of your stories, Dr. Doyle."

"Which one is that?" Doyle said.

"'The Adventure of the Cardboard Box,' of course."

"Mr. Mitchell, please explain," Doyle said.

"I shall. Your consulting detective tells us of the importance of ears in identifying victims of crime. Ears are so unique in structure that they may help investigators determine the gender and certain hereditary traits of a victim. Your tale has Sherlock Holmes sitting on a bench with Inspector Lestrade and Dr. Watson, examining two severed human ears that had been sent to a Croydon resident. As a result of his examination, he is able to discover and solve a double murder. Jack's horrific statement about amputating ears makes me wonder if the Ripper fell short of one of his goals that night."

"Mr. Mitchell, are you implying that Jack was serious about sending the police her ear?" Carrington said.

Doyle raised his hands. "Rein yourselves in for a moment. First let me read this to you." In a Cockney accent, he recited the letter, saying:

From hell

Mr Lusk
    Sor,
    I send you half the Kidne I took from one women prasarved it
for you tother piece I fried and ate it was very nise I may send you
the bloody knif that took it out if you only wate a whil longer
signed
Catch me when you can Mishter Lusk.

Doyle passed around the facsimile for inspection. Once it had made
its way back, Doyle returned it to his pocket and said, "Does anyone care
to interpret this letter?"

"I guess this is the information you were referring to earlier when
you suggested that Jack might have eaten her kidney. Do you really think
he did?" Evander said.

"There's no way to know for sure," Doyle said. "Please continue with
your analysis."

"Thank you, Sir Arthur. As was the case in his previous letters, there
were lots of spelling errors," Evander said.

"When we read the first letter, no consensus was reached as to
whether Jack was spelling words wrong on purpose." Doyle said. "Any
thoughts now?"

Matthew took over for his brother. "Once again, Jack made multiple
spelling and punctuation errors," he said. "But I do believe there was a
reason for them that I failed to see before."

"And what is that?" Doyle said.

"Jack was attempting to be true to the dialect of the East End,"
Matthew said.

"I am convinced that Jack was trying to conceal his identity," Dr.
Hammond said, taking Matthew's suggestion one step further.

"And how have you arrived at this conclusion?" Doyle said.

"The Ripper does not drop the 'k' at the beginning of the word
'knife,' yet he omits its 'e,' which indicates that he was toying with his
pursuers. Certainly a semiliterate person would have omitted the 'k.' And
certainly the correct spelling of the words 'half' and 'piece' implies that
this man had at least a partial education. The 'h' in 'Mishter' is strange,
unless, as Mr. Stanton suggested, he was imitating a certain pattern of
speech," Dr. Hammond said.

It was the evolution of the phrase "Catch me if you can" to "Catch me when you can" that had captured Stephen's interest, though. He was now convinced that the Ripper was egging on the police, proud in the belief that he was capable of remaining one step ahead of them.

"Interesting theory," Doyle said.

"Then the letter that was written in red ink probably wasn't penned by the Ripper," Evander said.

"Why not?" Doyle said.

"Because the 'Catch me' phrase does not appear in any form."

"Actually, it does. In the body of the letter, Jack asks the question, 'how can they catch me now.'"

"I stand corrected."

"This may be the opportune time to get back to Mr. Collins's query about the etymology of the name 'the Ripper.' Edgar, would you mind starting us off?"

"I have no brilliant thoughts to share with you," Edgar said. "As far as I'm concerned, it is a utilitarian epithet. To put it simply, that is what Jack did. He ripped women apart."

"Is that all?" Doyle said.

"I wouldn't offer such a banal interpretation," Matthew said. "I would think of the centuries-old abbreviation R.I.P., or 'rest in peace,' which we see so often in cemeteries."

Dr. Hammond responded to Matthew's comment with derision. "Isn't the bitter irony here palpable to you?" he said. "Don't you taste the venom? This man was devoid of conscience. He was an avenger who not only punished but also let his victims know through sheer savagery how he felt about those who had wronged him, those who had injured or insulted him. Yes, he might have used the term 'rest in peace,' but it was he who rested in peace as a result of sweet revenge. This is a portrait of a soulless man, a judge without mercy."

After a brief period of silence, Doyle asked if there were any other questions. Evander was still puzzled by the thimble that had been found next to the victim's right hand. Matthew said, "Either she was out here in a pitch-dark alley sewing while she was plying her trade, or this sewing implement has to have been some sort of clue deliberately placed for the police to find. The latter explanation seems most likely."

Doyle assumed that the appearance of the thimble was pure happenstance, but Stephen disagreed. He was convinced that the killer had purposely planted it for the police to find.

"There were many ideas put forth at the time in regard to Jack leaving clues deliberately," Doyle said. "In fact, one of my fellow members of the Crimes Club, Arthur Diosy, thought the locations of the murders were themselves clues. He claimed that the spots on which the killings took place formed a pentagram, or five-pointed star, when pointed out on a map and connected appropriately. Knowing that the pentagram is a symbol of black magic, Diosy conjectured that the murders had something to do with this practice, and that perhaps the killer was trying to concoct the fabled 'elixir of life,' a potion that could grant eternal life and youth, using the blood of his victims. As you can imagine, when he approached the Yard with his hypothesis, it did not receive the enthusiasm he had anticipated. It was summarily rejected as nonsensical. As for the thimble, considering the industries in this area, it had probably been lying on the ground for some time before the murder. Anyone else with any questions about what we have heard so far?"

"By the way, who was this Lusk?" Adelaide said.

"Just a local builder who also oversaw the area's vigilance committee," Doyle said. "He was a curious fellow, so when he opened the cardboard box that had been addressed to him and saw some flesh-like substance, he thought he might be the unsuspecting victim of a practical joke. He decided to bring it over to a local physician's office, and although the doctor was not in, his assistant was. He told him that it was human tissue, which prompted Lusk to bring it over to Dr. Thomas Openshaw, the pathological curator of the London Hospital Museum. He identified the tissue as a three-week-old piece of human kidney that belonged to a woman of approximately forty-five years of age, parenthetically adding that she had been suffering from Bright's disease."

"Pardon my ignorance, but Bright's disease—what is that?" Matthew said.

"It's an untreatable destructive kidney ailment in which the organ atrophies, or shrinks, and loses its ability to function. It can be a consequence of the lifestyle many of the women of this area are forced to adopt in order to survive," Doyle said.

"If we agree that the Ripper was after the kidney of Mrs. Eddowes," Dr. Hammond said, "is it possible that he knew of her affliction and targeted her because of it?"

Before Doyle could answer, Carrington chimed in. "How could he have possibly known that?" he said.

"He could have known, if she had told him," Dr. Hammond said.

Doyle coughed to gain the group's attention and put the focus back on himself. "The kidney in the cardboard box confirms two things: that the letter writer was the Ripper himself, and that financial gain was not part of his agenda," he said.

"What would financial gain have to do with this?" Carrington said.

"Although most of you are too young to remember it, twenty-five years ago, the going price for organ specimens was twenty pounds, and there were many researchers who could not wait to get their hands on these black market items. Just four days before Mrs. Eddowes was slain, the *Times* published an article reporting that the curator of the London Museum was being contacted often by many of these so called 'collectors.' This sensational revelation convinced a large segment of the public that Jack was one of these 'body snatchers.' But when he sent the half kidney to Lusk, he showed that money was not his motivation. It was the Ripper's refutation of those journalists who had written that financial gain must have been the underlying reason for his crime spree. The Ripper may have regarded this as an insult."

"Are you implying that this diabolical creature wanted the world to know he was not merely a selfish opportunist?" Dr. Hammond said.

"I would say that he perceived himself as the polar opposite: an altruistic disseminator of truth and virtue, the savior of a contaminated world," Doyle said.

"And what would this redeemer have looked like?" Evander said.

Carrington commented that this wasn't such an impossible question to answer, recalling that someone had furnished a description of Jack to the police at the time that had been taken quite seriously. From what he remembered, the killer had been described as having a shabby appearance and a small mustache, and as being approximately thirty years of age, five feet eight inches tall, of medium build, and of fair complexion. But Carrington had been more impressed by the description of the killer's clothing, which included a red neckerchief and a cap with a peak. Carrington also recalled Jack being depicted as a sailor type and asked Doyle if he could shed any light on the matter.

"You are bringing back some memories, Mr. Lambton," Doyle said. "Our friend Mr. Lambton is referring to a statement given to police by

Mr. Joseph Lawende, who had been out carousing that night with his drinking buddies at the Imperial Club only minutes before the tragic death of this poor woman. Mr. Lawende's dedication to detail conflicts with what the other two revelers had been able to offer the police, namely nothing. So this is more likely a tale told by an idiot, signifying nothing, a mere fabrication of an inebriated brain."

"But Dr. Doyle, there was no indication that Mr. Lawende was anything but sober when he told the Yard his story," Carrington said. "And his two friends were also sober when questioned. It was pure intuition that had told them that the man and woman they had come upon that night were up to no good, and this intuition had caused them to follow one of Whitechapel's laws of survival, which is to avoid eye contact with anyone who might interpret such an action unfavorably."

"Lawende's tale is not worth a tinker's curse," Doyle said. "These three bon vivants had plenty of time to sober up before giving their reports to the police, so there would have been no telltale signs of what they had been up to that evening. Is it not bizarre that the same man who was able to give such an eagle-eyed report of what he had seen, down to a red neckerchief, stated at the inquest he would no longer be able to identify the assailant even if he were to be placed in the same room? Ripper sightings were not unusual at the time, but they were usually figments of people's imaginations. Remember, London was plastered with reward signs, and anyone who could furnish information leading to the Ripper's capture was sure to inherit a king's ransom. It is poppycock to believe this description accurate."

"Actually, I don't think it all that difficult to believe," Stephen said, "when one considers the handful of other supposed Ripper sightings that were reported over the course of his reign of terror. Many of these potential witnesses described a man of approximately five feet eight inches tall, wearing a salt and pepper jacket or a navy pea coat, and sporting a dark cloth cap with a peak, sometimes characterized as a deerstalker cap or a sailor's cap. These depictions are all in keeping with Lawende's testimony, are they not?"

Before Doyle could voice his disagreement, Edgar, anxious to share a piece of information with the group, interrupted the conversation and stated that Catherine Eddowes had actually known the identity of the man who had brought Whitechapel to a fearful standstill. Apparently, twenty years earlier, when Edgar was just a young school boy, his father told him that Catherine Eddowes had been aware of the Ripper's real name, and that she had claimed as much to several others. Edgar had no precise idea of how his father had managed to obtain this information, but it had stayed with Edgar all this time. His father's words were so few and far between that they tended to stick.

Doyle acknowledged Edgar's statement. "I appreciate your devotion," he said. "I also hung on every word my father uttered. Quiet men tend to be misunderstood and oftentimes their greatness goes unappreciated. What your father referenced came off the presses of the *East London Observer*, although the story has never been substantiated. Nevertheless, the publication suffered no qualms about creating a fake 'exclusive,' which soon turned out to be a boon to the paper's circulation. Although I hadn't planned on mentioning this 'friendship' between Mrs. Eddowes and Jack, in retrospect, I think it is worthy of discussion. On the night of her murder, Catherine purportedly informed the superintendent of the casual ward at Mile End that she knew the identity of Jack the Ripper, and that she was going out to claim 'her' reward. The mammoth prize of several hundred pounds had everyone hoping to lay claim to it. Now I must ask you, if you knew the identity of the most brutal killer in the annals of the British Empire, what would be your next step?"

"If we are to assume that Catherine Eddowes knew the identity of the murderer, she may have been about to rendezvous with him in order to blackmail him," Stephen said. "But she would have had to make sure that she had an infallible bargaining chip when she met up with him."

"And what kind of bargaining chip could that have been?" Doyle said.

"If it had been me," Stephen said, "I would have created a signed and sealed document stating the Ripper's name and address. I would then hand over a copy of this letter to the Ripper, telling him that the original was in the hands of my solicitor, to be released to the police in the event of my death or disappearance. By taking these preemptive steps, I would be guaranteeing my future and my safety, along with a large down payment from the Ripper and a substantial monthly fee thereafter."

"Ah! Extortion par excellence, Mr. Mitchell," Doyle said. "Shades of Jekyll and Hyde! So, what you have so eloquently described to us is how Catherine Eddowes could have easily granted herself a lifelong endowment from the Ripper. Unfortunately for her, the fact that she was killed allows us to assume no such plan. Any other suggestions?"

"I would have informed the police that I had a planned tryst with the killer," Edgar said, "and would have made it a precondition that they write up a binding notarized contract naming me as the sole recipient of the reward money and guaranteeing that my identity would be held in perpetual anonymity."

"Very good," Doyle said. "So the police would have been there that night, waiting in the shadows to reel in Jack. As some of you may recall, Mrs. Eddowes would have had sufficient time to lay a trap for Jack while in police custody that night facing charges of public inebriation. The precinct's records specifically indicate that Mrs. Eddowes had reached a satisfactory state of sobriety prior to her release, after which, only moments later, she met her untimely demise."

"If the police's version of events is correct," Stephen said, "she would have been sober enough to tell the police to follow her. As she failed to do this, it can be further inferred that she had no idea who the Ripper was."

Doyle then gave a summary of Mrs. Eddowes's time in police custody. "The press reported that Mrs. Eddowes had been in a rush upon leaving the Bow Street Police Station, as if she were off to meet someone. Not only that, but she had also been adamant in her refusal to leave the station until she had been told the exact time. Constable Hutt had been on duty that night and had told her that it was too late at night for her to acquire any spirits, assuming her mind was on the procurement of alcohol. This failed to satisfy her. Once Hutt told her that it was precisely 1 AM, she told him she was surely going to receive a hiding from an unnamed person when she got home. Upon exiting the station, instead of heading in the direction of her home, she walked hastily towards Houndsditch. This incident is, in all probability, the source of the myth that she knew the Ripper's identity."

"Perhaps she did have a meeting with Jack," Edgar said, "but was too unwise to take the proper precautions."

"If so, what evidence here in Mitre Square would discredit this version of things?" Doyle said.

"Once again, the killing took place in the least accessible and darkest corner of the court yard," Carrington said, "and if Mrs. Eddowes had arranged a meeting with a man she knew to be the Ripper, she would not have chosen to do business in such a spot."

"Perhaps she just wasn't very bright," Adelaide said. "Or she was willing to take a chance. After all, none of us here today can ever determine what Catherine Eddowes knew or did not know about Jack. Life is a mystery, and there is nothing like suspense to make you appreciate it."

"Miss Oddie, I could not have said it better myself," Doyle said. "You are wise beyond your years. But the hour is getting late, and we still have a couple more places to visit."

11

1881

Becoming Doctor Doyle

March 1881

Once Arthur had returned from the Arctic, he received a telegram from George Budd asking him to visit his Bristol practice. Budd wished to see Doyle urgently, as he was in need of advice. Budd had gone to Bristol with the aim of resurrecting the practice that had belonged to his late father, William. He and his young wife made sure to rent the very home in which his father had lived prior to his death in 1880. Budd, however, had made a serious miscalculation, not realizing that his father's patients had transferred to other physicians during the seven years in which his father had lain ill. George Budd's ill-fated attempt to reestablish the practice had left him with a debt of £700 and a considerable amount of anger.

When Doyle first arrived in Bristol, Budd seemed too busy to talk to him, being involved in the supervision of his wife, who was mixing the "potions" with which Budd would treat his patients and, he hoped, make some money. Doyle finally cornered Budd and noticed the "queer stops, the sudden confidential whispers, the roar with which he triumphantly answered his own questions, the shrugs and slaps and gesticulations," but received not one "word all the time as to what it was that made him send [Doyle] that urgent wire which brought" his old schoolmate 100 miles to England's southwest coast.

Budd soon invited Doyle to dinner at his impressive house on a curving quiet avenue. Even though Doyle was greeted by a "footman with plush red knee-breeches," the evening seemed odd. Mrs. Budd seemed weary. Budd began acting strangely, looking around to see if anybody was "eavesdropping or conspiring against him." Doyle would attribute Budd's "brusqueness and frankness" to a "strange vein of suspicion" that "[ran] through his singular and complex nature." Budd finally convinced himself that there were no spies around and "threw himself down into his armchair."

After dinner, the two young men made their way to the smoking room, where they lit their pipes. Budd peered under the couches and chairs, scrutinized the pictures on the walls, and looked through the keyhole to make certain that no one would overhear what was about to be said. When he was satisfied that the room was secure, he poked Doyle with his pipe and said, "What I wanted to tell you is, that I am utterly, hopelessly, and irretrievably ruined." According to *The Stark Munro Letters,* Budd then provided Doyle with a better understanding of why he had been called to Bristol, saying that he would be "done for . . . unless some friend were to lend [him] his name on a bit of stamped paper." Doyle told Budd the hard truth, that he had no money at all, having given it to his mother upon his return from the *Hope* voyage. Hearing this news, Budd turned on him, saying, "Besides, as you have nothing and no prospects, what earthly use would YOUR name on a paper be?" Doyle told himself that if Budd had asked for the money a few months earlier, he might have been able to help, thinking, "What on earth could I do when affairs were in such a tangle?" Nevertheless, Doyle would write, "I could not help feeling complimented when so independent a fellow . . . turned to me in this way."

Doyle advised Budd to "call his creditors together" so they could see that Budd was "young and energetic" and "sure to succeed sooner or later." Budd disclosed that he was already considering such an idea, thanked Doyle for the advice, and then began drinking, his mood lifting shortly thereafter. After many drinks, Budd confessed that he was in need of some exercise and went over to a cupboard to fetch two pairs of boxing gloves. He "proposed that [they] should fight a round or two then and there." Doyle knew that he should not engage in fisticuffs, but the challenge was irresistible. He would later write, "The moment I looked him in the face I smelled mischief. He had a gleam of settled malice in his eye. I believe it was my refusal to back his paper which was running in his head. Anyway he looked as dangerous as he could look, with his scowling face sunk forward a little. . . ." As the bout began, Budd rushed Doyle, hitting him twice in the ear and declaring, "Say when you've had enough. . . ."

Doyle knew that he was the better boxer and soon proved it by clocking Budd in the nose and jaw and laying him flat across his own hearthrug. Budd got up in an instant, looking like a madman. Budd then commanded Doyle to take off his gloves and put his hands up. When Doyle refused, Budd became "mad with passion, and chucked his gloves under the table." Doyle tried to be the peacemaker, telling his opponent to have a glass of soda water. In the meantime, Budd's wife walked in and screamed when she saw what had befallen her husband. She demanded to know what had happened. Doyle said, "We've only been having a little spar. . . . Your husband was complaining that he never got any exercise." With the fight over, a calm came over the room and Budd invited Doyle to light up his pipe and join him in a chat.

April 1881

By the spring of 1881, Doyle was desperate to complete his medical studies on time. Although he had been adequately compensated for his position on the whaling vessel, he was now left with only "4 pounds/10," which made it virtually impossible for him to register for classes, let alone take his examinations. He contacted his mother, writing that they "must manage to save up the fees by hook or by crook." He neglected, however, to tell his mother that he was still a few credits short of being eligible to appear for his written and oral exams. Although his two stints at Dr. Hoare's had been granted accreditation by the University of Edinburgh, owing to Dr. Hoare having been recognized as one of Great Britain's elite physicians, his months aboard the *Hope* had not.

After Mary Doyle managed to come up with the funds Arthur needed to register for his oral and written examinations, it seems as though Arthur might have gained access to his school transcript, as it now appears altered in several places. When compared with historical record, the transcript seems to contain false dates, courses Doyle never took, and teachers Doyle never had. Doyle's stints at Dr. Hoare's practice also look to have been multiplied. The transcript reads that between 1877 and 1878, and 1878 and 1879, Doyle worked at Dr. Hoare's "outdoor dispensary practice." It also lists two years of practical midwifery with Dr. Hoare between 1878 and 1880, and twenty cases between 1880 and 1881. His letters home, however, contradict these dates. According to Doyle's own writings, he first met Dr. Reginald Hoare in the summer of 1879, two years later than his official transcript reports. In addition, his academic records from 1880 to 1881 seem to place him in two distant locations at once—Edinburgh's Royal Public Dispensary and Vaccine Institution under the supervision of Dr. William Husband for six weeks and Dr. Reginald Hoare's Birmingham dispensary. In contrast, his

UNIVERSITY OF EDINBURGH.

MEDICAL DEGREES.

FINAL MEDICAL EXAMINATION.

Candidate's Name in full Arthur Conan Doyle.

Date of Examination Summer 1881.

Birthplace.	Date of Birth.	Edinburgh Address.	Permanent Address.
Edinburgh.	May 22nd /59.	15 Lonsdale Terrace.	

PRELIMINARY EXAMINATION.

Board or Boards at which Preliminary Examination passed, or Degree in Arts and University, as the case may be.	Date or Dates of Examination, or of Degree in Arts.	Preliminary Subjects Passed.
London matric 1875.		Greek - Latin - French - Mathematics Euclid - Practical Philosophy - English Chemistry

COURSE OF STUDY.

See Directions, Page 4.

Class.	No. of Lectures in the Course.	Date of the Course.	Teacher's Name.	Name of University.	Name of Medical School.	Fee Paid to Extra-Academical Teacher in Edinburgh.
Botany	50.	76-77	Prof Balfour.	Edinburgh		

Doyle's Transcript

Doyle's school transcript shows dates that seem to have been altered, including the year of his birth and that of his matriculation examination, as noted above. By appearing one year older, Doyle would have become eligible to receive the prestigious doctor of medicine degree at the age of twenty-four instead of the mandatory age of twenty-five.

letters home during this time make no mention of him being in Edinburgh for six weeks. Despite the fact that Doyle was frightfully behind in his studies, his transcript belied this unpleasant reality.

Perhaps the biggest oddity in regard to Arthur's records is his date of birth, which is listed as "May 22nd/58," although his actual birth year is a year later. Coincidentally, a declaration signed by medical degree candidate Arthur Conan Doyle on April 22, 1881, seems to have been changed from "I Arthur Conan Doyle, hereby declare that the preceding statement is a true account of my Medical Education, &c., that I was born at Edinburgh on the 22nd day of May 1859 . . ." to ". . . that I was born at Edinburgh on the 22nd day of May 1858. . . ." It is unlikely that Doyle would have made such an innocent error on two occasions. Why Arthur would have wanted to age himself by one year is uncertain, but the prestigious doctor of medicine degree, which was available only to those who had reached their twenty-fifth birthday, may have been on his mind. Being a year older would grant him the opportunity to acquire this advanced degree one year earlier, which would allow him to command the higher fees associated with this degree sooner. Interestingly, Doyle's transcript fails to mention his studies at Stella Matutina, instead adding an extra year to his time at Stonyhurst. To coincide with this timeline, the date of his London University Matriculation Examination seems also to have been altered by one year. Whatever the reason for these discrepancies, Doyle's transcript makes it very difficult to pin down the true chronology of events.

Doyle took his written examinations in May of 1881, which, according to him, "were good fair papers." His written examination required him to compose an essay describing "a case of Acute General Peritonitis—its causes—its treatment." This task was reminiscent of his experience with the ill-fated seaman Andrew Milne while aboard the *Hope*. One month later, Doyle was assigned his "inquisitors" for his oral exams. They were Dr. Arthur R. Duffin in medicine, Dr. Alexander Keiller in midwifery, and Dr. James Spence in surgery. The diminutive Duffin proceeded to give him "a fearful raking over" the coals. Even when Doyle managed to come up with the correct response to one of his esoteric questions, Duffin tossed something even more difficult at him. Eventually, Arthur was forced to "confess" that he was totally bewildered by his evaluator's request for a more elegant test than the mere utilization of heat or acid to quantify albumen. Just when Doyle thought things could not get any worse, Duffin asked him to "put up the apparatus for the German yeast test for sugar. . . ." Thankfully, the bell rang, so Doyle "picked his pockets of some small change and shoved for home." Not only did the "malignant little scarecrow," as Doyle described Duffin, provide Arthur with some welcome vacation money, he also provided him with a "B" on the exam.

On June 11, Doyle met with Dr. James Spence for his oral exam in surgery. This great master of anatomy proved an even tougher examiner than Dr. Duffin. Before asking Doyle a single question, "Dismal Jimmy," as he had come to be known by his students, caught Arthur off guard by declaring that careful preparation and meticulous dissection were far more important than mere carbolic acid in bringing about a successful surgical outcome. This comment was an allusion to former department chairman Dr. Lister's theory of antisepsis, which involves using chemicals to kill disease-causing germs. Dr. Spence even boasted that Dr. Lister had acknowledged as much both in print and in front of all his peers when he had stated, "Spence's results are at least as good as mine." If Doyle were to have any chance at a passing grade, he would have to stifle his devotion to Lister in the face of this seventy-year-old man who resembled "three kicks in a mud wall."

Spence hurled a barrage of test cases at Doyle: ankle dislocations, tibial fractures, femoral artery wounds, the management of quinsy, and the treatment of eczema. At first Doyle was able to ward off these salvos with prompt and accurate answers, but the dour-faced interrogator would not be denied. "With his hat bashed over his left eye" he pranced towards Arthur with a total unwillingness to grant a ceasefire. Doyle was brought over to a "master tray" overflowing with forceps, curved knives, and all types of scoops and probes, and was ordered to construct a lithotomy kit that would contain only those instruments most essential to the removal of kidney stones. When Arthur laid out his tray with speed and finesse, Spence accused him of failing to provide the kit with a crucial artery forceps, adding derisively, "Well, why didn't you put one out—D'ye call that Surgery?" Doyle remained calm, responding, "I didn't lay it out, sir, because you forgot to put one in the tray." Dr. Spence would end up leaving a note of "less than satisfactory" on Arthur's transcript.

According to Arthur, he breezed through his oral examination in obstetrics and gynecology, areas of study still considered part of the practice of midwifery at the time. Thirty years prior to Arthur's enrollment, the University of Edinburgh had emerged as the world leader in the care of women before, during, and immediately after childbirth. It had been one of their own, Dr. James Young Simpson, who had guided the department to its position on the world stage. His use of chloroform as an anesthetic agent, his unique designs of surgical equipment used to deliver babies, and his adoption of hand-washing between deliveries combined to produce a drastic reduction in the mortality rate that had accompanied urban midwifery for years. The physicians of the Edinburgh were at the vanguard of a field that was rapidly emerging from centuries of ignorance and superstition, and was now grounding itself on a firm scientific and technical foundation. Doyle was keenly aware that achieving honors in such a crucial subject would only serve to make him a highly sought-after physician when the time came to establish a private practice. Ultimately, Dr. Keiller was only willing to place a grade of "S+," meaning less than good, although Arthur would describe his results slightly differently in a letter to Dr. Hoare, writing, "In Midwifery I took honours in my oral." Dr. Hoare must have been very proud to know that he had done such a good job preparing his disciple.

Arthur was now able to graduate, secure in the knowledge that he would soon be allowed to practice medicine and surgery anywhere in the British Empire. With this in mind, Arthur embarked on a mission essential to anyone who sought to build a thriving practice. He remembered something George Budd had told him: A suitable spouse was imperative to success. Unmarried physicians were at a distinct disadvantage in the competitive world of medicine, as bachelors were regarded as less stable and less dependable than married men. A young woman with an appreciable dowry, social graces, and decent looks would be quite helpful to a penniless new practitioner.

July 1881

Having just completed his examinations and with nothing much to do prior to his official graduation in August, Doyle set out to find himself a mate. He could think of no better place to look than Ireland, the "old family sod," especially since he had no wifely prospects in Scotland or England. The first part of his agenda included boarding the Zephyr, a new high-speed train that ran from Edinburgh to Liverpool. From there he boarded a steamer and sailed southwest on the Irish Sea with the intention of traveling to Ireland's first city, Waterford. When Arthur discovered that the ship had scheduled a six-hour layover in Dublin, he decided to pay a visit to Dr. Muggins, who had served with him as a fellow assistant to Dr. Hoare. After recounting the good old days with his old companion, he got back on board the boat and completed the journey to his destination.

From Waterford, he traveled by rail to the village of Lismore. When he disembarked from the train, he was greeted by the unexpectedly delightful sight of two liverymen, who ushered him onto a stunning carriage that displayed the Foley crest and its motto "Ut possum," which translates to "I can do that." Arthur was imbued with a renewed sense of pride, which had sprung from his mother's side of the family. He sat back in his well-upholstered seat and breathed in the delicious country air. Eventually he was transported down a private road five miles long, which led to the sprawling, 160-acre estate of Ballygally. This 300-year-old stone house had remained in the hands of the Foley clan since the very year it had been erected, and although the local government, through the two-year-old Fenian Land League movement, had recently seized more than 1,000 acres from the Foleys, the land that remained in the family's possession was teeming with rabbits, ducks, and water-hens, while the Blackwater River that flowed through it was the best river in all of Ireland for salmon fishing. The fact that the Foleys had the sole rights to its use insured their financial stability, as the angling fees collected for fishing with rod and reel on Foley-owned property brought in more than £1,000 each year.

It was Mary Doyle's first cousin Nelson Trafalgar Foley who provided the connection to Ballygally, but he had died three years before, and now his seven children, Arthur's second cousins, owned and ran the estate. Although the three brothers—Dick, Thomas, and Ned—and four sisters—Elizabeth, Mary, Alice, and Letitia—lived there, it was Dick alone who had been designated the official owner of the place in Nelson's will, and so Dick had become the manager of the manor. Doyle remained focused on his mission to find a wife, but it had never entered his mind until now that one of his cousins might fit the bill. He immediately began to analyze his chances of successfully wooing one of the distaff side of the clan, but his attempts to impress these ladies with his Scottish charm, wit, and intellect fell flat. At least he was able to find some relief from his social ineptitude when his cousin Ned invited him to play cricket for the Lismore team. At one match, Arthur found his eye wandering towards a pretty lady who was watching the action. He performed terribly both on and off the field, and when he asked the lovely spectator to join him for dinner, not only did she rebuff his advance, she also added insult to injury by proceeding to walk off alone.

Nevertheless, Doyle's obvious skill in outdoor activities impressed his relatives, especially his marksmanship in bringing wild ducks and geese down from the sky. Equally impressive was his talent to reel in fish from the Blackwater as if his rod were magnetized. But what most amazed his Irish kin was Doyle's ability to make his way through the property's labyrinthine unmarked areas. No one had ever been able to weave through the thickets and bushes and streams with such uncanny speed and instinct. The cousins wanted to make sure that each and every member of the Foley clan would have the opportunity to meet this "pathfinder." As Doyle would relate in one of his letters, "I find I am related to half the county."

During his stay, Arthur accompanied his cousins Dick and Ned to a Fenian League meeting, where they protested the actions of this anti-landholder, pro-tenant organization. Dick bravely, or crazily, "[i]nformed the president that he wished the whole league had one neck and he had his foot on it." Doyle's writings underline the fact that Dick "was not forcibly rejected," although Arthur would also tauntingly state, "I wish they would try some of their midnight business on us." Just a day or two later, after a night of dining and drinking "with another cousin four miles off," Doyle may have purposely made a late return to the manor house in order to perpetrate another one of his pranks. The place was supposedly locked up and Doyle had assumed that "everybody had gone to bed." In a letter to Amy Hoare, Doyle would write, "I slouched round the building not liking to knock them up, and at last—you know the habits of the beast, I shinnied up a waterpipe, found a window unfastened, and after some fumbling opened it, and tumbled in." The mildly inebriated Arthur decided to play a trick on his cousin Dick, pretending to be a member of the Fenian Land League who had come around to teach him "a lesson" for his ongoing disloyalty to its cause. But it was Doyle who was to pay the price for his antics. He received a "rapturous reception from Dick," one that Arthur felt was "rather too rapturous." Dick "sprang at [Doyle] with a double barreled gun in his hand, and would have put a charge of No. 12 through [his] head in another moment if [Doyle] hadn't mildly pointed out the inhospitality of such an action."

A very short time later, Doyle was still hoping to get into a fight with the Fenians. There was a perceived threat that the Land League was going to stage a boycott of the Cork Cattle Show. Although the Foleys "never intended to exhibit" there, Doyle tried his best to stir up his cousins, and succeeded with Ned, who "swore a priestly oath that he would take down the most mangy cow he had, and exhibit that cow." Doyle's writings depict his yearning for a tussle, as he states:

> Dick and I fostered the idea that if they persist in boycotting the show, we intend not to throw ourselves upon police or soldiers for protection, but simply to go down the three of us, armed to the teeth, and dare any man to lay a finger on the cow—I think my cousins will be as good as their word, and I know that I wouldn't like to miss the fun.

Evidently, the newly credentialed doctor from Scotland was risking time in jail and the possibility of having more family land confiscated by the Fenians simply to scratch his itch for a fight.

When it came to engaging the opposite sex, Doyle was doing poorly. An indication of how poorly may be seen in a letter to Amy Hoare in which Doyle describes a nineteen-year-old "young lady visitor" from Dublin's Trinity College who was first in her class in a very difficult program. Despite this fact, he characterizes her as "such an addle-headed womanly fool" and berates her every like and dislike. He finishes the letter by saying, "you never saw such an educated cabbage in your life." In what appears to be a case of severe sour grapes, he tells Dr. Hoare's wife, "You see, I am not getting limp, as the 'Doctor' used to say, over that girl."

Up to this point, Doyle's reconnaissance mission in the land of his ancestors had been a complete bust, but he remained determined to find himself an Irish belle. Having been told about a "fancy fair and rose show" that was guaranteed to attract the local ladies, he gladly joined his cousins at this fundraiser, which had been designed to raise money in the name of a recently deceased local philanthropist, Mrs. Welsted. It was there at Ballyin Gardens that he was introduced to "Miss Elmore Weldon of Belview." Although Miss Weldon may not have been a stunning beauty, she was alluring, especially in light of the fact that her family was well enough financially to rent a home from the Foleys during the busiest time of the season. Arthur made arrangements to rendezvous with Elmore at Monoman, her summer residence, a few miles east. He arranged for the liverymen to drive him over, and when he laid eyes on her this time, he felt that she was beyond "striking." As Arthur would relate to Amy Hoare, he had been swept away by a goddess and "By Jove! Such a beauty!" Doyle would also relate some gossip to Amy, saying that the two of them had "been flirting hard for a week or so and that things [were] about ripe." And yet, when not in Elmore's presence, Arthur still set his sights on other girls, but was rejected. By process of elimination, perhaps, Elmore, whom he would call Elmo, soon became his one and only. Upon leaving Lismore, Arthur had Elmore's picture in his bag, and he promised her that the two of them would soon meet again.

Once on the ferry home, Doyle had to face the reality that with graduation only a few days away, he had not received a favorable response to any of his job applications. The grim prospect of unemployment was reinforced when he arrived at his mother's new upscale Lonsdale address, at which point she told him there was no news to report on the job front. It was at this time that he took Elmo's picture and introduced "the fair maiden" to his mother. When Mary Doyle cast her eyes on the "splendid, well-developed firmly set lower jaw" and "a delicately molded chin" that was almost "masculine in its force," she became concerned with Arthur's choice for his potential bride, although she must have thought it wise to keep her thoughts to herself.

August 1881

Despite his lack of funds and his uncredited time spent aboard the *Hope*, Doyle managed to pull off the Herculean task of graduating with his entering class, and for once his mother was there with him at an occasion of importance. Although Doyle left no written record of the thoughts he must have had about his father's plight back at Blairerno, his perception of his mother and her lineage was clear. He regarded his ability to survive in hostile surroundings as attributable to the superior genealogy and intellect provided him by the Foley clan. After five years as a medical student, he was now concerned with making himself and his mother wealthy, influential, and properly respected members of high society.

As mother and son walked down the streets of the Old Town, their attention was drawn to the district's most prominent landmark, the graceful spire that stood atop the United Presbyterian Theological College. On this date, the first day of August, this building would be the graduation site of the University of Edinburgh Medical School class of 1881. The hall, which had a capacity of 2,500 souls, was already crowded to excess when the two arrived. Doyle and his mother managed to squeeze into this suffocating sardine can, but there were more than several disappointed ticket holders who were unable to gain entry to the festivities. Arthur separated from his mother and took his place alongside his fellow students in the front. He placed his black mantle over his suit and then donned his crimson hood bordered with white fur, which indicated that he would be receiving the MB and CM degrees, becoming a bachelor of medicine and master of surgery. Although most of the graduates wore academic costumes identical to his, there was a small minority of students in hoods of green or purple. These students would be receiving either a doctor of science degree or a doctor of divinity degree, with green signifying the former distinction and purple the latter.

Just after 10 AM, the university's chancellor, John Inglis, entered the majestic room, followed closely by the senatus academicus, which comprised the principal, vice chancellor, and the departmental deans. There was a silence as the front row of the auditorium filled with an impressive array of grey-haired professors and distinguished members of Edinburgh's literati. Doyle, his face aglow with hope and ambition, stood quietly with his classmates as Professor Wallace gave the invocation. Once the signal had been given for everyone to take their seats, Professor Annandale stood at the podium and offered an hour's worth of "a few introductory remarks" before calling the students up to receive their diplomas.

The first to be invited to the stage were those who were being awarded their MB and CM degrees with first and second honors. Altogether there were but thirteen of them, nine belonging to second honors, and four who were the year's stellar performers, a quartet of first honorees. The members of the faculty beamed with pride as the elite new physicians of the world passed in front of them to be capped by the chancellor himself. The remaining students were then given their turns to have Inglis "magically place" the venerable black velvet caps onto their heads. Unlike the first group, this assemblage was led through the ceremony quickly. Then, in what appeared to the audience to be a spontaneous event, the newly crowned physicians jumped up from their seats and burst into a song written by Professor MacLagan—an ode humorously dedicated to the celebrated chancellor:

> I'm passed, I'm passed,
> And capped at last
> I'm qualified and free now,
> on pasteboard neat,
> or brass door plate,
> To write myself MB now.

The paean went on and on for what seemed to be thousands of verses, but eventually things quieted down and the academic prizes were announced, with the coveted Eccles Prize, which was "awarded to the graduate who [had] distinguished himself most highly in all of the professional examination," going to Barclay Baron, and the Beaney Prize going to David Hepburn for his outstanding "proficiency in Anatomy, Surgery, and Clinical Surgery." Professor Annandale's valedictory followed, addressing the problem of medical quackery. The speech commenced with a reference to homeopathy, a method of practicing medicine that differed in many aspects from the allopathic or mainstream, methodology taught at Edinburgh. While Annandale made no derogatory remarks about those who were strict adherents to homeopathy's controversial central theory, which states that using highly diluted remedies allows the body

Licensed to Kill

While receiving a medical degree was a serious achievement for most, Doyle reveals a macabre sense of humor in a sketch of himself receiving his diploma.

to learn to heal itself, he was not nearly as kind to those who insisted on mixing homeopathy with mainstream medicine. Professor Annandale was harshest on the followers of the school's recently deceased professor of chemistry, Dr. William Gregory, who promoted suggestion and hypnotism in all therapeutic regimens. Annandale judged these mesmerists, as such practitioners were called, to be untrue to both their patients and themselves, and in strong words stated that he had no use whatsoever for these members of the profession. Annandale's concluding remarks were devoted to the tenets he had determined to be essential to the proper conduct of a medical practice:

> You are not to believe that you are fully equipped with all knowledge. You are to never stop learning the practical parts of your profession. You are not to consider that you have any vested interest in your patients. You are to expect proper remuneration from your patients for your services unless the patient is poverty stricken or suffering a misfortune. You are never to object to granting a patient a consultation with one of your fellow brethren if your patient so desires it. You are not to enter too actively into the region of politics, general, local, or theological.

Although Arthur was struck by these words, he was well aware that he had already broken at least several of Annandale's commandments. But on this glorious day he was not about to let such things bother him. Instead he joined in the celebration with the other new doctors, tossing his ceremonial cap high in the air and shaking as many hands as he could find. He then sought out his proud mother, who had already scheduled a photo session for her newly graduated son, and the two went into town. The day had been a splendid one indeed, and upon returning home, filled with an exhilaration he had never experienced before, Arthur drew a sketch of himself jumping off the ground with glee, holding his diploma container in one hand and his unfurled diploma in the other, with special emphasis placed on its stamp of authenticity. His macabre sense of humor revealed itself as he captioned the drawing with a three-word phrase: "Licensed to kill."

12

The Tour
Goulston Street, 4 PM

After visiting Mitre Square, Doyle's expedition proceeded a few short blocks where, without warning, its leader came to an abrupt stop. The entire party watched his eyes scan to the left and then to the right as they took in the street scene that lay before them. Thousands of people packed the streets, creating a mass of humanity so thick that it would be next to impossible for the group to make their way through it. Not even the carriage drivers were bold enough to navigate across this area, which was in actuality a gigantic marketplace where people were laughing, screaming, shoving, and buying all sorts of items, but mainly food. There were cattle stalls with at least a dozen cows, which were being milked under the supervision of bearded men in white shirts and large black hats. There were hundreds of booths selling everything from candles to chickens. Most of the women were wearing black wigs and long black dresses, and pushing their way through the street with their recently purchased fowl to have the birds' throats slit.

Although the group was waiting to hear why Doyle had brought them all to this place, Doyle said nothing for some time. After a long interval, he spoke. "Can't you feel the lust, the hunger, and the danger that lurks about here?" he asked. "Don't allow that street sign that reads Middlesex Lane to mislead you. Its recent renaming was strictly an attempt to rid this area of the stigma associated with Petticoat Lane. Our city fathers thought it would be best to reframe that which you see before you in effort to erase its negative connotations. The last time I was here, things were quite similar to what they are today. The streets were jammed and there was a similar flurry of activity. Come to think of it, I was in the company of your friends and family members as we tried our best to make our way through another crowd of Jews who had packed this place on the day of our stroll. We did not know that we had picked the eve of Passover for our Crimes Club excursion. Why the area is as busy as it is today I do not know. The fact that this over-crowded commercial center has had a bad reputation for centuries makes the Ripper's presence here on the night of the double murders appropriate."

"But Sir Arthur, how did you arrive at this conclusion?" Carrington said. "If no one caught sight of him, how can you state with such certainty that he was here?"

"When we arrive at our next site, it will be obvious that the Ripper walked this way," Doyle said. "For now, bear with me and accept my claim that Jack was here. Before I speak about this very interesting section, look around a bit and try to take in as much as you can. This place is very dynamic, with lots of diversions, so do your best to concentrate."

With the sole exception of Stephen, who had disappeared from sight, everyone stayed put. Doyle was the only one who noticed that Stephen had vanished, and when Stephen returned seven minutes later, Doyle simply asked him if he had discovered anything of note during his wanderings.

"Yes, Sir Arthur. I have," Stephen said.

"Would you like to share it with the rest of us?" Doyle said.

"My pleasure, Sir Arthur. On weekends, this street is converted into a marketplace specializing in secondhand clothing, crockery, vegetables, and fish. But today is an exception to the weekend rule."

"How is that?"

"Tonight marks the start of the Jewish New Year, Rosh Hashanah."

"How could you possibly have come up with that?"

"I asked one of the people down the road why it is so crowded here."

The group laughed as Doyle said, "Very good work. You're a dauntless young laddie. Go figure! On each of the two times in my life I have been here it has been a Hebrew holiday! Mr. Mitchell, what is it about this particular marketplace that differentiates it from any others that I know of in London?"

Stephen did not have a ready answer. He shrugged his shoulders slowly to indicate that he had been stymied by Doyle's query.

"Don't let it bother you," Doyle said. "I'll give you a hint. I'll give you all a hint. Let me remind you that Jack would have had to cross this street on that early Sunday morning back in 1888." He then looked around to see if anyone cared to hazard a guess at his question now, but there were still no responders until Dr. Hammond proposed an idea.

"The streets would have been cleared of its carts and customers long before Jack crossed its path—a virtual ghost town. Therefore, I don't think this street would have been relevant to the Ripper's activities, as far as I can see," Dr. Hammond said.

Doyle slowly and continuously shook his head, and Hammond knew that his response had been incorrect. "Au contraire, Dr. Hammond," Doyle said. "Perhaps you should scrutinize the area one more time, but this time, keep in mind the ethnicity of the people who live here. Look at the windows and the signs, and look carefully at the people who call this place home."

They all looked around, but it was Matthew who linked everything together. "Let me guess, Sir Arthur," he said. "The signs and symbols we see in the shop windows indicate that the people who live and shop here are Hebrews."

"Mr. Mitchell has already told us that, Mr. Stanton," Doyle said. "What would that mean for our marketplace shoppers, keeping in mind that most of them are of the Hebrew faith?"

"It means that there would be little happening here on any given Saturday, but a lot would be happening on Sundays," Matthew said. "The Hebrews observe their Sabbath differently than we do; they worship on Saturday, instead of on Sunday."

"Keep going, Mr. Stanton."

"A marketplace like this would start to get busy around 4 AM on a Sunday, but prior to that I assume that there would be very little going on, and that there would be very few people on this street."

"Brilliant. And can anyone see why this has relevance?"

Dr. Hammond now had a chance to redeem himself. "If Jack had been hiding out here, he would have had to wait until things started to get busy. Then it would have been easy for him to blend into the crowd," he said.

Carrington shook his head and curled his upper lip. "I find it difficult to accept your rationale, Dr. Hammond," he said.

"Why, Mr. Lambton?" Doyle asked.

"The killer was much too cunning to have entered any sort of labyrinth for any period of time," Carrington said. "He would have formulated an escape route that would allow him to slither out from the confines of this congested sardine can. From what I have gathered about the Ripper thus far, he was much too smart to have been cornered like a trapped animal, even if only for a split second."

"Your reasoning has lots of merit, and I have to agree with it," Doyle said.

Carrington questioned Doyle. "Then why do you believe that Jack hid here?"

"I never said anything about hiding here," Doyle said. "All I suggested was that Jack made his way over this bustling street."

Instead of moving on, Doyle stood there for a moment and looked around. He jabbed his index finger at the sky and said, "Actually, as I look around this place, I've just recalled something that may be of interest to you. Not only were these streets jammed with merchants and shoppers, they were also crammed to the gills with an influx of freshly drafted constables—all of Whitechapel was, in fact. But in those rare hours when there was no business being transacted and little foot traffic, every sound reverberated like thunder through these back alleys and main thoroughfares. In order to counter the possibility of the Ripper hearing the constables' footfalls, the new recruits came up with an ingenious idea. They nailed strips of rubber—usually bits of discarded bicycle tires—to the bottoms of their clumsy regulation boots."

"Improvised plimsolls, if you will," Stephen said.

"Precisely. Now, off we go."

Doyle escorted the group to a location called the cloth market area which was in close proximity. Again they waded through hundreds of vendors and workers who were wheeling their goods from one part of the place to the other. Doyle knew that he had no choice but to talk as loudly as possible in order to be heard above the thunderous noise that surrounded them. "Although none of the murders took place here, this is a very important spot in the chronology of the Ripper," he said. "Please cast your gazes at the narrow wall of 108 Goulston Street, and look at it very, very carefully. Not a single iota has changed since the Ripper's time, so scrutinize each brick for any cracks, and scan for any chip that might be in the mortar. See if this wall furnishes you with any information. Is there anything that could be construed as significant?" After a brief pause, Doyle continued. "My question is a rhetorical one. You could all stand here for years and nothing would be revealed."

Adelaide, who was rubbing her heels to help ease her pain, said, "Trust me when I say this, but I couldn't stand here for another minute." The entire group laughed.

"Understood, Miss Oddie," Doyle said. "I won't keep you standing here too long. As for this place, there is nothing to be seen aside from brick and mortar. So I ask you, how could this wall be relevant to the Ripper crimes, and what potentially important clue was purposely left here for the world to see?"

"This is where something was written on a wall?" Edgar said.

"Capital! But unlike the mysterious words that the biblical Daniel interpreted, the puzzling words that Jack left on this wall are still cloaked in mystery. For here on this wall the Ripper inscribed in white chalk his cryptic sentence. After Jack had slain Mrs. Eddowes, he came here to present this bizarre phrase to the public. It is quite unfortunate that Jack elected to employ such an easily erasable material like chalk instead of using something indelible."

Doyle took out a piece of chalk and wrote upon the wall:

> The Juwes are
> The men that
> Will not be
> Blamed for nothing

He then looked at his puzzled group for a moment. Adelaide was the first to speak. "The double negatives of 'not and nothing' are very confusing," she said. "Is the Ripper trying to absolve or blame the Jews as a people?"

"To blame, or not to blame, that is the question!" Doyle said. "And just like the words of Hamlet, these words are available for eternal interpretation. Apparently there were those in Scotland Yard who believed that this message would have been interpreted by the citizenry of London as an indication that a Jew was behind the murders. So what do you think the Yard did with the Goulston Street graffito?"

"I would think they went searching for a Hebrew murderer, whether rightly or wrongly," Matthew said.

"Actually, they had been doing as much prior to this find. Most of those who had been questioned by the police happened to be members of the Jewish faith. Therefore, this graffito in itself would not have affected the Yard's investigation. However, it would have added fire to the furnace for the newspapers of London, which had already reared their antisemitic heads."

"I think I can make the reasonable assumption that the first thing the Yard did was to compare the handwriting on the wall with the letters they had already received from Jack," Carrington said. "This may have been seen as the key to determining which letters were genuine."

"That would have been much too easy and logical," Doyle said. "Let me tell you what they chose to do with this treasure trove. They washed it away."

"They washed it off the wall?" Adelaide said.

"Yes, Miss Oddie," Doyle said. "Their ostensible reason for doing so was to protect the city's Jews from being subjected to terror by their fellow citizens. While their actions may have been deemed proper, they certainly failed to obtain a photographic record of that which Jack had written. To the dismay of many, they elected to sponge it off the wall."

"Dr. Doyle, do you think that Jack was surprised by the police's decision?" Stephen said.

"A good question. But why do you ask it?" Doyle said.

"The message suggests that Jack was highly manipulative," Stephen said, "and may have been attempting to create chaos out of order. If rioting had broken out, the police may have been forced away from investigating the Ripper's crimes, placing his case on the back burner and letting it go cold. Indeed, racial persecution would have been the center of attraction."

"In other words, Jack was trying to outmaneuver the police by keeping a step ahead of them—kind of a 'catch me when you can,' if you will, correct?" Doyle said. "Vigilance committees would have concentrated on suspicious-looking Jewish men, and would have given short shrift to other leads. Can anyone here offer me other options the Yard might have had in this matter?"

"They could have simply erased the word 'Juwes' from the wall," Edgar said, "and kept the remainder."

"A splendid suggestion. Erasing that one word would have been sufficient to protect the Jews of Whitechapel," Doyle said.

"They could also have done what you just suggested—taken a photograph of it," Adelaide said.

"Shocking that the Yard failed to utilize one of modern society's greatest inventions. Imagine that," Doyle said.

"Maybe there was more to it than this," Edgar said. "Maybe the Yard was afraid of the entire message and not only the word 'Juwes'."

"Can you elaborate?" Doyle said. "Why would they be fearful of Jack's entire message? It does not appear in any way to be threatening in nature. Actually, one could argue that it exonerates those of the Jewish faith rather than implicates them."

Dr. Hammond interrupted the conversation. "Dr. Doyle, could Jack's message have been an allusion to something else? Perhaps one or more members of the Yard or of the police saw something more in this phrase?"

"Are you suggesting that the decision to expunge the graffito could have had something to do with the police itself?" Doyle said.

"Yes," Dr. Hammond said. "Maybe some of them knew that the release of this message might harm one or more of their brethren."

"So the police hid this message from the public at large so they could protect one or more of their own, even as such a cover-up would allow Jack to continue on his merry way?" Doyle said. "Actually, Dr. Hammond, do not respond just yet. Just think carefully about what you have said. Now does anyone else have any other questions to ask or suggestions to make?"

"There is one other bothersome issue regarding the occurrence here," Evander said. "I am trying to think which is more logical: Did Jack come here directly after the killing, or did he remain out in the open, or did he go somewhere else first?"

"What Evander is trying to say is did Jack go from Mitre Square to Goulston Street immediately, or did he delay and wander the streets, or did he go to some other location?" Matthew said.

"While all three of these scenarios represent distinct possibilities," Doyle said, "the odds are against us ever finding out the truth. But let us poll our members."

Matthew, Evander, and Adelaide favored the "left the scene and went somewhere else" theory; Hammond, Edgar, and Carrington were proponents of the "remained on the streets" theory; and Stephen, ever the lone wolf, supported the "came directly to this site" theory. Doyle decided not to disclose his thoughts, but instead pointed out the flaws inherent to any hypothesis regarding the events of that night.

"Any of the three choices present difficulties in accounting for how a blood-stained, knife-carrying, street-roaming murderer could have managed to avoid being observed by someone," Doyle said. "Remember, two murders had already been committed that very night. The streets must have been swarming with constables and members of both the neighborhood watch and vigilance committees. Nevertheless, it seems as though Jack continued dauntless and finished his night's mission by writing on the wall."

Stephen, no longer listening to Doyle, decided to read the graffito once more. After a few seconds, he turned his eyes away from the wall and said, "I don't see how these phrases had anything to do with Jack's agenda. There are no catchphrases and no mention of the harm he had inflicted on his victims. Could these have been nonsense words coincidentally scribbled on the wall by some street urchins? Or maybe this message was just a prank?"

"Again, excellent theories," Doyle said. "The Yard could use you."

"Is that a compliment or an insult, Sir?"

"Don't be so skeptical in this instance. Of course it's a compliment. But to help resolve your doubts in regard to the authenticity and authorship of the brick writing, I am going to provide you with background information. While it is true that the police were being peppered with thousands of prank letters each month from the supposed Ripper, the real Jack was definitely the author of this phrase. A fabulous clue was discovered before the sun came up over Whitechapel, only an hour and a half after Catherine Eddowes's murder. Constable Long was able to spot and appreciate the significance of something others might have interpreted as a mere swatch of fabric next to the door of this building. This finding was the start of what would be a very controversial investigation by the police. Long was quite sure that the fabric was not present when he made his prior circuit of the area twenty minutes earlier, and he could not be shaken from this conviction. When he walked over to it and picked it up, he discovered it to be smeared with blood and fecal matter. It was only then that he saw the spooky note written above it, which suggested that Jack had been involved in this incident."

"But I still don't understand why these two findings would necessarily cause anyone to think they originated with the Ripper," Adelaide said.

"The police were on their toes with this one," Doyle said, "and quickly determined with absolute certainty that the piece of apron fabric found by the constable matched the piece of fabric cut away from Mrs. Eddowes's apron, right down to the stitching. It follows that Jack must have wiped his knife blade clean with the fabric and then discarded the swatch right here."

"That hardly makes any sense at all, Sir Arthur," Stephen said. "Wouldn't Jack have wiped his knife off on her clothing before he left the scene?"

"Ah," Doyle said, "but he may have been pressed for time, and he may have thought it quicker to cut a piece of fabric off and go rather than risk being spotted. As I said before, an officer might have been in Mitre Square as Jack was finishing up."

"No, Sir Arthur. The piece of cloth was cut from her apron with the intention of using it as a marker," Stephen said. "This was all premeditated. This message was left expressly with the police in mind. Jack made certain of it by leaving the matching fabric."

"So the fabric served as a calling card for the wall writing? A very interesting theory, Mr. Mitchell."

"And I think the white handkerchief on the knife had a similar meaning."

"But how can we put this all together and create a unifying theory? I alluded to some of the links in the chain back at Mitre Square. Remember whose jurisdiction we're now under."

"I've got it," Dr. Hammond said. "Mitre Square was in the City of London, which is not the Yard's bailiwick. Any item related to this murder but found outside the City of London would have brought the Yard into the investigation alongside the City of London Police."

"Dr. Hammond, you're quite the prophet," Doyle said. "But why would Jack want two sets of police after him? Wouldn't one be enough?"

"Now that I am aware of Jack's sociopathic nature, it doesn't surprise me at all that he would want two separate police forces on his trail. It was all fun and games for him, like watching two local baseball teams fight it out on the diamond."

"Precisely. And the battle was started right here when Commissioner Charles Warren demanded that the graffito be erased before a photograph could be taken of it. This rash action by the chief of Scotland Yard all but ensured that his agency would be butting heads with the London

Police. Very good, Dr. Hammond. Anyone else with any thoughts they would like to share?"

"What about the spelling of the word 'Juwes'?" Adelaide said. "Is not the correct spelling J-e-w-s? If what you have depicted is correct, then this word was misspelled, either by the police or by the message's writer."

"As I said, the phrase was hastily erased and not photographed," Doyle said, "but it was written down by the police—whether correctly or not is another story." Doyle then shook his head slowly. "Actually, the spelling of this one word sparked a battle between the two police forces, which eventually boiled over into the press. The word was the crux of a debate that would last for weeks, and which stemmed from the fact that the City Police and the Metropolitan Police had each managed to record the word differently in their respective pocketbooks. The City detective had recorded it as 'Juwes', while the Yard's constable had transcribed it as 'Jeuws'. This seemingly minor discrepancy would become the focal point of the murder inquest. After the press printed the startling revelation that no one had checked any of the rooms in this building despite its importance to the apron and the wall writing, the general populace began to lose faith in both departments.

"While it had not taken the Yard much effort to connect the discarded cloth to Catherine Eddowes's apron, a long period of time elapsed before the agency was able to discover the possible meaning of the writing on the wall. Of course, most of you think it has to do with the Hebrews that populate this area. However, in the minds of those who believed the spelling of the word on the wall that night was J-u-w-e-s, a hidden Masonic connection was made."

"Sir Arthur, I don't know much about the Masons, except that they are always present at important ceremonies in our community," Evander said.

"I fully understand that most of you do not know a great deal about the Masons, and I will not ask if any of you are Masons, for I know you are bound by oath not to reveal yourselves," Doyle said. "However, I will tell you a bit about this theory without divulging too much. According to Masonic lore, when the wisest of all the kings of antiquity, King Solomon, decided to construct the Holy Temple in ancient Jerusalem, a cadre of conspirators soon wove a plot designed to force Hiram Abiff, its chief architect and master of works, to reveal the secret word of the Master Mason, thus granting them the knowledge of this rank. Although most of the conspirators eventually withdrew from the scheme, the remaining three went through with their plan. Even after the first two men had attacked Hiram, he refused to yield to their demands. The third man, however, accidentally killed him with a blow from his weapon."

"Doyle, what does this have to do with the Ripper?" Dr. Hammond said.

"Bear with me for just a moment longer, my good doctor," Doyle said. "Before these three criminals were captured, they were overheard lamenting their actions aloud in a state of deep regret. One man wished that his throat had been cut and his tongue cut out before he could take part in the attack of Hiram. The next man longed that his left breast had been torn open and his heart and vitals thrown over his left shoulder to be eaten by beasts before he could take part in the ambush. The last man yearned that his body had been severed in two and his bowels burnt to ashes and scattered to the winds before he could take part in the beating. Does what you have just heard sound at all familiar?"

"Their chosen methods of torture are not unlike those inflicted on the murder victims," Adelaide said. The group nodded in agreement.

"There are members of law enforcement and academia who are still convinced that the techniques employed by the Ripper were inspired by the cries of this trio of villains," Doyle said. "But I now realize that I neglected to tell you the names of these bandits. They were called Jubela, Jubelo, and Jubelum." Doyle looked out on the faces of his audience. He was reminded of the expressions of horror he had seen on his classmates back at Stonyhurst after he had regaled them with his ghost stories. "Could Jack have been referring to these characters by devising a collective term such as 'Juwes'? It is a belief to which some adhere."

Knowing he had to temper his implication, Doyle cheerfully added, "Of course, Freemasons do not engage in human sacrifice or anything else of that ilk, nor do any of their members involve themselves in antisocial behavior. They are above reproach and are the absolute pillars of British society."

"Was there any chance that this was the work of a Mason gone astray?" Stephen said.

"I suppose there is no way to rule out the possibility that Jack was a wayward son," Doyle said.

"With what we have just learned about the Masonic legend, I am convinced at the very least that Jack must have been at one of this group's meetings at some point," Carrington said.

Stephen made another entry in his notebook, while Matthew proposed that perhaps the killer knew the ways and traditions of the Freemasons, even if he had not been a member. He went on to say that Dr. Hammond's earlier suggestion of a police cover-up of certain elements of the crime seemed valid. The American physician smiled, nodded his head, but said nothing.

"Perhaps one or more of the investigators from the rank and file, or even a member higher up the police hierarchy suppressed relevant information in order to veil the Order's involvement from the public," Edgar said.

"In spite of the fascinating coincidences we have just discussed, I really don't think so," Doyle said. "In the end, I attribute the erasure of the message to simple carelessness."

As Doyle was completing his words, Dr. Hammond emphatically cleared his throat, causing the group to turn towards him. "Thank you very much for redeeming my theory, Mr. Stanton," he said. "My career has been devoted to interpreting, if you will, 'the writing on the wall.' I might be able to cast a little more light on this baffling clue. A very powerful cause of morbid impulse is imitation. Many crimes have been committed by persons who have had this impulse excited by reading accounts of trials or the detailed particulars of an offense. Epidemics of murder may be the unfortunate result of reading such graphic accounts of criminal actions. So, the possibility looms that there was a ritualistic element contained within these horrendous atrocities, and that Jack may have been seized by a compulsion to exact revenge on the villains of the legend. With patience, he could have studied each and every component required to consummate this vengeful obsession, and may not have been a member of the medical community at all, just a man of talent."

"No doubt a perfect summary of the nature of the beast," Doyle said. "But time is of the essence, and we must move on to our last stop. Everybody please follow me closely, as we will soon be entering a particularly dirty little part of town, which reeks of the smell of its inhabitants. I hate to subject you to this ungodly place, but our outing would be woefully incomplete without its inclusion."

Doyle erased the chalk from the wall with his handkerchief, and Evander turned to speak to Matthew. "I thought we had already been through the worst part of the city," he said.

"I guess not," Matthew said.

13

1881–1882
An African Journey

October 1881

Despite his newly granted medical degree, Arthur had little money and no job. He had assumed that his previous assistantship with the noted Dr. Bell would have other physicians knocking at his door, but this was not to be. Without any other option, Doyle was forced to return to Birmingham to work for the meager sum of £2 a month. He settled back into his old routine very quickly, but even though he was privy to the company of the Hoares and their children again, the situation offered him little satisfaction, for he yearned to go back to the sea. Arthur read the want ads in the newspaper every day until he came across an interesting prospect. It had been posted by the African Steam Navigation Company, which specialized in transporting passengers and cargo, and read:

> Ships sail from Liverpool and Hamburg for St. Paul de Loanda, calling at Madeira, Teneriffe, and all ports on the West Coast of Africa. Voyage out and home in 84 days. Salary £8 per month. Surgeon ranks with chief officer and purser. Company finds instruments and drugs. Uniform optional; cap usually worn.

Doyle immediately sent a letter to the company's central office, and a few days later he received word that the position was his. The pay would be an improvement on his current salary—four times more than he was receiving from Dr. Hoare—and he would have no additional expenses. He was satisfied with the status a ship's surgeon enjoyed, which made him equal to the chief officer and purser, and the fact that he didn't have to purchase any instruments, drugs, or uniforms, save for a cap, sealed the deal. It was in the middle of October that Doyle, "with a light heart," packed up his boxes and set out for Liverpool. Arthur would later write, "[T]here was a charm about the great list of ports at which were advertised to call . . . whose very names had been hitherto unknown to me."

Reginald and Amy Hoare accompanied Arthur to Liverpool, where they spent the day with a family friend, Mrs. Dawe. Doyle would write to his mother that Reginald Hoare had given him "a splendid little revolving rifle." On the day following his arrival, October 22, Arthur went down to the Mersey pier. He was invigorated by being on the docks of such a great city. Each ship had its own past and future stories to tell, and he was sure that once aboard the vessel it would become a treasure trove of tales of adventure.

At the very top of the ship's gangplank, a group of African palm oil merchants spoke in an animated fashion about the ivory trade that was emerging deep in the heart of the Congo. Next to them, a group of well-dressed women of all ages were engaged in gentle conversation, while a few feet away from them an entourage of young missionaries surrounded a distinguished-looking Jesuit priest. Doyle expressed his disappointment when he compared the *Hope,* which looked "as clean as a gentleman's yacht, all shining brass and snow white decks," to the *Mayumba,* which "looked like a bit of a tub and very dirty." The ship was 288 feet long and carried two life boats and two oar-driven surf boats, as well as a small boat known as a gig for shoaling in shallow water. She had both fore and aft sails, and a maximum cruising speed of seven and a half knots. Although the ship had been given a recent name change to blur the fact that it had crashed into the S.S. *Severn* a few years before, it was still in desperate need of an overhaul. Doyle was not impressed.

Arthur was introduced by the purser to the ship's captain, Hamilton Gordon Wallace—a direct descendant of Scotland's national hero, William Wallace. After the meeting, he found his way to his portside cabin to stow his belongings. Once inside, he noticed it had only one sleeping berth. This time there would be no one sharing space with him. He also had the unexpected luxury of a porthole, which admitted just enough light to allow him to read. All in all, it would do.

Within minutes the wild screeches of steam whistles and the unearthly groans of foghorns reverberated in Doyle's "den." With a not-so-gentle rocking, the *Mayumba* left its moorings and headed out for open water. The ship navigated around an obstacle course of steamships and tugboats when a sudden shroud of dense fog came down upon it. Thirty minutes into the voyage, a surge of rough water smashed against the ship, and when Doyle looked out his cabin's porthole, he knew that the roaring ocean swells threatened to swallow up the dilapidated vessel. The captain and crew had just received a cable explaining how the *Clan MacDuff* had recently been caught in this same tempest and sunk, taking nineteen crew and twelve passengers to a watery grave. Captain Wallace, knowing that the *Mayumba* was in danger of meeting the same fate, took no risks and judiciously made for the first available port—Holyhead, in Wales. Doyle was forced to jump into his role as physician right away, as he began to take care of the "prostrate ladies" aboard the ship, among them the ship's stewardess, who "announced that she was going to die." Finally, after things had calmed down, the ship dropped anchor in Holyhead.

After weighing anchor from Wales, the ship sailed into the open seas under azure skies, but when it entered the Bay of Biscay off the French coast, once again the seas were "running like mountains," thanks to another great storm that was threatening to swallow up the ship. Torrents of phosphorescent water, which Doyle would describe as "liquid fire," accompanied each new wave, and soon everything on board the ship was afloat. Doyle watched in quiet horror as several of the ship's sails were ripped from their masts and thrown into the ocean. Finally, as the ship rocked towards the island of Madeira, the tropical sun appeared and the wind died down. The *Mayumba* had done it. It had successfully carried its crew and passengers to their first scheduled port of call. The beauty of the place was immediately apparent to Doyle. He was struck by its vegetation, which was lush and verdant, and which highlighted the brightly colored houses that dotted the landscape. The harbor depth was sufficient enough to allow even the biggest of ships to dock close to town, and allowed the crew the luxury of getting to shore in their surf boats within minutes.

Doyle went ashore and posted a letter to Amy Hoare, letting her know how much he appreciated all she had done for him and thanking her from the depths of his heart. Interestingly, in this letter he makes a point to tell her that he had "sighted the Tuskar light on the Waterford coast . . . ," and that "[n]othing of interest was observable either from the starboard or larboard bow . . . ," but fails to mention that he had saved the ship from being destroyed on a rocky promontory by pointing out the lighthouse—a detail that Doyle would relate years later in his autobiography, *Memories and Adventures*.

After the few hours spent in Madeira unloading passengers and loading cargo on and off the ship, the *Mayumba* headed out for Sierra Leone, which was much less civilized. Life there lacked European culture and was not comfortable. The smell of Freetown's muddy Sierra Leone River at low tide was unbearable, and the incessant buzz of the insects that inhabited the mangroves was all that could be heard. As soon as the sun had set, mosquitoes appeared, ready to suck blood from and inject disease into their defenseless prey. There, the tangled undergrowth along the riverbanks, where the water barely flowed, signaled potential disease for any newcomers. Doyle would spend much of his time practicing preventative medicine, later writing, "[T]he quinine bottle was more familiar to me than the developing tray." A lover of photography, Doyle had apparently constructed a makeshift darkroom to develop his pictures while aboard the *Mayumba.* He would later write an article in the *British Journal of Photography,* explaining how he had "used the bath-room of the ship as a substitute for a darkroom." According to Doyle, he had been able to do so "by closing the port with a towel, and using one of the ship's lanterns wrapped completely in red Turkey cloth." Although he does not say so, this "Turkey cloth" may have even been the red muffler he had worn during his visit to his London relatives while a student at Stonyhurst.

The next port of call was Liberia's capital city of Monrovia, whose strong coastal currents made it exceedingly difficult to dock the ship, creating a situation in which it was almost impossible to avoid damaging the other boats already berthed there. The city itself, which had been named in honor of the fifth president of the United States, James Monroe, was populated primarily by emancipated American slaves who regarded Africa as an appropriate place to enjoy their newly found freedom. Indeed, Monrovia was enjoying a period of dynamic growth and increasing prosperity when the *Mayumba* docked there that day. Doyle managed to find the time to disembark from the *Mayumba* and explore the city. He was particularly interested in American literature, and especially enjoyed learning any new Americanisms he had never seen before in books. Many of these idioms would appear in his future writings.

Unfortunately, by the time the *Mayumba* had made the trip from Sierra Leone to Liberia, the incubation period for the dreaded "coastal fever" was over. Its first victim reported to the infirmary with fever, severe fatigue, and a strange dull expression in his eyes. Doyle recognized the first symptoms of the fever and knew he had his work cut out for him. In a desperate attempt to control the spread of the illness, Doyle mandated that quinine be dispensed to all passengers and members of the crew. But just two days later, at least a dozen passengers began experiencing the effects of the sickness, which subjected them to agonizing bone and muscle pain, an inability to eat, fits of delirium, and explosive diarrhea. Arthur's infirmary became the hub of all activity on the ship. He was besieged by those who were ill and by those afraid of becoming ill. While he tried his best to maintain order, Doyle felt the situation could get out of hand. The unbearable coastal heat and the merciless insects only added to the misery, making it impossible for him to get any sleep.

When the ship docked at the city of Accra in what is now known as the country of Ghana, "a rather amusing incident occurred," as Doyle would later state. A large canoe carrying natives who were out fishing just twenty yards away from the *Mayumba* mistook Arthur's photographic equipment for a mounted Gatling gun. Fearing for their lives, they "gave a united yell and sprang overboard." In broken English, one of them identified himself as a veteran of a British man-o'-war and shouted, "Dem thing gatling gun—all same Queen's ship have in tops. What you want point him at [us]?" The fishing party refused to get back into their boat until Doyle had carried away the "obnoxious instrument."

Shortly after arriving at the port of Lagos, located in modern-day Nigeria, Doyle himself became the victim of fever and spent "several days fighting it out with Death in a very small ring." As "there was no one to look after" him, he passed in and out of delirium and pain for nearly three days. It was by some act of divine intervention that he was able to make a gradual recovery. Unfortunately, by the time he had enough energy to sit up in bed, he learned that a passenger, to whom he would have given medical care had he been lucid, had succumbed to this dreaded illness and was buried at sea.

Heading southeast, the ship docked next at Bonny. The passengers were advised to take great care should they decide to go ashore, as the Bonny River was known to be infested with sharks. Almost all made the judicious decision to remain on board. According to the *British Journal of Photography*, it was this place that afforded Doyle the opportunity to photograph "one of the great war-chiefs, Wawirra by name—a sort of African Duke of Cambridge," who told Doyle "that in his last campaign he had taken five hundred men." Doyle "remarked that [he] could 'take' as many as that in a single moment," referring to his ability to take a picture. Wawirra was unable to understand the joke and had to have it explained to him. Doyle was convinced that Wawirra had "the deeply-rooted impression that [he] was a blood-curdling warrior, and was consumed by a chronic thirst for human gore!" By strange coincidence, a short story Doyle had submitted for publication before leaving on the *Mayumba*, "The Gully of Bluemansdyke," which takes place in South Australia near the river Wawirra, would be published while Arthur was aboard the ship.

It was at the island port of Fernando Po that Doyle saw the "cruel green eye" of a shark that was looking up at him, and he knew that he had "seen the Devil, or as near an approach to him as is to be found in this world." Doyle would later describe photographing this shark, and would also state that he "put a bullet through his dorsal fin" at the time, an action which may have been a violation of maritime law, although there is no record of Captain Wallace having taken any disciplinary action against him for illegally carrying a firearm.

After leaving its next port, Victoria, the ship continued on to Old Calabar, located in present-day southeastern Nigeria. Although Old Calabar "seemed the largest and most prosperous place [he] had visited," it was clear that "here also the hand of death was over all." There the *Mayumba* was wedged into a waterway so narrow that the trees along each side brushed against the ship, and it would remain for a couple of days, loading and unloading cargo. None of the local workers could be found on this day, however, as it was, as the ship's captain would tell Doyle, "one of their confounded saint's days or Eboe days, or whatever they call them," so they would not be doing "a stroke of work" until the next day. As the locals could not be seen from the ship, Doyle hoped to take a few photographs of Old Calabar's inhabitants ashore. He agreed to join the captain and the purser on a trip up the Calabar River after hearing the captain say to the purser, "[T]he Doctor shall have the bows of the boat for himself and his camera. You and I will take our guns . . . and see if we can't get a shot." With Doyle set to take some photographs and the captain and the purser keen to hunt whatever creatures they might find, they bundled the camera, lenses, rifles, and provisions to bring with them. They followed a path of palms along a thin strip of yellow beach, and when they reached the end of the shoreline, they rented a canoe from one of the native inhabitants. From there, they headed towards their destination, the semi-remote village of Creek Town. As they moved deeper and deeper into the darkness of the mangrove swamp, Doyle spotted a three-foot-long snake, which he shot and then watched "drift downstream." Soon after, the settlement came into view.

The visitors left their canoe and stepped onto land. As a few of the village's buildings came into view, they spotted the local missionary's house and made his acquaintance. After talking with him a while, and with daylight waning, the group started back to the ship. As they were setting out again in the canoe, Doyle's autobiography states that they were confronted by a messenger from the king, who had "sent down a peremptory order that [they] should report [themselves] to him." It continues with Doyle writing, "[A]s it sounded ominous and might mean a long delay we got our paddles out and were soon back in British waters." While the order was likely a "courtesy call," there are other plausible explanations for its announcement. King Eyo Honesty VII, whom the British Consul had declared monarch seven years prior, had implored his people and the consulate "to aid him in doing good," asking the Scottish missionaries present at his coronation to "cease not day nor night to win sinners to Christ." The king derived the law from the Bible, and King Eyo Honesty VII had "prevailed upon the heads of the town to enact by proclamation, laws to provide for the better observance of the Sabbath in the town, and in country districts. . . ." These laws stated "that no canoe leave the beach, or come in, unless in a case of necessity." Coming into town on an "Eboe day," a saint's day on which all labor and travel is explicitly forbidden, would likely have been considered a violation, and perhaps the failure of the visitors to follow local observances had incensed the king, who may have wished to voice his displeasure.

In addition, the laws also stated, "No one, under a penalty . . . [could] fire a gun, or engage in any play. . . ." Any God-fearing man would have looked unfavorably at outsiders with weapons. In fact, it may not have been the mere presence of guns that had caused a stir, but rather Doyle's attempts to sell guns. "According to a story he told some while later at a public meeting," Doyle had taken along some firearms on the *Mayumba*, "which he hoped to sell for gold." But when he found that the local chiefs were "already supplied with the latest Remington and Winchester rifles," he found himself unsuccessful. The notion of the locals being armed, however, is dubious, as "tribes near the coasts, especially under colonial control in and around ports, were mostly unarmed for security reasons." While Doyle may have tried to traffic guns at Calabar, attracting the attention of the king, it is also plausible that this story of gunrunning was merely "the result of a fiction writer entertaining an audience" at the time. Nevertheless, Doyle and his companions did not wish to find out the exact reason for the king's order, and paddled back to the *Mayumba* without hesitation.

On the route home, Doyle reprised his role as the Great Northern Diver, lifting his body over the railing and dropping down into the water below at

Cape Coast Castle. He casually swam around the entire length and breadth of the ship, and when he was satisfied with the success of his performance, he calmly climbed back up onto the ship and began to dry himself off. In his auto-biography, Doyle would write, "Several times in my life I have done utterly reckless things with so little motive that I have found it difficult to explain them to myself afterwards."

Two days before the ship's scheduled return stop in Liberia, there was a changing of the guard in the country's capital city of Monrovia. Henry Highland Garnet had made the transatlantic crossing to Africa, which had taken him first to Liverpool and then to the sister ship of the *Mayumba*, the S.S. *Nubia*, which had deposited him in Liberia on December 22, 1881. On December 23, his birthday, Garnet was sworn in as the new US Minister to Liberia. Garnet had brought with him the pride and confidence of the "emancipated, enfranchised, and educated" black man and the religiosity of the new convert. This former slave believed that the governments of Liberia and the United States furnished the template for "a model Republic, founded on the principles of justice, and humanity, and Christian-ity, in which the burdens of war and the blessings of peace are equally borne and enjoyed by all." Indeed, this world-renowned former abolitionist bore the distinc-tion of being the first man of color to address the United States House of Repre-sentatives. In 1865, on what was to be Abraham Lincoln's last birthday, Garnet had stood before the House and delivered a sermon that so touched its members that he was asked to furnish Congress with a copy of his speech.

Doyle would write in his autobiography, "The most intelligent and well-read man whom I met on the Coast was a negro, the American Consul at Mon-rovia," a statement that has led most historians to believe he spoke to Henry Highland Garnet. The *Mayumba*, however, was traveling its homebound route back to Liverpool at the time. Upon its return stop at Liberia, Doyle states that this "well-read man" actually "came on . . . as a passenger," making it more than likely that Doyle got to spend time with the man Garnet had replaced, John Henry Smyth.

Doyle would confess to being impressed by Smyth's intellect, remarking upon the ability of "this negro gentleman" to feed his "starved literary side" with discussions of American and English literature, although he would also dis-play a negative opinion of the African natives, writing, "My own experience is that you abhor them on first meeting them, and gradually learn to hate them a very great deal more as you become better acquainted with them." Neverthe-less, Doyle would later show sympathy for these native peoples and respect for the citizens of the African coast, stating, "With the exception of the natives, who have been demoralized by contact with the traders and by the brutality of the slave trade, the inhabitants of the dark continent are really a quiet and inoffensive race of men, whose whole ambition is to be allowed to lead an agricultural life, unmolested and in peace." Doyle's writings also show that he whole-heartedly agreed with Smyth when the former US Minister to Liberia stated, "The only way to explore Africa is to go without arms and with few servants. You would not like it in England if a body of men came armed to the teeth and marched through your land. The Africans are quite as sensitive."

Towards the end of his journey, Doyle was awoken by the sound of clanging bells. The purser informed him that the ship was ablaze, and that all hands had been called and were working to extinguish the flames down below. Doyle grabbed his clothing and made his way quickly onto the deck as fire streaked from the coal bunker and black smoke filled the air. He fought his way to the engine room, where he was turned away and ordered to go about the ship and wake the passengers to inform them of the situation. Soot-covered sailors then pressed Doyle into the bucket brigade in a futile attempt to cool the now-glowing orange-red hull with water. The battle raged all night. The exhausted crew was put to the test, but eventually their bodies began to ache and fail. The ship was battered by high winds, which reignited the embers just as they were finally dying. Eventually water won out over fire and the *Mayumba* survived. The ship completed its voyage and docked at Liverpool. Arthur wrote a letter to his mother upon his arrival back in England, telling her that he had no intention of going back to Africa ever again.

January 1882

Once back in Edinburgh, Arthur discussed his future plans with his mother. It was decided that he should return to Dr. Hoare in Birmingham. Soon after his arrival at Dr. Hoare's, Arthur would write of a bizarre coincidence that had occurred, saying, "On the evening that I arrived here the Boss and I were standing at the door smoking our evening pipe when a cab drove up to the door out of which stepped Claud Augustus Currie." Apparently, Doyle's fellow student from the University of Edinburgh, and the man responsible for his stint aboard the *Hope,* had come to Dr. Hoare's residence without having sent his résumé in advance or forwarded a telegram to alert the doctor that he intended to apply for a position at his office. Perhaps Doyle had told Currie that Reginald Hoare would be sympathetic to the plight of an unemployed young physician who had once helped out his current assistant. Nevertheless, the two of them were put to work immediately, both of them being sent to Dr. Hoare's annex, which was being run by Dr. Aspinal.

Doyle, inspired by the "literary atmosphere" of Reginald and Amy Hoare's home, dashed off several articles to some of Britain's more scholarly medical journals. He admitted that the ideas contained within them had been "hatched" while he was working aboard the *Mayumba*. One of them, "Notes on a Case of Leucocythaemia," actually made it into the pages of the *Lancet,* the most highly regarded of them all. Although the case study was written in an erudite manner, Doyle describes it facetiously as sounding "very learnedly, don't it?" At times it sounds more like a tale whose storyline was derived from its author's recent experiences. In the article, the first therapeutic agent he relies on happens to be quinine, a medicinal he had been using routinely to treat the passengers and crew aboard the *Mayumba*. He then informs the reader that although the patient presented in Birmingham, he contracted his ailment while in "Aspinwall, on the American coast," which bears a curiously similar name to his overseer at the time, Dr. Aspinwal.

Around this time, Aunt Annette invited Arthur to visit her and her brothers in London. She was hopeful that they would be able to reestablish his faith in Roman Catholicism and convince him to accept their financial support. Despite their best attempts, however, Arthur remained headstrong and unyielding, and refused to agree to any of the terms that were attached to their monetary offer. His Uncle Richard even took him to lunch at his private club, the Athenaeum, where he was one of the few Catholic members. He was trying to show him that London was different from most cities, in that it was more liberal in its attitude towards those non-Anglicans. But even after meeting some of the club's famed members, who were "known for their Scientific or Literary attainments, Artists of eminence in any class of the Fine Arts, and Noblemen and Gentlemen distinguished as liberal Patrons of Science, Literature, or the Arts," Arthur stood adamant in his refusal to feign religiosity in return for the family's patronage. Doyle then sulked his way back to Birmingham with the impression that he would be forever regarded as an outcast by his father's side of the family.

As Easter season approached, Doyle set his sights on making it back to Edinburgh to spend some time with his mother and siblings. Just as he was bidding the Hoares a temporary farewell, a letter arrived from Elmo Weldon telling him that she was finished with him. Doyle would comment that she broke up their relationship "as cooly as if it was the most usual thing in the world." With his ego bruised, his financial situation in limbo, and his career opportunities limited, he thought about reprising his role as a ship's surgeon, but this time on a boat to Argentina. Despite looking forward to seeing his family in Edinburgh, Arthur was less interested in running into Bryan Waller, whom he had begun to perceive as a transgressor against his family's honor. It had become obvious to Arthur that Bryan had overstepped his bounds by assuming the role of head of household. Arthur may have suspected Waller of adultery with his mother, and may have even thought he had played a role in Charles Doyle's commitment to Blairerno House. A month after his return to Edinburgh, Arthur sent a letter to his sister Annette, saying that he had "put the finishing touch upon Waller," and that he had "nearly frightened his immortal soul out of him." Doyle then went on to boast that Waller had "utterly refused to fight," but that he had launched his physical assault anyway, making "such a mess of him that he did not leave the house for 23 days." Despite this physical confrontation, the Doyles remained lodgers in Dr. Waller's house. Waller, however, would soon close his practice and leave Edinburgh. Not long after his departure, Mary Doyle, Dodo, and Ida would join Waller at his country estate in Masongill, where they would live rent free.

The exact cause of the strain that Mary Doyle and Bryan Waller's relationship had placed upon Arthur and his mother's relationship has been the subject of speculation for decades. Whether Mary's feelings for Waller were romantic or merely maternal is not known. What is known for certain is that Mary Doyle and Bryan Waller shared a lasting bond, and she continued to live at Masongill for more than thirty years, even after her son had become a well-to-do household name.

As Doyle persisted in looking for a good job, "begging to offer [himself] for every vacancy," he was rejected "with a perseverance worthy of a better cause." Arthur continued to sink deeper and deeper into the throes of sorrow until he received a fateful telegram from his "old friend," the eccentric and unstable George Budd, who had wired him, stating:

> Started here last June. Colossal success. My example must revolutionise medical practice. Rapidly making fortune. Have invention which is worth millions. Unless our admiralty take it up shall make Brazil the leading naval power. Come down by next train on receiving this. Have plenty for you to do.

For once, Doyle showed a bit of restraint and resisted these wild ideas. He was not about to fall prey to Budd's antics. But even so, after a few days, he sent off a letter informing Budd that he would come down only if guaranteed a salary. Less than two weeks later, Budd cabled Doyle with words that suggested he felt insulted by the response:

Your letter to hand. Why not call me a liar at once? I tell you I have seen thirty thousand patients in the last year. My actual takings have been over four thousand pounds. All patients come to me. Would not cross the street to see Queen Victoria. You can have all visiting, all surgery, all midwifery. Make what you like of it. Will guarantee three hundred pounds the first year.

If Budd's words are taken at face value, he would have to have been examining and operating on more than 100 patients per day, and this omits the deliveries he would have been performing. He would have had no time off whatsoever. Budd's calculation seems impossible, and this fact should have been obvious to Doyle. Nevertheless, Doyle remained intrigued by Budd, with his "wonderfully ugly face and the ugliness of character which is as attractive as beauty."

It seemed that Budd was doing his best to lure the still poverty-stricken Doyle away from the security of Dr. Reginald Hoare's solid Birmingham practice to his own recently opened practice in Plymouth. Budd's insistence may have also been the result of enmity towards Doyle's boss. A year earlier, Budd had published an article in the *British Medical Journal*. A "Dr. Reginald R. Hoare, F.R.C.S." of Birmingham had responded in the "Clinical Memoranda" section of the journal to "Budd's proposition, that there is a law of compensation between the various organs of the body. . . ." Although Hoare had used the terms "extremely ingenious" and "bold and original theory" to describe Budd's work, he had also addressed many of the article's problems, and in his concluding paragraph had suggested that "apart from the physiologic facts, we cannot see how Mr. Budd can answer certain objections to his novel theory." Budd, well aware that Doyle was at Dr. Hoare's at the time, may have decided to steal Doyle away from his employer partly out of spite. Ironically, it is also entirely possible that Doyle may have been the author of the "Hoare" letter, as Reginald Hoare rarely wrote to any of the contemporary medical journals. It would not have been the only time that Doyle would have attributed his writing to someone else, as evidenced in a letter he sent to his mother from Aston Villa after he had returned from the *Mayumba*: "[I] shall write a rattling essay on 'Listerism—a success or a failure,' and send it in in Hoare's name."

Although Dr. Hoare, Amy Hoare, and Mary Doyle each advised him against taking the job with Budd, Arthur Conan Doyle boarded the train to England's southern coast, bringing with him all his possessions.

March 1882

Budd's guarantee that Doyle would make a minimum of £300 per year had played a big role in convincing Arthur to leave Dr. Hoare and join Budd in Plymouth. Even though it meant associating himself with a man who most regarded as repugnant, arrogant, and possibly even dangerous, Doyle's need for money had overpowered any rational evaluation of his "chum." Although Budd was almost four years Arthur's senior, they had both entered medical school in 1876. Doyle had come to know George Budd and his brother Arthur by watching them play for the Edinburgh Wanderers Football Club.

According to Doyle, Budd had gained a reputation for doing well on examinations with a minimum of effort. No one could recall seeing him with an open textbook, even though he had won the school's coveted anatomy prize, competing for it against the "ten hour a dayers," who had earned their nickname by studying almost incessantly. Budd's terrible temper, however, had been a recurring topic of discussion among the faculty and students of the University of Edinburgh, and Doyle would recall his first exposure to his fellow student as a situation in which Budd "had indulged in one of his wild escapes, which ended usually in a fight or in a transitory appearance in a police court."

Another of Doyle's favorite anecdotes reveals the time Budd got annoyed at a fellow student for having asked a "banal" question during a crowded anatomy lecture. When Budd's demands to end these "mundane inquiries" were not met, he took matters into his own hands. Budd stood up, walked over the desktops, and confronted his noncompliant classmate. Budd took the first blow, a punch to the nose that drew blood, but once he had recovered from this initial shock, he grabbed his opponent by the neck and dragged him outside the lecture hall. Before anyone could exit their seats to see what was going on, a noise akin to "the delivery of a ton of coal" was heard outside the door. A few minutes later, a saintly George Budd returned to the auditorium, where he casually sat back down and set his eyes on the lecturer as if nothing had happened. The other student would not return that day.

When Doyle arrived in Plymouth he found the Budds living in a large corner mansion on Elliot Street in the highly desirable "Hoe" section of town. This house had served as Budd's home office until enough money came in to prompt him to separate his work from his domestic life. He ended up renting a second house a mile and a half away on Durnford Street, which functioned solely as an office and surgery. His home, or "town residential," as Doyle would describe it, had more than two dozen bedrooms, although very few of them were furnished. Doyle was given one of these undecorated rooms, which contained only an iron bed and a wash basin.

After having ignored Doyle's advice to pay back his Bristol creditors, Budd had resolved that Plymouth was the logical place to set up shop. His family's roots to England's foremost naval port went back more than three centuries, and many of his relatives had served as physicians in the city. One relative, his beady-eyed uncle, John Wreford Budd, had managed to become "a widely-known and highly-esteemed practitioner" in this seaside metropolis, despite his eccentricities. An unfavorable depiction of him in the 1908 book *Devonshire Characters and Strange Events* portrays John Budd as an unbalanced and impulsive lunatic who threw food out into the street if wasn't cooked to his liking, a defender of people he did not know, a train jumper, and a charlatan who threatened his patients. George Budd was well aware that the city of Plymouth had accepted Uncle John with all his faults, allowing him to build up a large and profitable practice. Although his uncle had died almost a decade before, his children had remained in Plymouth, giving George Turnavine Budd the support system he needed to succeed.

Doyle was given the "grand tour" of the house, which had formerly been a gentlemen's club. Within minutes, Budd revealed his true colors, grabbing the arm of a servant girl and asking Doyle whether he had ever seen a prettier maid. Once Budd had shown Doyle the main floor, the two of them sat down for dinner. Halfway through the meal, Budd excused himself, returning a few minutes later with a money sack that contained the day's receipts, which amounted to almost £32. Doyle must have been quite impressed by this princely sum. After dinner, Budd took Doyle to his experimental laboratory, where he unveiled his latest invention, a magnetic bullet deflector. Budd's plan was to equip battleships with powerful electromagnets, which would be dragged behind vessels by large rafts. According to Budd, this plan would make the English fleet impervious to any missiles that might be thrust upon them. Doyle's response was similar to that of the admiralty—that is to say, less than enthusiastic. In order to lend credence to his theory, Budd pulled out a pistol and fired a bullet at a blob of sealing wax which he had attached to a wall four inches above his infallible "magnetic deflector." Doyle was taken aback when the bullet actually hit the magnet and not its target. But Budd himself was not totally satisfied with this demonstration. He wanted to prove unequivocally that his creation was beyond reproach. So, in a perverted attempt to recreate the William Tell legend, Budd placed the deflector under his wife's bonnet and invited his guest to fire six shots at her beautiful face.

Doyle did not take him up on his offer, but what is rather amazing is that neither she nor Doyle headed for the hills.

The next morning, Budd and Doyle traveled to the Durnford Street office,
where the first thing that caught Doyle's eye was a plaque that had been fastened to the building's stone wall. It read "Dr. George T. Budd, Physician and
Surgeon." Beneath it was a second plaque, which read, "Hours 10—6 Monday,
Wednesday, Friday." When Doyle realized that Budd worked only three days a
week, he became convinced that he had made the right choice to come. Even
Reginald Hoare had to work six days a week. More than ever, Doyle wanted his
own plaque placed directly next to Budd's. Apparently Budd's assertions that
his practice was a gold mine were true, as evidenced by the crowd of people
that had already gathered to see the good doctor that morning.

Budd took Doyle aside and offered him the secrets of his success. Consul-
tations were free, but medications were not. This "half genius and half quack"
had a client base that not even its three large waiting rooms or its multiple
examination and consultation rooms could contain. It was standing room only,
and so crowded that patients had to be given numbered tickets that corresponded to their places in line. As a "convenience" to those who could afford
it, and to those who were foolish enough to pay it, a "small fee" of "10/6," a
half guinea, would enable a patient to bypass the less wealthy and step to the
front of the queue. Over the course of the next three weeks, Doyle learned the
ins and outs of this ingenious operation. Upon completion of the free initial
consultation that was given to all comers, the patient was handed a prescrip-
tion, which was to be handed over to Mrs. Budd, who acted as the practice's
apothecary. This underage young lady—who possessed no formal training or
medical license—worked in a preparation room, diligently concocting the various elixirs and recipes that had been created by her husband. It was only after
she had collected payment that the patient would be handed his medication.
Many of the patients received placebos, while the therapeutic medicines were
used "in a heroic and indiscriminate manner which produced dramatic results
but at an unjustifiable risk."

On one occasion, instead of prescribing medication to a woman who had
come to him with a drinking problem, Budd made her swear on the "Holy
Bible," which was actually *Taylor's Textbook of Medical Jurisprudence,* that she
would drink only cocoa for two weeks. Another time, a woman who was complaining of a "sinking feeling" in her stomach was advised that if the prescribed
remedy failed to work, she was to swallow the bottle's cork, for there was
"nothing better than cork if you were sinking."

Arthur viewed Budd with a mixture of admiration, scorn, and pure amazement. In *The Stark Munro Letters,* Doyle portrays himself as someone who is able to "read" his own "nature" well enough to realize that he wishes only an amount of money sufficient to relieve his "mind of sordid cares" and enable himself "to develop any gifts which [he] may have, undisturbed." He states, "My tastes are so simple that I cannot imagine any advantage which wealth can give—save indeed the exquisite pleasure of helping a good man or a good cause." Doyle's actual letters, however, seem to contradict this idea, often focusing on his lack of money and his need to acquire it.

Budd, who had already amassed a small fortune and was adding daily to his wealth daily, hatched another scheme that included Arthur. Doyle and Budd were to join together "and charge families 2 guineas a year for all medical expenses." Although Doyle thought the idea was "rather thin," he had to consider it, for Budd's "extraordinary success hitherto" had made it "hard to say what is possible and what is not." Dr. Budd was actually years ahead of his time, as this type of system may be seen as a precursor of modern medical insurance. Budd also told his very impressionable partner that there was money to be made in eye surgery. In fact, the University of Edinburgh, the top medical school in Great Britain and possibly the world during Doyle's time, had a fledging ophthalmology department. Budd informed Doyle that "there was a fortune to be made in eyes. . . . A man begrudges having to pay for medicines . . . but he would give his last penny to save his sight." Just a few years later, Doyle would be specializing in this field in a London office.

Once Budd had been convinced that Doyle was willing to do things his way, he gave Arthur a consultation room right next to his own. Yet Budd's pockets were filled with at least £30 each day, while Doyle's remained empty. Adding insult to injury was Budd's ritual of strutting through the neighborhood known as the "doctor's quarter," where he, with Doyle at his side, would rattle his purse whenever he passed the office of another physician. Budd was in his glory when rival physicians would "come to their windows and gnash their teeth and dance" until Doyle and he were out of sight. Budd soon gave Doyle permission to affix his "Dr. A Conan Doyle Surgeon" name plate to the outside wall of the building, but there was one condition that Doyle had to accept. His plaque would be placed beneath the "office hours sign," where it would be barely seen.

Almost a week after joining the practice, Doyle still had not seen a single patient. Finally he was given "an old soldier with a cancerous growth on his nose." Although Doyle had no problem excising the lesion, his results were unspectacular, the poor man left with a deformed nose that pointed upwards. Doyle's description of his work bears notice as he writes, "I left him with an aristocratic, not to say supercilious organ, which was the wonder of the village, and might have been the foundation of my fame." After this instance, his patient load increased markedly. Most of them were unglamorous surgical cases that Budd was more than willing to hand over to his new associate.

Now that he was seeing patients, it was time for Doyle to learn how to mix the art and science of medicine. Budd shared his own unwritten guide on how to run a successful medical practice with Doyle. The first rule was to "never be polite to the patients," which Budd demonstrated by calling out from his upstairs hallway to the patients in the waiting room, "Stop your confounded jabbering down there! I might as well be living above a poultry show!" His second rule was that "[p]atients must realize that the physician is lowering himself to see a patient." This edict was vividly demonstrated when a crowd of people that had lined up to see him was told to go home, as "he had decided to spend the day in the country." The third rule must have been Budd's favorite, as it said to "[g]ive reason to make patients talk about you." Budd told Doyle that early on he had "[thrown] a man down the stairs after an argument about his condition." The upshot of this assault had been that "the man [had] talked about it so much in his village that virtually the entire population came to see him." Budd's rules, although nearly sociopathic in nature, were apparently just what the doctor ordered to firmly establish a medical practice.

Eventually, Doyle's financial situation began to improve on a weekly basis, and by June he would write to his mother, "I am keeping steadily out of debt. At present I owe for my plate and midwifery cards." He would also note, somewhat bizarrely:

> You must remember that if anything happened to Budd, (which God forbid) I should come in for a very good thing. In any case I hope before September to be doing well enough to start a house of my own, and to that end will save every penny I can. There is a fine opening here, a great many medical men have died lately and the survivors are awful duffers.

Why Arthur would think to hypothesize on the possible death of his robust and powerful twenty-seven-year-old associate is undoubtedly strange. His comment regarding the large number of medical men who had recently passed away is also odd in light of the fact that Doyle would later scout the area in an attempt to establish his own practice and lament, "Competition as you and I know is pretty brisk."

June 1882

Throughout Doyle's stay with Budd, Mary Doyle would take it upon herself to send her son numerous "letters of remonstrance" vilifying Dr. Budd. Apparently "her family pride had been aroused," and she feared for her son's reputation. Arthur, however, discounted her "dismal & lachrymose" correspondence. He much "enjoyed [Budd's] company and the extraordinary situations which arose from any association" with the man. When he informed his mother that Budd had no intention of being "crippled by debts owed to the tradesmen of Bristol," Mary Doyle urged her son in writing to get out of Plymouth as fast as he could, but Arthur simply tossed the letters into the fireplace.

According to Doyle, one morning, quite out of the blue, "the unscrupulous Budd" made his way across the hallway, entered his consulting room, and informed his young associate that he had been a destructive influence on the practice and had cut into its profits. Budd explained that some patients whose wish it was to see the senior partner were being placed in the room of someone whom they considered to be a less skilled physician. Budd believed that instead of subjecting themselves to an amateur, they were walking away and seeking help at the offices of rival doctors of the neighborhood. Budd admitted he had made a major error in having Doyle join him. Doyle displayed a tremendously forgiving nature in the face of this news, declaring it his absolute duty to remain with the practice for an additional "three weeks" after his former employer fell ill the next day and needed to be nursed back to health.

Doyle had his eye on Southsea as the location of his new practice, and Budd offered to pay his passage to the Portsmouth town and give him one pound a week until he could get on his feet. The prideful Doyle initially refused Budd's reasonable proposal, but reconsidered his decision after discussing the matter with his mother. In a letter to her, he writes, "I will accept it but only as a loan." Doyle insisted that he would not be beholden to Budd, and that he would repay the advance as soon as he could. When Arthur departed from Durnford Street, Budd made good on his promise, handing £2 over to him. With very little cash on hand to get started in Southsea and perhaps feeling slightly glum, Doyle sent a letter of apology to Elmo Weldon, who was still in Ireland, and who had been recently diagnosed with a terminal pulmonary illness. In it he states, "[B]oth men and women are incomplete, fragmentary, mutilated creatures, as long as they are single."

14

The Tour

Miller's Court, 5 PM

The streets were becoming less crowded and the group was able to negotiate Commercial Street with relative ease. The shopkeepers were beginning to close their doors and the peddlers were packing up their wares. A fruitmonger, hopeful of finding some last-minute buyers, spied Doyle and his company approaching and lifted a cart laden with overripe fruit, dragging it over to them as fast as he could. When they laid their horrified eyes upon the rotten, rancid stuff, they ordered the seller off at once.

"Was that purveyor of puckered and putrefied pears and apples serious about offering such vile produce for sale?" Carrington said.

"Survival, not pride, is paramount here in the East End," Doyle said.

"Where is that stinky mess going to be stored?" Edgar said.

"You don't seem to understand the nature of this place," Doyle said. "That man regards his unsold produce as precious cargo, and, in all likelihood he'll be hauling it up three steep flights of stairs to the tiny apartment where he and probably more than a dozen others live. It will then be further compromised by being exposed to the coughs and sneezes of the consumptive souls that dwell there. While hordes of unwashed and potentially disease-carrying hands have already touched this withered fruit, those who subsist in this district accept these conditions as their only way of surviving the desperate poverty that informs every aspect of their lives."

Doyle walked over to a vendor of maizypop and bought a bag of the popcorn treat for each member of his tour. "My friends, this is the one food item that tastes reasonably good, can be purchased at a fair price, and is relatively safe to eat," he said. "At least, I hope so—for your sakes and mine!"

As they devoured their snacks, Doyle led his guests through a narrow archway, where he stopped just short of a small courtyard. "Our focus now will be on the woman I consider to have been the final victim of Jack's murderous activities," he said. "Mary Jane Kelly lived and died right here in this apartment, yet on the surface her murder bore little resemblance to the others. Soon, you'll be able to see why I have included her on the roster of Ripper victims. On November 9, 1888, Jack the Ripper entered Mary Kelly's tiny room and killed her. Whether he was an invited guest or instead broke in is not known. But I ask you, is there anything I have said up to this point that might make you see this case as different from the others?"

Evander was quick to point out that, unlike the other killings, Mary Kelly's murder had not taken place in September. Doyle quashed this idea by reminding him that the murder of Mary Ann Nichols had taken place on the last day of August. Matthew then chimed in. "What Evander meant to say was that there was only one victim a month, and that September's double killing was an unintended anomaly," he said.

"Stantons, there were three separate killings in the month of September," Doyle said, "and one murder in August. Even if you consider the murders of Elizabeth Stride and Catherine Eddowes a single event, Annie Chapman's death also occurred in September, while the Ripper was inactive in October. I am hard pressed to believe that Jack made any real mistakes in regard to when he chose to take out his knife. Therefore, I am forced to conclude that both of you are overthinking things a bit."

"Perhaps the fact that this last victim was killed inside her apartment rather than out in the street is the discrepancy you are seeking," Adelaide said.

"Precisely, Miss Oddie. You've hit the nail on the head. But I ask you then, what would have caused Jack to alter his modus operandi?"

"Maybe he thought someone had come dangerously close to spotting him at one of the other murder sites and decided it would be best to move indoors."

"Indeed, his ability to circumvent the authorities at two sites, Dutfield's Yard and Mitre Square, may have been due to sheer luck," Carrington said. "We've already concluded that he had been forced to flee the scene prior to completing his mission in order to avoid being caught. It is safe to assume that the Ripper could have been somewhere within the confines of Mitre Square when Constable Watkins arrived on the scene."

"Interesting thought process," Doyle said. "And while this may have been the case, the more important question of how Jack managed to escape remains."

"Sir Arthur, I recall you saying that Constable Watkins left the crime scene to get some help from the night watchman at the tea factory," Adelaide said. "Wouldn't that have furnished Jack with an ample amount of time to make his exit?"

"Yes, my dear, it would have. But let us return to my original question. Is anyone able to see other advantages to moving indoors?"

"Absolutely!" Edgar said. "A move like that would have put an end to the possibility of being identified by a passerby and would have rid Jack of any time constraints, enabling him, in essence, to accomplish his task without having to look over his shoulder or at his watch."

"And by staying indoors, he would not have had to poke around in the dark for kidneys and livers," Carrington said.

"Perhaps, but I'm looking for something a bit different," Doyle said. "Any other suggestions?"

"Could Mary Kelly have had something inside the apartment that would have led the police to Jack had they found it?" Matthew said.

Doyle's eyes lit up. "Perhaps! But what could it have been?"

"That I do not know, Sir Arthur."

"Mr. Stanton, if your theory is correct, no one will ever know unless Jack is brought to justice. But there is one particular item that may be of interest here, especially to those of you who have read about the Ripper in newspapers and magazines: Mary's room key. The Ripper may have taken it with him to lock the door on his way out. If he had been apprehended that very day and brought in for questioning, the presence of this key on his person would have been extremely incriminating. However, I shall come back to this notion later."

Dr. Hammond was becoming agitated by this discussion. All he wanted was an explanation. "Why would someone who was able to commit a lightning-fast mutilation on a dark street switch gears and seek privacy and adequate illumination?" he said. "Dr. Doyle, things aren't making much sense here."

"Point well taken, Dr. Hammond," Doyle said. "What Jack did indoors was far more macabre and grotesque than what he did outdoors, if you can imagine. Poor Mary Kelly's body was ripped apart to the point of being unrecognizable. Let me just say that she was identified only by her ear lobes and the color of her eyes." Doyle allowed a few seconds to elapse without speaking so that the group could digest the horror of it all. "Let us stir the pot a bit, shall we?" he said. "Dr. Hammond's skepticism is warranted here. What are some of the barriers Jack would have faced working indoors?"

"I have a different interpretation of things," Stephen said. "The thought here is that good lighting would have aided him in his work, but darkness would have been a more valuable resource. A well-lit room would have exposed him to any eyes that might have gazed through Mary Kelly's window. If she had so much as whimpered or uttered a muffled cry, her killer would have run the risk of being easily apprehended by the police."

"Quite good, Mr. Mitchell," Doyle said. "So you are theorizing that light would have been a negative and not a positive?"

"Yes, light might have removed his cloak of secrecy, potentially bringing about his capture. But perhaps, Sir Arthur, he was one of those rare types that court capture. 'Catch me when you can,' his challenge to the authorities, may have been a particularly apropos statement. On the other hand, the Ripper may not have committed this murder."

"Once again we are back to the imitation theory, suggesting that Mary Kelly's killer may have been trying to copy Jack the Ripper. Although elements of this crime differ markedly from those of the previous four murders, I can guarantee you that Jack, and only Jack, was its perpetrator. In case you have forgotten, I have been privy to everything Scotland Yard has on record, so let us not get off track here. Instead, let us return to the events that led up to this gruesome murder. More than a month had passed since the double killings, and most of Whitechapel was under the assumption that the horror had finally ended. Everyday life was going back to its old routine. But one morning in November, at 10:45 AM, a local landlord, Mr. John McCarthy, was going over his accounts and realized that two of his tenants, Mary Jane Kelly and Joseph Barnett, had not yet handed in their rent. His assistant, Thomas Bowyer, was consequently sent over to where we are now, 13 Miller's Court, just off Dorset Street, to collect the 29 shillings owing."

Evander was startled to hear that an apartment like that would go for such a hefty sum, but Doyle told him that the rental was only 4 shillings a week, and that Mary was in arrears.

"A fortnight prior to the murder," Doyle said, "the couple had had some sort of argument, which wound up with Mr. Barnett being banished from this one-room apartment. Mary had been forced to fend for herself. Her circumstances would have caused her to exploit any method to come up with the back rent. Mr. Bowyer knew that Mary would be in her flat when he got there because she had specifically told him she would be watching the scheduled Lord Mayor's Day procession from her window as it passed by her apartment. He was puzzled when she failed to respond to his knock on her door. He jiggled the doorknob, but it wouldn't turn. He peeked through the keyhole, but could not quite make out what lay inside. He did not have a key to the apartment, so he decided to make his way over to the window you see there, remembering that it had been broken during the skirmish that Mary had had with her husband days earlier. Mr. Bowyer had not fixed it just yet. He figured that Mary was trying to dodge him, pretending not to be home when he knocked, and he was not going to fall for any ruse. He carefully passed his hand through the jagged glass, swept the muslin curtain to one side, and was greeted by the horrific sight of a blood-bathed sheet on which lay Mary Jane Kelly's lifeless nude body. His heart raced as he ran back to Mr. McCarthy. He tore open the door to McCarthy's headquarters at the chandlery and breathlessly informed his employer of the gruesome scene he had just encountered. Instead of notifying the police, the two of them went back to the scene, seeking out the constabulary only after Mr. McCarthy had laid eyes on the grisly aftermath of the crime."

"Dr. Doyle, are you saying that Mr. Bowyer was Mary Kelly's friend?" Dr. Hammond said.

"Why would you think so?" Doyle said.

"Because when someone tells you about their plans, some level of friendship may be inferred. And the fact that he was unafraid to stick his hand through a broken window and be spotted by the person within suggests the two of them shared some sort of camaraderie."

"Excellent work, Dr. Hammond."

"How do we know Mr. Bowyer wasn't the killer?" Carrington said. "After all, most victims of murder are killed by someone they know. As Dr. Hammond just pointed out, Mr. Bowyer certainly knew her."

"I'll answer your question quickly because time is short," Doyle said. "Later that day, the medical examiner concluded that many hours had elapsed between the time of Mary Kelly's death and Mr. Bowyer's arrival. Now, where was I? Oh yes, Mr. Bowyer left Mr. McCarthy and raced to the Commercial Street police station, where he was unable to speak coherently for some time before catching his breath. Not long after, Mr. McCarthy entered this same station and told Officers Dew and Beck about the terrible scene upon which he and his assistant had stumbled. McCarthy and Bowyer then led the officers back to the rooming house, where the policemen proceeded to take a look for themselves. After observing the corpse lying on the bed, they sent out a call for more assistance, believing the Ripper had returned.

"Let us move forward a bit to the arrival of Inspector Frederick Abberline, who had been placed in charge of the Ripper investigation because of his extraordinary knowledge of Whitechapel. He decided to maintain the status quo until two famed bloodhounds, Barnaby and Burgho, which had been requested by Commissioner Warren, could be brought to the scene. He kept the door to Mary Kelly's room locked so that the crime scene would remain pristine and uncontaminated by outsiders. He reasoned that once the dogs got there, they would be able to hunt down the killer."

"What could possibly have compelled the esteemed Sir Charles Warren to conclude that a pair of hounds would be able to track down this practitioner of evil?" Evander said. "The streets of the world's most populous city are not conducive to fox hunting!"

"What Evander is trying to get at is the fact that this city is a cauldron of odors," Matthew said.

"That Sir Charles deserved the fine reputation he enjoyed cannot be denied, but he was misguided in employing a military approach here," Doyle said. "Your skepticism rests on a solid foundation. It is my feeling that Warren was hoping to emulate the success of the Blackburn police force, which a dozen years before had attributed its success in apprehending the outrager and murderer of a little girl to a bloodhound-springer spaniel mix."

"Would you be kind enough to tell me what an outrager is?" Evander said.

"It is a term derived from the French word for 'beyond.' In other words, an outrager goes beyond the bounds of decency. Back in the

1870s, it was typically used to describe a rapist. In the Blackburn case, after the dogs had been sent to search the house of murder suspect William Fish, the bloodhound, Morgan, soon led the police to the bedroom fireplace, where charred pieces of the skull, hands, and forearms of Emily Holland lay hidden in a small hollow in the chimney. Fish was arrested, put on trial, and hanged. This case caused quite a stir during my final days at Stonyhurst and left an indelible mark on me, so Warren would not have been doing anything entirely new. And although as far back as half a millennium ago Robert the First of Caledonia issued a decree that no impediment to persons pursuing thieves with the help of dogs would be tolerated in his kingdom, hundreds of years later, a surrogate dog handler would be able to stand in the way of authorities."

"I don't understand," Evander said.

"My friends," Doyle said, "it is now important to note that the renowned Scarborough hounds never arrived in Whitechapel, as apparently the person in charge of their care and protection, Mr. Taunton, refused to 'endanger them.' He claimed that someone had told him of a burglary that had been committed in the vicinity, and he feared the perpetrator of this crime might have placed poison there. Warren had failed to make any financial arrangements with the owner of the dogs, Mr. Brough, to compensate him if any harm were to befall the animals. Nevertheless, even if Mr. Brough's dogs had been permitted to work on behalf of the criminal investigation department, it is unlikely that they would have been anything other than an impediment to progress. Bloodhounds, by their very nature, are extremely nervous in temperament and acutely sensitive to new or strange conditions. And by the way, Brough's hounds, which were in no way related to the celebrated Blackburn dogs, had no experience whatsoever in a large city. If they had been called out, it is likely that they would have run around in circles. But let us continue.

"The police remained outside Mary Kelly's apartment for two hours waiting for the dogs that would never arrive. At last, at 1:30 PM, Superintendent Thomas Arnold arrived and instructed Mr. McCarthy to smash in the door with his pickaxe. As the landlord chopped away, Superintendent Arnold declared that the order to bring Burgho and Barnaby to the apartment had been countermanded. Once the door was down, the police were greeted by the repulsive smell of rotting human flesh, an odor that permeated the entire room. They viewed what remained of a faceless woman whose body parts had been ripped out and arranged in a crude fashion atop a table, while her other organs had been placed under or around her corpse."

"Your choice of the word 'arranged' is a bizarre one, Sir Arthur," Carrington said.

"It may make sense to you once you've heard Dr. Bond's report of the scene, which was published in the *Lancet*," Doyle said, pulling a piece a paper from his pocket and proceeding to read:

> The body was lying naked in the middle of the bed, the shoulders flat, but the axis of the body inclined to the left side of the bed. The head was turned on the right cheek. The left arm was close to the body with the forearm flexed at a right angle and lying across her abdomen. The right arm was slightly abducted from the body and rested on the mattress, the elbow bent and the forearm supine with fingers clenched. The legs were wide apart, the left thigh at right angles to the trunk and the right forming an obtuse angle with the pubis. The whole of the surface of the abdomen and thighs was removed and the abdominal cavity emptied of its viscera. The breasts were cut off, the arms mutilated by several jagged wounds and the face hacked beyond recognition of the features and the tissues of the neck were severed all round down to the bone. The viscera were found in various parts. The uterus and kidneys with one breast under the head, the other breast by the right foot, the liver between the feet, the intestines by the right side, the spleen by the left side of the body. The flaps removed from the abdomen and thighs were on a table.

"Did he take any of her organs with him this time?" Edgar said.

"Excellent question, Mr. Collins," Doyle said. "At first it was believed that her uterus and other womanly organs had been removed from the scene, but after an exhaustive effort by the police surgeons, it was determined that not a single organ had made its way out of the room."

Dr. Hammond thought it odd that no viscera or other body parts had been taken, for he had made the erroneous assumption that organ collection had been the objective of several of the earlier killings. He thought that Jack, having all the time he needed in this instance, would not have been able to resist the opportunity to take away organs here, and told Doyle so.

"I am perplexed by the matter myself," Doyle said. "It may be that all that this vampire wanted was a bloodbath. For all I know, he may have guzzled down some of her blood. Sort of reminds me of my friend and distant cousin Bram's novels."

"Are you Bram Stoker's cousin?" Adelaide said.

"I am indeed! I guess you might say that the ability to write flows in our family's veins. No pun intended. Now, where was I? Oh yes, the flow of blood. Mary's bedclothes were saturated with blood, while a pool of it covered a two-foot-square area beneath her body. Additionally, blood had spattered on the wall to the right of her bed, with most of it concentrated directly in line with her neck."

"Sir Arthur, your description of this poor lady implies that she was both killed in her bed and mutilated there," Stephen said.

"How did you arrive at this conclusion?" Carrington said.

"It's all quite straightforward, my dear Mr. Lambton. The blood on the wall proves that Mary was alive when her neck was slashed. For blood to have sprayed forth, the heart must have still been beating."

"I see," Dr. Hammond said. "She couldn't have been standing in the erect position. She had to have been flat on her bed, as the blood found on the wall was at the same height as her mattress. Simply put, had she been standing, the trajectory of the blood would have put the stain somewhere else."

"Then something is not right here," Stephen said. "The details of Mary Kelly's death differ too markedly from the other four murders we've attributed to Jack, where the victims' necks were slit only after their bodies had been laid on the ground."

"What makes the position of the body and the spray of the blood so important to you, Dr. Hammond? Do these details really change anything?" Evander asked.

"Mr. Stanton, doesn't it seem a bit bizarre that someone who had always been so meticulous about keeping blood off of his garments would suddenly allow himself to be steeped in it?" Dr. Hammond asked.

"You're right, Dr. Hammond," Evander said. "It's more than bizarre. It doesn't make any sense at all."

"So how did the killer manage to get away without being spotted, Sir Arthur?" Matthew said.

"My 'Jill the Ripper' theory might be relevant here and could unify things," Doyle said. "It is my strong belief that Jack burned his clothing inside Mary Kelly's premises and then changed into a midwife's outfit. Having done so, any remnants of blood that might have remained on his shoes or cheeks would not have aroused suspicion. Further validation of my hypothesis may be found in the apartment's fire grate, where the inspector in charge of the case found a large accumulation of ashes, which he judged to be recent in origin. He assumed that these ashes had come from the victim's clothes, and felt that the killer had burned them to provide himself with light. But if we stick to our assumption that Jack was not in need of light, it is possible that his own clothes were the source of the ashes. Further confirmation of this idea is afforded us by the fact that Mary's entire wardrobe was found neatly folded on a chair, with her boots sitting directly in front of the fireplace. Although a skirt fragment and the rim of a velvet hat were present in the ashes, it is my feeling that the great majority of the clothing found inside the fireplace belonged to Jack, and that he burned his clothing in an attempt to make any potential evidence against him disappear."

"Did Scotland Yard hear any reports of midwives that had been seen walking in the area that day?" Adelaide said.

"Why would they, when midwives were so often found in the East End?" Doyle said.

Dr. Hammond became a bit agitated by what he regarded as too simplistic an explanation. He crossed his arms and moved his head from side to side. "Dr. Doyle, I'm still uneasy about attributing this particular murder to Jack," he said. "I'm just not convinced it's his work. It's so far afield from the first four, in which he committed the crimes in outdoor venues, positioned his victims, left clean crime scenes, and departed with certain mementos, if you will. This one doesn't match up with the others at all."

Doyle remained silent and reached into his pocket. He pulled out a yellowed piece of paper and unfolded it. It was a newspaper clipping dating back to 1888. He held it in his left hand and then looked out at the group, clearing his throat. "Earlier on I stated that a thorough search of Mary Kelly's place had failed to turn up the missing door key," he said. "After the police had searched the entire apartment and neighboring area for it without any luck, they deduced that Jack must have taken it with him. But this record stands at odds with Inspector Abberline's testimony at the inquest, which was held a week or two later at Shoreditch Town Hall. In it, he states, 'An impression had got abroad that the murderer had taken the key of the room away, but that was not so, as Barnett had stated that the key had been lost some time ago, and when they desired to get into the room they pushed back the bolt through the broken window.' It is conceivable, therefore, that Jack followed Mary back to her apartment, and after observing her place her hand through the window and unlatch the bolt to unlock her door, he did the same. Once he had gained entrance to her living quarters, he slaughtered her and left the ghastly scene with which we are now familiar."

Stephen pulled out his notebook and asked Doyle to repeat the portion of the article he'd just read, but a bit more slowly, so that he could jot down a few details. Doyle granted this minor request. Stephen listened carefully and then offered an idea. "Just a point of information," he said. "The bloodhounds would have been useless in this particular case, and Jack would have undoubtedly known it. But not for any reason we've discussed here."

"And why is that?" Doyle said.

"It's elementary, Sir Arthur," Stephen said. "Sir Charles Warren had likely been feeling pressure from all sides to unleash the hounds the next time Jack committed a crime. The Ripper was well aware of the possibility that when he committed his next murder, the dogs would be called upon to track him down. He was compelled to select the perfect day with the perfect conditions to commit another of his perfect crimes. This might explain why he chose to work indoors this one time."

"Mr. Mitchell, you have this armchair detective on the edge of his seat. You've offered a fascinating theory, but you still haven't answered my question," Doyle said.

"First I must recapitulate some of what you have just told us before I give the answer if you don't mind. A moment ago you said Mary Jane Kelly had told Mr. Bowyer that she intended to be a spectator when the Lord Mayor paraded by, and that she wouldn't be straying very far from her apartment."

"Keep going."

"On November 9, the people of Whitechapel would have been jammed in the streets of London like pilchards in a can. Events as important as this were, and still are, well publicized. Everybody would have known about it, even people like Mary Kelly and Mr. Bowyer. Many of the area's shops are temporarily shuttered during such events, while street vendors position their carts anywhere they can. All of this impedes movement, and the presence of the police tends to make the matter even worse."

"What does this have to do with the dogs?" Carrington said.

"The precise parade route would have been printed in all the local papers," Stephen said, "letting readers know which streets would be blocked off and which would remain open. An evil genius like Jack would have planned at least several potential escape routes well in advance, neutralizing any advantage Burgho and Barnaby would have brought."

"Mr. Mitchell's theory is a good one, and I completely agree with it," Doyle said. "Couple it with the fact that this isn't the Lancashire countryside. This is the East End of London. As noted, the number of people and scents on just one of its streets would have made it incredibly difficult for a dog to track someone down. Those poor beasts would have been running around like chickens without heads."

"So the annual Lord Mayor's Day parade provided Jack with the optimal circumstance under which to commit his crime," Adelaide said.

"Very good, Miss Oddie," Doyle said. "You've got it. Now any other questions regarding this murder before we go on?"

"Sir Arthur, you say that Mary Kelly was much younger and stronger than the Ripper's prior victims. Maybe he moved indoors because his hatred for women had reached the point at which he was looking for an out-and-out brawl, so he could truly rip someone apart," Evander said.

"Perhaps she was able to fight him off at first, but eventually he gained the upper hand and brought her inside," Matthew said.

Dr. Hammond summarily rejected both statements. "Poppycock!" he said. "I love that British term of yours. In America, we tend to use more profane and descriptive words for rubbish. Nevertheless, if things had unfolded this way, it would have been so noisy inside her dwelling that there would have been no way her neighbors would not have been made aware of the crime. Someone would have heard the commotion, and someone would likely have witnessed at least a portion of the assault. Dr. Doyle, am I correct when I say there was no evidence at the scene to suggest Mary had made an attempt to fend off her assailant?"

"No signs at all," Doyle said. "As a matter of fact, precisely the opposite. With the exception of her corpse and that two-foot square, everything was as neat as a pin."

"Mary Kelly unknowingly invited the Ripper into her apartment, and once inside, he did what he did best," Dr. Hammond said.

Doyle now looked at his watch and saw that it was close to 5 PM. "Time is growing short," he said, "and so I would like to open the floor to a discussion of some of the characters who became the suspects of the Yard and of the press. Is there anyone who would like to start?"

"I have heard others theorize that certain members of the royal family might have been involved, and that one of them in particular, the Duke of Clarence, had been suspected," Matthew said.

"Yes, the Duke, Queen Victoria's grandson, although at the time of the murders his title was Prince Albert Victor of Wales," Doyle said. "He would later become both Duke of Clarence and Duke of Avondale, and has long been rumored to have been the Ripper. Alas, this poor young royal has been unfairly accused of impregnating each of these women and then getting rid of them in order to maintain his rank. Another rumor, even more preposterous in nature, is that he had impregnated only one of these ladies, and it was her inability to keep the secret that had sealed her fate and the fates of her confidantes. I happen to know several of Dr. Hammond's American profanities, and even though I am tempted to yell one out, I will restrain myself. Not only was Prince Albert out of town when the murders were committed, he was out of the country, visiting Holyrood Castle in my beloved home city of Edinburgh.

"And how do I know that the theory of the pregnant prostitute is incorrect? I will tell you right now, Mr. Stanton. I have gone over each and every word of the autopsy reports with a fine-toothed comb, and the word 'fetus' does not appear in any of them. The fact is that all the women were malnourished, in poor health, and in the non-fertile age of their lives at the time of their deaths, save for Mary Kelly."

The group nodded in acknowledgement.

"While we are on the subject of royalty, however," Doyle said, "two of the Queen's surgeons were also put on the list of suspects, though the idea that either of these men would have been subjected to such disrespect borders on the absurd. The inclusion of Dr. William Gull on the list represents a most ludicrous choice, for at the time of the murders he was sixty-two years old and his right arm had been paralyzed by apoplexy. Imagine if you will, Her Majesty's Royal Physician huffing and puffing down Berner Street towards Mitre Square with his right arm dangling at his side. Now picture him slaying a woman twenty years his junior with an arm he hardly ever used, and doing so with meticulous skill. It defies logic. And pity poor old Dr. Edward Sieveking, the other suspect. The man was fortunate to be breathing at all. He was seventy-two years old, and with as many health problems as there are stars in the sky. Let us put this all to rest."

"You are quite right about those two, Sir Arthur," Edgar said. "But I have some information to impart to you that may be of interest to us all. One of my father's friends knew someone who had served as an investigator for the Yard back then, and who insisted that he knew Jack's identity. Evidently his claim was quashed by the authorities for some unknown reason."

"I'm dying to know! Who was the true killer?" Doyle said.

"I have been waiting for this moment to arrive, Sir Arthur, and I take further pleasure in revealing the identity of the perpetrator of the Whitechapel horrors. Not only did he reside in this district when these foul deeds occurred, he actually conducted a business here, so he knew this area like the back of his hand."

"I—we—are hanging on your every word!"

"Good! I am going to tell you. The name he went by when he dwelled here was George Chapman."

"George Chapman!" Carrington said. "I remember that name from a poisoning case that took place not much more than five or six years ago. Is that the same man?"

"It is. They are one and the same."

"Chapman!" Doyle said. "Allow me a wild guess. Your father's friend knew Frederick G. Abberline."

"Why, yes, he did. But how did you come up with that?" Edgar said.

"Mr. Collins, when it comes to old Fred, he should know better than to risk ruining his reputation by partaking in inane speculation."

"But, Sir Arthur, the facts all fit! For instance, the date of Chapman's arrival in England coincides with the commencement of the Whitechapel murders. And isn't it a bit odd that the murders seemed to have been transported onto American soil as soon as he made his transatlantic voyage just three years after these murders? And isn't the fact that he had studied medicine and surgery in Russia prior to his arrival here in London a bit macabre, especially when, in my estimation, the murders we're talking about were the work of a man with an expertise in surgical technique? Furthermore, the poisoning cases in question show a more than average knowledge of toxicology. This was a person who possessed a real knowledge of medicine, and we cannot ignore the story that Chapman's own wife told the American authorities about his attempt to do away with her with a long knife."

Stephen made more entries into his notebook, while Doyle lifted both his hands and made an "X" with them, signaling Edgar to stop talking at once. He took one step forward and slipped his hands into his vest pockets. "Mr. Collins, while some of your points may have validity," Doyle said, "it is more important to examine the facts and not the conjecture of a disgruntled, disappointed, and disillusioned old detective. Mr. Severin Antoniovich Klosowski, for that is George Chapman's real name, emigrated from Poland, not Russia, less than a year before any of the murders took place. He was in his early twenties then, and would have been far too young to have matched the description ascribed to the Ripper. As a relative newcomer to the East End, he would not have been familiar enough with the labyrinthine Whitechapel streets and alleys to have successfully evaded the police in darkness. There are very few who can wend their way through its maze without being trapped by dead ends suddenly encountered out of nowhere, and I include locals who have lived here all their lives. Chapman, as he called himself, had the additional obstacle of not being fluent in the English language. This would have surely impeded his ability to lure women into dark alleyways, or, as Mr. Mitchell pointed out, to get one to take out a cachou. Detective Abberline's statements about Chapman's preference for the use of poison over a knife, when combined with the other notions I have just pointed out, tend to discredit this accusation."

"My father also disclosed that a cryptic message had served as a heading for one of Jack's letters to the police," Edgar said, "but no one has ever been able to decipher its meaning."

Edgar's startling revelation took Doyle completely by surprise. "Cryptic message! I have seen the letters, all of them, and there was nothing cryptic about any of them," he said.

"I'm not talking about mere words or phrases, Sir Arthur. What I am referring to is the language of symbols and correspondences." Edgar reached into his pocket and asked Doyle to grant him another moment to finish up. "Actually," he said, "from the very moment we started this wonderful tour, I had hoped to be granted the opportunity to put this letter before you for your perusal. If there is anyone who has the God-given talent to solve this puzzle, it is you, Sir Arthur." Edgar deftly pulled out a crumpled piece of paper from his pocket, unfolded it, and proudly handed it over to Doyle.

Doyle's blue eyes moved back and forth across this facsimile of a supposed Ripper letter, scrutinizing the images before him. The smile on his face told the group that he was amused by what he was reading. "All right, my friends," he said. "What could have been going through the brain of a man who draws a coffin with a cross on it, a haloed skull and crossbones, a walking skeleton, a knife dripping with blood, and a honing stick? And Mr. Collins, there was one thing that had the potential of being overlooked on this paper, and that is the letters B, L, O, O, and D, which are scattered about the note. They do spell out the word blood, don't they? As our resident expert on what goes on inside the mind of a lunatic, Dr. Hammond, might you offer us your thoughts?"

"You're being facetious, Dr. Doyle," Dr. Hammond said.

"Not at all, Dr. Hammond. I would really like to hear your interpretation of these 'symbols and signs' that Mr. Collins has so generously put before us."

"As you wish. While the genesis of this imagery lies in the killer's twisted mind, his thoughts and dreams are certainly not buried too deeply beneath the surface. In truth, there's really nothing much hidden here."

"I have to agree with you. Have you any final thoughts to share?"

"Dear Dr. Doyle, has the Yard employed any fingerprint analysis to help them with this case?"

Evander chimed in. "Sir Arthur, hasn't the passage of time invalidated the usefulness of any of the remaining fingerprints?" he said. "Wouldn't they have faded away and become chemically incorporated into the paper?"

Doyle shook his head in disagreement. "Not at all, Mr. Stanton. The advent of fingerprinting vastly enhanced the crime-solving abilities of police forces the world over because prints are not transient, they are permanent. There are no inherent time constraints here, although in this case there are some factors that tend to diminish the usefulness of fingerprints. Does anyone want to hazard a guess as to what those factors may be?"

"Is one of them the fact that fingerprinting didn't come into existence until after the Ripper's crime spree had ended?" Matthew said.

"Yes, Mr. Stanton," Doyle said. "You see, even though Francis Galton was busy studying this new method of forensic science at the time, Scotland Yard was slow to appreciate how helpful fingerprinting could be in solving future, present, and past crimes. Unfortunately, this simple yet elegant practice continued to go unused for the classification of criminal records anywhere in the British Empire until 1897, when Her Majesty's Government published a directory of prints in India. It was only eight years ago, in 1902, that fingerprinting was first employed in the United Kingdom to convict an individual of a crime. It happened that a burglar had made his entry through a window whose sill had just received a fresh coat of paint, and in doing so had left a print of his left thumb. After comparing the print to the fingerprints of known criminals on file, the police were able to determine the identity of the perpetrator. He was brought to trial and sentenced to seven years of penal servitude. And although I included the use of fingerprinting in my story 'The Adventure of the Norwood Builder' a few years back, I doff my hat to Dr. Hammond's compatriot Mark Twain, who beat me to the subject by a full decade in his book *Pudd'nhead Wilson.*"

"Dr. Doyle, getting back to the Ripper's letters and the Yard, what is painfully unfortunate here is the fact that just about anyone was given unrestricted access to the Ripper letters," Dr. Hammond said. "What Scotland Yard failed to appreciate was that once the letters had been touched by anyone's hand, those prints would forever remain on them. Any fingerprints that would have come before a court of law would have had to be deemed inadmissible as evidence because all of these letters had been touched, smudged, and distorted by others. This flaw is compounded by sad truth that an insufficient quantity of prints had been obtained from the criminal population."

"Indeed, once again, you are on the mark, Dr. Hammond," Doyle said. "There aren't enough prints on file yet, and I must offer a confession to all of you who are standing before me today—I am one of those innocents who have actually held some of the Ripper's letters in their hands and been allowed to sift through their contents. But there is one saving grace. The Yard was not in any way remiss in the manner in which they handled the letters. Access to them was not granted to just anyone, only to those who were beyond reproach—people like the noted humorist Jerome K. Jerome; my brother-in-law, the writer Ernest Hornung, creator of that gentleman burglar A.J. Raffles; and me. We were fortunate enough to see the letters before a few of them were pilfered or misplaced. No one knows what happened to them, but those that remain are now kept under lock and key." Doyle scratched his head and looked up at the sky. "My goodness, almost twenty years have gone by since we did that. Where are the snows of yesteryear?"

A few second later, Stephen reached into his pocket, snatched out his notebook, and hurriedly jotted down another entry.

15

1882-1885
His Portsmouth Practice

June 1882

Arthur arrived in Portsmouth on June 24, 1882, with just enough money to subsist for a few weeks. The harbor was packed with British naval personnel who were in the preparatory stages of shipping out to protect the Empire's economic interests. The city was a bustling hub of naval operations and profitable business. It had more than an adequate supply of clubs and libraries for its wealthier and more educated inhabitants, and its railways made it easy to commute to London. The suburb of Southsea was especially attractive, as it was not oversupplied with physicians. On this blisteringly hot summer's day, Doyle left his box behind at the Clarence Esplanade pier and went off in search of a temporary place to stay. He was dressed in the only clothing he had, a heavy tweed suit. Eventually, having found a suitable lodging place, he returned to the wharf and hired a porter to carry his bags to his new quarters. Later that evening, he decided to take a walk through town. According to his account, he ended up walking right into the middle of a street fight around which a crowd of spectators had gathered.

Doyle pushed his way through the throng until he made it to center stage, where he found himself staring at a brawny drunk kicking his wife, who had a baby in her arms. He tried as best he could to act as a referee, but his efforts seemed to fall a bit short, as the irate husband turned and punched him in the throat. Of the experience, Doyle would write, "I found myself, within a few hours of my entrance into this town, with my top hat down to my ears, my highly professional frock coat, and my kid gloves, fighting some low bruiser on a pedestal in one of the most public places, in the heart of a yelling and hostile mob!" Doyle evidently escaped after the drunk turned his attention to a sailor who had been shoved between the two men, hurrying away before the police could arrive on the scene and question him.

On his second day in Portsmouth, he went to the post office and purchased an inexpensive map of the city. He returned to his room, laid the map on his table, and set up a daily itinerary designed to find a suitable location for his new practice. He covered the entire city by foot, recording on the map itself each and every brass nameplate that bore a doctor's name. Within days he "had a complete chart of the whole place, and could see at a glance where there was a possible opening, and what opposition there was at each point." What Doyle wound up with was an "empty, dust strewn" three-story redbrick house "wedged in between a church and a hotel," despite the fact that he was still virtually penniless. When asked for a reference for the house, Doyle was resourceful enough to give the name of his Uncle Henry to the landlord. Two years earlier, Henry Doyle had attained the impressive rank of Companion of the Order of the Bath, one of the highest honors granted by the Crown to civilians. The mere mention of his name exempted those he sponsored from being obligated to hand over a cash deposit when leasing or buying a home or apartment. In fact, it may have been the newly knighted Henry Doyle's name that George Budd had sought for backing when he had invited Arthur down to Bristol. The sophisticated Budd had likely known of the significance of the honor, though Arthur had probably been unaware of it at the time. By 1882, however, Doyle was cognizant of the importance and usefulness of his well-placed relative.

A few weeks later a notice appeared in the "Miscellaneous Wants" section of the *Portsmouth Evening News,* worded, "Dr. Doyle begs to notify that he has removed to 1, Bush Villas, Elm Grove, next to the Bush Hotel." Whether or not Doyle intentionally meant to mislead the public, a reader of such a public notice would have assumed that it represented a simple relocation of a practice from one part of town to another, not the inauguration of one. The nameplate Doyle used at his new office differed from the one that had been so unceremoniously removed from Budd's practice in Plymouth. The "Arthur" portion was now absent, and "Dr. Doyle" had become the more melodious and memorable "Dr. Conan Doyle." One element of convenience and professionalism, however, was still lacking at Bush Villas—namely, an assistant who could keep things in order, and who could mix medicines. Doyle immediately dashed off a letter to his mother in the hopes of getting her to send down his fourteen-year-old sister, Connie. Mary Doyle astonished her son with her response that Southsea was no place for such a young girl, and that there was no way she would allow Connie to leave home. Doyle then pleaded with his mother to send his younger brother, Innes, whom he called Duff, instead. He implored his mother in letter after letter, stating:

> Since I can't get Conny send down Duff. I shall at once put him in buttons when he arrives if I can raise the capital. I might pass him for my eldest son but it would never do to acknowledge such a youngster as a brother—however he and I will arrange the matter between us.

Doyle, well aware of the importance of public perception, wanted the public to think that he was a gentleman in his early thirties who had been charged with the unexpected responsibility of caring for his "son" by himself—a fraternal attachment was absolutely unacceptable. In this same missive, Doyle also tells his mother to have Duff bring "a pair of blankets & as many books" as she could spare. Knowing that his brother's wardrobe was quite limited and that his mother might use this fact as an excuse to keep him at home, Doyle then strategically adds, "Never mind the clothes. I'll manage to rig him out." Although her oldest son had no visible means of adequately supporting her youngest, Mary sent Innes to Arthur anyway.

En route to Southsea, the nine-year-old Innes visited his London relatives. Shortly after his departure, these same Doyles decided they would make the best effort they could to assist his older brother in growing his practice. They enlisted the support of the local Southsea curate, who paid a visit to their nephew so that his name could be spread around the Catholic community, but Arthur would have none of it and sent the priest on his way. The accomplished and wealthy Doyles of London would not abandon their wandering nephew, despite his lack of faith in Catholicism.

After he had officially moved into his home office, Doyle sent a letter to George Budd, providing his former colleague with his new address, so that Budd would know where to send the promised sum of one pound weekly. True to his word, Budd's money arrived soon thereafter. But a telegram Doyle would receive from Budd a week later would not be so kind, stating:

> When the maid was arranging your room after your departure, she cleared some pieces of torn paper from under the grate. Seeing my name upon them, she brought them, as in duty bound, to her mistress, who pasted them together and found that they formed a letter from

your mother to you, in which I am referred to in the vilest terms, such as "a bankrupt swindler" and "the unscrupulous Budd." I can only say we are astonished that you could have been a party to such correspondences, and we refuse to have anything more to do with you in any shape or form.

In *Memories and Adventures*, Arthur suggests that Budd may have read the letters from his mother while the two of them were still working together, and that Budd, having assumed that Mary's opinion was also Arthur's, may have simply been waiting for Doyle to open a practice of his own so that he might cease his weekly payment and push Arthur closer to financial ruin. In this same autobiography, however, Doyle also tells the reader that Budd "died in early middle age, and I understand that an autopsy revealed some cerebral abnormality, so that there was no doubt a pathological element in his strange explosive character." Despite the fact that it had been Mrs. Budd who had supplied her husband with the excuse he required to free himself from any responsibility to Doyle, Doyle began sending money to Mrs. Budd on a regular basis after her husband's death, ensuring that she and her young children would be able to make ends meet.

When Doyle realized that patients were coming "in at the rate of about two a week," he felt compelled to nurture his talents as a writer, submitting for publication a number of stories and "several other articles fluttering round the country looking for homes." While he never stopped working, he was forced to confess that his efforts never earned more than "50 pounds in any year. . . ." To his great relief, the floundering solo practitioner received an unexpected visit from Reginald Hoare, Mickey Hoare, and Claud Currie. They joined Doyle on a short ferry trip to the Isle of Wight, where they had a great time at the "thriving watering-place" and its famous town, Ryde. While on their way back to Portsmouth, Hoare advised Doyle to rent out his basement floor to a "decent woman" in exchange for cleaning services. Curiously, upon their return to Bush Villas that evening, Reginald, Mickey, and Claud soon left. Some sort of confrontation may have transpired between Doyle and Dr. Hoare at the time, as months later Doyle would write a letter to his old employer, asking, "Do you still feel as bitter against me as you did that evening? . . . There is no other man in the world to whom I would humble myself by repeating a thing which has once been disbelieved—but whoever has made mischief between us has lied."

People were not "flocking in with startling rapidity" to his practice, so Doyle did his best to attract new patients. Although Arthur had been admonished by William Royston Pike, a respected local physician, to take down the "free visit" plate he had mounted on an outside wall of his office, Doyle refused to accede to Pike's request. He stood firm when Pike told him that this type of chicanery might work in "some towns" but would not pass muster "in an exclusive place like Southsea." Having Innes around helped Doyle create the image for himself of a responsible and competent physician, but it was no substitute for the presence of a spouse, and Arthur was again feeling the pressure to get a wife. Once more he contemplated marriage to Elmo Weldon. Elmo would eventually inherit £1,500, although she would not be able to "touch it until the death of [her] old Aunt with whom she [lived] at Lismore." Doyle wrote to his mother, informing her that "marriage would double [his] income," but that he would marry Elmo only if he were taking in no more than £2 a week from his practice. He asked his mother if she thought it was "sensible" that Elmo come down to Ventnor on the Isle of Wight, where she and Arthur would be close to each other. It may have been that Doyle was suffering not from a broken heart as much as from empty pockets. In fact, he would write, "I wish her money was not tied up so. If I could marry it would fetch the practise up with a rush."

In the meantime, Doyle, who was in desperate need of food and cash, gave serious thought to abandoning his practice and relocating to Nepal, where he would serve as "a doctor to attend collies in the tea gardens of the Terai." While the position paid an amazing £400 a year, Doyle remained skeptical about the offer, for he believed that tea was "not one of the exports of the country, nor could it possibly grow in the marshy basin" of the region. He called upon the knowledge of his former Stonyhurst and University of Edinburgh classmate James Ryan, now the owner of an 800-acre tea plantation and 300 acres of rubber trees. Ryan informed him of Terai's location directly south of Darjeeling, and that this area grew tea very similar to that of its northern neighbor. Ryan's response, however, would not convince Doyle to accept the very lucrative post, especially after he had learned the region had seen a recent cholera epidemic, which had killed off a lot of the local labor force.

Once Doyle had decided that he would be staying put in Southsea, he set out to find a woman to handle the upkeep of his house and office. After all, the people of the Elm Grove district of Southsea expected a successful physician to have a full-time housekeeper. Doyle states that he "had a brainwave" and "put an advertisement in the paper that a ground floor was to let in exchange for services," forgetting that Hoare had told him to do this very thing a month prior. Two elderly women—Mrs. Gifford and Mrs. Smith—

replied jointly to Doyle's offer. Mrs. Smith resigned almost immediately, but her friend stayed on. Doyle was startled by the amount of furniture Mrs. Gifford had brought with her and how she had "made the plate & door knob beautiful." Bizarrely, in a letter to his mother, Doyle would also write, "[T]hat is as far as I would let her for she has been given to understand that if she comes through the door of the bedroom she leaves through the window. Luckily she has no friends about here, but still I would sooner she had no chance of telling anyone the secrets of our prison house." To what exactly he is referring here, whether in jest or in earnest, is unclear. Things soon brightened up for the twenty-three-year-old physician's practice, as he would report:

> I was sitting writing when I saw a crowd before the door—a peal at the bell—and a gentleman was carried in, just thrown from his horse. I doctored him—took him home in an open carriage (think of the advertisement!)—saw his wife—was thanked & complimented by all—and handed him over to the family doctor who bowed to my diagnosis. Ha! Ha! Wasn't that good.

Reminiscent of a short story he had written the year before called "Crabbe's Practice," in which Doyle's characters concoct a complex scheme to bring notice to a youthful doctor's practice, Doyle saw this occurrence as an opportunity to promote his business and "sent Innes off to get it into the evening papers." To Doyle, the notoriety would be "far better than the money." For the first time since Dr. Hoare's visit, Doyle dispatched a letter to his former employer, telling him about "the man who had the good taste to fall off his horse," and stating, "I stuck him together again, and it got into all the papers and got my name known a little."

By strange coincidence, the proverbial bolt of lightning struck twice in the same spot when a similar accident occurred soon afterwards right in front of Doyle's building. Once again, Doyle found his name in the papers. He would write to his mother about the matter, saying, "[W]e have had another lucky hit—A man broke his jaw & fractured his skull just outside the house today in a carriage accident." Doyle would "take him home and receive 2 guineas for [his] trouble."

The New Year was quickly approaching, and with his brother's invaluable assistance, Doyle had managed to stay afloat in Southsea. A few more fortuitous accidents and multiple referrals from Wiliam Henry Kirton, a dentist who lived across the street from him, had helped quite a bit. Doyle purchased a Christmas present for himself with £4 his Aunt Susan had sent from London. It was a red lamp that indicated the presence of a doctor's office inside a building. Arthur had enrolled Innes in a local school and would replace his "adorable door opener" with a housekeeper. In the meantime, the two brothers were preparing for one of their mother's rare visits. They sent her a list of items they wanted her to bring along, which included a "[g]lass for gas globes . . . the lamp . . . the sofa . . . two or three chairs and a table . . ." and "anything in the way of carpet." Upon her arrival, Mary Doyle voiced her pleasure with how Arthur had decorated the office as well as with his choice of location.

Now that the practice was showing signs of growth and stability, Mary Doyle withdrew her approval of Elmo Weldon as Arthur's potential spouse, despite Elmo's attractive dowry. Arthur sent a letter to Elmo telling her of his change of heart, which led to further correspondence, some of which aimed to "put [him] in the wrong," as Doyle would later say. The relationship ended, and after a final letter from Elmo, Arthur would write to his mother, telling her, "You shall see all the correspondence when you come back." This statement implies that Doyle had held on to some of the letters at least, and contradicts earlier claims that he had kept none at all. Nevertheless, Elmo vanished from Doyle's life.

January 1883

In 1883, Doyle had the good fortune of making the acquaintance of one of the Gresham Life Assurance Society's local agents, George Barnden, who provided him with a few physical examinations to perform on prospective clients. Soon after, Barnden decided to make Doyle an official "Gresham man," ensuring the survival of Arthur's practice in Southsea, at least for the time being. The job also gave Doyle the opportunity to travel to London, where the company was headquartered in the city's financial district, the Poultry. As a result, Doyle would be afforded the opportunity to visit his friend, William Burton. As a token of his appreciation for his sixty-pound annual allowance from Gresham, Arthur dedicated a song to his employers called "The Lay of the Grasshopper," which goes:

> When pestilence comes from the pest-ridden South
> And no quarter of safety the searcher can find
> When one is afraid e'en to open one's mouth
> For the germs of infection are borne on the wind

When fruit is cheap, and when coffins are dear;
Ah then, my dear friend, 'tis a comfort to know
That whenever betide, we have by our side,
A policy good for a thousand or so

In the midst of these good tidings, Doyle learned that his mother was clearing out from what she called the "deserted Edinburgh." After more than thirty years of wandering about the Athens of the North, she was abandoning it for the Yorkshire countryside. Knowing that her husband would be confined to an asylum for the remainder of his life, and aware that her oldest son was now in Portsmouth and had no intention of ever returning to Edinburgh, this was an opportunity that the forty-six-year-old Mary Doyle could not resist. She was to become the matriarch of Masongill Cottage, the ancestral home of the Waller family. Bryan Waller had come back to Edinburgh to teach pathology but still owned his place at George Square and could travel back and forth between Edinburgh and Masongill at will.

Coincidentally, Doyle's "infernal neuralgia" returned around this time. His affliction was accompanied by other signs and symptoms of disease: "colic & indigestion . . . a week's cough . . . sore throat . . . and bad dreams." Whether there was an infectious or physical component to all of it or whether all his medical problems originated in his mind cannot be determined. It is clear, however, that Doyle once again turned to self-experimentation, employing one of his photographic chemicals, pyrogallic acid, instead of the time-honored remedy of chrysarobin, to treat what he had determined to be psoriasis. The end of Doyle's four weeks of self-prescribed pyrogallic acid treatment coincided with the beginning of his letter campaign to the editors of the *Medical Times and Gazette,* which called for the immediate reinstatement of the Contagious Diseases Acts. Suspended earlier in the year, the Contagious Diseases Acts were a national mandate that placed all blame for the ravaging effects of venereal diseases squarely on the shoulders of women. Until the day on which Josephine Butler's fight against the legislation bore fruit, women who worked as prostitutes in port cities and army posts risked being incarcerated in lock hospitals, which were essentially clinics that focused on the treatment of venereal diseases. Once inside, they would be subjected to internal examinations and would not be released until doctors had "cleared" them. As a young physician working in a naval town, Doyle would have been familiar with the signs of various venereal diseases. He voiced his indignation with the suspension of the Acts in a letter to the editors of the *Medical Times and Gazette,* in which he called for the government to immediately reinstate it, writing:

As an ounce of fact is proverbially superior to an indefinite quantity of theory, I think that I am justified in citing one or two instances of the effects of the present suspension of the Acts. Being in practice as a medical man in the town most affected by the measure, I am able to speak with some authority on the subject. Last week a large transport entered Portsmouth Harbour with time-expired men from India. Upon the same day several diseased women left the hospital presumably with the intention of meeting that transport, and there was no law to prevent it. I say that if an unfortunate soldier, coming home to his native land after an absence of years, and exposed to such temptations, should yield to them, and entail disease upon himself and his offspring, the chief fault should not lie at his door.

Doyle was firm in his conviction that a central registry of prostitutes was imperative to protect the soldiers and sailors against venereal diseases. He issued a demand that all women who had been diagnosed with a sexually transmitted disease be arrested on the spot and hospitalized under lock and key until they could be declared "cured," prostitute or not. Doyle closes this same letter with the following pronouncement:

Property has depreciated near all the public-houses since the suspension of the Acts, on account of the concourse of vile women whose uproar and bad language make night hideous. I venture to say that, were the old laws enforced again tomorrow, there would still in a hundred years' time be many living who could trace inherited mental or physical deformity to the fatal interregnum which the champions of the modesty of harlots had brought about.

These words were not taken lightly, and in a letter published on June 20 by the *Medical Times and Gazette*, Frederick C. Banks of London lashed back at Doyle's statements, writing:

Nothing but sheer ignorance of the powers of the Acts, as still enforced, could have led Dr. Doyle to believe such a cock-and-bull story, or respectable journals like yours to quote it as a weapon against the late action of the Government. On reading Dr. Doyle's letter in your local contemporary, I knew at once that somebody had misled him. I wrote to him and he courteously replied that he had been misinformed, and that the Resident Medical Officer at the Portsmouth Lock Hospital had assured him that there was no foundation for the story.

In this same letter, Banks goes on to defend the Portsmouth Lock Hospital and the government's repeal of the Contagious Diseases Acts, both of which Doyle had condemned in no uncertain terms previously. After reviewing the "errors" of his hastily written letter, however, Doyle issued a retraction of his earlier words, which very few actually saw, as it appeared on an obscure page of the newspaper. Shortly thereafter, Doyle would write to his mother, telling her that there had been "a lull in the practice. . . ." Perhaps word had spread that Doyle was casting aspersions on Portsmouth and its inhabitants. For the time being, Doyle would take a strategic withdrawal from the critical arena and focus instead on writing fiction. He would also decide to be more sociable, in the hope that meeting more people might improve his reputation and practice.

November 1883

By November, Doyle had reinvented himself, becoming the "most popular man" in Portsmouth, and getting on "splendidly with everyone." Accompanying this sudden elevation in status was his induction into the Portsmouth Literary and Scientific Society, which "kept the sacred flame burning in the old city with [its] weekly papers and discussions during the long winter." Inside the Penny Street lecture hall, where this group met, Doyle claimed to have "learned to face an audience, which proved to be of the first importance for my life's work." Doyle praised the collective, saying that it was in this urbane and intellectual group that he "learned to speak out, to conceal [his] trepidations, and to choose [his] phrases."

Eager to display his talents, he volunteered to give a lecture on the Arctic seas, basing some of it on his adventures aboard the *Hope*. In a desperate attempt to impress an audience filled with military men of high rank, physicians and surgeons, men of the cloth, and prosperous businessmen, he thought he would need animal specimens to bring about his desired result. Feeling he had an insufficient number of samples, he asked his mother to send him his prized seal and bird, which he had stored in Edinburgh for safe-keeping, but these items failed to arrive in time. Doyle also needed to look the part of a gentleman explorer, and just days before his speech, he received a package from family friend Charlotte Drummond that contained an assortment of shirts and well-crafted collars. To display his appreciation, he would write to her, "I have a crutch stick of ebony and silver which I won as a prize and with the collar I am more than a masher—I am a dude—which is an Americanism for the masherest of mortals." Doyle ended up employing about "30 birds from a local stuffer," and assumed that "the audience [would] give [him] credit for having bagged the lot."

On December 3, 1883, Major-General Alfred W. Drayson, the president of the Society, called Doyle up to the lectern to commence his speech. Doyle spoke about the British expedition of 1875, praising the English seamen of the current era and expressing confidence that the Pole would be reached if future efforts were "attempted in the manner which was most calculated to lead to success." His lecture was met with loud applause. With his place in the Society now established, Doyle found it much easier to make new friends and acquaintances, one of them being Major-General Drayson himself. A Renaissance man, Drayson was a historian, an artillery professor at Woolrich Academy, a noted writer, and a world expert on billiards and the card game known as whist. He was also an astronomer, although his view on the heavens was regarded as a bit unorthodox by the Royal Academy. What charmed Doyle most, however, was Drayson's expertise on all things occult. Doyle would be taken under Drayson's wing to learn about Spiritualism and, twelve years later, would join the Society of Psychical Research, a group dedicated to examining these phenomena.

A few days after his successful lecture, Doyle received word that his favorite uncle, Richard, had suffered a stroke on his way home from the Athenaeum Club, and that after slipping into a coma, he had died the next day. Arthur and Innes took a train to London to attend the funeral service, where the two of them served as the representatives of Charles Doyle's side of the family. Although Arthur considered his father a man of elegance, charm, wit, and morality, he may have been embarrassed by his father's illness and by any questions that may have arisen in regard to his father's well-being. Alcoholism was regarded as a dire curse in Victorian England, with epilepsy not far behind. After the service, Arthur was miffed when he discovered that his name had been left off the published list of funeral attendees. He even wrote an angry letter to the papers demanding that they print an addendum that would acknowledge his presence that day.

Innes and Arthur went their separate ways, with Innes heading to Yorkshire to visit his mother at Masongill and Arthur returning to his Portsmouth practice. Two weeks later, Arthur decided to ring in the New Year in Birmingham with the Hoare family. He asked his mother's permission to allow Connie to come down to Birmingham. Connie was scheduled to go on to London afterwards, but Doyle had other plans for his sister. According to Arthur, "Aunt Annette was not ready to receive her & B'ham was getting rather dull," so he nobly volunteered to take Connie to Southsea with him. During her brief sojourn there, her big brother was proud to show her off at any upscale events he could—formal dances, Literary and Scientific Society gatherings, and dinner parties. Everyone she passed was mesmerized by her aristocratic aura, noting that "her beauty [was] only equalled by the sweetness of her manners." It was at this time that Doyle's short story "John Barrington Cowles" was in its embryonic stages, and soon after Connie's departure, Doyle was once again "grinding away all day at the extraordinary circumstances in connection with the death of John Barrington Cowles."

Having paid his respects, Doyle directed his mother to tell Innes that it was both his right and duty to "load himself with plunder" from their recently departed beloved uncle's estate. Over the course of the next few weeks, Arthur was able to secure six of Richard Doyle's "rosewood chairs—a sofa—and a table." With his home and office teeming with valuable furniture, paintings, illustrations, and accessories, Doyle would tell his mother, "I have now in the consulting Room 16 pictures hung—including 9 Charles Doyles—which 16 pictures I value at something over 100 pounds. Ha! Madam, see what a great thief you have for a son." Within a month, however, his health took a turn for the worse, and by February Doyle was revisited by what he thought was his "old African fever." His bones felt as if they were about to break, his hands shook to the point where he could no longer hold a pen, and he was experiencing chills and night sweats. Adding insult to injury was the sad fact that just when he was rallying, he was challenged with "a few slight bladder symptoms." Doyle had stubbornly coped with these symptoms in silence, but after a time he was forced to ask Dr. William Pike to look after his practice so that he could attend to his illness.

January 1884

Doyle's short story "J. Habakuk Jephson's Statement" was published by the *Cornhill Magazine,* England's most highly regarded literary journal, in January of 1884. Its new editor, James Payn, printed the story anonymously and presented it to the public as a true account of the discovery of the ghost ship the *Mary Celeste,* a British-American merchant vessel that had washed up off the Gibraltar coast some twelve years earlier. Although it became popular with the public, this so-called firsthand account also elicited an angry response from Her Majesty's Advocate-General of Gibraltar, Sir Frederick Solly-Flood, the principal investigator of the actual incident, who criticized the tale as "a fabrication from beginning to end." In truth, even those only vaguely familiar with the incident could have easily determined that it was just a story and nothing more. Doyle subtly changes the name of the boat to the *Marie Celeste*, is off by one year regarding the date of its recovery, has it departing from Boston rather than New York, and renames its captain. Nevertheless, publications from far and wide picked up the story and ran it as gospel. In the end, the twenty-four-year-old Doyle came away with an increased confidence in his ability to write convincing tales.

Arthur was then invited by the *Cornhill Magazine* to be among the literati at a social event that was held in Greenwich at the famed pub the Ship Tavern. There Doyle met the "shrewd rather mercantile looking" James Payn for the first time, and was also introduced to botanist Allan Grant; artist George Du Maurier, who would reach greater fame a decade later with his gothic novel *Trilby;* Fred Boyle, author of *Camp Notes;* and Thomas Anstey Guthrie, author of *The Giant's Robe.* At the end of the festivities, Doyle and a few others strode along the streets of London. After more drinking, Doyle left the group underneath the Adelphi Arches. From there he went to William Burton's house, where the two of them spent the entire night reminiscing about old times.

April 1884

It was the Easter season and Arthur rewarded Innes, who was enamored of all things military, with a four-mile walk to what had been dubbed Palmerston's Folly twenty-five years before. Portsdown Hill was a collection of forts that Prime Minister Lord Palmerston had constructed to protect the city from the possibility of a French cross-channel invasion. Presently the public would be able to enjoy a full week of military exercises there designed to enlist support for the Crown's imperialistic agenda. The streets were flooded with civilians, an estimated one hundred thousand of them, and soldiers of all types, including "linesmen, marines, artillery, blue jackets, cavalrymen, grey clad London highlanders with woodcock crests," and more. Flags waved in the breeze below every window.

The two Doyle brothers fought their way through the madding crowd, finally making it down to the chalk bluffs of Portsdown Hill, where they got to witness firsthand the Cambridge University Rifle Volunteers, the Fourth Middlesex regiment, and representatives of the Inns of Court, who were firing their rifles in unison to ensure that the festivities got off to a flying start. Battle reenactments of all kinds made the crowd feel as if actual warfare was being waged. Arthur, however, was less than impressed with the skill level of the troops, and would write that many of them would have had "a premature interview with their creator" had this been the real thing. At the "hurly-burly" evening's end, the young physician and his brother returned home and sat down to tea. Arthur wrote a letter to his mother at the Waller Yorkshire estate: "The tide of battle has rolled over us, the rival armies have disappeared, and on the field of carnage the foul bird flaps its heavy wings over the empty ginger beer bottle. While it lasted we had a great carnival."

May 1884

The two oldest Doyle girls, Lottie and Annette, decided to take some time off from their roles as governesses in Portugal and made the voyage back to Liverpool. Rather than traveling to nearby Masongill, where they could have seen their mother, they chose to head straight down to Southsea to visit their brother, who had recently observed his twenty-fifth birthday. During their stay, Arthur showed them around town whenever his schedule permitted, and when it did not, the two ladies simply set off on their own. A couple of weeks into their visit, their close friend, Jessie Drummond, traveled down by rail from Edinburgh to join the Doyle siblings. Upon her arrival, the group decided to ferry over to the Isle of Wight for a day trip. The trio of modern women evoked in Doyle a combination of shock and humor whenever they unabashedly lit their cigarettes and discussed controversial issues that hitherto had been taboo for Victorian ladies to mention. He was proud to be in their company, and was impressed by their spunk and independence.

One month later, after everyone had cleared out of Southsea, Arthur served as Lottie's adviser after she wrote him a letter from Lisbon telling him that she was considering marrying a man that she had met on her return to Portugal. He furnished her with some "brotherly" advice about matrimony, warning her it would be a violation of propriety to rush into marriage. He added that she of all people should never allow the possibility of tarnishing her reputation by making a rash decision. It was imperative for her to investigate the social and medical histories of this man and of his family, his prospects of making an adequate living, and the stability of his personality. Lottie found her brother's concerns to be well founded and rejected her suitor's proposal.

Lottie's issue made Arthur realize that the time he had spent focusing on his medical studies and now on his practice had afforded him little opportunity to secure a relationship with a member of the fairer sex. The short stay of his sisters and Jessie Drummond emphasized the idea that he needed a woman in his life. Even before the girls' departure, Doyle dashed off a letter to Jessie's mother, stating, "I don't know what I shall do when the three of them go off and leave me in my primitive loneliness." While his relationship with Jessie Drummond was strictly platonic, the way in which she laughed at his witticisms, as well as her genuine interest in his adventure stories, afforded Arthur the chance to gain the self-confidence required to pursue a relationship with a woman.

Around this same period, Arthur would describe his financial situation to his mother, telling her of his recently self-imposed austerity program. Always selective about his choice of stationery, he would begin with a small request, stating, "I hope this will reach you in time to tell you that the black edge crested paper is the best in my opinion and I am somewhat short of it." He would then move on to more serious issues of necessity, writing:

> The only other thing that I can think of which you might have better & cheaper than us is butter. My friend Lloyd has promised to send me down a sack of potatoes which will come useful during the winter. I am economizing very hard just now for the reason that it seems very probable that I may not get any more Gresham examinations to do, and as I drew about 70 pounds from them last year that would make a difference in the income. It seems that some of the old original examiners here have complained to the head office that I am taking all the work, and head office are inclined to favour their appeal by stopping my exams for a year or two so as to give them a turn. Nothing is decided yet, but the matter is being discussed up there and it is very likely to go against me. In case it does it will not do me any permanent harm for I can keep going without their aid very nicely now, though it was invaluable at the time. I shall drop my policy, apply for an examinership in another office and by cutting down some of my unnecessary expences such as egg for breakfast, newspapers &c (including my holiday by the way) I shall more than cover the amount. I shall also pitch into the writing very hard this winter, as indeed I am doing now. So don't annoy yourself about this—even if it goes against me—for it may do me good rather than harm.

A subsequent letter home confirms further adversity, explaining that one of the stories he had submitted would not see publication, as Arthur states,

"'Professor Baumgarten' came back from [the *Cornhill Magazine*] as I prophesied it would. I have had a great run of bad luck of late."

February 1885

In need of respite from his everyday life, Doyle headed straight to William Burton's place to engage in their usual photographic research, and to read him excerpts from a story that five years later would be published as *The Firm of Girdlestone*. Soon after, he went over to his Aunt Annette's house, where he convinced her to give him a valuable clock. While there, he overheard a conversation involving the sale of his Uncle Richard's childhood journal for £200 and immediately posted a letter to his mother about the matter, saying that, as Charles Doyle's wife, she was absolutely entitled to a quarter of the proceeds. His health soon began to pose problems for him again, and when he left London he was suffering with an upper respiratory infection, a dental abscess, and an exacerbation of his dreaded neuralgia. Once back in Southsea, he would express his plaintiveness, stating, "Things are dull here—weather, trade, spirits, and all things else. Nobody seems to have any money—and I am no exception to the general rule."

It seemed that everything he had tried had come to nothing—his partnership and friendship with George Budd had failed, his relationship with Elmore Weldon had flickered out, and his practice in Southsea was fading. But money was not the only thing on his mind. It was the disintegration of his dignity that bothered him as well.

Although Arthur had been granted the paired degrees of bachelor of medicine and master of surgery in 1881, which allowed him to practice medicine anywhere in the Empire, he perceived the doctor of medicine degree, for which he was now eligible, as the ultimate prize. To be granted this postgraduate research degree, Arthur was required to submit a successful thesis to the University of Edinburgh's Faculty of Medicine. Arthur would write to his mother at Masongill and state, "I am going to take my MD this coming year, if I can. I find it will be useful to me. I have too many irons in the fire to hope to write anything elaborate, so I shall content myself with a little treatise on locomotor ataxy, with some theories of my own concerning that disease. To that end I wish you to get me through Livingstone a copy of Julius Althaus' recent monograph on Locomotor Ataxia."

Locomotor ataxia refers to the sudden stabbing pains in the trunk and extremities, loss of muscle coordination, bone and joint problems, and other neuralgic disturbances that follow tabes dorsalis, the degeneration of the spinal cord and nerve roots. It is most often the result of an untreated case of the sexually transmitted disease syphilis, manifesting itself late in the course of the illness. This was the subject that would become Doyle's topic of discussion for his MD degree. Although syphilis was running rampant throughout Europe, much about the illness was unknown. In fact, Doyle had been taught by his professors that although it could be spread from person to person during sexual relations, it was more frequently passed down from generation to generation, from mother or father to the offspring. This concept, known as "Lamarckian inheritance," ruled the day.

The Althaus report unequivocally states, "[I]n all cases before ataxy is observable, is the abolition of the patellar tendon reflex, or knee jerk (Westphal's symptom)." This particular finding may have concerned Arthur, as his father had already been noted as having lost this reflex. In fact, it was Charles's only abnormal physical finding in all his years of institutionalization. If the loss of this reflex was the first sign of locomotor ataxia, and locomotor ataxia was most commonly caused by syphilis, Doyle may have worried about his father having the disease. And because he believed the illness to be inheritable, he may have worried about himself as well. This thesis topic may, in fact, have been chosen to allow him to research the subject without revealing any ulterior motive for doing so. Doyle committed himself to reading every article that existed about locomotor ataxia, perhaps praying that a more benign disease than tabes dorsalis might offer an explanation for his father's problems. Arthur would tell no one other than his mother about his choice of topic, and just a few weeks before he submitted his thesis, he even did his best to throw his sister Lottie off the track by writing to her and saying, "I am working at my MD thesis—on inflammation of the sebaceous glands at the base of the ortho fotio sukafantadika teleiporos" (*sic*).

Doyle knew that his essay would have to be skillfully done if it was to convince the medical faculty of its worth, as he had no real clinical element to help him present a cogent argument. He called upon his literary prowess to persuade the university that he merited an MD degree. In his thesis, he states, "There are few diseases which possess a more extensive literature than does tabes dorsalis, and none perhaps, considering the short time since Duchenne first drew attention to it, which has attracted the attention of so many brilliant investigators." Doyle was likely counting on the possibility that his opening statement would suggest to his reviewers that they were about to evaluate a work of great importance. He then directs a subtle barb at some of the giants of nineteenth-century medicine as he writes, "Yet in spite of the researches of such men as Erb, Charcot, Leyden and a host of others, our knowledge of the initial lesion in tabes, and still more of a course of treatment which may cause permanent improvement in the patient, is scanty in the extreme." By downplaying the accomplishments of these devoted clinicians Doyle may have been hoping to elevate himself in the eyes of those who would judge him.

Doyle then displays humility to the judges, saying, "It is with diffidence that a young medical man must approach a subject upon which so many masterminds have pondered—more particularly when the views that he entertains differ in many respects from any he had encountered in his reading." Although the word "diffident" implies a certain reserve and timidity, Doyle's suggestion that his theories are totally without precedent nevertheless shows a strong sense of ego. He goes on to disparage the well-situated and sufficiently cultured city of Portsmouth, which he and his mother had carefully selected as the right location to set up his practice, by writing, "Doubly diffident must he be when enforced residence in a provincial town cuts him off from the pathological and histological aids which might enable him to strengthen his argument." This jab at Portsmouth seems totally unwarranted, as the city was easily accessible by rail to London and had a thriving and accomplished medical, literary, and philosophical community of its own. The employment of the words "provincial" and "cut off from knowledge" had little basis in fact, and may be interpreted as a self-serving vehicle for unmerited advancement.

Doyle continues to lay blame on his environment in order to excuse any shortcomings of his thesis, as he states, "In the preparation of a thesis upon such a subject the post-mortem room and the microscope are of more value than the writing desk and the library. A workman must however work with such tools as he finds to his hand and this I have endeavoured to do to the best of my ability." If Doyle had truly been deprived of the "tools" of his trade, it is difficult to explain why he would have selected such a potentially problematic topic as the subject of his thesis. His claim that he had no access to sophisticated instruments and apparati, and that he had no access to autopsies, is actually unfounded. Certainly his friendship and association with the Royal Portsmouth Hospital's chief medical officer (and his own personal physician), William Royston Pike, would have given Doyle unlimited and unhindered access to a sprawling world-class medical complex that at the time had never been busier. This meant that cadavers, microscopes, chemical reagents, and anything else needed for clinical and academic research would have been within Doyle's reach. Indeed, the very same Dr. Pike had authored a recently published article in the *Pharmaceutical Journal,* in which he boasts that he "made a post-mortem examination" and after a careful "examination by the microscope" proved a case of murder by arsenic poisoning.

In a depiction of a typical victim of locomotor ataxia, Doyle makes vast generalizations, stating, "In many cases he is of that swarthy neurotic type which furnishes the world with an undue proportion of poets, musicians, and madmen. In nine cases out of ten he has had syphilis, possibly a year ago, more probably four, eight, twelve or even twenty years before." This description is Lamarckian in its emphasis on a specific "type" of individual who would be genetically susceptible to the ravages of locomotor ataxia. Doyle appears to be alluding to an 1869 publication by Francis Galton called *Hereditary Genius: An Inquiry into its Laws and Consequences,* which divides natural genius into two components, one classifying men according to their reputation and the other classifying them according to their natural gifts. Indeed, three sequential chapters in the book are "Poets," "Musicians," and "Painters." Substituting the term "madmen" for "painters" may have been Doyle's way of giving a nod to the public perception of his father.

It is fascinating that the following vignette in Doyle's thesis contains almost all the signs and symptoms that had finally driven him to seek the help of his colleague Dr. Pike the year before. In it, he writes:

> Various little symptoms show him however that the demon which has seized him has not relaxed its grip. He may have fleeting attacks of facial neuralgia and even of facial paralysis. Strange flushes come over him and he perspires profusely without obvious cause. Numbness and prickling alternate in different parts of his frame. His sexual desire which has possibly for some time back been inordinate begins to wane. Vague pains which have been flitting about his lower limbs and which he has probably ascribed to rheumatism, become more intense and sudden in their character until he can only compare them to electric shocks. The sufferer's appetite has been probably capricious for some time back and his digestion uncertain. Suddenly someday after a meal he is seized by an irresistible attack of nausea. He vomits for hours, throwing up not only all that he has eaten but also many pints of a clear mucoid fluid, occasionally stained with blood or mixed with bile. The attack continues until he is utterly exhausted. This is a gastric crisis. Or it may be a violent attack of diarrhoea with tenesmus and innumerable watery stool. Or it may be a sudden cough with difficulty of breathing.

Later on in his paper, Doyle details some of the nerve derangements that accompany tabes dorsalis, stating, "The fifth nerve shows signs of derangement early in the course of the disease. Lightning pains frequently occur along its course. Anaesethesia of the head and face is also a common symptom." Considering his own bouts with neuralgia, these facts may have caused him to consider quite seriously the possibility that he himself was afflicted with locomotor ataxia.

Doyle also makes sure to include some words from the "great German Jewish" poet Heinrich Heine, who was a victim of neurosyphilis, and who so poignantly describes his own bodily disintegration in his work. Although Doyle's long discourse on the poet makes for interesting literature, it has no scientific bearing whatsoever. Among Doyle's final words to the arbiters are, "In concluding this thesis, of the imperfect nature of which I am deeply conscious, I must acknowledge thankfully the assistance which I have received from various publications upon the subject." It would surely seem as though Doyle, a master of the written word, had hoped to get his essay approved on the basis of its literary merits instead of its scientific ones. Ultimately, his writing talent would pay off, and this very incomplete work would be considered acceptable to grant Doyle his MD, elevating his status among his peers and in the public eye in general.

16

The Tour

Miller's Court, 6 PM

It was 6 PM and the group had officially finished its circuit. Doyle pulled out his pipe, stuffed some tobacco into its chamber, and lit it. After two puffs of smoke, he asked what might rightfully have been interpreted as his final question, "Why are we ending our day here at Miller's Court and not somewhere else?"

"Could it be that any slayings after this one were not necessarily the work of the Ripper?" Matthew said.

"Not exactly." Doyle glanced over at Stephen and had no difficulty at all interpreting his body language. "Mr. Mitchell, I can see you are itching to say something. Go ahead."

"Sir Arthur, our tour must end here because this is the X that marks the spot where Jack's criminal activities came to an abrupt conclusion," Stephen said. "There's absolutely nothing beyond this point worth a visit." He held up one finger with each of his following statements. "No avenue on which he was captured by the police, no place of incarceration, no plaza to mark his public execution, no street to memorialize where he was lynched by an angry mob. It's somehow so sad and distant. As Ernest Dowson once wrote, it's all gone with the wind."

"Precisely," Doyle said. "I couldn't have said it any better myself. Old Jack managed to outwit them all, and amazingly, more than two decades later, his identity remains unknown and his legend continues to grow. I ask you, where did he go? Did he vanish into thin air? Did he descend into the depths of hell? Take a few minutes, gather your thoughts, and see if you can come up with something." He left the group to its thoughts and began to walk slowly up the street. While most of the members were busy thinking of what to say upon the return of their host, Carrington's attention was exclusively focused on Adelaide's eyes and not at all on Doyle's assignment. Three minutes later, Doyle strolled back to the group and immediately asked Adelaide for her thoughts.

"I believe he must have been a Navy man on leave here in London, and that once he returned to his ship and set sail, he became forever free," she said.

"Very good," Doyle said. "But what do you think would drive a man of the sea to commit such gruesome atrocities?"

"Sir Arthur, I don't think this man needed any motive to do what he did. Ars gratia artis—art for art's sake, and murder for murder's sake."

"A bit terse, Miss Oddie, but once again, very well considered. And I do appreciate the Poe reference. Let us assume that this was the case. Dr. Hammond, I want to ask you something now. Do you believe that Jack would have picked up his knife again and made our tour longer than it was today, had he returned to London after another voyage?"

"Nothing tempts like temptation," Dr. Hammond said, pushing his glasses a bit higher on his nose with one finger. "But I want to go back to Miss Oddie's statement for a moment. It is true, merchant ships provide havens for many men with backgrounds steeped in mystery. There is an unwritten code that their privacy is inviolable. Their secrets are forever their own. No breeches of this strange etiquette are ever tolerated. And to your question, Dr. Doyle, the opportunity to kill again would have been too much for a man with such a psychopathic nature to resist."

"Well done, Dr. Hammond," Doyle said, turning his attention to Carrington. "Mr. Lambton, where do you think the Ripper went?"

"I agree with Miss Oddie and Dr. Hammond," he said.

Unwilling to let Carrington off the hook, Doyle asked him to explain how and why he had come to this same conclusion. Now Carrington was forced to expound upon the mariner theory.

"Having returned to his ship, Sir Arthur, he would have resumed his assigned duties," Carrington said. "But with each opportunity to leave his vessel at its many ports of call, there is no reason to expect that he would have controlled his malevolent impulses."

"Interesting. And I must admit that once the killings ended here in London Town, I began to study newspaper accounts of other murders committed in Europe and the Americas to see if any of them conformed to Jack's style. While I found gory slayings in each of the four corners of the globe, none of them had been performed with the Ripper's precision. But thank you, Mr. Lambton. Quite good." Doyle pointed politely at Evander and asked him if he had any theories.

Evander stood up straight, pulled his shoulders back, and raised his chin. It was almost with delight that he offered his take. "Yes, I do have a theory," he said, "and a good one at that. It is my contention that Jack was apprehended right here in London for some other crime or crimes that were completely unrelated to the murder of the five prostitutes. Yes, it would have been true that the Whitechapel murders would have come to an abrupt stop, but it would not have been because the Ripper wanted it so."

"What you're implying is that he was arrested and taken into custody for robbery, arson, or some other criminal activity, and was therefore prevented from continuing his murderous spree. I like that," Doyle said.

Matthew meekly tilted his head to the right, elevated the palm of his hand to ear level, and asked Doyle permission to raise a question of his own. Doyle smiled at him, nodding his head in the affirmative.

"If Evander is correct, then Jack would not have been arrested for something trivial, but for a crime that would have placed him behind bars for a long time," Matthew said, narrowing his brother's theory.

"Why do you say that?" Doyle said.

"I am using retrospective analysis. After all, twenty-five years have gone by, and if the Ripper had been incarcerated for simple robbery or arson, he would have been out of prison by now. Am I right, Sir Arthur?"

"That depends on other factors. Sometimes a criminal will have something on his record that will add years to his sentence. Nevertheless, both Stanton brothers have done outstanding work here today."

Adelaide raised her hand and waited patiently for Doyle to call on her.

"Yes, Miss Oddie?" Doyle said.

"Jack the Ripper's criminal bent may have been the very reason why the month of October of 1888 saw no activity by him. He may have been arrested for something minor, something that called only for a few weeks behind bars. This short period of incarceration would have put him on temporary hiatus," she said.

"Could be," Doyle said.

"I'm pretty sure I know the kind of place in which the Ripper resides now," Edgar said. "That is, if he is still among the living."

"And what kind of place would that be, Mr. Collins?" Doyle said.

"A lunatic asylum somewhere in Britain. For although he may have managed to escape the law, there was no escape from his irrational mind. And while he may not have killed again, I cannot conceive of him behaving normally for more than a short time. Eventually, he would have been committed to a mental institution. Jack was probably an individual prone to periodic fits of homicidal mania—a Jekyll and Hyde. Madmen tend to be quite astute in masking their afflictions, and Jack may have perpetrated murder both prior to and after his 'official' Ripper crimes. I can easily visualize Edward Hyde revering back to the irreproachable Dr. Jekyll immediately after each and every killing."

"You can, Mr. Collins?"

"Yes, I most certainly can."

Doyle voiced his approval of Edgar's hypothesis and then turned once again to Matthew for his thoughts. Surprised by Doyle's attention, he regained his composure before responding. "Jack would have been keenly aware that the police and the neighborhood vigilance committees were out in full force looking for him," Matthew said. "He would certainly have known that by continuing his rampage much longer they would track him down and bring him to the gallows. But I disagree with Mr. Collins's assessment that Jack would have found it difficult, or even impossible, to stop his misogynistic butchery and blend into the mundane activities of his district. For all we know, he may have been counted amongst its most respected citizens."

"Capital!" Doyle said. "I like that." He turned to Dr. Hammond. "Professor Hammond, how do you see things?"

"Thank you for giving me the floor, Dr. Doyle," Dr. Hammond said. "My many years of clinical and academic practice in the field of neuropsychiatry have given me the rare opportunity to deal with patient populations from all walks of life and all socioeconomic groups. I have treated those who have shown difficulty coping with the stresses of daily life, as well as those who have been classified as criminally insane. As one of the few acknowledged experts in my field, it is not presumptuous to believe that I have earned the right for my theory to supersede any of those we have heard up to this point. I do not say this to disparage the others. I am impressed by what I have heard thus far, but I must remind all of you that the desire to destroy life is often exhibited during the earliest stages of infancy. In fact, the wish to perpetrate violence against other human beings and the lower creatures is inborn and instinctive. No amount of civilization or refinement is sufficient to abolish it in its entirety, and while most individuals succeed in suppressing this violent impulse, even the most mild-mannered of men possesses it. It is ever present and ready to dominate when a sufficient cause arises. Many of those who yield to it ultimately destroy themselves. Jack belongs to this group, so I must assume that he took his own life."

"A very interesting theory, Dr. Hammond," Doyle said.

"Any notion that suggests Jack had no motive when he murdered and mutilated these poor women is entirely without merit," Dr. Hammond said. "My clinical experience tells me that there is no such thing as a murder without a motive. It also tells me that those who possess to an inordinate degree the propensity to kill their fellow creatures are generally skillful at concealing their motives. Often, in fact, a murderer is driven by reasons that fail to explain his actions—if those actions are viewed from a normal standpoint. There is no delusion or emotional disturbance, nor does he exhibit any deficiency of intellect. He is perfectly aware of the nature of the act and simply feels moved by an irresistible force. Very often he manifests calmness and deliberation. At other times, he may display agitation or excitement. Once his impulse has been satisfied, he recollects distinctly all the circumstances of the occasion.

"I am inclined to think that our perpetrator was a reasoning maniac, one who had received or imagined he had received some injury from the class of women upon which his crimes were perpetrated. He assumed the role of reformer, one who thought he would either annihilate these women one by one or strike such terror into them that they would abandon their unsavory ways. He was probably a person whose insanity was not suspected. If it wasn't suspected, it certainly would not have been detected, even by those who were in constant association with him. It is quite conceivable that our killer may have passed a dozen policemen on his way towards the accomplishment of his nefarious purpose. It would be to his advantage if he were high up in the social scale, for if he were of a lower echelon, he would be subject to more suspicion.

"I would like to share one final thought with you. We can all see that this man was a veritable genius, even though he was a psychopath. Unfortunately, the two can paradoxically reside in the same body, as Robert Louis Stevenson reminds us. Jack was a man who was convinced beyond all doubt that his intellect would enable him to elude police detection and any vigilance organizations."

"Dr. Hammond, do you think Jack might have been a member of the scientific community—a chemist or biologist, perhaps?" Adelaide said.

Dr. Hammond stood in silence but managed to nod his head a few times. "The great biologists and chemists who have become insane are so few in number that I cannot at this moment recall a single one," he said. "But the contrary holds for those who are artistic. Among the great poets, painters, novelists, and musicians who along with their genius have shown symptoms of insanity are many. The names Tasso, Burns, Swift, Mozart, Hayden, Scott, Blake, and Poe come to mind at once. And there are many more. This Jack, this Ripper, this murderer, surely had a purpose, a motive, and a calling to carry out his acts. But once he had completed his crimes, he may have been unable to go on, knowing how evil his actions had been—his only remaining option being the destruction of self: suicide."

"Dr. Hammond, a brilliant presentation, and I hope that all of us have been able to digest a large part of it," Doyle said. "What you have brought to us today makes it difficult for me to allow this meeting to end. Your erudite speculations, which are founded on a scientific basis, remind me of an interesting event that occurred three or four years after Mary Kelly's murder. It tends to merge your theory with Mr. Lambton's. Some of you may be old enough to recall the case of Dr. Thomas Neill Cream. After he had completed his medical studies at the prestigious St. Thomas's Hospital Medical School here in London, he returned to his native Canada for a while, but eventually made his way back to England. In 1892, he was apprehended for the poisoning deaths of four street women. Several witnesses to his hanging swear that he uttered, 'I am Jack the . . .' before the rope snapped his neck. Even though it was impossible for him to have been the Ripper, as he had been imprisoned in a Chicago penitentiary in 1888, the desire for fame or infamy resided in his soul. So it does for many a man, and for many a woman, too, as our absent friend Miss Pemberton might have wished us to point out.

"Now I shall make reference to another story of how the Ripper may have met his end. A newspaper account at the time reported that a lodging-house keeper had informed the Yard of a young medical student boarding there who had acted bizarrely on each of the nights of the murders. According to the lodging-house keeper, on the nights in question, this young man had returned to the dwelling dressed in clothes that differed from those in which he had left, wearing shoes that appeared stained with blood. A short time later, this same medical student's body was found in the Thames. While it is presumed that the poor lad had drowned himself, which goes hand in hand with Dr. Hammond's theory, I am certain that much of the story about the nights that preceded his death were fabricated by his landlady."

Doyle had been so impressed by Stephen earlier in the day that he made sure to save the young man's comments for last. When Stephen was called upon to add his thoughts to the conversation, he methodically slid his notebook from his pocket into his hand, opened it up, and thumbed through its contents until he found his desired page. While the group cast its eyes upon him, he looked back with a profound intensity in his gaze.

"My approach to our illustrious tour guide's question has been following a different track than everyone else's," Stephen said. "You may have noticed that I have been penciling in those items I regard as salient features of this case, which, if interpreted correctly, might enable us to identify this master criminal. What he may or may not have done in the years following his reign of terror is of little importance to me. And it should be of little importance to you. Rather, we should be limiting ourselves to studying the clues that might reveal his psyche, physique, educational background, and profession or trade. It is this information that will furnish the civilized world with Jack's true name. Sir Arthur, I would like your permission to mull over certain aspects of today's tour. These details may tell us who Jack is, not where he might be."

"You're free to do so, Mr. Mitchell. We have pretty much summed up what Jack could have done in the aftermath of his crimes. So, go ahead with your analysis," Doyle said.

"Thank you, Sir Arthur. After viewing the first four murder sites, we came to the conclusion that Jack preferred dark streets and alleys to well-lit indoor locations. Our friend Mr. Collins is a proponent of the 'lunatic theory,' which states that certain members of society can be deemed to be moonstruck. Those who accept this arcane proposition would consider this malady the consequence of a full moon exerting its effects upon the susceptible. But we know that all of the outdoor murders were committed in almost total darkness, making it impossible for any madman of London to have been exposed to the light of a full moon on those nights. Those who accept the aforementioned proposition will have to admit that on the nights Jack chose to commit his crimes, he would not have been under the moon's influence.

"As for the murder of Mary Jane Kelly, we must err on the side of caution before attributing her horrible death to the Ripper. Instead we should look in the direction of her irate former live-in boyfriend, Joseph Barnett, the man she had cast out. As for me, except for the lamentable fact that an innocent woman was brutally slaughtered by an evil person, I have no particular interest in this case."

"What are you talking about?" Matthew said.

"Sir Arthur shared some vital information with us. I'll find it in a trice." Stephen opened his notebook to the back and flipped through a few pages. "Ah, here's what we've been told. You see, when Barnett was questioned under oath, he asserted that the key to their flat had been 'lost some time ago,' and had remained so both before and after her killing. He stated that access to the apartment could only be achieved by reaching one's hand through a broken window pane and sliding open the door bolt. You do remember Sir Arthur saying this, don't you?"

"I remember it. Please go on, Mr. Mitchell," Adelaide said.

"This window had been smashed by the quarrelsome couple only days before the murder, which suggests that their altercation had escalated from the verbal to the physical—a fact that tends to incriminate Barnett, for it is not uncommon for an angry lover to return to his mate's premises, even after being ordered not to do so. In my estimation, Mary Kelly's murder was in no way a Ripper killing."

Stephen flipped back to the beginning of his notebook and the group remained attentive. "Let's move away from copycat killings and return to the genuine article. Let's start with Jack's physical appearance. The best composite sketch I can draw of him is that of a muscular, mustachioed man of approximately thirty years of age, who stood about five feet nine inches tall. He was significantly taller than almost all the people of the East End. And how do I know this last fact? Thanks to Jack London, currently America's most famous author. He lived here, a place he called London's underworld, for an entire summer. Let me paraphrase the observations he made during his sojourn in Whitechapel. He was struck by a conspicuous physical characteristic of its male dwellers, namely that he, who regarded himself as someone of only medium height, was able to look over the heads of nine out of ten men here. Evidently the great majority of its natives were short, as were the foreign sailors. The only exceptions were the Scandinavians, Americans, and Englishmen not of the area.

"As for Jack's age, it is easy to guess. Almost all the accounts I've read, as well as the supplemental information provided by Sir Arthur, approximate the Ripper's birth year to be between 1856 and 1862. So, if he's still on God's earth, he's around fifty years of age. In terms of his educational background, I'm assuming our gentleman Jack went on beyond the preparatory level and had at least a modicum of university training, probably in the field of medicine. But his training did not occur here in London, for if it had, the likelihood of his being pointed out by someone he knew would have been . . ."

"Yes, I understand what you're saying, and I agree," Doyle said. "Your point has been well made. I concur that the chances of him being identified had he studied in London proper would have been too high."

"But, Sir Arthur, somehow he managed to learn every nook and cranny of Whitechapel. He was able to maneuver into dead ends those who thought they knew the place better than anyone. Of all the mazes in the history of mankind, this city of four million is the most confusing and challenging. Even when I have a map with me, I am still forced to rely on landmarks to prevent myself from getting utterly lost. And Jack's cunning didn't end there. He manipulated the police, the newspapers, and the vigilance committees the way a master puppeteer controls the rods and strings of his marionettes. This was no ordinary man. He was always more than a step ahead of his rivals. And Sir Arthur, I must respectfully disagree with you when you hypothesize that the Ripper may have been an American. There is no doubt he was from somewhere in Great Britain. But I do agree that he knew a lot about the jargon, idioms, and customs of Dr. Hammond's native land. How did he get to know this country so well? He read and studied its literature: Mark Twain, Harriet Beecher Stowe, Edgar Allan Poe. He might even have read books written by English writers who employed Americanisms in their stories. Actually, Jack might have read *A Study in Scarlet* or one of your non-Sherlockian stories, Sir Arthur, like 'The American's Tale.' That is a jolly good one, especially the bit about the man-eating plant. I loved it."

Doyle's cheerful nod of the head let Stephen know that he was impressed by his well-considered inferences and refined literary taste.

"Mr. Mitchell, your theory implies that Jack must have been well-educated," Adelaide said, "for books like *Adventures of Huckleberry Finn* and *Uncle Tom's Cabin* were not designed for the barely literate. In fact, one must also be able to read between the lines to appreciate them fully."

"Your point is well taken, but I still have more to say," Stephen said. "Mr. Stanton's recollection of that mysterious 'Jacky' who was so flamboyantly brazen about his ability to elude any potential captors merits some discussion here. I know the source, and it is not Mother Goose's 'Little Robin Redbreast.'" Stephen recited the following words in a hushed tone:

> Pouring rain! Pouring rain!
> We must stop at home again.
> Let us have a game of play
> On this cold and rainy day!
>
> "Catch me! Catch me! If you can!"
> Jacky cried, and off he ran.

Stephen paused briefly. "It is a strange little thing," he said. "And it is my belief that the Ripper's message was derived from this nursery rhyme, which is known as 'Catch me!' by Alexander John Ellis. My mother read this creepy rhyme to me when I was little, and it has never left me."

"That's the one!" Matthew said. "Evander, you are so fortunate that you don't remember it."

"Perhaps Mother never read it to me because she liked me best," Evander said.

"Sir Arthur has been kind enough to paint a picture for us of what Jack's personal life might have been like as he embarked on his criminal career," Stephen said. "The Eddowes murder suggests he may have been a Freemason, as the arrangement of the poor woman's organs seems to echo an ancient Masonic ritual. Additionally, the message on the wall that was erased in haste by the police may have had Masonic undertones. If Jack had been a Mason, it is unlikely he was living in poverty, for members of this order tend to belong to the well-to-do class. And I don't know if it fits here, but I don't want to forget this note I jotted down. It has to do with the letter that Jack supposedly wrote to Mr. Lusk, the leader of that so-called vigilance committee. I wonder if the addition of the letter 'h' to the word 'Mister' was meant to let Lusk know that he knew him personally and did not like him."

"How so?" Doyle said.

"Well, if Lusk himself actually pronounced the word in this manner, it follows that the Ripper would have met him somewhere along the line. Makes me wonder if our Mr. George Lusk was ever a Mason."

"Maybe it's not Lusk's pronunciation of the word that should concern us here. Maybe it was the Ripper himself who used this sound when he spoke," Dr. Hammond said.

"Excellent!" Doyle said. "Perhaps a subtle clue, the nuance of which would have been discerned by only the brightest minds of Scotland Yard."

Stephen went on. "What's more, the rounded, easy handwriting and occasional embellishment of the letters with illustrations lead me to believe that Jack possessed a slightly artistic bent. But let us get to the description of Jack's outfit, which apparently included a cap with a peak—perhaps a deerstalker cap or a sailor's cap—a red neckerchief, and a grey or navy pea coat."

"Aha! So you're the Ripper, Mr. Mitchell!" Carrington said, pointing to Stephen's cap. "Stop in the name of the law!"

"You've got me. Shall I wait for the police to arrive?" Stephen let the entire group join in the fun before continuing. "But the cap I wear as a tribute to my literary hero elicits one question that demands an answer, as I shall now explain. Whenever I wear it, it draws the attention of others, for it is not part of the regular costume worn in a sophisticated city. Yet somehow, when the Ripper wore it in combination with his red muffler, he somehow managed to remain just another face in the crowd. Certainly Frederick Abberline's theory of Jack being a foreigner loses all credibility if my description of him holds water. And I assure you, it does.

"And although the Ripper performed his work in sheer darkness, he also made the paradoxical decision to do so out in the open, and in highly trafficked areas. It is clear that he never gave a thought to the possibility of being apprehended. He had no concerns about doing away with any law enforcement official who might interfere in his nefarious activities. This was a man who was absolutely sure of his invincibility, who believed he had the perfect method, and who was certain that none of his victims would be able to emit any more than a last gasp before leaving this world. There is no doubt that he was in superb physical condition when he butchered Catherine Eddowes, for when Constable Watkins arrived at the scene, the Ripper remained as quiet as a mouse. Anyone else would have been huffing and puffing audibly, becoming extremely easy quarry for the policeman.

"I have no cause to question my powers of reasoning, which have convinced me that Jack did not have to chase down Catherine Eddowes before mutilating her. Nevertheless, he must have been well prepared to defend himself against anyone who posed a potential threat to him. While he was likely experienced in some form of combat, somehow he was able to hold back the aggressive instincts that otherwise might have done him in. And as for the pea coat he was seen wearing, it suggests that he was a merchant seaman or perhaps a member of Her Majesty's Royal Navy. The discipline required in each of these vocations offers us a satisfactory explanation for his ability to control himself."

Doyle put both his hands on the ivory ball atop his cane and leaned forward. "Keep on," he said.

"As my notes state, the murderer displayed a combination of anatomical accuracy and surgical speed. Jack was able to identify, dissect, and remove a kidney with one fell swoop of his knife, despite operating in the darkest recesses of Mitre Square. Yet he had sufficient time to poke holes in her liver and take samples of it home with him. At the very least, he had to have attained the position of surgical assistant or dresser, and had to have been blessed with the eyes of an eagle. There can be no other explanation. The description of him as a man of thirty years of age tends to be confirmed here, for no one much older could have worked so accurately in such unfavorable conditions. I now proclaim myself judge and jury and hereby acquit Dr. Gull and Dr. Sieveking of the unfounded allegations lodged against them!"

Stephen paused to look over at Dr. Hammond. He could see by Hammond's facial expression and body language that the American physician knew full well that Stephen had a firm grasp on the key elements of this case. Stephen then read excerpts from the next few pages of his notebook. "Strong, agile, fast, able to outthink Scotland Yard's best, always a step ahead, taunted police with clues." Stephen paused to gather his breath and then went on. "Highly intelligent, hid his educational background, possibly a clergyman, lawyer, physician, or even a member of the titled aristocracy. And let me not forget, an able seaman or officer in Queen Victoria's Navy."

Dr. Hammond patted Stephen on the shoulder, congratulating him on the way he had been able to summarize the man behind the horror.

"Thank you, Dr. Hammond, but I'm not quite done yet," Stephen said. "Does anyone here have any misgivings about the strange fact that all the victims, save the now-excluded Mary Kelly, were in their early-to mid-forties? Harlots of that age are not the ones a man in his late twenties or early thirties would generally seek out. No, I would have expected him to pursue tarts a score younger than those, unless he had an ulterior motive to make women of a slightly older age his victims. Perhaps something compelled him, or impelled him, to render what he perceived as a deserved fate unto these women. He may even have been acting as a surrogate for someone else, exacting revenge on behalf of another.

"And Dr. Doyle, I absolutely reject any notions that have our murderer eloping overseas or committing suicide. Someone like Jack would never have willingly left London, nor would he have ever considered doing away with himself. I also cannot conceive of him being arrested for any other crime or institutionalized. Even though a quarter century has passed, we do not know who he is or what he may have been avenging. But the great city of London still remains the logical choice in regard to his whereabouts. After all, it is here where it all began." Stephen paused, leaned back a little, lifted his chin, and placed his notebook back into his coat pocket. "Somehow I envision him still toying with the Yard."

Doyle took a slow puff of his pipe and created a ring of smoke that wafted up into the East End twilight and dissipated gradually. He decided that this was the proper moment to address his amateur detectives for the final time. "So, without taking sides," he said, "there are several possibilities regarding the Ripper's ultimate fate. Jack may still be lurking about the streets of the East End; he may be under lock and key in an asylum somewhere in our beloved realm; he may have given in to his demons and done away with himself; or he may have been a merchant seaman who, having left London, carried himself and the answers we now seek to some land beyond the sea. The fact is that any one of these notions might be the correct one. So, let us return to the London Hospital, where our day began."

17

1885-1887
Of Marriage and Masons

March 1885

Despite facing the challenge of completing an entire medical thesis by month's end, Doyle somehow managed to find the time to take advantage of the many social outlets that the "provincial" town of Portsmouth afforded him. The same Dr. Pike who had taken care of him during a recurrence of his "African fever" was now his teammate as a member of the Southsea Bowling Club. The two had so much mutual respect for each other that when Dr. Pike asked Doyle to offer a second opinion on one of his patients, a very ill twenty-five-year-old man named John Hawkins, Doyle took time off from preparing his medical thesis to evaluate him. The patient had received the devastating provisional diagnosis of terminal cerebral meningitis from Dr. Pike, but before accepting the finality that accompanied such an illness, the Hawkins family wanted to ensure that no other possibility, however remote, had been overlooked. Dr. Pike escorted Doyle to the upscale home of the patient's wealthy uncle, where poor John Hawkins's twenty-seven-year-old sister, Louisa, and his mother, Emily, had been staying for the past few months.

The Hawkins family had been living on the financial edge for a dozen years, after the patriarch of the clan, Jeremiah Hawkins, had died at the age of seventy-eight, leaving behind a wife thirty years his junior and seven children. Although his fairly substantial landholdings in Minsterworth, Gloucestershire, were sufficient to support the family, it was not able to provide them a lavish way of life. And each time one of the adult Hawkins children moved out, money had to be further divided. The only way to make the income go as far as it could was to live frugally and adopt an off-season lifestyle. This was the very reason that these members of the Hawkins family were in Southsea before the fashionable people arrived there in May.

Pike brought Doyle to the patient's bedside, and Doyle performed a brief examination, informing John's uncle, sister, and mother that he concurred with Dr. Pike's initial assessment. Young Mr. Hawkins had indeed been stricken with an infection that had invaded the lining of his brain during the family's annual "slightly off-seasonal" sojourn to Southsea. Both Doyle and Pike were likely unaware that just two years earlier the family had mourned the loss of John's sister Mary. Doyle, in his most impressive tone and demeanor, told the anxious onlookers that although their loved one was presently stable, he could not be expected to live more than ten to twelve weeks. With the knowledge that John Hawkins's uncle did not want anyone dying in his house, and knowing that no hotel or lodging-house would take in such a desperately ill person, Doyle offered to take in John as a boarder at his place. For a modest fee, he would be willing to see to the patient's needs. This would make things easier for Dr. Pike, whose responsibilities as chief medical officer at the Royal Portsmouth Hospital made it impossible for him to render the services that such a patient required. Despite the severity of the illness, Doyle was keen to acquire a "resident patient."

The family agreed to transport their mortally ill relative to Doyle's place, where Doyle's housekeeper had prepared a room on the third floor for the new lodger. Doyle's memoirs imply that Louisa was immediately drawn to him, while he makes mention of her "trusting green eyes and brown curly hair." During the few moments they were able to spend alone together, the two shared a certain kindness and compassion that neither had ever known before. On the evening of March 24, Dr. Pike paid a surprise visit to Bush Villas and asked to take a look at "his" patient. He observed that John was "dozing peacefully," and that his body temperature, though still feverish, had dropped to 101.5 degrees Fahrenheit. According to Doyle's account of the matter in *The Stark Munro Letters*, the patient "was taking medicine with a little chloral in it at this time." The "chloral" was, in fact, chloral hydrate, which was a rel-atively new addition to the pharmaceutical preparations used at the time. A sedative and hypnotic agent, it was a potentially dangerous drug because it was difficult to distinguish its therapeutic level from its toxic level. When com-bined with alcohol, it took on the name "knockout drops." It may have been Doyle's employment of this medication that allowed a feverish patient with seizures to sleep through the night.

The next morning, Doyle was awakened by the sound of a cup and saucer smashing to the floor, immediately followed by the screams of his housekeeper, who immediately burst into Doyle's room and cried, "My God! He's gone!" After rushing into John's room, Doyle found Louisa's brother "stretched sideways across his bed, quite dead. He looked as if he had been rising and had fallen backwards." Doyle's next comments on the death, as illustrated again in *The Stark Munro Letters,* seem to indicate his attraction to Spiritualism and his belief in the afterlife, as he states, "His face was so peaceful and smiling that I could hardly have recognized the worried, fever-worn features of yesterday. There is great promise, I think, on the faces of the dead. They say it is but the post-mortem relaxation of the muscles, but it is one of the points on which I should like to see science wrong."

After a brief period of private mourning with his housekeeper, Doyle laid the patient straight in his bed, and his housekeeper placed a sheet over the corpse. Arthur then ventured off to the Hawkins house, where breakfast was being served. Doyle would write of the meeting, "[S]ympathy was all for me, for the shock I had suffered, and the disturbance of my household. I found myself turned from the consoler into the consoled." Doyle told them that "since the poor boy could not tell [him] his symptoms," there was no way he could have foreseen any problem arising that fateful night. Although Doyle confessed that both he and Dr. Pike should have recognized the fall in John's body temperature and his sleepiness as "really the beginning to the end."

The Hawkins family turned to Doyle to "see to everything, the formalities, register, and funeral." And Doyle did just that—he signed the death certificate, met with the undertaker, and arranged the funeral. Two days later, at 8 AM on a Friday, the body of John Hawkins was laid to rest. Only one of his five siblings, twenty-seven-year-old Louisa, was in attendance. When Doyle returned home after the service, he saw an unfamiliar, burly man with bushy whiskers waiting at his door. The man introduced himself to Doyle as a police detective assigned to investigate an anonymous letter, which stated that one of Doyle's recently deceased patients "was to be buried at an unusual hour" that day, and that "the circumstances were suspicious." Doyle was asked to furnish the officer with a detailed description of Hawkins's affliction and the medical services that had been rendered. After doing so, Doyle informed the officer that none other than the esteemed Dr. Pike had personally examined the patient on the night before his death and could corroborate his statement. "The detective shut his note-book with a snap," saying that he would have to interview Dr. Pike as a mere formality, apologizing in advance for the unjustified intrusion.

Doyle thanked his good fortune that Dr. Pike had visited him on the night of John's death and could back up his story. Otherwise, any suspicion of wrongdoing may have resulted in the exhumation of the deceased, which may have revealed the presence of chloral in the body. This discovery could have raised the possibility that John had been poisoned by too high a dose of the drug, and as "some money interests *DID* depend upon the death of the lad—a sharp lawyer might have made much of the case." Thankfully, Doyle's good reputation and a bit of luck had combined to keep even "the first breath of suspicion" from blowing his "little rising practice to the wind."

John Hawkins's death brought Arthur close to the Hawkins family. He started making frequent trips to their residence, and at first engaged both mother and daughter in casual conversation. Within a few weeks, he began to call solely on Louisa, whom he called Touie, and soon the two were tightly bound to each other in love. Their bonds were tightened when she told him of her older brother and father's namesake, Jeremiah, who had been incarcerated in Barnwood Mental Hospital outside of Gloucester for almost seventeen years. Her description of him as a young artist who would never be able to fully reach his potential no doubt reminded Doyle of his own father. In fact, by mid-May, Charles Doyle would be expelled from Blairerno after becoming violent during one of his routine "escape" attempts. Labeled as "dangerous," he would be placed in the Montrose Royal Mental Hospital on or near Arthur's twenty-sixth birthday.

By the end of April, Arthur and Touie were betrothed, and Doyle, who had just submitted his MD thesis, suggested that they get married right away. Touie was a bit reluctant to take such a dramatic step, fearing that the wedding might be too soon after her brother's death. Around this time, Doyle wrote "Saucy Kate," a poem that warns about the dangers inherent in post-poning marriage. The title's adjective could have been seen as a twist on the pronunciation of Southsea, and "Kate" as the literary representation of his wife to be. In the poem, Doyle never fails to admonish Kate that by putting off marriage to a later date, she may wind up a spinster.

They settled on a six-month waiting period, but soon moved the date up by several months. Arthur and his future mother-in-law went to the Hawkins's solicitor in Monmouth, a small town in Southeast Wales, to write up a marriage agreement. The solicitor showed Doyle a collection of documents that confirmed the true worth of the properties that the Hawkins family owned outright, as well as the income they were guaranteed by the tenants who were leasing these landholdings. Currently there were at least six people who were dependent on the income generated by these landholdings. Touie's mother was won over by Doyle's charm and eagerly signed the contracts that would serve the couple very well in the future. Adding to these good tidings was the fact that Doyle's thesis paper had recently been approved by his alma mater. He was now entitled to be known as Arthur Conan Doyle, MD. With the knowledge that he would have to return to Edinburgh in early August to have this degree conferred on him, the couple moved the wedding date to coincide with his diploma confirmation.

Although he had avoided stepping on Masongill property up to this time, Arthur agreed to hold the wedding reception on Bryan Waller's estate. Three weeks prior to the festivities, Arthur sent Touie to Masongill to plan the details with his mother. As his fiancée became close with his mother while making the arrangements, Doyle stayed behind in Southsea, where he was competing in lawn bowling as late as July 29. One week before his scheduled marriage, he took the train to Edinburgh where he received his diploma. Not long after, he boarded a train to Preston Station and took a carriage over to Stonyhurst. He knew the school was not in session at the time, but he was also aware that the Stonyhurst Wanderers would be meeting the Stonyhurst College cricket team in a match that day. Arthur was invited to play for the Wanderers against his former school. Arthur scored eight runs, helping to defeat his alma mater, and the team's captain extended him an offer to join the team for the next series of games on the schedule. Although he could not make it to the game in Liverpool due to his prior obligation, he agreed to play two games in Dublin on August 12 and 14.

On August 6, 1885, Arthur Conan Doyle and Louisa Hawkins became husband and wife at St. Oswald's Church in Thornton in Lonsdale. In attendance was Mary Doyle, a formerly staunch Roman Catholic who had now become a registered parishioner at Bryan Waller's Protestant church. Interestingly, Bryan Waller was chosen to be Arthur's best man instead of his younger brother, Innes, who was deemed "too young" to serve in this capacity. True to his word, when the wedding ceremony was over, the groom told Arthur's new bride that he would be heading out the next day to join the Wanderers, who would be leaving for Dublin to play cricket. Touie, ever the dutiful Victorian wife, agreed to stay on at Masongill and spend some quality time with her mother-in-law.

Upon returning from his one-man "honeymoon" in Ireland, Arthur offered James Hogg the opportunity to publish *The Firm of Girdlestone*. Arthur would describe it as a book that "abounds in exciting scenes, murder and sudden death," stating, "[I]n fact I would need a private graveyard to plant all my characters in." But Hogg turned it down. After receiving multiple rejections from other publishing houses, Doyle buried "the disheveled mass of manuscript at the back of a drawer."

January 1886

By 1886, Arthur's interest in Spiritualism had begun to take shape, despite his previous academic training in hard science and perception of himself as a "convinced materialist"—someone who sought to find and accept only what was undeniably true. It is difficult to account for Doyle's dualism. After all, he had abandoned Roman Catholicism, which had at one time been so important to him, on the grounds that its basic tenets were incapable of being proved. It was Major-General Alfred W. Drayson, the President of the Portsmouth Literary and Scientific Society, who had the greatest influence on Arthur's developing interest in and acceptance of psychic phenomena, which ran the gamut from mediumship, mesmerism, and thought-transference. From the moment he met Drayson, one of England's pioneers of the spiritualist movement, Arthur recognized his "great force of character" and his "singular gift of exposition." Doyle was bowled over by Drayson's "clever analogies," and came to the conclusion that somehow Drayson had acquired a new type of awareness. Although Doyle would tell others that he was not entirely convinced that Spiritualism was a true science, he fell under Drayson's sway and began accompanying him to numerous social events, séances, and table-tipping sessions throughout England, all in an attempt to contact the unseen world. Whenever Doyle would comment that things appeared to be orchestrated or that incorrect information was being conveyed from the spirit world, Drayson would try to right the ship, so to speak, by explaining that there are different types of spirits, some of which are good and tell the truth, and some of which are up to no good and deliberately mislead their audience. Amazingly, Doyle seemed to accept anything that Drayson proposed.

Drayson had been following a Scottish "mystic" named Daniel Dunglas Home for more than twenty years. Prior to his death in 1886 at the age of fifty-three, Home had lived a life that roughly paralleled Doyle's. Both men had fathers who were talented but troubled by drink, both had been sent away from home before the age of ten, both had studied medicine, and both had seen their faith in the Roman Catholic Church evaporate. Doyle came to regard Home as a kindred spirit, and when the Scot died, Doyle became incensed when he read the obituaries in the newspapers. Years later, Doyle would write of Home, "When his most useful and unselfish life had come to an end, it must be recorded to the eternal disgrace of our British Press that there was hardly a paper which did not allude to him as an impostor and a charlatan." Doyle had witnessed several of Home's séances, and had become certain that the transference of ideas and concepts between both the living and the dead was possible. He eventually even considered himself capable of the practice. He recruited architect and friend Henry Joseph Ball to assist him in conducting a series of "scientific" experiments in which Doyle would "secrete" his thoughts across a room to Ball, who then, after having received the "secretion," would draw the "thought" on paper. Of these experiments, Doyle states, "I showed beyond doubt that I could convey my thought without words."

It was during this time that Doyle came up with an idea for his next literary creation. He would draw inspiration from Edgar Allan Poe's C. Auguste Dupin and Émile Gaboriau's Monsieur Lecoq, though his admiration for these characters would be tempered by the deficiencies he perceived in both their personalities and their crime-solving abilities. Doyle was more impressed, in fact, by the investigative powers of his medical professors back at Edinburgh—men like Joe Bell, Henry Littlejohn, and William Rutherford. The consulting detective of Doyle's imagination would be a blend of these fictional sleuths and the men of science he knew, though he would also include certain aspects of himself. In addition, the character would have an assistant to chronicle his triumphs. After jotting down some ideas for the histories and traits of these partners in private investigation, Doyle focused on coming up with just the right name for each. The first name he came up with—Sherringford Hope—did not have a nice ring to it, according to Arthur's wife, Touie. But she did like the name Sherlock Holmes. Ormond Sacker, the original name given to Holmes's sidekick, soon evolved into John H. Watson, MD. Although Doyle was immersed in the irrational world of Spiritualism at the time, the notes for his new characters' first story read, "I must say that I have no patience with people who build up fine theories in their own armchairs which can never be reduced to practice." He certainly did not want his detective to be a mere Lecoqian "bungler" or, like Dupin, "more sensational than clever."

He tentatively named the first novella featuring Holmes and Watson *A Tangled Skein*, but felt a new title was needed once he had completed the tale six weeks later. He called upon his artistic background and came up with the word "study," which refers to a preliminary sketch before the final product is unveiled to the onlooker, and then inserted the word "scarlet," which adds a touch of the exotic and the literal element of color to something that might otherwise be construed as bland. Once finished, Touie dispatched a letter to Arthur's sister Lottie, saying, "Arthur has written another book, a little novel about 200 pages long, called 'A Study in Scarlet.'" But just like Doyle's other book, *The Firm of Girdlestone, A Study in Scarlet* traveled the same "circular tour," sent off only to come back with a notice of rejection. Doyle would write of his disappointment to his mother, stating, "My poor 'Study' has never even been read by anyone except Payn."

By late 1886, Arthur would receive a message from the publishing firm of Ward, Lock & Co., which stated, "We have read your story *A Study in Scarlet*, and are pleased with it." To Arthur's chagrin, the next few sentences would not be as encouraging, as the publisher would explain, "We could not publish it this year, as the market is flooded at present with cheap fiction, but if you do not object to it being held over until next year we will give you £25 for the copyright." Doyle replied, stating that he would rather receive royalties based on sales instead of a flat fee, but his request was categorically denied. Doyle would later write about this incident, saying, "I was heart-sick, however, at repeated disappointments, and I felt that perhaps it was true wisdom to make sure of publicity, however late." Arthur ultimately agreed to accept the firm's one-time payment.

January 1887

In January of 1887, Drayson invited his protégé to join him at a meeting of the Society of Freemasons at Phoenix Lodge number 257. Around this same period, Doyle's other mentor, Dr. William Royston Pike, was selected to be the incoming Worshipful Master of the Prince Edward of Saxe-Weimar Lodge number 1903, on the other side of Portsmouth. The relatively favorable political and judicial climate of Great Britain at the time had allowed Freemasonry to propagate its doctrines throughout the Empire, thus allowing for the preservation of its ancient landmarks and symbols. In England and in Scotland, initiation into the Order was viewed as a great honor. Indeed, many a king's hand has held the gavel of the Grand Master. It is entirely possible that Arthur had first heard about the Society from Bryan Waller, who while residing with the Doyles in Edinburgh had served as the poet laureate of the Lodge Canongate Kilwinning number 2, one of the oldest and most respected Masonic lodges in Scotland.

Doyle made his way up the stairs and entered the lodge, which was in its centennial year. There he saw many of the city's power brokers—barristers, men of science, prominent businessmen, and even police officials—wearing the customary Masonic apron. This was a fraternity whose members served as a type of chamber of commerce, involving themselves in charitable works, including significant financial support for the Royal Portsmouth Hospital. Three weeks into 1887, Doyle would join this lodge. For almost fifty years, it had been housed in an impressively columned two-story temple in Old Portsmouth, High Street. Although it was Major-General Drayson who had served as Arthur's mentor in all matters involving the occult, it was the city's mayor, William David King, who had put forth Doyle's name for membership, and it was John Brickwood, a prominent local brewer and football teammate of Doyle's, who seconded the motion. Fifty other pillars of the community were in attendance on the evening of his inauguration, and once he had been confirmed by Worshipful Master W.P.G. Gilbert, Doyle so embraced the teachings of the Order that within two months, he would attain the rank of third-degree Mason, or Master Mason.

Part of the ceremony that marked a member's attainment of third-degree status at this time was the member's participation in the performance of a play reenacting the death of Hiram Abiff, also known as the widow's son. According to the story, Hiram was selected by one of the most powerful and wisest kings of ancient times, King Solomon, to design and supervise the construction of a magnificent temple built in God's name. One day, after entering the sanctum sanctorum of the temple to pray and draw designs upon his trestle-board, Hiram, a Master Mason, is confronted by a workman, who demands that he reveal to him the Master Mason's "word," which would imbue him with all the secrets of a Master Mason. Hiram tells the man that he will receive the word when the temple is completed, if he is worthy. Unsatisfied with this answer, this "ruffian," Jubela, strikes Hiram across the throat with a twenty-four-inch instrument of measurement known as a gauge. As Hiram attempts to retreat through the west passage, he is attacked by a second conspirator, Jubelo, who hits him with another tool known as a square. Hiram still does not comply, and tries to escape via the east gate, where a third man, Jubelum, knocks him on the forehead with a gavel, ultimately killing him. Realizing their deed, the three workmen bury Hiram, mark the grave with a sprig of acacia, and endeavor to flee to Ethiopia.

Worshipful Master, represented by King Solomon, and the remaining craftsmen soon discover that Hiram is missing. The identities of the three ruffians and the details of their conspiracy are then confirmed by twelve Masons who had earlier refused to conspire against their Master. These twelve are tasked with seeking out the three criminals. In their search, one of the men comes across the sprig of acacia and asks two of his brethren to join him and have a look. They begin to suspect the presence of a grave, but are distracted by the audible laments of the three ruffians, who are nearby, having been unable to secure passage out of the area, and who have become penitent in the face of their act. First Jubela states:

> Oh, that my throat had been cut across from ear to ear, my tongue torn out, and my body buried in the rough sands of the sea at low-water mark, where the tide ebbs and flows twice in twenty-four hours, ere I had been accessory to the death of so good a man as our grand master Hiram Abiff!

Jubelo continues the plea by saying:

> Oh, that my left breast had been torn open, and my heart and vitals taken from thence, and thrown over my left shoulder, carried into the Valley of Jehoshaphat, and there to become a prey to the wild beasts of the field, and the vultures of the air, ere I had conspired the death of so good a man as our grand master Hiram Abiff!

Finally, Jubelum begins to groan:

> Oh, that my body had been severed in two in the midsts and divided to the north and south, my bowels burnt to ashes in the centre, and the ashes scattered by the four winds of heaven, that there might not the least track or trace of remembrance remain among men or Masons of so vile a wretch as I am; ah! Jubela, Jubelo, it was I that struck him harder than you both; it was I that gave him the fatal blow; it was I that killed him.

The listening craftsmen immediately seize the ruffians and bring them to Worshipful Master, who sentences each attacker to die in the manner described in his respective lament. Worshipful Master then directs the men to search for Hiram's grave in the area where the ruffians were overheard. While the body is found, no ordinary craftsman can lift it, and the Masons fear that the secret word has been lost forever. Only a Master Mason may lift Hiram's body, so it is Worshipful Master who exhumes the body, stating, "[T]he first word spoken after the body is raised shall be a substitute for the master's word, until future generations shall find out the right."

In the reenactment, Doyle would have played the part of Hiram, and with his body now "raised from the grave," this new third-degree Mason would have been given the tools of a Master Mason and then taken his seat. He would also have received his personal copy of a book containing the history and rituals of the Freemasons, covering three millennia of Masonic history, starting with the reign of King Solomon through the year 1885. The architectural figures, diagrams, songs, and poems found on its pages represent the building trade and its accomplishments, and include images of masonry tools such as compasses, squares, and rulers; depictions of the magnificent historical structures built by masons, such as the Great Pyramid of Giza; and sketches of other ritualistic symbols, such as the skull and crossbones, coffins, and daggers.

From this point on, Doyle would have been able to enjoy the perks available to those of this exclusive rank, including free lodging at any Masonic house in Great Britain. Nevertheless, despite Arthur's desire to become a Freemason and his ability to achieve a high Masonic rank within only two months of membership, he would never again participate in any of the activities of Phoenix Lodge number 257 after receiving his Master Mason apron. By February of 1889, he would officially hand in his "demission," and later neglect to mention the fact that he had been a Mason in his official autobiography.

November 1887

Even with an MD degree, a marriage certificate, and a Masonic apron, Doyle still seemed to be in a state of limbo. His medical practice was going nowhere and he had little reason to believe that his literary career would blossom. His father had been made a permanent inmate of Scotland's highest-security lunatic asylum, and his mother had become solidly entrenched in her role as the matron of Masongill, remaining there even after Bryan Waller's marriage many years later. His beloved brother Innes was about to be sent off to military school in northern England, and his sister Annette had written that she was about to embark for Brazil to work as a governess, quite possibly remaining there permanently. Lottie, who had always been dedicated to her older brother, apparently despised his mother-in-law, and added fuel to the fire by telling him it would be a long time before she would be visiting Bush Villas again. Doyle's sense of uncertainty increased even more when his most trusted friend, William Burton, informed him he would be leaving England for a year to assume a professorship at Tokyo's Imperial University. In fact, Arthur's "old friend" was destined to spend the rest of his life in Asia, where he would win wide acclaim for his achievements in sanitary engineering, architecture, and photography.

Although the year 1887 drew to a close with the publication of the first Sherlock Holmes tale, *A Study in Scarlet*, in *Beeton's Christmas Annual*, Doyle, having sold all his rights to the story for a one-time payment of twenty-five pounds from the magazine, "never at any time received another penny for it"—not that there were many pennies to be had, as "[t]he book had no particular success at the time." It would take four more years for Doyle's consulting detective to bring him fame and fortune, but both would arrive quite suddenly after the publication of his Sherlock Holmes short stories in the pages of the *Strand Magazine*.

18

The Tour

The London Hospital,
6:30 PM

uring the solemn, silent walk back, Stephen lagged behind, escaping everyone's notice. His forehead furrowed and his eyes peered downwards. His notebook remained open in his hands. Once the façade of the London Hospital had come into view, Doyle gave his farewell address.

"So, my friends, we have reached the final phase of our day's adventure," he said. "Hopefully, our tour of the notorious Jack the Ripper's hunting grounds will prove the source of interesting memories in the future. It is most regretful that Miss Pemberton chose to depart prematurely, for had she stayed, I am sure she would have been an invaluable contributor to our little jaunt. Nevertheless, the seven of you have given me extraordinary new insights into this most mystifying and ghastly period in history. Thank you for your interest and your time. Your carriages will be here shortly."

Four carriages, for which Doyle had made advance arrangements, arrived one by one. Doyle extended firm, cordial handshakes to Carrington, Adelaide, and Edgar, and wished them a good evening and good luck. As the three of them were going places in close proximity to each other, they shared the first carriage. Doyle then shook the hands of the Stanton brothers, and as the two of them entered the Landau he told them how proud he was to have met two siblings so able to read each other's thoughts. Dr. Hammond made sure to use both hands to bid

Doyle farewell and complimented him on his Sherlock Holmes-like detection skills. Doyle laughed and told Dr. Hammond that the pleasure had been all his, adding that he had never before met such a well-trained American physician.

Stephen Mitchell failed to seek out Sir Arthur and was about to step aboard his carriage when Doyle came over to him, grabbed his right hand, and refused to let it go. "Mr. Mitchell, you've left an indelible imprint on me today and I would like to thank you for your well-constructed analysis of Jack's personality and behavior," Doyle said. "It is you whom I will remember best out of an outstanding group of individuals."

"Thank you," Stephen said.

Doyle watched Stephen's carriage depart. As it turned off Whitechapel Road, the dust that had been made airborne by its wheels started to clear, and Sir Arthur Conan Doyle observed Stephen's hand extending from the window of the cab, dropping an unknown object to the street below. Doyle approached the item and soon discerned Stephen's deerstalker cap lying in the middle of the road. Making no move to pick it up, the world's most celebrated mystery writer turned and began the long walk back to his Kensington home.

19

1890–2011

The Game Is Afoot

January 1890

Now the father of a one-year-old daughter, Mary Louise, Doyle decided to terminate his rather unsuccessful general medical practice, opting instead to travel with his family to Vienna to study ophthalmology. After returning from his training, he set up a new practice as an eye doctor in London, although he would later declare that "not one single patient . . . ever crossed the threshold of [his] room." In spite of the less-than-stellar performance of his first two Sherlock Holmes novels, he continued to write, now using a shorter format featuring the same characters. It would be the publication of the short story "A Scandal in Bohemia" in the July 1891 edition of the *Strand Magazine* that would capture the imagination of the British public and catapult him to success, allowing him to end his career in medicine and begin his life as a full-time writer.

December 1892

At the close of 1892, Scotland Yard invited Doyle and a couple of other noted writers to stop by police headquarters and look at the collection of crime artifacts the force had amassed, which had become known as the Black Museum. Once there, Doyle's main focus was on a single letter purportedly written by Jack the Ripper, known today as the "Dear Boss" letter. On July 4, 1894, the *Evening News* of Portsmouth reprinted an interview Doyle had given an American journalist in which he furnishes his analysis of the "Dear Boss" letter and discusses how Sherlock Holmes would track Jack the Ripper. Doyle describes the letter as having been "written in red ink in a clerkly hand," adding that it "had been written by someone who had been in America," for "[i]t began, 'Dear Boss,' and contained the phrase 'fix it up' and several others which are not usual with the 'Britishers.'" He also remarks on "the quality of the paper and the handwriting," which seems to suggest "the letters were not written by a toiler," concluding that the author "was therefore a man accustomed to the use of a pen." Not long after this time, the press reported that some or all of the alleged Ripper letters had mysteriously disappeared from Scotland Yard.

September 1894

Having attained fame and fortune with his Holmes stories, Doyle was transformed into the consummate British gentleman, becoming a regular attendee and participant in athletic activities—cricket, soccer, bowling, ballooning, riflery, billiards, motor car racing, and even transalpine skiing (which he had introduced to Britain). He was soon embraced by the nation's most influential publishers, editors, and writers. In September of 1894, he made a transatlantic crossing and toured the United States, where he expanded his literary circle. By 1900, he was in South Africa, although he had solemnly vowed never to return there after his *Mayumba* voyage, practicing medicine during the Boer War, and would go on to act as a pamphleteer for his nation's role in this conflict.

In 1906, his wife Louisa succumbed to tuberculosis, leaving behind their daughter, Mary Louise, and their son, Arthur Alleyne Kingsley, whom they simply called Kingsley. In 1907, Doyle remarried to a woman he had met years before, Jean Elizabeth Leckie, for whom, it is said, he had long harbored a secret love. They would remain together for the rest of Doyle's life and have three children together, Denis, Adrian, and Jean.

In 1900 and 1906, Doyle attempted to win a seat in Parliament, but found no success. In 1909, he agreed to serve as the president of his country's divorce law reform union. The major plank of his platform was that a woman should be permitted to terminate a marriage to a spouse who had effectively abandoned her. On the issue of suffrage, however, he stood steadfastly against granting women the right to vote, stating that such a right would doubtless lead to the destruction of marriages due to the domestic bickering that was sure to follow if such legislation were to be passed.

At times, his total immersion in certain causes left him in the crosshairs of his critics. Even though as a public figure he was an easy target, he remained totally unfazed by any threats or taunts. His writing was so stylish and his personality so disarming that the public tended to side with him in his social, economic, and political opinions. But his devotion to and his proselytizing on behalf of Spiritualism would have an adverse effect on his reputation, especially in his later years. His 1922 book *The Coming of the Fairies* failed to convince his readers that there existed photographs proving the existence of sprites. The scientific community made short work of his claims and the press mocked him, sometimes accusing him of being a ranting madman. Even his friendship with the great illusionist Harry Houdini was irreparably fractured when Houdini publicly stated that all mediums should be looked upon as frauds and charlatans. Doyle refused to yield, insisting that Houdini himself was hiding the fact that he was a medium empowered with supernatural abilities.

Despite these criticisms, when Sir Arthur Conan Doyle died in 1930, he was mourned the world over. His literary work, of course, lives on.

November 1987

As 1987 was coming to an end, almost 100 years after Jack's last act of murder, the Ripper's "Dear Boss" letter was returned anonymously to the Metropolitan Police. Upon receipt of the letter, Scotland Yard requested a recall of all Ripper documents, which were being held at the Public Record Office. The police did not publicly announce the return of the document until 1988. According to Scotland Yard's records, Arthur Conan Doyle was one of the last people to have handled the letter.

December 2011

Through firsthand accounts and Doyle's own words, the authors of this book began to uncover a number of previously unexamined facts, which now serve to clarify many of the ambiguities found in previous accounts of Doyle's early history. With all the clues gathered, the strange case of Dr. Doyle may be considered a mystery worthy of the Sherlock Holmes in each of us.

Afterword

In Search of the Truth

"What one man can invent another can discover."
—*Sherlock Holmes in "The Adventure of the Dancing Men"*

A cascading series of events led my father and me on this journey and compelled us to learn more about the life of Arthur Conan Doyle—specifically, the years that preceded his rise to worldwide celebrity. The first of these events occurred in 1997, when I came across an article in *Science* magazine. I was drawn to its intriguing title, "The Perpetrator at Piltdown," and as I read it, I was startled and mesmerized by the authors' bold allegation. They claimed it had been none other than Sir Arthur Conan Doyle who had orchestrated the greatest archeological hoax ever: the discovery of the missing evolutionary link between man and ape. This link was, in reality, nothing more than a cap of a fragmented human skull that had been planted in the dirt alongside the jaw bone of an orangutan. The article hypothesized that Doyle had sought to ridicule several of the British scientific community's most esteemed members. Each of these targets had previously taken stances against Spiritualism and other unorthodox beliefs that Doyle strongly endorsed. If Doyle had, in fact, been the perpetrator of this hoax, then he had elected to go to his grave without ever revealing his involvement in this cruel prank. It wasn't until 1953, twenty-three years after Doyle's death, that fossil remains of the Piltdown man were exposed as fraudulent.

Years later, in the spring of 2007, I read two more articles on Doyle that further strengthened my suspicions about the man. One of the articles detailed Doyle's compulsive nature in his defense of a series of photographs taken by teenager Elsie Wright, in which she had supposedly captured images of sprites and pixies. At the time, Doyle defended the existence of these "Cottingley Fairies" and launched a crusade to validate these photographs. At his own expense, he hired experts from the Eastman Kodak and the Ilford film companies to verify the authenticity of the pictures. When he failed to gain their support, he made it a point to share his opinions and beliefs with the general public by putting out a short book in 1922, *The Coming of the Fairies.*

The second article discussed Doyle's medical school thesis, "An Essay upon the Vasomotor Changes in Tabes Dorsalis." A slow and inevitable degeneration of the nerves of the spinal cord, tabes dorsalis is caused by the syphilitic bacteria *Treponema pallidum.* I obtained a copy of this manuscript, and after subjecting it to careful scrutiny, concluded that Doyle had, indeed, written a brilliant paper, though I also felt something deeper was at play—something I could not yet put my finger on. Knowing of my father's interest in Doyle, I immediately contacted him to discuss my thoughts. Unbeknownst to me, my father had also come to believe that Doyle was much more than he seemed.

Together, we set off to read the great Doyle biographies, novels, and short stories—not to mention the previously unpublished collection of Doyle's private correspondence, *A Life in Letters.* Once we had finished our preliminary work, we embarked on our own in-depth research to see if anything of relevance might have been missed (see Annotated Bibliography on page 299). We began to scour old newspapers and magazines, and amassed quite a few books written by Doyle's fellow members of the Crimes Club, looking for any references that might help us understand the man. Our search led us to *Inquest,* a book written by Doyle's friend Samuel Ingleby Oddie and published in 1941. The two men had been members of the Crimes Club—in fact, both had been members of the original group on which we would base our fictionalized Whitechapel tour—and had graduated from the University of Edinburgh Medical School.

As we would learn, Oddie and Doyle spent lots of time together after their 1905 excursion through the notorious hunting grounds of Jack the Ripper. Oddie, a former London coroner, reveled in sharing his tales of the sea and his knowledge of criminology with his nation's most famous writer, and didn't balk at the idea of accompanying Doyle to séances and table-turnings, at least at first. But he soon became disenchanted with his friend's "childlike faith in the . . . ridiculous antics and trickery of a certain spiritualistic medium." What irked him most was that Doyle had willingly abandoned his "robust common sense and shrewdness and his extraordinary mental acuity," and even more disconcertingly had "founded his belief on evidence which not ought to have deceived a fairly intelligent and observant youth of sixteen."

We then acquired the 1978 book *The Doyle Diary,* which we discovered was about Arthur's father, Charles Altamont Doyle. Leaving no stone unturned, we read it, analyzing the notes and sketches it contained. Doing so turned out to be a watershed event. We learned of Arthur's father's numerous incarcerations in psychiatric hospitals throughout Scotland. Charles had been admitted to Royal Lunatic Asylum, Infirmary, and Dispensary of Montrose on May 26, 1885, after being declared a lunatic by Dr. James Ironside and Dr. James Duffus, the psychiatric evaluators for Blairerno House, a home for alcoholics in northern Scotland to which Charles had been initially sent. Around that same time, the newly twenty-six-year-old Arthur had recently submitted his thesis on tabes dorsalis to the University of Edinburgh. It struck us immediately that tabes dorsalis is the result of an untreated case of the venereal disease syphilis—a disease associated with madness.

We looked for signs indicating that Charles might have been afflicted with the very condition, tabes dorsalis, on which Arthur had written. We sent emails to the previously mentioned mental asylums in the hope of gaining more knowledge concerning the cause of Charles's symptoms. Answers came when Jennifer Johnstone, an assistant archivist at the University of Dundee in Northern Scotland, was kind enough to forward us some crucial information pertaining to Charles's transfer from Blairerno to Montrose. His physical examination upon admission indicated that he had exhibited an abnormal and telltale neurological sign: the loss of his knee-jerk reflex. Known as Westphal's sign, it was exactly what we had been looking for—the same indicator about which Arthur had written in his treatise on syphilis. We asked ourselves if Arthur might have seen his father exhibit this sign, and whether this recognition would have had an adverse effect on Arthur's psyche, possibly sparking a vendetta against prostitutes, the likely source of Charles's syphilis. We were reminded of Arthur's letter to the *Medical Times and Gazette* in 1883, which called for the reinstatement of the Contagious Diseases Acts—legislation that meant to curb the spread of venereal disease through the regulation and forced hospitalization of prostitutes.

It was the combination of Oddie's *Inquest, The Doyle Diary,* and Jennifer Johnstone's invaluable notes that finally enabled us to link Arthur's choice of thesis topic to his own life, and indirectly to his irrational conviction in the occult. My father thought back to his medical school psychiatric rotations at Metropolitan Hospital and Manhattan State Mental Hospital, where he had been captivated by the concept of paranoia vera, a psychiatric disorder that German psychiatrist Emil Kraepelin defined in 1893 as an "insidious development of a permanent and unshakeable delusional system from inner causes, in which clarity and order of thinking, willing, and action are completely preserved. It effects a deep-seated change of the total outlook on life, and a derangement of standpoint towards a surrounding world." This revelation cast new light on Doyle's possible predisposition to delusional mania. But how could we accuse this gifted, logical figure of being mentally unstable, of being a murderer?

In a paper featured in the 1981 book *Psychiatric Diagnosis,* noted psychiatrist Yehuda Fried asks whether "a deep-seated change of the total outlook on life" is a derangement in itself, describing a person with the rare condition of paranoia vera as presenting "a delusion and a particular one at that," and going on to say that the condition itself is paradoxical since, by definition, the delusion of the paranoiac person is a logical and systematic one. Back in 1911, Paul Eugen Bleuler wrote that paranoia is based on "the construction of false premises of a logically developed unshakeable delusional system," which is now known as the concept of the "fixed idea." But what was fact and what was imagination, especially in someone obsessed by a fixed idea? Bleuler went on to write, "[T]he common denominator is the logical nature of the delusion, and therefore, it is not the content of the delusion that defines it as a disease but rather the former structure."

Even though Doyle as a young man appeared to be meticulously accurate in his thoughts and perceptions, we kept noticing his one basic problem: his inability to consider views that differed in any way from his own, as evidenced by his absolute faith in what he was "seeing" when he went to occult meetings. He refused to acknowledge anything that contradicted his beliefs, and when others disputed his claims, he would insist that their opinions merely confirmed rather than disproved his own theories. Interestingly, these thought processes are very similar to those of someone afflicted with paranoia vera. Could Doyle's intractable nature point to this psychological sydrome? And could the combination of paranoia vera and an unmistakable grudge against women of the night have created a killer?

A person with Doyle's inflexibility would make him "rather unintelligent in a deep sense though his thinking outwardly is both logical and intelligent in the strict sense." In the words of Kraepelin, a person with paranoid delusions possesses an exalted self-consciousness, and so will often boast of his "sense of duty and unwearied diligence," claiming that "he is a respectable citizen, he only wants what is right, he helps everyone if he can, and if it is right." Doyle was invited to and attended numerous social events at which he found it easy to impress the other invitees and draw them into his world, but only temporarily. Then things fell apart. An example of this may be found in Doyle's relationship with Harry Houdini. While initially Doyle was able to establish a tight bond with the great magician, it wasn't long before he tried to convince his new friend that Houdini himself possessed powers that went far beyond those of mortal men. Houdini was astonished and frightened by Doyle's beliefs, and when Doyle attempted to defend Margery, the famous Boston medium, Houdini stated in front of an audience that men like Doyle were "a menace to mankind." The two of them never reconciled their differences.

In December of 2011, my father and I found a clue that would lead us down another avenue: the disappearance of Jack the Ripper's famed "Dear Boss" letter from within the walls of Scotland Yard. Knowing full well that in 1892 Doyle had visited the Black Museum, the Yard's collection of crime artifacts, we decided to investigate things a little bit more. It was commonly assumed that the entire Ripper letter collection had disappeared around the time of Doyle's visit. Based on a hunch, we sent off several emails to Scotland Yard, asking whether this was indeed the case, for we had been under the impression that only the "Dear Boss" letter—the one with which Doyle had been fascinated—had been taken. We were informed that our understanding was correct. We were also told that the stolen "Dear Boss" letter had been returned to the Yard in November of 1987, almost 100 years after the last Ripper murder.

Doyle's visit to the Black Museum sparked further research, and this time not just on Doyle himself. Our focus widened to include the subject that had so interested Doyle that day: Jack the Ripper. We read many magazines and newspaper articles covering the Ripper murders, never losing sight of Doyle's history during the years surrounding the Whitechapel killings. Most interestingly, we learned of Doyle's two-year membership in the Freemasons. What struck us as odd was the rapidity with which Doyle had been able to rise up the ranks and become a third-degree Master Mason. Even stranger was the fact that, after this amazing accomplishment, Doyle immediately stopped all participation in the Freemasons, and by the winter of 1889, had officially resigned from the organization. Fascinated, we decided to read through some of the Masonic books and magazines in print during Doyle's association with the brotherhood. We found notable similarities between certain Masonic rituals and the Ripper murders, and a striking resemblance between Masonic artwork and a group of sketches found on one of the Ripper letters. We had to keep digging.

The information we uncovered is contained within this book's pages, through its biography, tour, and comprehensive bibliography. By providing the reader with public statements made by Arthur Conan Doyle as well as other compelling evidence, we believe that only one conclusion can be reached. As Sherlock Holmes himself states, "When you have excluded the impossible, whatever remains, however improbable, must be the truth."

The person brought to light by looking at Doyle from his formative years to the age of twenty-nine was different from the man described in his biographies. Time after time, we found an impulsive individual with a taste for aggressive behavior, a lack of empathy, an aversion to rules and regulations, and a proclivity for deception and trickery—as well as a man of remarkable strength and athleticism. We could not help but be taken aback by certain revealing aspects of his life during his first three decades.

His impulsive personality was evident on numerous occasions: as he climbed Goatfell Mountain with his friend and younger sister despite warnings against doing so, as he self-medicated with dangerous gelsemium to treat his facial neuralgia, as he sprayed an unsuspecting young lady with a water launcher as a joke, as he picked the pocket of one of his exam inquisitors, as he dived off the ship into the water at Cape Coast Castle while on his African trip, and as he suddenly left to play cricket in Dublin the day after his marriage to Louisa. In fact, in his autobiography, Doyle himself says, "I have done utterly reckless things with so little motive that I have found it difficult to explain them to myself afterwards."

During our research, Doyle's aggressive nature often came to the fore. He got into scrapes with rival neighborhood toughs as a child. He was especially drawn to the sport of boxing. He took no thought in jabbing his fellow student with bed shears at Stella Matutina. He lamented his absence at a tavern brawl at his first port of call on the *Hope* and asked the captain if the crew could go back the next night to start another row. He yearned to stir up an altercation between the Fenian Land League and his cousins while visiting the Foley clan in Ireland. He became involved in a street fight within hours of arriving in Portsmouth to set up his new practice. And when he had had enough of him, Doyle physically assaulted former lodger Bryan Waller, who purportedly did not leave his residence for weeks thereafter.

Even more distressing was that this aggression and impulsiveness seemed to be combined with a distinct lack of empathy. Doyle's behavior appeared to us almost devoid of remorse. One unsettling example of this is an early letter to his mother, in which he writes of the death of two Stonyhurst boys, only to transition immediately to the joy he feels at the arrival of "50 new books" at the library. A lack of empathy was apparent throughout his life: in the pleasure he took in setting off firecrackers in a passenger train, in the laugh he had in his cutting off the flippers of seals and using them as makeshift mittens, in his experiments on sea birds while aboard the *Hope* (in which he placed different poisonous substances on bread to see which would kill the birds quickest), and in his request to his brother to "plunder" his recently deceased uncle's estate. Of course, his cartoon celebrating the attainment of his medical diploma, with its caption "Licensed to kill," may be the clearest example of a merciless soul.

Doyle's distaste for rules and regulations was also quite clear to us in the countless disciplinary actions taken against him by numerous professors in more than one school. Throughout his early days, Doyle was often reprimanded as a stubborn, slovenly, uncivilized buffoon by his superiors. Doyle, of course, put his aversion to authority front and center by publishing critiques of professors and classmates in his school magazines. Moreover, his inclination to take pleasure at other people's expense was part and parcel of his fondness for deception and trickery. He had a devious bent, obvious in a number of his actions: sending papers to medical journals under the names of other doctors he knew in hopes of discrediting these individuals, posting invitations to a fake "Mayor's Ball" to his employer's clientele, possibly doctoring his school transcript to further his medical education, and perhaps even planting a "sea monster" at Sannox Rock on Arran during his visit there.

Realizing that these troublesome inclinations existed in a young man of great strength, speed, agility, and stamina was a turning point for us. It was the moment we realized that Arthur Conan Doyle might be Jack the Ripper—and that every new detail we learned about Doyle supported this idea. He was naturally athletic, both quick and powerful. Even as a small child he climbed trees with ease, often with his friend Willie Burton. He was an avid sportsman, playing cricket and football, and falling in love with boxing. He became extremely well conditioned by his hikes at Stonyhurst, his walks through treacherous terrain in the dense forest near Stella Matutina, and as a member of a marching band in which he carried the heaviest instrument. As a young adult, his physical prowess impressed his captain on the *Hope* so much that he was recruited to club seals upon the dangerous Arctic ice floes. Doyle stripped the seals of their blubber after hauling them aboard the ship. This immensely hard work was done with ease and relish, and only increased Doyle's strength and stamina.

Doyle had the mind, the physique, and the medical training to do the terrible things attributed to the Ripper, and his motive was clear. Doyle suspected his father's madness to be the result of syphilis contracted from prostitutes. Doyle went so far as to write his medical thesis on a condition caused by syphilis. In light of his peculiar facial neuralgia and the experimental treatments to which he subjected himself, Doyle might have thought he'd inherited the disease from his father. In someone prone to paranoia vera, a psychological state defined by obsessive delusion, these beliefs might have led to an uncontrollable compulsion to get even. Doyle certainly had a strong stance against prostitutes. He even argued in favor of forcibly confining them to specialized hospitals until cured of any venereal disease.

Here was a man with the impulsiveness, aggression, deceptiveness, brute strength, and surgical skill to perform the Ripper murders. Here was a man who felt he had good reason to detest the streetwalkers of the day, who enjoyed settling scores, and who might have been in the throes of paranoia vera—consumed by a desire that had to be fulfilled. And once the score was settled and the urge satisfied, the paranoia vera waned and the killings stopped. Before long, the man was famous and the whole world was a different place. Yes, it may seem improbable. But it might just be the truth.

Annotated Bibliography

Books

The African Repository. Washington, DC: The American Colonization Society, 1883. Notes that the new ambassador to Liberia, Henry Highland Garnet, sails aboard the steamship *Nubia,* not the *Mayumba.* The departing ambassador, John Henry Smyth, boards the steamship *Mayumba* on the first leg of his return to America.

Ainsworth, William Henry. *The Lancashire Witches.* London: Henry Colburn, 1849. Popular tales of the Pennine district that would have been familiar to the boys at Stonyhurst.

Anderson, James. *The Constitutions of the Free-Masons.* New York: Robert Macoy, 1859. In 1887, Doyle joins the Freemasons Phoenix Lodge 257 in Southsea, England. He demits in 1889.

Atlay, J.B. *Famous Trials of the Century.* Chicago: Herbert S. Stone & Company, 1899. Discusses the Tichburne case, the Madeleine Smith case, and the Burke and Hare case.

Baines, Edward. *The History of the County Palatine and Duchy of Lancaster.* London: John Heywood, 1891. Describes the origins and architecture of Stonyhurst College.

Baker, Michael. *The Doyle Diary: The Last Great Conan Doyle Mystery.* London: Paddington Press, 1978. Brief biography and sketches drawn by Charles Doyle while he was confined in an asylum.

Baring-Gould, Sabine. *Devonshire Characters and Strange Events.* Plymouth: William Brendon and Son, 1908. Insights into George T. Budd from his relative, John Wreford Budd.

Bell, Joseph. "Some Hints By a Medical Examiner." *Transactions of the Insurance Society of Edinburgh.* Edinburgh: H. & J. Pillans & Wilson, 1904. A primer on the proper performance of insurance physicals, with special emphasis on occupation, hereditary, vices, and environment.

The Bengal Catholic Expositor. Calcutta: P. S. D'Rozario and Company, 1840. An overview of Stonyhurst College that mentions its most illustrious graduate, Charles Waterton.

Bennett, Arnold. *Books and Persons.* New York: George H. Doran, 1911. Includes an obituary of John Churton Collins.

Benson, Lionel. *The Book of Remarkable Trials and Notorious Characters,* London: John Camden Hotten, 1874. Details the wax figures of Edward Oxford, William Burke, and James Greenacre that fascinated fifteen-year-old Arthur Conan Doyle.

Besant, Walter. *Children of Gibeon.* London: Chatto and Windus, 1886. A poignant depiction of life in London's East End.

Booth, Charles, ed. *Life and Labour of the People in London: East, Central and South London.* MacMillan and Company, 1902. Description of London's East End by the founder of the Salvation Army. Mentions ginger beer.

Booth, Martin. *The Doctor, the Detective, and Arthur Conan Doyle.* London: Hodder and Stoughton, 1997. Biography of Arthur Conan Doyle.

Burton, John Hill. *The Book-Hunter.* New York: Sheldon and Company, 1863. Biography of Burton; contains description of his famous library.

Burton, William K. The *A.B.C. of Modern Photography*. London: Piper and Carter, 1886. Innovative photographic techniques devised by Doyle's best friend, William K. Burton. NB.

Byrne, Mrs. William Pitt. *Gossip of the Century*. London: Ward and Downey, 1892. The identity of H.B. is known only to John Doyle's daughter, Annette, until Doyle reveals it to former Chief of Police Robert Peel.

Carr, John Dickson. *The Life of Sir Arthur Conan Doyle*. New York: Harper & Bros., 1949. "Novelized biography" of Arthur Conan Doyle.

Carson, William English. *The Marriage Revolt*. New York: Hearst International Library Company, 1915. Notes that Arthur Conan Doyle helped found the Divorce Law Reform Union.

Chambers, Robert. *The Book of Days, a Miscellany of Popular Antiquities*. London: W. & R. Chambers, 1869. Biographical information on Madame Tussaud and history of her wax museum.

Chiene, John. *Looking Back, 1907–1860*. Edinburgh: Darien Press, 1908. Notes that Doyle is Joseph Bell's favorite student.

Christison, Robert. *The Life of Sir Robert Christison*. Edinburgh: William Blackwood and Sons,1886. The controversial Robert Christison defers to William Rutherford and Arthur Gamgee in performing liver research.

Collins, L.C. *Life and Memoirs of John Churton Collins*. London: The Bodley Head, 1912. Information pertaining to the 1905 Whitechapel tour in which Doyle and Churton Collins took part.

Cook, Joseph. *Life and the Soul*. London: Ward and Lock, 1892. Doyle attends one of Cook's famed Boston Monday Lectures while living and working with Dr. Reginald Hoare in Birmingham.

Crowe, Fred J.W. The *Scottish Master Mason's Handbook*. London: George Kenning, 1894. A detailed look at the inner workings of Scotland's Masonic Order.

Didier, Franklin James. *Franklin's Letters to his Kinsfolk*. Philadelphia: J. Maxwell, 1822. "Catch me when you can" appears in print. Later, this phrase is used by the Ripper.

Diver, Ebenezer. *The Young Doctor's Future*. London: Smith, Elder, and Company, 1881. Doyle accepts the position as ship's surgeon aboard the *Mayumba* after failing to find other viable work opportunities.

Doyle, Arthur Conan. *The Captain and the Polestar: And other Tales*. London: Longmans, Green, and Company, 1892. In the story "The Great Keinplatz Experiment," Doyle describes a case of taking "a man's soul out of his body." Mentions syphilologist von Althaus, whose book on spinal cord diseases was critical to Doyle's medical thesis on locomotor ataxia.

—. "Bones." In *Tales from Many Sources. Vol. 4.* New York: Dodd, Mead, and Company, 1885. Principal character Jack Morgan is referred to as "Boss."

—. *The Case of Oscar Slater.* New York: George H. Doran Company, 1912. Doyle pleads for the full pardon of the man convicted of murdering Marion Gilchrist with a hammer.

—. *The Coming of the Fairies.* New York: George H. Doran Company, 1922. Doyle provides a spirited and bizarre defense of alleged photographs of sprites and fairies.

—. *A Duet with an Occasional Chorus.* London: Grant Richards,1899. Doyle creates a bookcase reflecting his literary tastes and takes the reader on a tour of Westminster Abbey's Poets' Corner.

—. *The Field Bazaar: A Sherlock Holmes Pastiche.* Summit, NJ: Pamphlet House, 1947. Sherlock Holmes deduces that "Doctor" Watson had been asked to help raise funds for Edinburgh University's cricket field just by analyzing the contents of an envelope.

—. *The Haunted Grange of Goresthorpe.* Ashcroft, British Columbia: Ash Tree Press, 2000. Despite its evocative title, this early ghost story by Doyle is unsophisticated.

—. *Letters to the Press.* London: Secker & Warburg, 1986. A collection of letters written by Doyle that appeared in England's newspapers, literary periodicals, and medical journals.

—. "Life and Death in the Blood." In *Good Words for 1883.* London: Isbister & Company, 1883. An article written from the perspective of a traveler microscopically placed inside the human body.

—. *Memories and Adventures*. Boston: Little, Brown, 1924. Doyle's autobiography; does not discuss his medical school thesis, Freemasonry, or father's battle with mental illness.

—. *The New Revelation*. New York: George H. Doran Company, 1918. Doyle's writings on Spiritualism, psychic experiences, the afterlife and other metaphysical topics.

—. "The Silver Hatchet." In *My Friend The Murderer and Other Mysteries and Adventures*. New York: Lovell, Coryell, and Company, 1893. Contains reference to Thomas De Quincey.

—. *The Stark Munro Letters*. New York: D. Appleton and Company, 1895. A semi-autobiographical account of Doyle's years immediately following his graduation from the University of Edinburgh Medical School.

—. "The Third Generation." In *Round The Red Lamp*. 1894. Reprint. Richmond, VA: Valancourt Books, 2007. A case of congenital syphilis is described as having been passed down for three generations, according to the basic tenets of Lamarckian theory.

—. *The Vital Message*. New York: George H. Doran Company, 1919. Doyle's thoughts on the Second Coming.

—. *The Wanderings of a Spiritualist*. New York: George H. Doran Company, 1921. Doyle uses the words of Teddy Roosevelt to open his book, 'Aggressive fighting for the right is the noblest sport the world affords.'

—. *The Works of A. Conan Doyle*. New York: D. Appleton and Company, 1902. A compilation of some of Conan Doyle's greatest literary works.

Drayson, Alfred Wilks. *The Gentleman Cadet*. London: Griffith and Farran, 1875. While living in Southsea, Doyle was taken under the wing of the author, a noted polymath. This book chronicles Drayson's adventures at the Royal Military Academy at Woolwich, a school that Conan Doyle's brother Innes would attend before launching his outstanding military career.

An Evening From Among the Thousand Evenings Which May Be Spent with Punch. London: Bradbury, Agnew & Company, Ltd., 1900. Describes Richard Doyle's work and his rationale for leaving *Punch*.

Feasey, Henry John. *Westminster Abbey Historically Described*. London: George Bell, 1899. Reverently describes those who are commemorated in the Abbey's Poets' Corner.

Fitzgerald, Percy Hetherington. *Stonyhurst Memories*. London: Richard Bentley & Son, 1895. A contemporary of Doyle shares his recollections of his life as a student at Stonyhurst College.

Fournier, Alfred. *Syphilis and Marriage*. Translated by P. Albert Morrow. New York: Appleton and Company, 1882. A Lamarckian disciple gives his thoughts on the transmission of syphilis at the same time Doyle is preparing his medical school thesis.

Fraser, Norman. *Student Life at Edinburgh University*. Paisley, Scotland: J. & R. Parlane, 1884. Mentions the table at which Napoleon Bonaparte dined during his final exile on St. Helena.

Fried, Yehuda. "Reflections on the Diagnosis of Paranoia." In *Psychiatric Diagnosis*, edited by Joseph Agassi. Philadelphia: Balaban International Science Services, 1981. A presentation delivered by Fried, a master of psychiatric diagnosis, on paranoia.

Fry, Danby. *The Lunacy Acts*. London: Knight and Company, 1864. Lists Bryan Waller Procter (Bryan Charles Waller's uncle) as one of the appointed Commissioners in Lunacy.

Fry, Herbert. *London in 1880*. London: David Bogue, 1880. A description of the London of Doyle's youth.

—. *London in 1887*. London: W.H. Allen, 1887. A description of the London of Doyle's youth, accompanied by maps of Whitechapel.

Galton, Francis. *Hereditary Genius*. London: MacMillan and Company, 1869. Galton, the father of eugenics and fingerprinting offers his opinions as to the inner workings of the minds of poets, musicians, and painters. Doyle, in his thesis, tellingly discusses poets, musicians, and madmen.

Geddie, John. *The Water of Leith from Source to Sea*. Leith, Scotland: W. H. White and Company, 1896. Describes John Hill Burton's home and its centuries-old spectre, the Green Lady.

Gerard, John. *Centenary Record. Stonyhurst College, Its Life Beyond the Seas, 1592–1794, and on English Soil, 1794–1894*. London: Marcus and Ward and Company, 1894. Although Doyle describes a Mr. Chrea as being a Stonyhurst prefect, no such person appears in the college's registry.

Gibbon, Charles, ed. *The Casquet of Literature*. London: Blackie and Son, London, 1882. The phrase "Get Buckled" appears; it was also used in one of the Ripper's letters.

Gibbon, Eduardo A. *Nocturnal London* (1890). Reprint of the original volume. Whitefish, Montana: Kessinger Publishing, 2010. Contains reference to Madame Tussaud's Wax Works.

Graham, Richard. *The Masters of Victorian Literature, 1837–1897*. Edinburgh: James Thin, 1897. In a section devoted to Arthur Conan Doyle, Graham claims that Sherlock Holmes was based on Dr. Joseph Bell.

Grant, Alexander. *The Story of the University of Edinburgh*. London: Longmans, Green, and Company, 1884. Summarizes the first three hundred years of the University's history. Also includes short biographies of the medical school's outstanding faculty members.

Grant, James. *Cassell's Old and New Edinburgh*. London: Cassell, Petter, Galpin and Company, 1880. Contains references to the Morningside Asylum and to John Hill Burton's Craigshouse, with its library and Green Lady.

Greene, Joseph M. "In the Interests of Humanity, Should Vivisection Be Permitted, and If So, Under What Restrictions and Limitations?" In *Vivisection: Five Hundred Dollar Prize Essays*. Boston: American Humane Education Society, 1891. Attests to the worldwide influence of Dr. William Rutherford, the leading vivisectionist of his time.

Greenwood, James. *The Seven Curses of London*. Boston: Fields, Osgood, and Company, 1869. Depicts pauperism, gambling, and debauchery in the London underworld.

Gruggen, George, and Joseph Keating. *Stonyhurst: Its Past History and Life in the Present*. London: Kegan Paul, Trench, Trübner, and Company, 1901. Mentions that Stonyhurst has devoted a special room for the teaching of gymnastics, fencing, and boxing.

Hadden, Robert. *An East-end Chronicle*. London: Hatchards, 1880. Describes tendency of Whitechapel murderers to throw their victims into the Thames.

Hammond, William Alexander. *Treatise on Insanity in its Medical Relations*. New York: Appleton and Company, 1883. Hammond, a former U.S. Surgeon-General, offers his views on mental illness.

Hare, Augustus John Cuthbert. *Walks in London*. London: Smith, Elder, and Company, 1883. Describes a walk through Lambeth, a rough section outside London, just before Jack the Ripper's reign of terror.

Hassell, Joseph. "A Silver Thimble." In *Common Things and Elementary Science in the Form of Object Lessons*. London: Blackie and Son, 1884. A silver thimble becomes a possible clue in the Ripper killings. Birmingham was the thimble capital of the world when Doyle lived there.

Henley, W. E., and John Stephen Farmer. *A Dictionary of Slang and Colloquial English*. London: George Routledge and Sons, 1905. Jargon of the Victorian and Regency eras.

Hewitson, A. *Stonyhurst College: Its Life Beyond the Seas, 1592–1794, and on English Soil, 1794–1894*. London: Marcus Ward and Company, 1894. Refers to the legend and ghost of Richard Francis Sherburne, a student at Stonyhurst who inadvertently ate some yew-berries and died. Also mentions the Gentlemen Philosophers' dog kennel—perhaps the inspiration for "The Hound of the Baskervilles."

Hogg, James. *Men Who Have Risen*. New York: Townsend and Company, 1861. Contains illustrations by Charles Doyle.

Holden, Edith. *Blyden of Liberia*. New York: Vantage Press, 1967. Notes that ambassador Henry Highland Garnet arrives in Monrovia on

December 22, 1881, on the English steamer *Nubia.*

Holland, Thomas. *Freemasonry from the Great Pyramid of Ancient Times.* London: R. Folkard and Son, 1884. Refers to Hiram Abiff, King Solomon's master architect and a hero of the Freemasons.

Hollingshead, John. *Ragged London in 1861.* London: Smith, Elder, and Company, 1861. Contains compelling description of London's lower classes.

How, Jeremiah. *The Freemason's Manual; or; Illustrations of Masonry.* London: Simpkin, Marshall, and Company, 1862. Details the criteria for attaining the rank of third-degree Master Mason.

Hugh, Goldie. *Memoir of King Eyo VII of Old Calabar.* Old Calabar: United Presbyterian Mission Press, 1894. Notes that Doyle violated King Eyo VII's decree by firing a gun on the Sabbath. Doyle was also violated international maritime law by bringing a gun onto his ship and, also by carrying it ashore.

Hutchings, W.W. *London Town Past and Present.* London: Cassell and Company, 1909. Details the Stepney and Whitechapel districts; includes map and other illustrations.

Hutton, Laurence. *Literary Landmarks of Edinburgh.* New York: Harper and Brothers, 1891. Discusses Professor Adam Ferguson's home at 2 Sciennes Hill; mentions that it was the location where Robert Burns ordained Sir Walter Scott.

Irving, H. B. *A Book of Remarkable Criminals.* New York: George Doran and Company, 1918. Irving recalls a conversation between his father, the well-known actor Henry Irving, and Great Britain's poet laureate, Alfred, Lord Tennyson.

Jack, Thomas. *The Waverley Handbook to Edinburgh.* Edinburgh: Thomas C. Jack, 1876. A guide to Edinburgh.

Jambon, Jean. *Our Trip to Blunderland.* Edinburgh: William Blackwood and Sons, 1877. Includes sixty illustrations by Charles Doyle.

Jerome, Jerome K. *My First Book.* London:

Chatto and Windus, 1897. Arthur Conan Doyle contributes the piece "Juvenilia" to this collection of essays written by famous authors about their first works.

Knott, George. *Trial of Sir Roger Casement.* Philadelphia: Cromarty Law Book Company, 1917. Contains Conan Doyle's petition to the prime minister on behalf of Roger Casement.

Lambton, Arthur. *Echoes of Causes Célèbres.* London: Hurst and Blackett, Ltd., 1931. Dedicated to "My Fellow-Members of 'Our Society.'"

—. *The Salad Bowl.* London: Hurst and Blackett, Ltd., 1927. Discusses formation of the "Crimes Club," which counted Doyle, Max Pemberton, and John Churton Collins among its first members. Remarks upon exemplary memory of Collins.

—. *Thou Shalt Do No Murder.* London: Hurst and Blackett, Ltd., 1930. Acknowledges friendship with Doyle, research assistance by Doyle on essay "The Psychic in Crime." Also discusses case of Thomas Neill Cream.

Landsborough, David. *Arran: Its Topography, Natural History, and Antiquities.* London: Houlston and Sons, 1875. Details Arran as "Scotland in miniature" and describes a trek up Goatfell Mountain.

Lankester, Ray. *Science from an Easy Chair.* New York: Macmillan Company, 1911. Collection of articles and illustrations from the Director of the British Natural History Museum's Daily Telegraph column.

Lellenberg, Jon, Daniel Stashower, and Charles Foley. *Arthur Conan Doyle: A Life in Letters.* New York: Penguin Press, 2007. Selections from Doyle's correspondences; provides commentary and photos.

Le Queux, William. *The Crimes Club.* London: Evenleigh, Nash & Grayson, 1927. A record of the Crimes Club's secret investigations, written by Le Queux, a member of "Our Society."

Lodge, Oliver. *Pioneers of Science.* London: Macmillan; 1893. Discusses Copernican theory of the revolution of Earth around the Sun; insults Alfred Drayson.

London, Jack. *The People of the Abyss.* New

York: Macmillan Company, 1904. London documents time spent living on the streets of London amongst the city's poor.

Lovechild, Lawrence. *The Book of Nursery Rhymes, Tales, and Fables: A Gift for All Seasons.* Philadelphia: George B. Zieber, 1847. Contains two references to "Little Robin Redbreast."

Lycett, Andrew. *The Man Who Created Sherlock Holmes.* New York: Free Press, 2007. Biography of Conan Doyle.

MacDonagh, Michael. *The Book of Parliament.* London: Isbister and Company, 1897. Traces the history of Big Ben.

Machray, Robert. *The Night Side of London.* Philadelphia: J.B. Lippincott Company, 1902. Describes London, and the East End in particular, at night.

Macnaghten, Melville Leslie. *Days of My Years.* New York: Longmans, Green and Company, 1914. Macnaghten, Chief of the Criminal Investigation Department during in the 1880s, describes his career at Scotland Yard.

Madame Tussaud and Sons' Catalogue. London: Nassau Steam Press Company, 1866. Describes contents of Madame Tussaud's exhibition.

Maunder, Samuel. *Treasury of Knowledge.* London: Longman, Orme, Brown, Green, and Longmans, 1840. Describes Old Town as resembling a turtle, with the castle as head, High Street as back ridge, the narrow lanes as sides, and Holyrood House as tail.

McClenachan, Charles T. *The Book of the Ancient and Accepted Scottish Rite of Freemasonry.* New York: Masonic Publishing and Manufacturing Company, 1868. The history, poetry, and symbolism of the Freemasons; includes the story of Hiram Abiff. Contains illustrations.

McLaren, Elizabeth. T. *Dr. John Brown and his Sister Isabella.* New York: Anson D.F. Randolph and Company, 1891. Mary Doyle's friend and confidant, Dr. John Brown, was the author of *Rab and his Friends.*

McLean, Thomas. *An Illustrative Key to the Political Sketches of H.B:1829 to 1832.* London:

Howlett and Brimmer, 1902. Analysis of H.B.'s (John Doyle's) political cartoons.

Miltoun, Frances. *Dickens' London.* Boston: L. C. Page & Company, 1908. Describes Whitechapel in Dickens' time and present day.

Mitchell, David. *The History of Montrose.* Montrose, Scotland: George Walker, 1866. Describes the Montrose Old Asylum and Sunnyside Royal Hospital, to which Charles Doyle was sent after a failed escape attempt.

Morrison, Arthur. *A Child of the Jago.* Chicago: Herbert S. Stone and Company, 1896. Novel functioning as a sort of survival guide to the East End.

Oddie, Samuel Ingleby. *Inquest.* London: Hutchinson and Company, 1941. Oddie gives both favorable and unfavorable opinions of his friend, Doyle.

Oliver and Boyd's New Edinburgh Almanac and National Repository. Edinburgh: Oliver and Boyd, 1884. Contains official information and statistics on commerce, agriculture, law, chronology, and government of Edinburgh. Reginald Hoare's name appears on the roster of the Royal College of Surgeons for the year 1879.

Pankhurst, Emmeline. *My Own Story.* London: Eveleigh Nash, 1914. Autobiography of Pankhurst, a leader of the British suffragette movement.

Pond, James Burton. *The Eccentricities of Genius.* London: Chatto and Windus, 1901. Includes chapter on Doyle, featuring several letters written by Doyle that discuss his lecturing tour in America.

The Popular Guide to The House of Commons; London: Pall Mall Gazette, 1892. Mentions the owners of the Kearley and Tonge warehouse, which was located in Mitre Square.

"Portobello." In *The Topographical, Statistical, and Historical Gazetteer of Scotland.* Edinburgh: A. Fullarton and Company, 1853. A description of the seaside resort town where Doyle spent several of his early boyhood years.

Post Office Edinburgh and Leith Directory, 1859–1860. Edinburgh: Ballantyne and Company, 1859. Notes residence of the Doyles.

Post-Office Edinburgh and Leith Directory, 1862–63. Edinburgh: Ballantyne and Company, 1862. Doyle name spelled incorrectly.

Richardson, Frank. *The Worst Man in the World.* London: Eveleigh Nash, Fawside House, 1908. Suggests that Jack the Ripper is a "medical man."

Ross, Janet. *Three Generations of English Women.* London: John Murray: 1888. Includes letters written by Doyle's uncle, Richard "Kitkat" Doyle.

Roughead, William. *Trial of Dr. Pritchard.* London: Sweet and Maxwell, 1906. Includes testimony by Douglas Maclagan and Henry Littlejohn, both professors at the University of Edinburgh Medical School.

Rules and Regulations and List of Members. London: Athenaeum Club, 1874. Lists Richard Doyle as member of the Athenaeum; "Kit Kat" suffered a stroke after attending a meeting there and died a day later.

Rutherford, William. *An Experimental Research on the Physiological Actions of Drugs on the Secretion of Bile.* Edinburgh: Adam and Charles Black, 1880. Refers to vivisections performed by Rutherford and his associates.

—. *Outlines of Practical Histology: Being the Notes of the Histological Section of the Class of Practical Physiology.* London: J. and A. Churchill, 1875. Recommends drawing paper similar or identical to type used in some of the Ripper letters.

"Rutherford and the Liver." In *Physiological Fallacies.* London: William and Norgate, 1882. The process by which the liver secretes bile is explained.

Scott, Walter. *The Pirate.* London: George Routledge and Sons, 1880. Describes the technique of seal flinching.

Shakespeare, William. *King John.* New York: MacMillan and Company, 1890. In Act V, the Bastard says, "And you degenerate, you ingrate revolts/You bloody Neroes, ripping up the Womb/Of your dear mother England, blush for shame/For your own ladies and pale-visaged maids/Like Amazons, come tripping after drums/Their thimbles into armed Gauntlets change/Their needles to lances, and their gentle hearts/To fierce and bloody inclination." Was the thimble left at Mitre Square meant to represent the Ripper's challenge to any women who dared leave the hearth?

—. *Othello.* London: George Kearsley, 1806. The handkerchief serves throughout the play as a symbol of love and fidelity. The Ripper may have used handkerchiefs in his crimes to denigrate liberated women.

Sidney, James Archibald. *Alter Ejusdem.* Edinburgh: Maclachlan and Stewart, 1877. Includes illustrations by Charles Doyle.

Sieveking, Edward Henry. *The Medical Adviser in Life Assurance.* Hartford, CT: N. P. Fletcher and Company, 1875. Handbook for physicians who perform life insurance physical examinations.

Smith, Alexander Duncan. *The Trial of Eugene Marie Chantrelle.* Glasgow: William Hodge and Company, 1906. Discussion of the poisoning case that includes testimony from Dr. Henry Littlejohn, one of Doyle's teachers at Newington Academy. Includes photo of Littlejohn.

Smith, John Thomas. *Mendicant Wanderers through the Streets of London.* Edinburgh: William P. Nimmo and Company, 1883. Sketches of London's homeless inhabitants.

Speight, Harry. *The Craven and North-west Yorkshire Highlands.* London: Elliot Stock, 1892. Describes Bryan Waller's family genealogy.

Stevenson, Robert Louis. *Edinburgh.* Philadelphia: J.B. Lippincott Company, 1905. Stevenson describes his home city.

—. *Letters and Miscellanies of Robert Louis Stevenson.* New York: Charles Scribner's Sons, 1900. Reprints letter addressed to Doyle, complimenting him on his Sherlock Holmes adventures and noting the resemblance of Holmes to "Joe Bell."

Stoker, Bram. *The Watter's Mou.'* New York: Appleton and Company, 1895. The author of *Dracula* describes Peterhead, Scotland, the town from which the *Hope* departed.

Stratton, J. Y. *Hops and Hops-Picking.* London: Society for Promoting Christian Knowledge,

1883. Notes that the people of Whitechapel flock to Kent in order to earn money by gathering hops.

Taylor, Alfred Swaine. *The Principles and Practice of Medical Jurisprudence*. London: J & A Churchill, 1883. Comprehensive textbook on causes of death by hanging, strangulation, and suffocation.

Thom's Irish Almanac and Official Directory of the United Kingdom. Dublin: Alexander Thom and Sons, 1857. Lists Charles Doyle among members of the Office of H.M. Works.

Waller, Bryan Charles. *The Twilight Land, and Other Poems*. London: George Bell and Sons, 1875. A collection of poems written by Mary Doyle's boarder and friend.

Ward, Thomas Humphry. *The Reign of Queen Victoria*. London: Smith, Elder, and Sons, 1887. Includes a short sketch of Richard Doyle.

Wells, Carolyn. *The Technique of the Mystery Story*. Springfield, MA: The Home Correspondence School, 1913. Investigates how crime writers, including Doyle and Gaboriau, create their characters.

Wensley, Frederick Porter. *Forty Years of Scotland Yard*. Garden City, NY: Doubleday, Doran, and Company, 1931. One of Scotland Yard's detectives describes his long career. Mentions use of rubberized shoes by detectives during investigation of Ripper murders.

Williams, Montagu Stephen. *Round London, Down East and Up West*. London: MacMillan and Company, 1893. Discusses wax representations of confirmed and unconfirmed Ripper victims.

—. *Later Leaves*. London: MacMillan and Company, 1891. Discusses the Whitechapel Murders.

Journals

Ad for Edward's XL Dry Plates. *Journal and Transactions of the Photographic Society of Great Britain* 7 (October 1882): xii. Includes endorsement of Edward's photographic plates by Doyle, who mentions taking them on trip to Africa, though none of the resulting photographs were ever published elsewhere.

"After Office Hours." *New England Medical Monthly* 18 (February 1899): 67. Doyle's newest work receives a chilly reception from his medical peers in the United States.

"An Important Sanitary Fact." *Popular Science* (November 1876): 123. Quotes Dr. Littlejohn describing the old town of Edinburgh as overcrowded and unsanitary.

"The Annual Dinner." *Journal of the British Dental Association* 9 (1888): 486–501. Notes that "Coran" Doyle attended the annual dinner of the British Dental Association. Discusses gratitude of doctors for the assistance of dentists on difficult cases. Portsmouth and its suburb, Southsea, are mentioned.

"Art Chronicle." *The Portfolio* 15 (1884): 24. Obituary of Richard Doyle. Mentions that John Doyle had "three sons, all more or less gifted in art"; Charles Doyle is significantly not included in this description.

Bell, Joseph. "Somewhat Unusual and Complicated Case of Inguinal Hernia." *New York Medical Abstract* 2 (December 1882): 472–473. Bell notes that he makes a groin incision after chloroform has been administered to his patient.

Benham, Allen. "John Churton Collins: A Review." *Modern Language Notes* 24 (November 1909): 204–208. Obituary. Notes that Collins dies "under circumstances somewhat obscure."

Bishop, Joseph B. "Early Political Caricature in America." *Century* 44 (June 1892): 219. Claims that John Doyle was the "real founder" of the *Punch* political caricature style.

Brough, Edwin. "The Bloodhound." *Century Illustrated Monthly Magazine* 2 (June 1889): 189. Brough states that he was consulted by the Chief Commissioner of the Metropolitan Police as to the feasibility of employing bloodhounds to track the Whitechapel murderer. Article includes pictures of Brough's dogs, Barnaby and Burgho.

Brownrigg, Henry. "Midnight at Madame T's." *New Monthly Magazine* (1837): 392–400. Includes reference to Madame Tussaud's "Chamber of Horrors," predating the so-called "original" use of that term by *Punch* magazine in 1846.

Burton, William. "Precipitation Methods and Green Fog- Alcohol in Emulsions." *British*

Journal of Photography 30 (January 26, 1863): 44–45. Burton introduces a method for eliminating green fog from photographic plates; thanks friend Doyle for contributing information to article.

"A Chat with Conan Doyle." *Idler Magazine* 6 (August 1894): 340–349. Doyle discusses the state of current literature.

Chiene, John. "Chloroform." *Practitioner* 18 (January 1877): 25–32. Chiene describes the physiological actions of the new anesthetic agent, chloroform; also criticizes how the "eyeward" at the Edinburgh Royal Infirmary (Joseph Bell) use a "flannel cap covering the nose and mouth" instead of a "towel or handkerchief."

"Chronicle and Comment." *Bookman* 22 (1902): 113–128. Biography of Conan Doyle with photographs.

"Conan Doyle's Rapid Work." *Phrenological Journal and Science of Health* 103 (April 1897): 198. Report on Doyle's uncanny ability to perform difficult tasks speedily.

Cortie, A.L. "The Scientific Work of Father Perry, S.J." *Month* 68 (March 1890): 474–488. Discusses career and educational techniques of Father Perry, noted Stonyhurst teacher and astronomer.

Craig, J. M. "Observations on Impaired Lives." *Transactions of the Actuarial Society of America* 2 (1889): 52. The Gresham Life Assurance Society helped keep Doyle afloat financially.

Damon, F. William. "Rambles in the Old World." *Friend* 29 (July 1880): 49–52. Contains detailed description of the capping ceremony at the University of Edinburgh Medical School.

"The Demeanour of Murderers." *Time* 1: (1879) 284–290. Describes Madame Tussaud and her wax museum.

Diogenes [pseud.]. "A Letter from the West Coast of Africa." *Fettesian* 4 (November 1881): 3–10. Describes a voyage aboard the *Mayumba* prior to Conan Doyle's own journey a few months later.

"Diseases of the Nervous System." *London Medical Record* 11 (December 15, 1883): 518–519. Alice Ker reviews Lecoq's paper on apoplectiform attacks in ataxy. Lecoq's work was cited by Doyle in his medical thesis, and may have influenced his understanding of his father's seizures.

Dolman, Frederick. "Two English Authors of Repute." *Ladies' Home Journal* 11(October 1894): 7. Notes that Doyle's fame "bids fair to eclipse" that of his relatives.

Doyle, Arthur Conan. "The American's Tale." *London Society* (1879): 185–196. An early short story written while Doyle was still a medical student displays his interest in and knowledge of America and of Americanisms.

—. "Crabbe's Practice." *Boy's Own Paper* (December 1884): 54–57. Doyle humorously describes the skills and skulduggery required to build a new medical practice.

—. "De Profundis." *McClure's Magazine* 3 (November 1894): 513–518. Discusses Ceylon tea fields, the family business of his friend, James Ryan. Also mentions the Thames shipping towns of Gravesend and Falmouth. The story itself features elements of telepathy.

—. "Doyle's Crowborough Home." *Bookman* 36 (February 1913): 604–605. Doyle produces a sketch of himself after receiving his medical degree. Its subtitle reads, "Licensed to kill."

—. "The Gully of Bluemansdyke." *London Society* 40 (December 1881): 23–37. The Warirra, an Australian river, is referenced by Doyle in this short story, which was submitted prior to his employment on board the *Mayumba*.

—. "Dr. Koch and His Cure." *Review of Reviews* 2 (December 1890): 552–560. Doyle tenders a harsh but respectful critique of Dr. Koch's purported cure for tuberculosis.

—. "Is Sir Oliver Lodge Right?" *Metropolitan* 46 (September 1917): 20–21. Doyle explains his conversion to Spiritualism.

—. "J. Habakuk Jephson's Statement." *Cornhill Magazine* 2 (January 1884): 1–32. Published anonymously, and once assumed to be written by Robert Louis Stevenson, this short story is a fictionalized account of the ghost ship *Mary Celeste*. Mistakenly taken to be a true eyewitness record by many readers.

—. "Life on a Greenland Whaler." *Strand Magazine* 13 (January 1897): 16–25. Doyle records his adventures in the Arctic Seas; includes photos of Colin McLean, Captain John Gray, Doyle, polar bears, walruses, and narwhals.

—. "Mr. Stevenson's Methods in Fiction." *Living Age* 69 (March 1890): 417–424. Doyle analyzes Stevenson's fiction, including *The Strange Case of Dr. Jekyll and Mr. Hyde.*

"Dr Joseph Bell's Introductory Address." *Edinburgh Medical Journal* 26 (January 1871): 577–590. Bell offers his views on the teaching of botany and natural history; also explains differences between medical school in London and medical school in Edinburgh.

F., H.G. "Reminiscences of School Life at Feldkirch." *Month* 81 (May 1894): 98–104. An alumnus recounts his life at Stella Matutina.

Griffiths, Arthur. "Unsolved Mysteries of Crime." *Cassell's Family Magazine* (1896): 381–387. Griffiths contends that the Ripper was either a foreign-born seaman or a person with a split personality, one superior to and more respectable than the other.

Hammond, William A. "Madness and Murder." *North American Review* 147 (December 1888): 626–637. Hammond, a noted neurologist and the eleventh US Surgeon General, offers his theories on madness.

Hedley, J.C. "Pope Leo XIII and the Freemasons." *Dublin Review* 12 (July 1884): 144. Notes recent dissociation of English Freemasons from French Freemasons, who repudiated belief in God and immortality of soul.

"How Jack The Ripper was Caught." *Deseret Weekly* 50 (1895): 658. Intimates that a "celebrated" West End physician is the Ripper.

"Industries of the European Paper Trade. Alexander Pirie and Sons." *American Stationer* 7 (December 1879): 20–21. Paper by Pirie and Sons was recommended by Dr. Rutherford..Includes picture of the Stoneywood Works.

Innes, Cosmo. "'Smoke Rockets' For Testing Drains." *Sanitary Record* 6 (February 1885): 385–386. With no concern for his own financial benefit, Cosmo Innes altruistically forgoes the copyright on his drain-testing invention, and instead gives it to society.

Irwin, Francis. "Stonyhurst." *Catholic Encyclopedia* 14 (1912): 309–310. Includes images of Stonyhurst from the western and southern fronts.

"J. Doyle, Esq." *Gentleman's Magazine* 224 (February 1868): 251–252. The obituary of John Doyle fails to acknowledge his son, Charles Altamont Doyle, though it notes that "[t]he best character of himself may be found in the career of his children, all in different paths and careers, individual as artists."

"Jack the Ripper." *Alienist and Neurologist* 10 (1889): 97–98. Notes that criminals like to visit areas where their crimes are discussed; posits that it is "entirely within the bounds of possibility that the Whitechapel murderer is now present in this room."

"Jack the Ripper." *American Practitioner and News* 12 (December 1891): 392. Notes phenomenon of Ripper copycat killings around the world.

Keith, Mercia Abbott. "Stately Edinburgh Throned on Crags." *Churchman* 90 (July 1904): 186–189. Photographs of Holyrood Palace, etc.

Lethaby, W.R. "The Priory of Holy Trinity." *Home Counties Magazine* 2 (1900): 45–53. Describes Mitre Square.

Littlejohn, Henry Duncan. "Report on the Sanitary Conditions of the City of Edinburgh." *Edinburgh Medical Journal* 11(May 1866): 1028–1031. Littlejohn, a noted toxicologist at the University of Edinburgh and an inspiration for the character of Sherlock Holmes, discusses crowding and decrepitude in Edinburgh.

"The London Factory Girl." *Temple Bar* 122 (January 1901): 315–327. Refers to 1888 match-girl strike.

"The Man-hunting Bloodhound." *Baily's Magazine of Sports and Pastimes* 71 (June 1899): 413–417. Discusses use of bloodhound in the murder of Emily Holland in Blackburn.

"Medical News." *Edinburgh Medical Journal*

37 (September 1891): 283–285. Indicates that Crosse and Oddie were classmates at the University of Edinburgh.

"Medical Schools of Scotland." *Edinburgh Medical Journal* 26 (October 1880): 354–355. Describes Bryan Charles Waller's job as a pathologist.

Mee, Arthur. "Papers communicated to the Association. A Visit to Stonyhurst." *Journal of the British Astronomical Association* 13 (December 1902): 68–70. Discusses contributions to astronomy by Fathers Perry, Moore, and Sidgreaves at Stonyhurst College.

"Meetings of Societies." *Edinburgh Medical Journal* 12 (June 1871): 838–847. Describes the methods of Doyle's teacher Dr. Keiller for incising the cervix; the Ripper's mutilations seem to have been informed by these methods.

"In Memoriam of Thomas Irwin and Henry Doyle." *Donahoe's Magazine* 27 (1892): 446–447. Obituary of Doyle's uncle, noted for his role in establishing the National Gallery of Ireland.

Moore, J. Murray. "The Hand as an Indicator of Disease." *Journal of the British Homeopathic Society* 10 (1902): 249–264. Quotes from Sherlock Holmes story noting characteristic pyrogallic acid stains on the hands of the photographer. Doyle used pyrogallic acid to treat his psoriasis.

"Notes and Notices." *Zoophilist* 8 (April 1889): 214. 'We are very often told that vivisection is right and proper because, in the opinions of experts, it "does good." A Bishop lately remarked, in a public speech in London, that, "the Whitechapel Murders had done much good."We should like to know whether the advocates of vivisection would, on their own principle, license the Whitechapel murderer to do a little more good, in the same way, in other districts?'

"Obituary: John Doyle." *Art Journal London* 7 (March 1868): 47. Obituary for John "H.B." Doyle, Doyle's grandfather.

"Obituary Notices." *Journal of the Chemical Society* 59 (1891): 453. Obituary of Cosmo Innes Burton, William K. Burton's younger brother, who died of smallpox while living in Shanghai.

"Obituary Notices." *Musical Times* 21 (September 1880): 469. Notes death of Reginald Hoare.

"The Original of Sherlock Holmes." *Book Buyer* 11 (March 1894): 61–64. Discusses Bell as inspiration for character of Sherlock Holmes; relates story illustrating Bell's prowess as a detective.

"The Pictures of Richard Doyle." *Edinburgh Monthly Magazine* 137 (April 1885): 485–491. Author claims that if a poet is "the man who has been in hell," Richard Doyle could be considered "the man who had been in Elfland."

"Poisoning Cases." *Law Times* 72 (1882): 425–426. Notes expert testimony of Professors Penney, Christison, Maclagan, Littlejohn, Crum Brown, and Fraser in recent Scottish poisoning cases.

Preston, W.C. "Hop-Picking in Kent." *Sunday Magazine* 13 (1884): 575. Mentions that Whitechapel poor clear out of town in late summer and early fall to find work gathering hops.

Ringer, Sydney, and William Morrell. "On Gelseminum Sempervirens." *London Lancet* 4 (April 1876): 164–168. Doyle used gelseminum in a failed attempt to cure his chronic neuralgia.

Robinson, Fred Byron. "A Sketch of Mr. Lawson Tait and His Work." *Journal of the American Medical Association*, January 30, 1892: 129–133. Discusses Lawson Tait's reputation as a detective; notes that he consults in high-profile criminal cases, including the Whitechapel murders.

Rodin, Alvin, and Jack Key. "Arthur Conan Doyle's Thesis on Tabes Dorsalis." *Journal of the American Medical Association*, February 5,1982: 646–650. Discusses Conan Doyle's medical school thesis.

Scott, Clement. "Back in London." *America* , October 4, 1888: 8. Offers graphic description of events in Whitechapel when the Ripper murders were being committed.

"Sealing." *Adventures Round the World* (March 1881): 88–93. Notes that the "molly" is a "sacred bird" and that "no sailor ever thinks of killing one."

"Stonyhurst Life." *Month and Catholic Review*

20 (1874): 325–336. Describes life at Stony-hurst; includes brief section on noted alumnus Charles Waterton.

"Sunday in East London." *Sunday at Home* 42 (1895): 88–93. Describes Spitalfield ghetto and Petticoat Lane; mentions the activity of the Ripper in this area.

"Vivisection." *Edinburgh Medical Journal* 21 (July 1875): 53–54. Criticizes two anti-vivisection bills; defends vivisection.

"W.K. Burton." *Photographic Times* 17 (June 10, 1887): 295–296. Discusses W.K. Burton; attributes genius to legacy left by father.

Wakefield, W. Walsham. "The East End." *Contemporary Review* 54 (December 1888): 793–805. Describes East Enders as simple-minded children "whose toys are vices" and who thus play at criminality.

Waller, Bryan Charles. "To Annette." *Popular Monthly* 43 (May 1897): 507. In this poem, Waller laments the death of Doyle's older sister, Annette. Contents imply that Waller was present in the Doyle household prior to Annette's departure for Portugal.

Watts, M.T. "The mysterious case of the doctor with no patients." *Journal of the Royal Society of Medicine* 84 (March 1991): 165–166. Describes Doyle's failure to establish a successful practice.

"Whitechapel, London." *Freemason's Repository* 18 (July 1889): 506–510. Describes the slums of Whitechapel.

Whittingham, Charles. "Modern Stony-hurst." *Downside Review* 2 (1883): 146–151. Describes inner workings of Stonyhurst College.

Winslow, John Hathaway, and Alfred Meyer. "The Perpetrator at Piltdown." *Science* 83 (September 1983): 32–43. Claims that Doyle perpetrated one of the biggest archaeological hoaxs of the twentieth century.

Periodicals

Adamson, W.M. "To the Editor of the Times." *Times* (London), October 13, 1888: 7. East End clergyman Adamson critiques proposals to help prostitutes.

"Another East End Murder." *Evening News* (London), November 10, 1888: 3. Notes presence of Vigilance Committee and police following recent murder. Mentions a Mrs. Kennedy, witness who heard the cry of "murder" coming from victim, and the schedule of cattle deliveries via the Thames.

"Another Horrible Murder in Whitechapel." *London Standard*, September 10, 1888: 3. Recounts testimony of witnesses who last saw Annie Chapman; describes her murder.

"Another Murder and Mutilation." *Evening News* (London), October 3, 1888: 3. Describes a mutilated female corpse found in Pimlico; efforts made to link this murder to Annie Chapman's.

"Another Murder in Whitechapel." *New York Times*, September 30, 1888: 5. Notes two new Whitechapel murders, similarities to previous Ripper victims.

"Another Murder in Whitechapel." *Times* (London), September 1, 1888: 6. Contains quotes from victim Mary Ann Nichols; notes that facial bruises result from mouth being covered.

"Another Terrible Crime." *Echo* (London), November 9, 1888: 3. Describes Mary Kelly murder crime scene, testimony of those who last saw her, concern over failure to use bloodhounds.

"Another Whitechapel Murder." *Echo* (London), September 8, 1888:3. Details writing purported to be on the wall of a building near the Annie Chapman murder crime scene.

"Another Whitechapel Murder." *Times* (London), November 10, 1888: 7. Describes Mary Kelly, Kelly's last known interactions, and circumstances surrounding the discovery of her body.

"Arthur Conan Doyle." *British Medical Journal*, January 2, 1932: 25. Review of John Lamond's biography of Doyle; notes that Doyle was "a many-sided personality" who struggled with poverty while a doctor in Southsea.

Banks, Frederick C. "The Contagious Diseases Act." *Medical Times and Gazette*, June 23, 1883: 710. Banks responds to a letter by Doyle published a week earlier. Doyle had lobbied for the restoration of the Contagious Diseases Acts; Banks objects to Doyle's arguments as "absolutely untrue" and resulting from "sheer ignorance."

Barnett, Samuel A. "Whitechapel." *Times* (London), October 11, 1888: 5. Describes Whitechapel as "a nursery of crime."

Bedford, R.C. "Whitechapel." *Times* (London), October 9, 1888: 12. Discusses need to provide for older women forced into prostitution.

—. "Whitechapel." *Times* (London), October 13, 1888: 7. Pleading for more donations.

—. "Funds for Whitechapel." *Times* (London), October 30, 1888: 6. Donations for Whitechapel.

Besant, Annie. "White Slavery in London." *Link*, June 23, 1888. Discusses "phossy jaw," a disease afflicting those who worked with white phosphorus, causing necrosis (death) of the the jaw bones and teeth. Also mentions the "matchbox girls'" strike.

"Bloodhounds for Murderers." *Echo* (London), October 1, 1888: 1. Bloodhounds to track the Ripper first suggested at the inquest of Mary Ann Nicholls and again at the inquest of Annie Chapman.

"British Leaders in Medicine During the Victorian Age." *British Medical Journal*, June 19, 1897: 1579–1582. Homage to the great physicians of the reign of Queen Victoria—Gull, Christison, Simpson, Addison, Stokes, Clay, Snow, and Lister.

"British Political Feuds." *New York Times*, November 14, 1888: 1. Claims that Ripper murders are not the reason for the resignation of London Police Commissioner Charles Warren.

Campbell, Maurice. "Sir Arthur Conan Doyle." *British Medical Journal*, May 23, 1959: 1341. Biographical entry on Doyle; discusses his childhood, education, literary career, and time in South Africa.

"Canon Jessop and Sir Conan Doyle on Medicine." *British Medical Journal*, October 15, 1904: 1026. Notes that Doyle's "short and chequered career as a doctor" included time served

as a ship's surgeon and army doctor; practiced in both the country and in city slums.

"A Central Mortuary for London." *Lancet*, September 15, 1888: 527. Arguments for the institution of a central mortuary in London, allowing for potential witnesses to view murder victims and thus confirm or reject their connection to specific cases.

"Cesare Lombroso." *Journal of the American Medical Association*, November 13, 1909: 1644–1645. Discusses Dr. Lombroso's attempt to identify the "criminal born" with the "primitive savage." Lombroso's theories influenced medicine and criminology for decades.

Chiene, John. "Promoter's Address." *Lancet*, August 8, 1896: 361–364. Dr. Chiene, Professor of Surgery at the University of Edinburgh Medical School, alludes to Lamarckian theory during his address to the graduating class of 1896, noting the presence of both a male and a female element in each cell.

"Conan Doyle's MD Thesis." *British Medical Journal*, March 27, 1982: 985. Doyle is able to complete his medical dissertation in a remarkably brief period of time. This, despite the death of a patient under his personal care, an interrogation by the police regarding his possible culpability in the patient's demise, and the courting of his future wife (the sister of his dead patient) all during this precise time frame .

"A Confession." *Evening News* (London), September 27, 1888: 3. A "shabby genteel" man is sought as a witness in the Chapman murder. Jack the Ripper purportedly asked his victim, "Will you?"

D. "The Detection of Crime." *Times* (London), October 11, 1888: 3. Anonymous author explains that criminals make mistakes that result in valuable evidence; article refers to "dynamite outrages" that occurred in Mitre Square and various crime writers and fictional detectives.

"Death of Sir William Gull." *Lancet*, February 1, 1890: 256. Reports death of William Gull "after only two days' acute illness," though indirectly the result of cerebral hemorrhage suffered in October 1887.

"Dismay in Whitechapel." *New York Times*,

October 1, 1888: 1. Details murders of Stride and Eddowes; notes that Mitre Square is deserted but patrolled every half hour by police.

Doyle, Arthur Conan. "The 'New' Scientific Subject." *British Journal of Photography*, July 20, 1883: 418. Here, Doyle argues against the credibility of the pseudosciences. "He tells us that scientific men have discovered a force in all living things which they have named 'Od'. What scientific men? At the risk of being flippant I should submit that it is very odd that such a force should be mentioned in non text-book of science"

—. "The Edalji Case." *British Medical Journal*, January 19, 1907: 173. Doyle deduces that George Edalji, who gained notoriety in the cattle mutilation 'outrage', could not possibly have been guilty of the crime as he suffered from myopic astigmatism.

—. "Gelseminum as a Poison." *British Medical Journal*, September 20, 1879: 483. Doyle mentions personal use of gelseminum to treat neuralgia; notes that he frequently exceeded accepted maximum dosage and experienced no ill effect beyond diarrhea.

—. "On the Slave Coast With a Camera." *British Journal of Photography*, March 31, 1882: 185–186. Doyle recounts his use of the ship bathroom as a darkroom.

—. "On the Slave Coast With a Camera." *British Journal of Photography*, April 7, 1882: 202–203. Doyle mentions that he had the opportunity to photograph a war chief named "Wawirra." In a bizarre coincidence, Doyle had just written about an Australian river named Wawirra a few weeks earlier.

—. "The Remote Effects of Gout." *Lancet*, November 29, 1884: 978. Doyle examines the effects of gout on three generations of a single family. Indicates an interest in tracking disease within families that may have contributed to his selection of tabes dorsalis as a thesis topic.

—. "Where to Go With the Camera: Southsea: Three Days in Search of Effects." *British Journal of Photography*, June 22, 1883: 359–361. Doyle refers to two friends, the "Lunatic" and the "Man of Science," and mentions that a

Mr. Barnden of the Gresham Insurance Society joins them on the excursion to Southsea.

—. "Where to Go With the Camera: To the Waterford Coast and Along It." *British Journal of Photography*, August 24, 1883: 497–498. Doyle writes about an 1881 trip to Dublin and the Blackwater Valley on which he was accompanied by his friend Cunningham, who does not appear in his letters from that time.

Doyle, Richard. "Madame Tussaud Her Wax Werkes." *Punch*, September 15, 1849: 112. Illustrates Chamber of Horrors and contains character sketches of "Ye Celebrated Murderers."

"The East-End Atrocities." *Echo* (London), October 2, 1888: 3. Notes that a "man with a Black Shiny Bag" asked a guest in the Three Nuns Hotel for the exact ages of the local prostitutes. Mentions that Catherine Eddowes had a tattoo of the initials "T.C."

"The East-End Atrocities." *Echo* (London), October 3, 1888: 3. Newest Ripper victim identified as "Catherine Kelly"; initials T.C. on her tattoo stand for Thomas Conway, former husband or boyfriend.

"The East-End Atrocities." *Echo* (London), October 10, 1888: 3. Reports that prostitutes are avoiding common lodging houses for fear of the Ripper.

"The East-End Atrocities." *Echo* (London), November 12, 1888: 3: Reports that a doctor is acting as an amateur detective; Whitechapel locals sought to lynch him.

"The East-End Atrocities." *Echo* (London), November 14, 1888: 3. Describes Mary Ann Kelly's murderer.

"The East-End Horrors." *Lloyd's Weekly News*, October 7, 1888: 1. Denounces Whitechapel killings as "war against a class, and. . .therefore all the more terrible."

"The East End Murders." *Echo* (London), September 14, 1888: 3. Private Reward offered by Mr. Samuel Montagu, M.P, is mentioned; "Pearly Poll" knew "Dark Annie"—The press tags descriptive adjectives onto the victims and the local prostitutes. Funeral of Annie Chapman takes place in utmost secrecy.

"East End Murders." *Echo* (London), September 15, 1888: 3. Ripper suspect Edward Stanley is released from police custody, considered to be a "pensioner." In fact, he is a militiaman.

"The East End Murders." *Lloyd's Weekly News*, October 14, 1888: 1. Police presence increased at night; murders have caused uptick in amateur detective work/letters to police.

"The East End Murders." *London Mid Surrey Times and General Advertiser*, October 13, 1888: 3. Claims Ripper had knowledge of throat cutting; includes portraits of the supposed murderer. Mentions use of bloodhounds Barnaby and Burgho in tracking the Ripper, discusses funeral of Catherine Eddowes.

"The East-End Murders." *London Standard*, October 3, 1888: 3. Possible significance of pawn tickets discussed at latest inquest.

"The East-End Murders." *London Standard*, October 4, 1888: 3. Catherine Eddowes identified at Golden Lane Mortuary. References made to a horse falling in the street and a knife being observed on the steps at that precise location.

"The East-End Murders." *London Standard*, October 5, 1888: 3. Coroner at the Mitre Square Inquest claims that the murderer must have possessed anatomical knowledge. Torn apron piece found at Goulston Street is the portion missing from the apron of the victim.

"The East-End Murders." *London Standard*, October 6, 1888: 3. Ripper is described as an educated man "from the way he spoke"; is said to have worn a deerstalker. Various aspects of Elizabeth Stride's story are debunked, cachous mentioned. Divisional Police Surgeon Phillip believes that the Ripper must have some anatomical knowledge.

"The East-End Murders." *London Standard*, October 9, 1888: 3. Warren arranges for use of Edwin Brough's bloodhounds to hunt Ripper, increases the number of officers on patrol.

"The East-End Murders." *London Standard*, October 10, 1888: 3. Bloodhounds Barnaby and Burgho are mentioned.

"The East End Murders." *Times* (London), October 10, 1888: 10. Body of "Long Liz" Stride identified by Elizabeth Tanner, described as found on murder scene by Dr. Phillips. Thomas Coram testifies that he found a knife with a blood-stained handkerchief wrapped around its handle on a doorstep.

"The East End Murders." *Times* (London), October 11, 1888: 5. No trace of narcotics found in Stride's stomach.

"The East End Murders." *Times* (London), October 12, 1888: 4. Recounts testimony of Constable Hutt, Gordon Brown; significance of "Juwes" discussed at length.

"The East End Murders." *Times* (London), October 16, 1888: 10. Thomas Conway meets with police.

"The East-End Tragedy." *Echo* (London), September 10, 1888: 3. Amelia Farmer identifies body of Annie Chapman; deputy at Chapman's lodging house testifies as to Chapman's inebriation, lack of funds on night of murder.

"The East End Tragedy." *Echo* (London), September 11, 1888: 3. Ripper suspect John Piser is taken into police custody; suspect William Henry Pigott also monitored.

"The East-End Tragedies." *Echo* (London), October 11, 1888: 3. Recounts testimony of policemen who interacted with Catherine Eddowes before her demise. Mentions writing on the wall, portion of women's apron.

"The East-End Tragedies." *Echo* (London), October 12, 1888: 3. Suspect John Foster is arrested in Belfast, Ireland.

"The East-End Tragedies." *Echo* (London), October 13, 1888: 3. Discusses spelling of the word "Juwes," possibility of governmental reward for information on Ripper, increased police presence.

"Easter Monday Review." *Hampshire Telegraph and Sussex Chronicle:* April 12, 1884. Mentions Portsmouth's mock artillery skirmishes, which Doyle had taken his brother Innes to see.

"An Elderly Gentleman." *Times* (London), October 15, 1888: 13. Describes widespread panic over Ripper in London and surrounds.

"Events Beyond the Sea." *New York Times*, September 12, 1888: 1. Notes that several suspects have been arrested in Ripper murders; all discharged.

"Exciting London Events." *New York Times*, November 10, 1888: 1. Contains lurid description of Mary Jane Kelly's corpse.

"Good Out of Evil." *Lloyd's Weekly*, October 14, 1888: 1. Author opines that Ripper murders bring attention to the need to improve lives of East End inhabitants.

Hazell, Walter. "Friendless And Fallen In Whitechapel." *Times* (London), October 6, 1888: 12. Letter to the editor emphasizing need to help vulnerable women who are being victimized in Whitechapel.

"History of Seven Days." *Illustrated American*, July 16, 1892: 427. Claims that Dr. Neill Cream is Jack the Ripper.

"Horrible London: Or, The Pandemonium of Posters." *Punch*, October 13, 1888. Billboard posters depicting the Ripper murders.

"Home for Incurables, Cork." *British Medical Journal*, July 9, 1881: 57. Mentions fancy fair held at Lismore, where Doyle would met Elmore Weldon.

"In Whitechapel Jewry." *Boston Evening Transcript*, July 20, 1901: 24. Contains description of Petticoat Lane.

J.F.S. "The State of Whitechapel." *Times* (London), September 14, 1888: 6. Notes that robberies are still being committed within 100 yards of the killings.

Jones, Harold Emery. "The Original of Sherlock Holmes." *Collier's*, January 9, 1904: 14–15. Cites teachers at the University of Edinburgh Medical School.

Kelly, Howard A. "The Whitechapel Murders." *Medical News*, October 13, 1888: 430–431. Speculates that Ripper might be a woman.

Kinnaird, Mary J. "A Whitechapel Fund." *Times* (London), October 26, 1888: 10. In letter to the editor, Kinnaird announces she is raising a fund to bring Christianity to Whitechapel.

"The Latest Horror." *Evening News* (London), November 12, 1888: 3. Relates personal history of Mary Kelly and notes near-lynching of amateur detective investigating the Ripper mur-

ders; detective used disguise and identified self as "a medical man."

"The Latest Whitechapel Murder." *Lloyd's Weekly*, November 11, 1888: 1. Reports that the police believe the Ripper took a souvenir body part from the scene of Mary Kelly's murder.

"Letters, Notes, and Answers to Correspondents: The Condition of the Pupils by Chloral Hydrate." *British Medical Journal*, September 20, 1879: 481. Mentions use of chloral hydrate for hypnosis; quotes Dr. Hammond.

Lewis, Edward Dillon, "To the Editor of the Times." *Times* (London), October 4, 1888: 10. Letter to editor notes that Ripper murders require anatomical knowledge.

"Literary Notes." *British Medical Journal*, January 28, 1899: 224. Discusses the theory that the Ripper died or became insane after his last murder.

"London Crime and Gossip; A Terribly Brutal Murder in Whitechapel." *New York Times*, September 1, 1888: 1. Reports on a "strangely horrible murder" in Whitechapel, the third of an apparent series.

"The London Paranoiac." *New York Times*, October 8, 1888: 4. Notes that paranoiacs exist in every class and at every level of intellectual ability.

"London Tragedies." *The Daily Telegraph*, October 5, 1888: 1. Reports £500 reward for the capture of the Ripper.

"London's Awful Mystery." *New York Times*, October 2, 1888: 1. Notes "daring character" of murderer in perpetrating crimes in area with police presence and plenty of potential witnesses.

"London's Record of Crime." *New York Times*, October 3, 1888: 1. Writes that "[t]he carnival of blood continues," noting that London has also seen an increase in crime this summer apart from the "master murderer's work."

"London's Small Police Force." *New York Times*, November 10, 1888: 1. Reports newest Ripper murder (Kelly), expresses concern that London police "seem absolutely powerless to put an end to these mysterious crimes."

Mack, Michael. "A French Chapter of Whitechapel Horrors." *Times* (London), October 6, 1888: 12. Discusses a series of Ripper-like crimes that were committed in France.

Maurice, Arthur Bartlett. "Concerning Mr. Sherlock Holmes." *Collier's*, March 28, 1908: 12–14. Discusses the genesis of Sherlock Holmes.

— "Sir Arthur Conan Doyle." *Collier's*, March 28, 1908: 11–12. Discusses Doyle's career and personality.

—. "Concerning Conan Doyle." *Collier's*, March 28, 1908: 14. Elaborates on Doyle's dramatic power.

"The Medical Evidence and an Abstract of the General Evidence Adduced on the Trial of William Palmer." *Lancet*, May 24, 1856: 563–585. Discusses murder-by-poisoning case of John Parsons Cook, which Drs. Littlejohn and Maclagan were instrumental in solving.

"Medical Freemasons." *Lancet*, May 16, 1896: 1369. Explains why physicians join the Order of Freemasons. Includes Frederick Gordon Brown on list of Grand Officers.

"Medical News." *Medical Times and Gazette*, August 7, 1869: 179. Announces marriage of Reginald Hoare to Amy Jane Tovey.

"Medicine in the Novel." *Medical Press*, February 1, 1905: 119. Criticizes Doyle for medical errors made by Sherlock Holmes and Dr. John Watson in stories; errors undermine genius of Holmes and offend doctors' "professional pride."

"The Method of Sherlock Holmes." *British Medical Journal*, December 30, 1893: 1442–1443. Reports that Doyle's medical education, particularly training under Joseph Bell, was critical to creation of Sherlock Holmes.

"The Mitre Square Murder." *Evening News* (London), October 4, 1888: 3. Reports testimony of local fruit seller who claims to have sold grapes to the Ripper.

"The Mitre Square Murder." *Evening News* (London), October 5, 1888: 2. Reporter spends a night in a doss house and interviews several of its residents.

"The Mitre Square Murder." *Evening News* (London), October 19, 1888: 3. Reports that

half a human kidney—suspected to be Catherine Eddowes's—was received by George Lusk, a Freemason and chairman of the Whitechapel Vigilance Committee. Parcel is accompanied by a letter from the Ripper: "Catch me when you can Mishter Lusk."

"The Mitre-Square Victim." *The Echo* (London), October 4, 1888: 3. Describes testimony at inquest on Catherine Eddowes's death. Reward of £500 offered for capture of killer.

"The Mitre Square Victim." *Evening News* (London), October 11, 1888: 3. More testimony at Catherine Eddowes inquest; no poison found in stomach. Dr. Gordon Brown testifies on details of murder; Brown would later serve as guide of Crime Club's 1905 Whitechapel tour.

"More East-End Tragedies." *Lloyd's Weekly News*, September 30, 1888: 1. Describes condition of Eddowes's body. Dr. Brown offers pencil sketch of body position at crime scene.

"The Murder in Hanbury Street." *Saturday Review of Politics, Literature, Science and Art*, September 15, 1888: 311. Objects to police scrutiny of "Leather Apron" suspect John Piser.

"Murder in Whitechapel." *London Standard*, September 1, 1888: 2. Describes murder of Mary Ann Nicholls, considered to be the third in a series of crimes.

"Murder Theories." *Lloyd's Weekly News*, September 23, 1888: 1. Describes theories of Dr. Phillips, the police divisional surgeon, whose examination of latest murder victim led him to believe perpetrator had "considerable anatomical knowledge."

"The Murderer at Large." *New York Times*, October 22, 1888: 1. Notes Ripper copy-cat killing in Columbia, South Carolina.

"The Murders." *Evening News* (London), October 6, 1888: 3. Mentions letters purportedly sent by the Ripper to the police, Charles Warren, bloodhounds.

"The Murders." *Evening News* (London), October 8, 1888: 3. Reports on message supposedly written by Ripper upon the wall: "The Jews Shall Not Be Blamed For Nothing." Police sponge it off to prevent a riot. Bloodhounds mentioned.

"The Murders." *Evening News* (London), October 10, 1888: 3. Notes decreased presence of amateur detectives, increased presence of professional detectives in Whitechapel.

"The Murders and Sir Charles Warren." *Lloyd's Weekly*, November 11, 1888: 1. Indicates that the Mary Jane Kelly murder differs only from the preceding Ripper crimes in that it was perpetrated indoors.

"The Murders at the East End." *Times* (London), October 2, 1888: 6. Reports testimony from members of the International Working Men's Educational Club, discusses letter assumed to be written by the Ripper.

"The Murders in the East-End." *London Standard*, October 2, 1888: 3. Discusses murders of Stride and Eddowes; reward offered. Reports testimony of International Working Men's Educational Club members at inquest.

"The Murders in London." *New York Times*, October 6, 1888: 1. Warren decides to bring out the bloodhounds to track down Jack the Ripper.

"The Murders in London." *Times* (London), October 20, 1888: 7. Notes that Mr. Lusk, of the Whitechapel Vigilance Committee received a parcel containing half a kidney.

"News of the Day Abroad." *New York Times*, September 4, 1888: 1. Describes Ripper crime spree as a cross between "Poe's 'Murders of the Rue Morgue' and 'The Mystery of Marie Roget;'" notes mysteriousness of Ripper's identity.

Nunn, Thomas Hancock and Thomas G. Gardiner. "Whitechapel." *Times* (London), October 6, 1888: 12. Authors comment that "[t]hose of us who know Whitechapel know that the impulse that makes for murder is abroad in our streets every night."

"Obituary: Charles Clay." *British Medical Journal*, September 23, 1893: 712–713. Obituary of Dr. Clay, pioneer of abdominal surgery "Father of the Ovariotomy."

"Obituary: George T. Budd." *British Medical Journal*, March 16, 1889: 628. Notes death of D. George Budd at age 34; in his memoirs, Doyle would attribute this premature death to some sort of cerebral anomaly.

"Obituary: William Budd." *British Medical Journal*, January 31, 1880: 163–166. Obituary of William Budd, father of Doyle's friend, George T. Budd. The Budds lived in Dartmoor, later to become the setting for Doyle's works "The Hound of the Baskervilles" and "The Cardboard Box."

"Old World News by Cable." *New York Times*, September 9. 1888: 1. Describes fourth murder of the Ripper, here called "Leather Apron." Comments on strange coincidence that murders are taking place "while everybody is talking about Mansfield's 'Jekyll and Hyde' at the Lyceum."

"Old World News by Cable." *New York Times*, October 7, 1888: 1. Notes that failure to find the Ripper would reflect poorly on British government.

"The Police and Sir Charles Warren." *London Standard*, November 16, 1888: 3. Reports resignation of Charles Warren as Police Commissioner.

"Professor Annandale on Homeopathy, etc." *Michigan Medical News*, October 10, 1881: 296. Reports on Doyle's capping-ceremony on the day he received his MB degree from the University of Edinburgh.

"Professor Annandale on Quackery." *London Medical Press and Circular*, August 24, 1881: 179. Transcribes valedictory address given by Annandale to Doyle and the other new graduates of the University of Edinburgh; Annandale warns that quackery is extending into the medical profession.

"Public Mortuaries." *Lancet*, September 22, 1888: 583. Discusses proposal to institute public mortuary in Whitechapel.

"The Repeal of the Contagious Diseases Act." *Lancet*, October 20, 1888: 778. Reports that Whitechapel murders have brought attention to issue of prostitution and shown the validity of the Contagious Diseases Acts.

"Report of the Lancet Special Sanitary Commission on the Polish Colony of Jew Tailors." *Lancet*, May 3, 1884: 817–818. Describes Hanbury Street and its environs; area is closed down each Saturday so that its Jewish residents can observe the Sabbath.

"Resignation of Sir Charles Warren." *Evening News* (London), November 13, 1888: 3. Warren complains that he had all the responsibility but relatively little freedom to act; cannot continue as Police Commissioner.

Robinson, Arthur J. "Whitechapel Fund." *Times* (London), October 29, 1888: 3. Robinson offers another reformation plan for Whitechapel.

"A Sad East-End Exhibit." *Echo* (London), September 15, 1888: 1. Describes a waxwork exhibit (later detailed by Montagu Williams in his book *Round London*) containing figures of murder victims Martha Turner and Mary Ann Nicholls.

"Sanitary Administration of London." *Lancet*, October 6, 1888: 679–680. Explains that the Whitechapel murders call attention to need for better government of poorer urban areas.

"Scottish Hospitals and Medical Schools." *Lancet*, September 12, 1868: 370–371. Notes that Joseph Bell owns the most modern ophthalmologic equipment available; Doyle would later specialize in ophthalmology under Bell, using his knowledge to try to free George Edalji.

"Sensational Placards Incentives to Crime." *Lancet*, September 29, 1888: 641–642. Echoes Dr. Hammond's theory that visual cues can act as triggers for violent actions.

"A Serious Question." *Lancet*, September 15, 1888: 551. Discusses possibility that "highly-coloured pictorial advertisements" might act as visual triggers for violence.

"Sexual Perversion and the Whitechapel Murders." *Medical Record*, March 16, 1889: 296–297. Suggests that the Ripper is "a well-meaning, though excessively zealous man."

"The 'Social Evil' in London." *Lancet*, December 8, 1888: 1146. Author opines that "men should be able to walk to and from their business without having the social evil thrust upon them night after night and year after year."

"Social Whirl." *Motor Car Journal*, October 31, 1908: 751. Describes Doyle and Max Pemberton as avid motorists.

Steer, Mary H. "Ratcliff Highway Refuge." *Times* (London), October 11, 1888: 14. Steer details how East End women turn to prostitution to earn money for food and shelter.

"Stephen Joseph Perry, F.R.S." *Nature*, January 23, 1890: 279–280. Discusses Perry, Stonyhurst teacher noted for his contributions towards astronomy.

"Still Uncaptured." *Bridgeport Morning News* October 8, 1888: 4. Notes that Whitechapel is "swarming with detectives" talking to prostitutes and trying to find new leads.

Stoker, Bram. "Sir Arthur Conan Doyle Tells of His Career and Work, His Sentiments Towards America, and His Approaching Marriage." *New York World*, July 28, 1907: 1. To Stoker, his interviewer and distant relation, Doyle reveals character names considered before settling on "Sherlock Holmes." Also discusses how Doyle "drifted into the study of medicine" and erroneously lists order of medical assistantships.

"The Story of an Outcast." *Speaker*, April 19, 1890: 425. Obituary of Joseph Merrick, the Elephant Man.

"The Streets of London." *Lancet*, March 11, 1865: 265–266. Describes London fog.

"Talked about in London." *New York Times*, September 29, 1888: 2. Discusses discharge of Ripper suspect who made false confession.

"Tee Shots." *Golf Illustrated*, September 29, 1899: 445. Describes Joseph Bell as enthusiastic golfer.

"Topics of the Day." *Medical Times and Gazette*, June 16, 1883: 671. Reprints part of letter by Doyle condemning the repeal of the Contagious Diseases Act.

"Two Americans Arrested." *New York Times*, October 4, 1888: 1. Reports that two Americans have been arrested as Ripper suspects.

"Two More Murders." *Times* (London), October 1, 1888: 9. Reports on Stride and Eddowes murders.

"Two More Women Horribly Murdered." *London Mid Surrey Times and General Advertiser*, October 6, 1888: 3. Discusses other potential victims of the Ripper, offers map of crimes, reports on most recent inquest.

Warren, Charles. "Lord Mayor's Day, 1888" *Times* (London), November 6, 1888: 8. Advance notification of the traffic routes and road closures that are to be in effect on Lord Mayor's Day.

Waterson, Davina. "Dead Men Do Tell Tales." *Scientific American*, October 24, 1914: 271–272. Claims that the mutilations perpetrated by the Ripper demonstrate "considerable anatomical knowledge."

"What They Have Come to In Whitechapel." *New York Times*, October 21, 1888: 12. Describes Whitechapel in lengthy and unfavorable detail.

"Whitechapel." *Saturday Review of Politics, Literature, Science and Art*, November 24, 1888: 607. Opines that the Ripper murders have become "a standing nuisance"; hopes that they "will lead to some good if the wretched women who have been the victims of these outrages do begin to suffer from panics."

"The Whitechapel Horror." *Evening News* (London), September 10, 1888: 3. Stepfather describes "Leather Apron" suspect John Piser to reporter. Discusses inquest on "Annie (Sievey) Chapman."

"The Whitechapel Horrors." *Evening News* (London), October 1, 1888: 2. Describes Stride and Eddowes murders; mentions presence of grapes and sweeteners.

"The Whitechapel Horrors." *Evening News* (London), October 2, 1888: 3. Reward now at £1200 for the Ripper's capture. Questions failure to use bloodhounds; records testimony of a Mr. Baskert, who believes he saw the Ripper.

"Whitechapel Horrors Due to Free-trade Wages." *Tariff League Bulletin*, December 21, 1888: 284. Claims that 10 to 12 percent of Whitechapel's women and girls are or have been prostitutes; denounces fact that women there "practically choose between semi-starvation and harlotry."

"The Whitechapel Murder." *British Medical Journal*, September 22, 1888: 672. Speculates on the psychology of the murderer.

"The Whitechapel Murder." *British Medical Journal*, September 29, 1888: 729. Mentions that an American requested uterus specimens for research at an unnamed pathological museum attached to a medical school.

"The Whitechapel Murder." *Echo* (London), September 1, 1888: 3. Discusses and discards possibility that recent murder perpetrated by a "'High Rip' gang"; most detectives credit crime to single "maniac."

"The Whitechapel Murder." *Echo* (London), September 3, 1888: 3. Police say that Mary Ann Nicholls was killed at the spot where she was found, and was not transported from another location.

"The Whitechapel Murder." *Echo* (London), September 4, 1888: 3. Describes writing found on the slaughterhouse gate reading, "This is where the murder was done."

"The Whitechapel Murder." *Echo* (London), November 13, 1888: 3. Portion of body is missing. The Echo asks, 'Why weren't the bloodhounds used?'

"The Whitechapel Murder." *Evening News* (London), September 14, 1888: 3. Describes bloodstained newspapers believed to have been used by the Ripper to wipe his hands after a murder.

"The Whitechapel Murder." *Evening News* (London), September 28, 1888: 3. Reports arrest of Ripper suspect; prints letter by James Risbon Bennett supporting theory that Ripper "possessed some knowledge of anatomy."

"The Whitechapel Murder." *Evening Standard* (London), November 16, 1888: 3. Funeral services held for Mary Jane Kelly.

"The Whitechapel Murder." *Lloyd's Weekly News*, September 2, 1888: 6. Discusses different theories about perpetrator or perpetrators of Ripper murders.

"The Whitechapel Murder." *Times* (London), September 3, 1888: 12. Notes similarities between three Whitechapel murders; suggests they are "the work of one and the same villain."

"The Whitechapel Murder." *Times* (London), September 4, 1888: 8. Discusses murder of Mary Ann Nicholls.

"The Whitechapel Murder." *Times* (London), September 11, 1888: 6. Discusses crimes supposedly committed by "Leather Apron."

"The Whitechapel Murder." *Times* (London), September 12, 1888: 6. Notes "peculiar marks" on wall near Chapman murder scene.

"The Whitechapel Murder." *Times* (London), September 13, 1888: 5. Relates probable time of Chapman murder; notes that "the murderer must have walked through the streets in almost broad daylight without attracting attention, although he must have been at the time more or less stained with blood."

"The Whitechapel Murder." *Times* (London), September 14, 1888: 4. Details Chapman crime scene; notes presence of pills and an envelope with the seal of the Sussex regiment.

"The Whitechapel Murder." *Times* (London), September 27, 1888: 5. Describes the Ripper as calculating and medically skilled, one who had a compulsion to order and arrange things.

"The Whitechapel Murder." *Times* (London), November 12, 1888: 6. Notes that a "fierce fire" had been made in fireplace at Mary Jane Kelly's.

"The Whitechapel Murder." *Times* (London), November 13, 1888: 10. Reports that some body parts are still missing from Mary Jane Kelly crime scene; Charles Warren resigns.

"The Whitechapel Murder Mysteries." *New York Times*, October 12, 1888: 2. Discusses message purportedly written by Ripper near murder victim: "I have murdered four and will murder 16 before I surrender myself to the police." Message erased on order of Charles Warren before photographic documentation possible.

"The Whitechapel Murders." *Echo* (London), September 17, 1888: 3. Government retracts offer of reward. New details in death of Mary Ann Nichols; new Ripper suspects possible.

"The Whitechapel Murders." *Evening News* (London), October 5, 1888: 3. Discusses Americanisms, theories on Ripper's motivations.

"The Whitechapel Murders." *Evening News*

(London), September 19, 1888: 3. Reports on meeting of the Vigilance Committee, of which Mr. Lusk is president. Discusses roposals for reward for the capture of Ripper, better lighting for the streets of the East End, and the removal of slaughterhouses.

"The Whitechapel Murders." *Lancet*, September 15, 1888: 533. Discounts theory that Ripper murders are "the work of a lunatic."

"The Whitechapel Murders." *Lancet*, September 22, 1888: 603. Notes that "it is well known to experts in insanity that although the anticipation of the deed may be long cherished, yet the act itself is sudden, unexpected, uncomplicated by any subsequent mutilation, or attempt to conceal the act, and very frequently followed by some suicidal attempt."

"The Whitechapel Murders." *Lancet*, September 29, 1888: 637. Discusses possibility that motivation for Ripper murders was the procurement of the uterus.

"The Whitechapel Murders." *Milwaukee Sentinel*, June 10, 1894. In interview, Doyle recounts examination of Ripper documents at Scotland Yard's Black Museum. Doyle notes that "Dear boss" letter is written on "good paper" with "red ink"—indicating he saw original letter, not facsimile.

"The Whitechapel Murders." *New York Times*, September 19, 1888: 1. Reports that the police have arrested a German named Ludwig in connection with the Ripper murders.

"The Whitechapel Murders." *New York Times*, October 4, 1888: 1. Discounts the coroner's theory that Ripper's murders were "carried out under the impulse of a pseudo-scientific mania." Notes that "a foreign physician" of "highest respectability" had looked into possibility of obtaining body parts for research a year earlier.

"The Whitechapel Murders." *Saturday Review of Politics, Literature, Science and Art*, November 17, 1888: 574. Claims that a murderer who is not motivated by money/revenge and whose victims are from an overlooked class will be able to continue his crime spree unimpeded.

"The Whitechapel Murders." *Sydney Morn-*

ing Herald, May 21, 1896: 3. Reports that an ex-con named Seaman was found guilty of a double murder in Whitechapel; a man with same name was implicated in a robbery during the Ripper's spree.

"The Whitechapel Murders." *Times* (London), September 15, 1888: 6. Discusses other Ripper suspects, none particularly promising.

"The Whitechapel Murders." *Times* (London), September 18, 1888: 12. Reports on inquest of Mary Ann Nichols.

"The Whitechapel Murders." *Times* (London), September 19, 1888: 3. Details suspect who changed clothes in lavatory of City News Rooms on day of Chapman murder.

"The Whitechapel Murders." *Times* (London), September 20, 1888: 4. Reports on Annie Chapman inquest; black eye possibly due to fight prior to murder. Witness claims Ripper wore "a brown deer-stalker hat."

"The Whitechapel Murders." *Times* (London), September 24, 1888: 3. Reports on inquest of Mary Ann Nichols.

"The Whitechapel Murders and Sanitary Reform." *Lancet,* October 6, 1888: 683–684. Opines that Whitechapel murders help bring attention to need for reform in Whitechapel.

The Whitechapel Mystery." *Evening News* (London), September 8, 1888: 3. Describes Annie Chapman murder.

"Whitechapel Tragedy." *Echo* (London), September 12, 1888: 3. Interviews released Ripper suspect Piser; Chapman identified by brother; bloodstained papers noted.

"The Whitechapel Tragedies." *Echo* (London),

October 5, 1888: 3. Reports that constables are wearing "galoshes" to keep tread quiet and carrying "stout sticks" to protect selves.

"The Whitechapel Tragedies." *Echo* (London), October 6, 1888: 3. Notes that suspect is believed to wear deerstalker hat and carry a black shiny bag; "vigilance force" is working "with a level of secrecy equal to that of the trained men."

"The Whitechapel Tragedies." *Echo* (London), October 8, 1888: 3. Describes Ripper suspect as wearing deerstalker hat. Reports testimony by a medium as to identity of Ripper; police to train bloodhounds to follow the Ripper's scent.

"The Whitechapel Tragedies." *Echo* (London), October 9, 1888: 3. Notes Dublin police received letter from a "Jim the Ripper." Introduces idea that Ripper mutilations are in keeping with tradition of German thieves.

Williams, Rowland Addams. "The Whitechapel Murders." *Times* (London): September 26, 1888: 3. In letter to editor, Williams, former deputy coroner for Crickhowell, Breconshire, criticizes Dr. Phillips's handling of the Chapman autopsy. Notes that the Ripper "is probably a person making research from motives of science or curiosity, and not a drunken loafer."

Winslow, L. Forbes. "To the Editor of the Times." *Times* (London): September 12, 1888: 6. Winslow believes "that the murderer is not of the class of which 'Leather Apron' belongs, but is of the upper class of society."

"Yesterday's Whitechapel Tragedy." *Lloyd's Weekly News,* September 9, 1888: 1. Reports on violence against Jews in East End resulting from rumors about identity of "Leather Apron."

About the Authors

Daniel Friedman, MD, received his BA from Stony Brook University, and his medical degree from St. George's University School of Medicine. He is currently a practicing pediatrician in Floral Park, New York, and is also an active member of the Cohen Children's Medical Center, where he sits on the voluntary staff advisory committee. In addition to being an amateur sleuth, he spends his spare time as singer/songwriter and bass guitar player for the Friedman Brothers Band. Dr. Friedman resides on Long Island with his wife, Elena, and their three children, Amanda, David, and Andrew.

Eugene Friedman, MD, received his BA from New York University, and his medical degree from New York Medical College. He was chief resident in pediatrics at New York Medical College and later served as assistant chief of pediatrics at Martin Army Hospital at Fort Benning, Georgia. Dr. Friedman has been in private practice for more than forty years. He has held multiple leadership positions in organized medicine and has devoted himself to the education of future physicians. He is an avid gardener and a translator of late nineteenth-century French poetry. He and his wife, Sheryl, live on Long Island and have five children and fourteen grandchildren.

Index

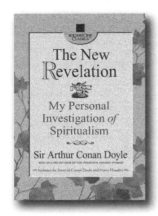

THE NEW REVELATION

My Personal Investigation of Spiritualism

Sir Arthur Conan Doyle

The spiritual movement in the early part of the twentieth century had few, if any, proponents greater than Sir Arthur Conan Doyle—a medical doctor, soldier, intellectual, and world-renowned author. He believed fully in the principles of Spiritualism, which embraced areas that we refer to today as ESP, New Age philosophy, metaphysics, and psychic experiences. It accepted the existence of a soul and an afterlife, and it offered an intriguing view of our existence in relationship to a greater being. Life was a continuum—a progression into ever-greater knowledge and understanding that linked the souls of all people. Doyle was convinced that the principles of Spiritualism were both reasonable and able to be proven.

In 1918, Sir Arthur published The New Revelation—a firsthand account of his personal investigation into the world of Spiritualism. This work became the most influential statement of the movement. In it, Sir Arthur presents his case on the merits of Spiritualism in a clear and concise manner. The reader follows along as Sir Arthur, in a voice reminiscent of Dr. Watson, calmly and deliberately examines psychic experiences, life after death, mediums, automatic writing, and more.

Sir Arthur Conan Doyle tirelessly lectured around the world on behalf of Spiritualism. It was a task he carried out until his death in 1930. While some may view this work as a historical footnote, the answers to Sir Arthur's basic questions regarding life and death are as relevant today as they were then.

In addition to this classic work, readers will find an original Introduction, which provides an insightful look at Doyle—the man and his passionate pursuits. It recounts his personal life and explores his experiences with Spiritualism. Also included is an Afterword that brilliantly captures Sir Arthur's friendship with famed magician Harry Houdini as documented through their personal correspondence.

$12.95 US • 120 pages • 5.5 x 8.5-inch quality paperback • ISBN 978-0-7570-0017-1